11 95

D1806598

JAZZ ON RECORD

A critical guide

JAZZ ON RECORD

A Critical Guide

Charles Fox, Peter Gammond
Alun Morgan

with additional material by
Alexis Korner

GREENWOOD PRESS, PUBLISHERS
WESTPORT, CONNECTICUT

Library of Congress Cataloging in Publication Data

Fox, Charles, 1921-
   Jazz on record.

   Reprint of the 1960 ed. published by Hutchinson,
London.
    1. Jazz music--Discography. I. Gammond, Peter,
joint author. II. Morgan, Alun, 1928-   joint author.
III. Title.
[ML156.4.J3F7 1978]   789.9'136'542   78-8189
ISBN 0-313-20513-2

*Warning: Although every effort has been made to ensure the
correctness of record numbers, neither the publishers nor the
authors hold themselves responsible for purchases made with
reference to this book*

Reprinted in 1978 by Greenwood Press, Inc.
51 Riverside Avenue, Westport, CT. 06880

Printed in the United States of America

10 9 8 7 6 5 4 3 2 1

INTRODUCTION

A BRIEF introduction to this book is necessary if only to anticipate
certain criticisms. Although a large amount of jazz history gets into
its pages it is not the aim of the book to present a potted history.
There are already plenty of books attempting to do that. The slant
is entirely from the point of view of the record collector and of the
records at present available. Thus certain jazz musicians may appear
to have been forgotten – to pick a random few: Eddie Lang, the
poetical Bix of the guitar; Frank Teschemacher, the spiritual ancestor
of the spiky school of reed players like Pee Wee Russell and Lester
Young; Adrian Rollini, Jimmy Blythe. But, in fact, none of these
people has an EP or LP record available to his credit and therefore
does not appear under a separate entry. They are nearly all mentioned
somewhere in the book but still may appear to have unfair represen-
tation compared with some lesser musicians. Others, although in a
similar state of unavailability, have been accorded an entry largely
because of their seeming forgotten talents.

Comparing this book to others of a similar nature our main claim
to pre-eminence is the wideness of our coverage. Our bias may seem
to be toward mainstream and modern jazz, but this is simply because
there are other excellent books available which have covered the
traditional ground so thoroughly. It is also because our collective
sense of perspective tells us that a number of interesting but slight
talents of the early days of jazz should not now be over-written.

So this is a record guide, not a jazz textbook. It attempts to sort out
for the jazz enthusiast the enormous number of records available to
which the writers of the book, in their constant preoccupation with
gramophone records, have easier access and perhaps a wider knowledge than the average collector can usually afford. The plan of the
book is simple and hardly needs explaining – it will immediately
become obvious. Some readers may feel the lack of discographical
details, but again these are available elsewhere and were omitted to
get in more practical criticism and to save the book from becoming an

immense volume instead of the pocket book it was intended to be.

The task of preparing a book like this is not made any easier by the illogical whimsy of the record companies. A classic example is given by one of the most famous and oldest of the American record companies which sits on one of the finest collections of classic jazz with apparently no sense of obligation toward the public's requirements and our voracious appetite for the vast and valuable archives that they have complete control of. Nobody, unfortunately, can touch this glittering store except the company which hold the copyright, for the whole history of jazz is too brief for it to have got beyond this tiresome stage. It is our feeling that such companies have a duty to keep most of these recordings in circulation. It is almost as if a book publisher was able to decide that they would suppress half the classics of English literature. In England, moreover, one of the two major companies which have the rights to issue the above-mentioned American company's products, not only does nothing to persuade them from their dog-in-a-manger policy and to open the vaults, but fails to issue many of the records that are made available to them on the grounds that they are not commercial. This would have a more convincing ring if it wasn't for the fact that they do issue the most curious, ill-assorted, and, even odder, short-lived rubbish that they imagine has some glittering appeal to the fickle teenagers and the dulled wits of the mums and dads. Whenever a classical jazz issue of great merit has managed to slip through the ring of prejudice and ignorance it has always justified itself by good, regular and lasting sales.

From the unbalanced plenty that we are allotted, we have attempted to select, sift and review to the best of our ability. We hope that our guidance will be of some value to the collector of every degree, and may possibly be a slight persuasion to the record companies to take a saner attitude toward their jazz issues.

CHARLES FOX
N.B: The collective opinions expressed in this book are not necessarily those held by each individual writer.
PETER GAMMOND
ALUN MORGAN

A

JULIAN 'CANNONBALL' ADDERLEY   *alto saxophone*

Like so many of his contemporaries, Cannonball Adderley started
out as a devout admirer of Charlie Parker; in fact there was virtually
no originality in Adderley's work for some years. Even on first
hearing, some of his records give the vague impression that the
listener has experienced the music before. His first LP (1) was made
within days of his dramatic appearance at the Café Bohemia but his
playing fails to justify the breathless adulation heaped on him at the
time. He plays with confidence and a full tone on the ballad *Flamingo*
but otherwise fails to create jazz of merit or originality. Over the
years he has been recorded in a number of lack-lustre settings (including, inevitably, an album with strings) but it was not until 1958 that
he began to make an impact on the more discerning listeners. On (3)
he is the chief soloist in a big band assembled by arranger Gil Evans
and provides the right kind of contrast between the written and
improvised sections. (2) finds him near his best in a quintet which
contains his brother Nat on cornet; gone are most of the slithering
neo-Parkerisms and in their place is a more direct and personal
approach. *What's new* is something of a *tour de force* for Adderley's
extrovert passion as he plunges head-first into a lengthy transformation of the tune from the first bar of the opening chorus. Throughout
most of 1958 and 1959 Cannonball worked with Miles Davis's group
where he seemed to blossom forth as a better soloist than before.
Unfortunately this is not reflected on all the records he made during
this period and his own *Somethin' else* LP ((A) BN 1595) finds him
below form; the rest of the group succeeds in cutting the leader
with ease and it is guest soloist Miles Davis who emerges as the star
of the session.

(1) INTRODUCING CANNONBALL – 12 Lon LTZ-C15015. (A) 12 Sav
    12018. *1955.*

(2) CANNONBALL'S SHARPSHOOTERS – 12 Mer MMB12008. (A) 12
    EmA 36135. *1958.*

(3) GIL EVANS AND HIS ORCHESTRA – 12 Vog LAE12173. (A) 12
    WP 1246. *1958.*

HENRY 'RED' ALLEN (1908)   *trumpet, vocal*

The influence of Louis Armstrong is strong in many jazz trumpeters; certainly it is in Red Allen; at least in the broadest possible sense, in approach, phrasing and the particular jazz language used. But in detail, Allen is too much of an individualist to sound exactly like Armstrong in the way that Jabbo Smith, for example, generally did. To begin with he has none of Armstrong's serenity and control. Allen is one of the most variable players in jazz because he is a highly emotional musician. Jazz obviously excites him, at times to the point of incoherence, and his playing is often wild. Many of his recordings belong to a period which might be described as the growing pains of swing, the big-band jazz whose essence is excitement, drive and power. Allen has all these elements. One could take his 1940 recordings on (4) to portray him at his most subdued, at least on the delightful *Canal Street blues* where he falls in with the good behaviour of Benny Morton and Edmond Hall. We see him in the next stage of intoxication on (1) where he uses his powers to great advantage to lead a band in exuberant performances in the well-known Luis Russell mould, whose band it was. *Swing out* and *It should be you* both contain rather breathless, erratic Allen solos, while *Feeling drowsy* and *Biff'ly blues* show him playing under the sobering influence of the blues in his most lyrical vein. Allen at his most exciting and effective can be heard on the sides made under the name of Billy Banks and his Rhythmakers, *Yellow Dog blues, Spider crawls, Yes suh, Margie* and *Oh Peter* once available on now deleted Parlophone recordings made with the Luis Russell band between 1929 and 1931; nearly all worth having if you like the curried and spiced flavour of the vintage music of that period. The later recordings have their moments, especially (6), but often the flavour and the spirit has been supplanted by a group of weary veterans with only an occasional spark lighting the proceedings. (5) is downright awful.

(1) RED ALLEN AND HIS NEW YORK ORCHESTRA – 7 HMV 7EG8112 (d). (A) 10 Vic LVA3033 (d). *1929.*

(2) RED ALLEN AND HIS ORCHESTRA – 7 HMV 7EG8136 (d). (A) 10 Vic LVA3003 (d). *1929.*

(3) TRUMPETERS HOLIDAY (also Frankie Newton) – (A) 12 Ep LN-3253. *1935.*

(4) NEW ORLEANS JAZZ (also Armstrong, Dodds, Noone and Singleton) – 12 Br LAT8146. (A) 12 Dec DL8283. *1940.*

(5) JAZZ AT THE METROPOLE CAFÉ – 12 Lon LTZ-N15010. (A) 12 Beth 21 (*d*). *1955.*

(6) RIDE RED RIDE IN HI-FI – 12 RCA RD-27045. (A) 12 RCA LPM-1509. *1957.*

(7) AT NEWPORT (also Teagarden and Ory) – 12 Col 33CX10106. (A) 12 Ver 8233. *1957.*

(8) DIXIELAND ALL STARS – 12 Col 33SX1030 (*d*). (A) 12 Rou 25015. *1957.*

MOSE ALLISON (1927)   *piano, trumpet, vocal*

Mose Allison is virtually unique in that he is one of the few 'modern' musicians to formulate a piano style combining elements of Charlie Parker (via Bud Powell and Horace Silver) and the country blues singers of his childhood environment. Born and brought up in a small town near the Mississippi delta, Allison has retained a great admiration for such artists as Tampa Red and Sonny Boy Williamson; consequently, although he has worked with such contemporary-styled soloists as Zoot Sims and Stan Getz, his keyboard work is reminiscent of the astringent guitar style associated with blues singers. He claims to have been influenced, since 1946, by Al Haig and Bud Powell although his style seems closer to that of George Wallington. Mose is at his best interpreting his own compositions and the majority of his writing so far consists of vignettes based on childhood memories. *Back Country Suite* (which occupies one complete side of 1) is an attempt to convey an impression of the delta country; there is no real link between the ten 'movements' other than their common geographical tie but the melodies have great charm and occasional poignancy. *Blues* has a vocal by Allison who sings in a somewhat nasal, unpleasant manner although he has a great understanding of the idiom. The reverse side of (1) is more conventional with a swinging version of *Blueberry Hill* and a further vocal on Mercy Dee Walton's *One room country shack*. The second Allison LP (2) is titled 'Local Color'; in five movements this is a sequel to the *Back Country Suite*, and contains a better vocal on *Parchman Farm*, an authentic-sounding lament with the sting in the tail. On the reverse side Mose plays middle-period trumpet on *Trouble in mind* and shows

[9]

that he is less impressive as a horn player than as a pianist. (3) conforms with the expected piano trio format and contains only one Allison original amongst its ten tracks. Apart from *Stroll*, a pleasant but innocuous trumpet solo, Mose remains at the piano and the Latin-American treatment given to *I told ya I love ya* provides the most memorable music on a consistent but not outstanding record.

(1) MOSE ALLISON TRIO – 12 Esq 32-051. (A) 12 Pre PRLP7091. *1957*.
(2) MOSE ALLISON TRIO – 12 Esq 32-071. (A) 12 Pre PRLP7121. *1957*.
(3) MOSE ALLISON TRIO – 12 Esq 32-083. (A) 12 Pre PRLP7137. *1958*.

ALBERT AMMONS (1907–49) *piano*

With the obvious exception of Fats Waller, no one played the piano with more emphatic enjoyment than Albert Ammons. Even a blues was given a sort of pensive gaiety. Ragtime was made to sparkle, and boogie, in his hands, was an extrovert romp. There was nothing crude in his approach for he was an expert and professional type of musician, with enough basic ability to overcome technicalities and suggest careless abandon. His boogie was simple but not stereotyped; in the manner of Yancey he developed a tidy train of thought as he played; which is not the same thing as merely keeping to a rigid pattern as the more commercialized boogie does. On his first session recorded in 1936 with admirable support from Guy Kelly, Dalbert Bright, Ike Perkins, Israel Crosby and Jimmy Hoskins, a tidy little group with which he was playing in a Chicago Club at the time, he gives a good cross-section of his abilities. *Boogie woogie stomp*, a vigorous runaway bash, one of the most infectiously gay pieces of boogie woogie on record in which Ammons shepherds the band in front of him at a breakneck pace; *Nagasaki*, a bright emphatic number; *Early mornin' blues*, one of the finest instrumental blues on record ; are all on (1). His 1938 Columbia *Shout for joy*, an exhilarating performance, is again available (TFR6018), while his 1939 Blue Note session, including *Boogie woogie stomp* and *Boogie woogie blues* (2), demonstrates his power as a soloist. The celebrated sides made as a duet with Pete Johnson for Victor in 1941, are a tonic of unrepressed enjoyment as extroverted and as uncomplicated as jazz can be. *Cuttin' the boogie* and *Barrelhouse boogie*, two of the best known, are not at present available but, oddly enough, the previously

[10]

unissued *Boogie woogie jump* is – a single track on GREAT JAZZ PIANISTS
– 12 Cam CDN 118, (A) 12 Cam CAL-328.
(1) ALBERT AMMONS AND HIS RHYTHM KINGS – 7 Br OE9325.
1936.
(2) ALBERT AMMONS – 7 Vog EPV1071. *1939.*
(3) GIANTS OF BOOGIE WOOGIE (with Meade Lux Lewis and Pete
Johnson) – (A) 12 Riv 12-106. *1939.*
(4) ALBERT AMMONS – 10 Mer MG25012. *1947.*

GENE AMMONS (1925)   *tenor saxophone*
   Son of the famous boogie pianist, Gene Ammons' career in jazz
has been dictated, to some extent, by changing fashions. Starting out
as an admirer of Lester Young he was at his coolest with the Woody
Herman band, when his lengthy solo on Shorty Rogers' arrangement
of *More moon* (Cap LC6560, (A) T324) would pass muster as the work
of Zoot Sims or Allen Eager. Later he formed a seven-piece band
with Sonny Stitt and altered his manner of playing to suit the superior
rhythm-and-blues music of the day. The Stitt-Ammons group
specialized in such extrovert material as *Seven eleven*, *Chabootie*,
Stringin' the jug, etc., while Gene was featured as a ballad soloist on
Blue and sentimental, *My foolish heart*, etc. Stitt played baritone much
of the time and the band contained, at various periods, such individualists as Bennie Green, Duke Jordan, Matthew Gee and Junior
Mance. After some years of touring with a rhythm-and-blues unit
Ammons returned to jazz as leader on a session which produced
Woofin and tweetin' and *Juggernaut* (1). Unfortunately Gene's sidemen
(Art Farmer, Lou Donaldson and Freddie Redd) revealed the weaknesses in the construction of their leader's solos by playing with
greater fluency and originality. Much the same sort of thing happened
on the next LP (2) although the stilted conga drumming of Candido
tended to bog down even the most inventive members. One track,
Madhouse, culminates in a wild attempt at collective improvisation
by the front line men (Art Farmer, Ammons and Jackie McLean).
(3) is much better for here Gene seems capable of putting together a
series of ideas to form solos of merit. The very quality of his tone
indicates his potentialities as he lays the foundations for a memorable
version of *Laura*. Art Farmer again graces the front line (as does
Jackie McLean, although McLean tends to be the stylistic oddity

[11]

here) but the presence of guitarist Kenny Burrell in the rhythm section ensures a steadiness of pulse and a consistency of quality.

(1) GENE AMMONS ALL STARS – 10 Esq 20-078. (A) 12 Pre PRLP 7050 (with four titles added). *1955.*

(2) GENE AMMONS ALL STARS – 12 Esq 32-047. (A) 12 Pre PRLP7039. *1956.*

(3) GENE AMMONS ALL STARS – 12 Esq 32-077. (A) 12 Pre PRLP7083. *1957.*

JIMMY ARCHEY (1902)   *trombone*

A bright and brassy player with a bold technique, playing a powerful New Orleans style with enough polish to make him sound really professional. His music is simple and often very moving. Has recorded with Oliver, Bechet, Mezzrow and Bob Wilber. (1) is a programme of smooth Dixieland by a French band dominated by Archey.

(1) JIMMY ARCHEY WITH MICHEL ATTENOUX AND HIS ORCHESTRA – 10 Fel EDL87019. *1955.*

LOUIS ARMSTRONG (1900)   *trumpet, vocal*

Louis Armstrong was and is the pivot, leader and inspirer of a greater part of the jazz played between 1925 and the present. Without needing to claim that he has been the greatest jazz musician, though many critics would unhesitatingly do this, it is only justice to say that he has been one of the most important, not only for his own achievement as a musician but also in his responsibility for the way in which jazz has developed. Now that jazz is commonly accepted and has a respectable history behind it, it is difficult to look back to about 1925 and judge exactly what Armstrong's achievement was. So much of what he played, so many of the phrases he used, the possibilities of the trumpet in jazz which he disclosed, have seeped into the language of jazz that it would require considerable space to analyse his contribution to the music. There was a vigorous jazz before Armstrong came on the scene but his stature as a musician was so much greater than any who had gone before him that he dictated not only how the trumpet should be played but most of the other instruments of jazz – the saxophone, for instance, through the playing of Coleman Hawkins.

He developed the vocal technique of jazz playing, using his instrument as a voice and a mind. Basically his approach was simple. Often it amounted only to the reshaping of a melody, and at no time did he ever stray very far away from the tune he was using. But his presentation of even the tritest melody was always inspired and logical, quintessentially jazz because he has always spoken and thought pure jazz, and spoken it with clear authority. He was able to do this because of a truly remarkable technical command of his instrument. It can never be pointed out too often how much a great jazz player can do with an instrument like the trumpet, trombone or clarinet – far more than was ever attempted or imagined by even the most skilful orchestral player. This is worth pointing out, for if we need to defend jazz – and it still is often necessary – this is a major consideration. Armstrong's playing has not changed much over the years. If we ignore the backing on any recording of his and listen only to his trumpet we find the same authoritative approach. He has not needed to change – because he started with the most inspired and accomplished playing that it was possible to achieve within a certain form of jazz and, although there are different approaches, and more subtle approaches, there will never basically be a better.

This brings us to the curious contradiction in Armstrong's position in jazz. Considering him as a musician – there can be nothing but praise. His playing is sheer magic, strong, pure, using the whole range of his instrument, even the highest notes which lesser musicians strain toward with alarming squeaks, achieved with easy assurance and a beauty of tone and musical thought which are absolutely undeniable. It makes it more difficult therefore to fault Armstrong as a leader in the jazz field. In discussing jazz with Armstrong one finds that he lives only for his music; he gets a vast enjoyment out of it and this he communicates to everyone around him. It seems that he has never considered jazz as anything but entertainment, except – humanly – as a living, and he has not the nature of a man like Charlie Parker or Duke Ellington who assumes and worries about his position as a jazz mentor. As long as Armstrong is surrounded by highly professional musicians who enter into his enjoyment and do not hamper his playing then he is quite happy. He never pauses to consider whether what he is doing is artistically satisfying or correct as a whole. Perhaps it is only critics who should consider such questions as these.

[13]

The problem, however, in assessing his recorded work is that, while he himself always plays superbly, he is not always playing against the ideal backing. Either he must have players of his own stature if it is to be a collective work in the early New Orleans tradition; such a group is not easily assembled, and does not always work when it is owing to irreconcilable temperaments; or he must have a backing which is subdued to the role of non-conflicting support. In this last manner, Armstrong has recorded some of his best work, as a strong, soaring solo voice above a comparatively large band, in other words, a backing in which other individual voices except his lost their identity. In spite of these problems he has led, amongst a mass of not entirely successful material, some of the greatest jazz recordings ever made.

One other criticism levelled against Armstrong is that he uses the same material, in the same way, over and over again. The only answer seems to be that he has done work that cannot be done better so how can it be altered. The attacks on Armstrong were at their worst when he visited England in 1956 at the head of what appeared to be a touring circus which played on a revolving stage in a vast ice rink. The band with him then seemed about the least inspired and worst balanced that he had ever fronted. Since then he has redeemed himself by some new, excellent and varied work. But it is probably on his early recordings that his true status will be assessed.

His earliest recordings with King Oliver's Creole Jazz Band (1) are discussed in the Oliver section. It was this period as second cornettist to Oliver in which Armstrong gained experience and confidence so that when he joined Fletcher Henderson in 1924 he immediately became the dominating voice in that orchestra. Many comparatively dull Henderson performances like *Money blues*, *What-cha-call-'em-blues*, in which most of the musicians seem to be doing nothing in particular, spark into life as soon as Armstrong takes a solo. The accompaniments to blues singers like Bessie Smith (*St. Louis blues Cold in hand blues, Reckless blues, You've been a good old wagon*, etc.), Ma Rainey (*See see rider blues, Jelly bean blues, Countin' the blues*) and with Maggie Jones, Clara Smith and Trixie Smith, are great examples of trumpet vocalization, so that the trumpet comments on the vocal makes the performance a tightly knit duet with both the performers encouraging each other to greater sensitivity and feeling. Also during this time he recorded with various small groups (with Clarence Williams and Sidney Bechet) sides like *Terrible blues* and *Santa Claus blues* (2) which have powerful moments but do not give Armstrong full freedom or an entirely cohesive backing. Two interesting sides by Perry Bradford's Jazz Phools, *Lucy Long* and *I ain't gonna play no second fiddle* (on a deleted Voc V1030), are worth finding.

The classic period of Armstrong Hot Five and Hot Seven recordings is an artistic adventure of goods and bads with the superb thrown in at regular intervals. Armstrong rides along on a constant stream of invention that sometimes inspires his group and sometimes leaves it standing.

In 1925 he embarked on what, for convenience, is called the 'Chicago' period, with a group that was to be the nucleus of his studio groups for some time to come; it included Johnny Dodds, Kid Ory, Lil Armstrong and Johnny St. Cyr, all powerful, direct and individual players who gave Armstrong admirable if sometimes unsubtle support. It must be remembered that this was not a regular group, so when they were collected in the studio they were not necessarily playing as a practiced and smooth combination; hence some of the roughness of their work. They recorded *My heart*, *Yes I'm in the barrel* (3) and *Gut bucket blues* (3), three spirited but decidedly rough performances. In February 1926, the same group recorded *Come back sweet papa* (4), *Georgia grind* (4), *Cornet chop suey* (3), *Heebie jeebies* (3) *Muskrat ramble* (3) – these last three being highly successful sides in which the drive is increased, the roughness somewhat diminished and the results very exciting – *Oriental strut* (4) and *You're next* (4). In May 1926, Armstrong recorded with an orchestra with which he was working at the time, Erskine Tate's Vendome Theatre Orchestra, and produced two highly exciting sides with the larger band drive and sound, in which his trumpet is featured in a hectic but exact and skilful ride-out with the orchestra – *Stomp off, let's go* (2) and *Static strut* (2).

These were followed by two fine recordings under the name of Lil's Hot Shots with the usual small group, *Drop that sack* (2) and *Georgia bo bo* (2). These are masterpieces, the first a piece of calculated elation, the second a bouncy and yet slightly mournful bit of lyricism.

[15]

Four sides, *Don't forget to mess around* (5), *I'm gonna gitcha* (5), *Dropping shucks* (5) and *Who's it* (5) were not so successful and have only recently been reissued since their original pressing. The same group recorded again on 23 June, 1926, *The King of the Zulus*, *Lonesome blues* (4), *Big fat ma and skinny pa* (4), *Sweet little papa*, earthy and spirited sides without ever rising to the true greatness; the same may be said of four sides recorded in November, *Jazz lips*, *Skid-dat-de-dat* (3), *Big butter and egg man* (4) and *Sunset Café stomp* (4) and, later the same month with John Thomas replacing Ory, *You made me love you* (4), *Irish Black Bottom* (4), and *Leave mine alone*.

In April, 1927, with a group under the name of Johnny Dodds' Black Bottom Stompers which included Dodds, Stomp Evans, Earl Hines, Bud Scott and Baby Dodds, Armstrong recorded four classics sides which for sheer lyricism and beauty he rarely surpassed: *Weary blues* and *New Orleans stomp* (both on a now deleted Vocalion V1008) and *Wild man blues* (2) and *Melancholy* (2). These sides foreshadowed the great Hot Five sides of 1928 in which Hines was again to feature with such classic results. The Hot Seven recordings of 1927 featured the original five with Pete Briggs (tuba) added and Baby Dodds. The series started with the exuberant *Willie the weeper* (6), with its punching final stop-chorus, and *Wild man blues* (6), followed by a series of recordings each of which has some special merit and all of which should make a basis of any jazz collection: *Alligator crawl* (6), *Potato head blues* (6), *Melancholy blues* (6), *Weary blues* (6), *Twelfth Street rag* (6), *Keyhole blues* (6), *S.O.L. blues* (6), *Gully low blues* (6), *That's when I'll come back to you* (6). A return to the Hot Five formula produced more magnificent recordings: *Put 'em down blues*, *Ory's creole trombone* (3), *The last time* (3), *Struttin' with some barbecue* (3), *Got no blues* (3) and, with Lonnie Johnson added, *Once in a while* (7), *I'm not rough* (7), *Hotter than that* (7) and the beautiful *Savoy blues* (7), one of the greatest sides Armstrong ever recorded.

1928 saw a strange but bountiful change, with a group of completely different character, a comparatively sophisticated group which included Hines, and Zutty Singleton and some musicians of lesser stature who gave Armstrong greater room to develop his own voice while they gave a grave and balanced support. This was the first step towards Armstrong the virtuoso soloist. The sides recorded in 1928 included: *Fireworks*, the immortal and perfect

West End blues (8), *Skip the gutter* (8), *A Monday date*, *Sugar foot strut* (8), *Two deuces* (8), *Squeeze me* (8), *Don't jive me* (8), *Knee drops*, *No* (8), *Basin Street blues* (8), *Weather bird* (8) – a remarkable duet between Armstrong and Hines, *Muggles* (8), *Heah me talkin' to ya*, *Tight like this* (8), *St. James' Infirmary* (8). Again we can only add that this is a collection that no one can be without.

1929 brought the next step which emancipated Armstrong as the star soloist, this time with the orchestral backing of secondary importance, usually with a larger group, and featuring Armstrong a great deal as a vocalist. The curious *Knockin' a jug*, a strangely beautiful recording with Teagarden, Sullivan and Lang (9), is an exception. The orchestral series starts with *I can't give you anything but love* (9), with an instrumental styled vocal which marks the beginning of Armstrong's equality as a vocalist and trumpeter, followed by *Mahogany Hall stomp* (10). From the 1929–30 recordings in this vein the following are at present available: *Black and blue* (9), *After you've gone* (10), *St. Louis blues* (11), *Dallas blues* (10), *Dear old Southland* (9), *Tiger rag* (11), *I'm a ding dong daddy* (9), *Confessin'* (9), *If I could be with you* (9), *Body and soul* (9), *You're driving me crazy* (10), *Shine* (9), *Lazy river* (9), *Stardust* (9). The Victor recording period which followed this has mostly been withdrawn from the HMV label and not yet reissued on RCA, but some of the following records are still to be found and are well worth the search (DLP1105, DLP1036, SEC8028). Two fine tracks which have been reissued are *Basin Street blues* (12), and *When it's sleepy time down south* (12). A Decca recording with a Dixielandish flavour follows and (13) contains *When the Saints*, *Bye and bye*, *West End Blues*, *Mahogany Hall stopm*, *Dippermouth blues*, *Save it*, *pretty Mama*, *You rascal you*, and *When it's sleepy time down South*.

Scattered amongst the 1935–42 period on American Decca are a number of fine sides currently only to be found on deleted 78s. The British gramophone companies have never shown much initiative in selecting their own jazz records. Instead they wait for the ready made assortments from America. These offerings include some very pleasant and amusing sides with the Mills Brothers (14); the four admittedly commercial but still fine spirituals including *Shadrack* and *Johan and the whale* (15), two consistent Armstrong best-sellers; and four superb sides available on an LP with sides by Dodds, Noone and

[17]

others (16), *Perdido Street blues*, the superb *2.19 blues*, *Down in Honky Tonk Town* and *Coal cart blues*. These sides on which Armstrong played with a musician of his own calibre in Sidney Bechet, are amongst the greatest he ever made.

In 1946, Armstrong made four tracks which are a collector's item now issued on an EP (17), *Long long journey* and *Snafu* with Leonard Feather's Esquire All-Americans, a high-falutin' title which encompassed an Ellington contingent – Ellington himself, Greer, Hodges; also Byas and Shavers; and two fine performances with Vic Dickenson, Bigard and Singleton amongst others, *I want a little girl* and *Sugar* (17).

Now began a series of recordings with the All Stars, a concert group designed to entertain in a high-powered way. The first All Stars was a mixed batch in all ways, Teagarden, Hackett, Hucko and Catlett playing some very unco-ordinated jazz (18), to be followed by a series of groups of very unequal quality. For a time the personnel included Teagarden, Bigard, Cary (later replaced by Hines) Shaw and Catlett, with Velma Middleton as resident vocalist. There are great moments on these records (19–23), particularly some Hines solos and, of course, Armstrong himself, but on the whole it is a brash, often tasteless, cellophane-wrapped period, and needs to be explored with caution. The collector would do best to let the last of this series (27) give him the flavour. Here is a concert performance which will nostalgically conjure up the All Stars as we heard them in Paris and in London 1956, after a long period when records were our only contact with Armstrong. By this time Trummy Young, Kyle and Deems were in the group and they provide breezy entertainment and atmosphere but rarely the great jazz we would expect from the master. During these years Armstrong also made a series of more commercial recordings with big bands led by Sy Oliver or Gordon Jenkins (20), including a series of vocal recordings – *I get ideas* (26), *C'est si bon* (26), *The gypsy* (25), *Kiss of fire* (25) and the like, which are likeable if not exactly jazz-crammed performances.

Whether or not it was the result of hard criticism, which Armstrong claims to ignore, the All Stars, by now with Edmond Hall replacing a disappointing Bigard, suddenly sparked into life and coherence with a much-acclaimed record on American Columbia (28) on which they concentrated on the works of W. C. Handy. These were powerful though often harsh performances which excite but don't induce much desire to hear again. (29 and 30) followed in the same vein. A series of recordings with Ella Fitzgerald were a great success although most people thought Ella outshone Armstrong (31, 34, 35); these are novelties for those who mainly want Armstrong as a vocalist. The reassuring and exciting series of recordings in which Armstrong recorded a musical autobiography for American Decca (33) were the greatest event in Armstrong's career since his 1920 and 1930 triumphs. The great freshness of these sides was partly because they contained material which hadn't been worn threadbare by continual All-Star performances, ranging from the old jazz standards which we had hardly heard Armstrong play for years – a highly professional *High society*, slick and polished in contrast to the out-of-tune, ragged revival performances and wonderful tracks like the sub-dued but powerful *All the wrongs you've done to me*. Listen to Armstrong's exciting second entry – in *Mandy make up your mind* for example, and all the way through the series Kyle, Hall and Barnes in great form, only Trummy Young persisting with some vulgarity. Here Velma Middleton, so often a disappointing singer indulging in ungainly antics on the stage, shines as a great blues singer in memories of Bessie Smith and Ma Rainey. So the four LPs continue with a sprightly *Cornet chop suey*, classic performances of *Weary blues*, *Knockin' a jug*, revived in a performance nearly as great as the original a delightful *Song of the Islands* and performances like *Them there eyes* where Armstrong rides in triumph and elation above an augmented group with a biting saxophone section. This is an expensive buy, as the four records are not available separately, but everyone ought to have it.

A few more vocal records since then (36, 37, 39) are an anti-climax, but Armstrong has restored our faith. He is still one of the greatest and towers above jazz on an undestroyable pedestal. Personally he is magnificent – a genius – without any apologies for the use of this much over-used word.

(1) YOUNG LOUIS ARMSTRONG – (A) 12 Riv 12-101. *1923–4.*

(2) JAZZ CLASSICS – 10 Br LA8597. (A) 10 Br BL58004 (d). *1924–7.*

(3) LOUIS ARMSTRONG STORY, Vol. I – 12 Ph BBL7134. (A) 12 Col CL-851. *1925–7.*

(4) HOT FIVE – 10 Fon TFR6003. *1925–6.*

(5) THE HOT FIVE AGAIN – 7 Par GEP8768. *1926.*

(6) LOUIS ARMSTRONG STORY, Vol. 2 – 12 Ph BBL7189. (A) 12 Col CL-852. *1927.*

(7) HOT FIVE – 7 Par GEP8730. *1927.*

(8) LOUIS ARMSTRONG STORY, Vol. 3 – 12 Ph BBL7202. (A) 12 Col CL-853. *1928.*

(9) LOUIS ARMSTRONG STORY, Vol. 4 – 12 Ph BBL7218. (A) 12 Col CL-854. *1929–31.*

(10) LOUIS ARMSTRONG AND HIS ORCHESTRA – 12 Fon TFR17073. *1929–30.*

(11) LOUIS ARMSTRONG AND HIS ORCHESTRA – 12 Fon TFL17106 *1929–30.*

(12) LOUIS ARMSTRONG – 7 RCA RCX-1007. (A) 7 RCA Vic EPA-5000. *1932–47.*

(13) LOUIS ARMSTRONG CLASSICS – 10 Br LA8528. (A) 10 Dec DL5225 (*d*), 12 Dec DL8284. *1936–9.*

(14) LOUIS ARMSTRONG AND THE MILLS BROTHERS – 10 Br LA8681 (*d*). *1937–40*

(15) SATCHMO SINGS SPIRITUALS – 7 Br OE9310. *1938.*

(16) NEW ORLEANS JAZZ (also Dodds, Noone, Singleton, Allen) – 12 Br LAT8146. (A) 12 Dec DL8283. *1940.*

(17) LOUIS ARMSTRONG – 7 RCA RCX-105. (A) 12 RCA Vic LPM-1443. *1946.*

(18) LOUIS ARMSTRONG – 7 RCA RCX-1031. (A) TOWN HALL CONCERT PLUS – 12 RCA Vic LPM-1443. *1947.*

(19) SATCHMO AT SYMPHONY HALL – 12 Br LAT8017–8. (A) 12 Dec DL8037-8, or DXB-108. *1947.*

(20) WITH GORDON JENKINS – 10 Br LA8700. (A) 12 Dec DL8840. *1949–52.*

(21) NEW ORLEANS DAYS – 10 Br LA8537. (A) 10 Dec (*d*) DL5279. (A) (NEW ORLEANS NIGHTS) Dec DL8329. *1950.*

(22) JAZZ CONCERT – 10 Br LA8534. (A) 10 Dec (*d*) DL5280. (A) (SATCHMO ON STAGE) Dec 8330. *1950.*

(23) SATCHMO AT PASADENA – 12 Br LAT8019. (A) 12 Dec DL8041. *1951.*

(24) MUSIC FROM 'THE GLEN MILLER STORY' – 10 Br LA8691. *1951–4.*

(25) SATCHMO SINGS – 12 Br LAT8243. (A) 12 Dec 8126. *1951–5.*

(26) SATCHMO SERENADES – 10 Br LA8679. (A) 12 Dec 8211. *1951–5.*
(27) LOUIS ARMSTRONG AT THE CRESCENDO – 12 Br LAT8084-5,
   (A) 12 Dec DL8168-9. *1955.*
(28) LOUIS ARMSTRONG PLAYS W. C. HANDY – 12 Ph BBL7017.
   (A) 12 Col. CL-591. *1954.*
(29) SATCH PLAYS FATS – 12 Ph BBL7064. (A) 12 Col CL-708. *1955.*
(30) AMBASSADOR SATCH – 12 Ph BBL7091. (A) 12 Col CL-840.
   1955-6.
(31) ELLA AND LOUIS – 12 HMV CLP1098. (A) 12 Ver 4003. *1956.*
(32) LOUIS ARMSTRONG AT NEWPORT (also Condon) – 12 Ph BBL7151.
   (A) 12 Col CL-931. *1956.*
(33) SATCHMO: A MUSICAL AUTOBIOGRAPHY – 4-12 Br LAT8211-4.
   (A) 4-12 Dec DXM-155. *1956-7.*
(34) ELLA AND LOUIS AGAIN – 12 HMV CLP1146. (A) 12 Ver 4017.
   1957.
(35) ELLA AND LOUIS AGAIN, Vol. 2 – 12 HMV CLP1147. (A) 12
   Ver4018. *1957.*
(36) LOUIS AND THE ANGELS – 12 Br LAT8210. (A) 12 Dec 8488.
   1957.
(37) LOUIS AND THE GOOD BOOK – 12 Br LAT8270. (A) 12 Dec
   8741. *1958.*
(38) SATCHMO THE GREAT – 12 Ph BBL7216. (A) 12 Col CL-1077.
   1955-6.
(39) LOUIS UNDER THE STARS – 12 HMV CLP1247. (A) 12 Ver 4012.
   1957.

MARVIN ASH (1914)   *piano*
A skilful pianist who has polished his jazz to the point of glitter and
occasionally lapses into that Joe 'Fingers' Carr sort of glib technique
that has recently had such popularity. The jazz breaks through
however and (1) is an entertaining record.
(1) NEW ORLEANS AT MIDNIGHT – 12 Br LAT8191. (A) 12 Dec 8346.
   1956.

B

BUSTER BAILEY (1902)   *clarinet, saxophone*
A skilful clarinettist in the traditional mode but with a very individual approach of his own. Plays in a very melodic style with long

slurred phrases and very neat and accurate ornaments, classically toned and very controlled. He found his best niche in the John Kirby group which played a concise and original type of chamber-music jazz of a fairly sophisticated kind. Played with Fletcher Henderson from 1924 to 1937, with a break from 1930-3 during which he was with the Noble Sissle Band. Played with John Kirby from 1938-47. His background is not therefore the small hot group but rather the cultivated jazz of the larger or the more polished kinds of band. A recent LP (1) shows him applying this sort of technique to small group jazz portraying his home town of Memphis, making a pleasing and interesting record.

(1) ALL ABOUT MEMPHIS – 12 Fel FAJ7003, (S) SJA2003. (A) 12 Fel FAJ-7003, (S) SJA-2003. *1958*.

MILDRED BAILEY (1907–51)   *vocal*

Only two white girls, during the entire 1930s, sang jazz with any real degree of success. They were Mildred Bailey and Lee Wiley, and by an odd coincidence both were of American Indian descent. Mildred Bailey had joined Paul Whiteman's orchestra back in 1929 (it was there she met and married Red Norvo); in 1936 she became joint-leader of the Red Norvo orchestra. Her small, sweet, high-pitched voice was unique, even quaint – in the best sense of that word. Where she scored over her white contemporaries was in the easy, relaxed manner in which she sang, and in her understanding of the blues (she was influenced by Bessie Smith as well as Ethel Waters). None of her best work, unhappily, still remains in the record catalogues. An outstanding performance was of *Someday sweetheart* (78 Br 02106, deleted many years ago), made in 1935 with Chu Berry and Teddy Wilson in the accompanying group. Four recordings also made that year (this time especially for issue in Britain) were *Honeysuckle rose, Willow tree, Downhearted blues* and *Squeeze me* (1), with Bunny Berigan, Johnny Hodges, Teddy Wilson and Grachan Moncur. (Try to get the original Parlophone 78s, where the recording quality is superior to that on the EP.) During the late 1930s Mildred Bailey also appeared on many records by the Red Norvo orchestra. On (2) and in CURTAIN CALL, Vol. 6 (10 Br LA8655, *1941*), she sings *Rockin' chair*, a song which became closely associated with her.

(1) MILDRED BAILEY AND HER ALLEY CATS – 7 Par GEP8600. (*d*). *1935*.
(2) 'THE ROCKIN' CHAIR LADY' – 10 Br LA8692. (*d*), (A) 12 Dec 5387
   (*d*). *1941*.
(3) ME AND THE BLUES – (A) 12 Reg 6032. *Late 1940s*.

CHET BAKER (1929) *trumpet, vocal*

Pitch-forked into the limelight with the original Gerry Mulligan
Quartet, Baker has shown himself to be an inconsistent jazz soloist.
The early falterings had a certain charm and his pleasing, mellow tone
seemed to indicate that when he matured he would be an important,
lyrical jazzman. In fact Chet's career has taken several steep nose-
dives and it seems unlikely now that he will ever be more than just
an average soloist. He has appeared on several LPs, most of them
recorded in Los Angeles, and many of them drab and lifeless. Therefore the albums discussed here are considered to be amongst his best
or to contain work of merit by some of Chet's sidemen. Apart from
his earliest appearances with Mulligan (1), where his perky, singing
lines complemented the avuncular story-telling of the leader, one of
his best albums is (2). Backed by Russ Freeman, Leroy Vinnegar and
Shelly Manne – a rhythm section not given to sympathy towards
recalcitrant soloists – Chet sweeps through a varied programme with
a welcome display of guts and attack. Putting a mute into the bell
of his trumpet he plays a lively and compelling *Love nest* which ranks
as one of his best solos on record. (3) is an equally good LP by Baker's
then regular group and it is due principally to the sterling efforts
of Phil Urso and Bobby Timmons that the album rates so highly;
Bill Loughborough is added on chromatic tympani for one track
(*Mickey's memory*, a thinly disguised *I'll remember April*) and gives the
music an unusual, intriguing quality. Although entitled 'Big Band'
(4) is played by nine- and eleven-piece units and is somewhat disappointing. Art Pepper is heard in some pleasant solo passages and
Baker is melodic and tasteful on *Worrying the life out of me* (a small
band version of the same tune is included in (3)) but the band is
neither big enough nor strong enough to kick Chet along in anything
more than his usual enervated manner. The chief assets of (5) are the
saxophonists (Art Pepper and Phil Urso) and the pianist (the late
Carl Perkins), all of whom successfully carve the leader on nearly
every track.

(1) GERRY MULLIGAN QUARTET – 12 Vog LAE12050. Most of the tracks on (A) 12 WP1207. *1952* and *1953*.

(2) RUSS FREEMAN-CHET BAKER – 12 Vog LAE12119. (A) WP1232. *1956*.

(3) CHET BAKER AND CREW – 12 Vog LAE12076. (A) WP1224. *1956*.

(4) CHET BAKER BIG BAND – 12 Vog LAE12109. (A) WP1229. *1956*.

(5) PLAYBOYS – 12 Vog LAE12183. (A) WP1234. *1957*.

HAROLD BAKER (1914)   *trumpet*

'There's a saying that all St. Louis trumpeters sound alike,' Clark Terry told one of the editors in 1958, 'Miles, Harold Baker, Joe Thomas, Mouse Randolph and me, we're all from the same place.' Certainly all these St. Louis musicians display some concern for the texture of their playing, for getting a mellow sound, and none more than Harold 'Shorty' Baker, a veteran of the Don Redman, Andy Kirk and Duke Ellington orchestras. Few trumpeters in jazz can equal his keen melodic sense, the elegance with which his ideas are converted into flowing cadences. (1) presents him with a quartet, performing in a subdued but always interesting fashion. Most of Baker's solos, though, are usually played on sessions organized by other musicians, mostly with the Duke Ellington orchestra or various groups led by Johnny Hodges. Perhaps the most notable of his recent solos with the Ellington band (he only left it in 1959) have been the lyrical *All heart*, the second section of 'Portrait of Ella Fitzgerald', contained in Vol. 2 of 'Ella Fitzgerald Sings The Duke Ellington Songbook, No. 2' (12 HMV CLP1228, (A) 12 Ver 4009/2 (*1956*)), and his duet with Ray Nance, *Mr. Gentle and Mr. Cool*, in 'Duke Ellington at Newport' (12 Ph BBL7279, SBBL526 (A) 12 Col CL1245, CS8072 (*1958*)). Baker provides the main solo interest in four tracks by the Al Hall Quartet on 'Cascade of Quartets' – *Should I* and *Honeysuckle rose* (Vol. 1, 12 Col 33SX1191), *St. Louis kid* and *I didn't know what time it was* (Vol. 2, 12 Col 33SX1218). Finally, he and trombonist Quentin Jackson infuse life into what is otherwise a rather languid set of tracks by Billy Strayhorn's Septet, 'Cue For Saxophone' (12 Fel FAJ7008, SJA2008 (*1959*)), second-string Ellingtonia partly rescued by Baker's versatile and witty playing.

(1) THE BROADWAY BEAT – 7 Par GEP8772. (A) (incl. other titles) 12 King 608. *Late 1950s*.

KENNY BAKER (1921)   *trumpet, flügelhorn*

Kenny Baker has an affection for, and a natural ability to play in, the Swing Era style. He has recorded on many occasions during the last two decades, with big bands and small groups, and was an important member of the Ted Heath brass section for some years. Many of his records have not been aimed at the jazz market and it would be patently unfair to criticize them for their lack of jazz content. Several more of his LPs have rung the changes on the skilled personnel which he employed on his highly successful radio series, a series aimed at a non-specialist late-night audience but catering at the same time for the jazz enthusiast. Kenny is one of the most accomplished, technically, of all European trumpeters and his presence in a section is a guarantee of quality. As a soloist he tends towards a certain brashness of expression on occasions and alternates stylistically between Billy Butterfield, Charlie Shavers and Ruby Braff. Of the two records listed below (1) is by a small group containing the talented Johnny Scott on flute and the under-appreciated Bruce Turner on one track (*Baby*). The LP is devoted to tunes by composer Jimmy McHugh and the excellent rhythm section includes drummer Lennie Hastings whose playing deserves mention. (2) is by a studio-assembled big-band which contains the sax section heard later as part of Woody Herman's Anglo-American Herd (Don Rendell, Johnny Scott, Art Ellefson and Ronnie Ross; Rendell and Ross appear under pseudonyms). In many ways this is the finest big-band record to have been produced in Britain; the section work is excellent and there is a spirit present which is sometimes missing in even the best of the American orchestras. Baker is content to lead the band most of the time, but emerges from the ranks to play an effusive solo on *Sunrise serenade*. The remainder of the material was written by Bill LeSage, Andre Previn, Johnny Scott, Ray Bryant and Baker; Baker's own *Influential character* (dedicated to Duke Ellington) is one of the high-spots of the LP and contains a Cootie Williams-style solo by the leader.

(1) KENNY BAKER AND HIS RHYTHM – 10 Nix NJT517. *1958.*
(2) KENNY BAKER AND THE BAKER'S DOZEN – 10 Col 33S1140. *1959.*

BURT BALES (1916)   *piano*

A Jelly Roll Morton disciple who alternates between Morton

interpretations and the Spanish-tinged style with some ragtime thrown in. He is a modern primitive in approach, sometimes a little heavy and plodding but, at his best, a pleasant enough pianist who does some sincere, accurate and interesting private revivalism.

(1) AFTER HOURS PIANO – 10 GTJ LDG1316. *1949.*
(2) WITH THE RAY ELLIS ORCHESTRA AND CHORUS – 7 GTJ EPG1179. *1949.*
(3) JAZZ FROM THE SAN FRANCISCO WATERFRONT – 10 HMV CLP1218. (A) 10 Cav 5007, 12 ABC 181. *1950s.*
(4) THEY TORE MY PLAYHOUSE DOWN (also Paul Lingle) – (A) 12 GTJ 12025. *1950s.*
(5) BURT BALES WITH MARTY MARSALA'S BAND – 12 HMV CLP1218 *1957.*

PAUL BARBARIN (1901)   *drums*

A jazz musician whose history goes back to 1915 at which time, age 14, he was already a professional drummer, and later played with Keppard and Buddy Pettit. His subsequent career with King Oliver, Luis Russell and Louis Armstrong established him as a respected drummer able to swing almost any sort of band. It is obvious, however, that his real inclination is towards the rougher, primitive jazz of his native New Orleans, with its basic leanings towards the Creole element as illustrated in the joyous *Eh la-bas* on (3). The whole of this LP is full of genuine New Orleans jazz of which Oliver would have approved, the spirit completely captured without resorting to mere roughness, making up one of the most successful New Orleans records of recent years. (1) is rather less successful, while (4) is of a high standard and very well recorded.

(1) PAUL BARBARIN AND HIS NEW ORLEANS BAND – 10 Vog LDE013. (A) 10 Cir C408 (*d*). *1950.*
(2) NEW ORLEANS CONTRASTS (with Sharkey Bonano) – (A) 12 Riv 12-217. *1951.*
(3) PAUL BARBARIN AND HIS NEW ORELEANS JAZZ – 12 Lon LTZ-K15032.
(4) RECORDED IN NEW ORLEANS, Vol. 1 (with Bonano, Matthews and Girard) – 12 GTJ LAG12083. (A) 12 CTJ 12019. *1956.*
(5) PAUL BARBARIN JAZZ BAND (with Johnny St. Cyr) – 7 Tem EXA98. (A) 12 Sou 212. *1956.*

[26]

CHRIS BARBER (1930)   *trombone, bass*

A thoroughly schooled and skilful musician, as a change from the traditionalists who play and lead bands after three months' payments on their instruments, Chris Barber is one of the best trombonists in England, and a fine bass-player, though not heard so frequently on this instrument. Sometimes he also breaks into song, but this is better forgotten. He found his true metier in the crisp-sounding band led by Ken Colyer in 1953 and which, soon after, became Chris Barber's own band. They were distinctive as being perhaps the first group to hit on what might be called an English style of jazz. It had little of the New Orleans tone about it but played in a style (especially noticeable on the ECHOES OF HARLEM LP) which came close to the California Ramblers bands of the '20s. There is no great depth to the music but the crisp, almost staccato sound, and the authoritative playing of Barber and Monty Sunshine, were combined to produce some pleasing and very successful jazz. As with most British groups the rhythm, particularly in slow numbers, is inclined to be plodding, with often weak bass playing and monotonously unenterprising drumming and banjo strumming. If only some of the leaders would spend as much time instructing their rhythm sections as they do their front-lines. It is a fitting place to make these few carping remarks because here is a band which is certainly as good as any white American band heard on record in the last few years and, except for its rhythm section, as good as many Negro bands. Moreover, the better the material selected, the better they play. Generally, however, there is not enough thought given to form (in this they should be compared to the Wilbur de Paris band which excels in creating shape and musical form) and a lot of performances, particularly the concert ones, end up as a rambling string of solos without any structure. These remarks are not only applicable to the Barber band.

The 1954 recording on Decca started this band on its remarkable career. Here tracks like *Bobby Shaftoe* and *The Martinique* illustrate the strength of the band's ensemble playing and the advantages of some careful arrangements. Halcox at this stage was a little weak as a lead trumpet, a fault soon rectified, and with tracks like *Merrydown rag* and the commercially successful *Rock Island Line*, led by Lonnie Donegan, this LP (2) is a notable milestone in British jazz history.

There is an excellent (apart from the vocal) *It's tight like that* on (4) and some delightful sides made at a Festival Hall concert on (5) with some of their best '20s-sounding efforts in *I'd love it* and a fine *Skokiaan*. The band was abetted here by Bertie King on alto. (9) introduced Ottilie Patterson to British audiences and they were captivated by this miniature Bessie Smith when she sang *St. Louis blues* and *Reckless blues*, still two of her best performances. The band fell into a smooth rut at times now but made some of their finest sides in the ECHOES OF HARLEM LP which are absolute gems of rejuvenated period jazz (11), and tracks like *Doin' the crazy walk*, *Sweet Savannah Sue* and *Magnolia's wedding day* are really enjoyable and accomplished sides. All three are on a fine EP, NJE1007, rightly called 'Chris Barber Special'. A series of LPs called Chris Barber in Concert are full of atmosphere and excitement but are apt to get monotonous because they degenerate into strings of solos which may have been fun on the night but sound pretty thin after a couple of playings. Pat Halcox on these plays some confident and exciting music on sides like *Bugle boy march* (23) and the band is best where most arrangement is evident, as on *Majorca* (23), but dreadful where they give Ellington's *Rockin' in rhythm* (23) a Dixieland mauling.

The Barber skiffle group without the ebullient Donegan is a disastrous affair. Copies are never as good as the original and, apart from their thin and callow efforts to sound happy, the tracks on an EP like (18) deserve the censure that would be given to a serious composer who modelled himself on Mozart or a novelist who tried to imitate Dickens today. They are doomed to failure from the start. Young Englishmen cannot sing Negro songs like Negroes, as is amply demonstrated in an EP like (26) where the band accompanies Sonny Terry and Brownie McGhee. The rhythm sparkles with the added power of these natural jazzmen. We cannot review all the Barber records individually but suggest that (28) is a very good sample of their present highly professional and still beautifully crisp playing. All the players have steadily improved and play with great confidence, and Ottilie Patterson's delightful piano and vocal performance on *Squeeze me* shows that her promise has been fulfilled. The band is wonderfully recorded here.

(1) CHRIS BARBER'S NEW ORLEANS JAZZ BAND – 7 Tem EXA6. *1951.*

(2) NEW ORLEANS JOYS – 10 Dec LF1198. *1954.*

(3) Chris Barber's Jazz Band – 7 Tem EXA22. *1954.*

(4) Chris Barber at The Royal Festival Hall, Vol 2 – 7 Dec DFE6344. *1954.*

(5) Jazz at The Royal Festival Hall – 7 Dec DFE6238. *1954.*

(6) Jazz—Sacred and Secular – 12 Col 33S1112. *1954.*

(7) Chris Barber Plays Spirituals – 7 Col SEG7568. *1954.*

(8) Chris Barber at The Royal Festival Hall – 7 Dec DFE6252. *1955.*

(9) Ottilie Patterson with Chris Barber's Jazz Band – 7 Dec DFE6303. *1955.*

(10) Barber's Best – 12 Dec LK4246. *1954–5.*

(11) Echoes of Harlem – 12 Nix NJL1. *1955–6.* (Also 7 NJE1007.)

(12) Barber Goes to Town With Ellington – 7 Col SEG7586. *1955.*

(13) Chris Barber Plays, Vol. 1 – 10 Nix NJT500. *1955.*

(14) That Patterson Girl, Vol. 1 – 7 Nix NJE1012. *1955.*

(15) Chris Barber Plus 1, Minus 1 – 7 Nix NJE1013. *1955.*

(16) Chris Barber Plays, Vol. 2 – 10 Nix NJT502. *1956.*

(17) That Patterson Girl, Vol. 2 – 7 Nix NJE1023. *1956.*

(18) Chris Barber Skiffle Group – 7 Nix NJE1025. *1956.*

(19) Chris Barber Plays, Vol. 3 – 10 Nix NJT505. *1957.*

(20) Chris Barber in Concert, Vol. 1 – 12 Nix NJL6. *1957.*

(21) Chris Barber in Concert, Vol. 2 – 12 Nix NJL15. *1957.*

(22) Chris Barber Plays, Vol. 4 – 10 Nix NJT508. *1957.*

(23) Chris Barber in Concert, Vol. 3 – 12 Nix NJL17. *1958.*

(24) Sonny, Brownie and Chris – 10 Nix NJT515. *1958.*

(25) Chris Barber Jazz Parade, Vol. 1 – 7 Nix NJE1068. *1955–8.*

(26) Chris Barber Jazz Parade, Vol. 2 – 7 Nix NJE1075. *1958.*

(27) Chris Barber International, Vol. 1 (Barber in Berlin) – 12 Col 33SX1189. *1959.*

(28) Chris Barber Band Box – 12 Col 33SX1158. (S) SCX3277. *1959.*

(29) Here is Chris Barber – (A) 12 Atl 1292. *1959.*

COUNT BASIE (1904) *piano, organ*

During the early and middle 1930s big-band jazz was dominated by the orchestras of Duke Ellington and Jimmy Lunceford, bands which played jazz both complex in structure and subtle in harmony.

Then, in 1935, Fletcher Henderson began writing arrangements for Benny Goodman's new orchestra, arrangements in which Henderson employed the same 'call-and-response' pattern that he used when scoring for his own band. It was a pattern many 'swing bands' were to copy. There were two methods, in fact, practised at this time, one emphasizing harmony and texture, the other predominantly formal. In opposition to both these approaches, therefore, was the robust almost bludgeoning music of Count Basie's orchestra, a band which only arrived in New York during the autumn of 1936. A New Yorker himself, Basie had been the pianist with Bennie Moten's Kansas City orchestra. The Moten band had played violently, aggressively; so did Basie's, although with vastly more relaxation. Basing most of its performances upon the blues, the Count Basie orchestra brought a new sense of power to big-band jazz.

The truth was that where other bands experimented with tone-colouring, counterpoint, or other sophistications, Basie's orchestra concentrated upon swinging, upon achieving the maximum rhythmic impetus. The band's Kansas City origin was reflected in its obsessive use of riffs, the repetition of a single, simple musical phrase over and over again, a device that might seem tedious in the hands of dullards but never sounded so when deployed by Basie's musicians. Most of the time the band performed 'head' arrangements, arrangements worked up on the stand by the musicians themselves, arrangements loose enough to allow the full-sized brass and reed sections to swing with a spontaneity which up to then had been the monopoly of small jazz groups. In those days the rhythm section sounded really phenomenal (it still does), a stimulating mixture of verve and relaxation. Basie himself, a master of understatement, has always been a superb orchestral pianist (perhaps the finest apart from Duke Ellington), interjecting single notes at dramatic moments, timing his pauses as skilfully as a great actor. Alongside him in the section were Freddie Greene (still with Basie in 1960, and still the finest of rhythm guitarists), Walter Page (bass) and Jo Jones (drums). In his concentration upon the high-hat cymbal, his shifting of the rhythmic emphasis away from the bass-drum, Jones was already foreshadowing one of the innovations which the modern jazz experimenters were to develop during the 1940s. The lightness and crispness of Basie's rhythm section can be experienced on *Shoe shine swing* (1) and *Lady be good* (2), the work of a sextet, made in 1936 and featuring the earliest recorded solos of a tenor saxophonist who was also the greatest musician in the Basie band – Lester Young. Basie can be heard alone with the rhythm section on two tracks (*Fare thee honey, fare thee well* and *Red wagon*) on (4), an LP which also includes such early yet classic band performances as *Roseland shuffle*, *Shorty George* and *Sent for you yesterday* (with Jimmy Rushing shouting the blues).

Those early years, that period between 1937 and 1941, were the greatest in Basie's career as a bandleader. At that time his orchestra possessed a splendid ferocity and was also wonderfully relaxed. There were often rough edges to the section work, but this band scarcely aimed at sounding immaculate. And just as remarkable as the band's constant ability to swing was the brilliance of the individual soloists. Outside of the Ellington and Henderson orchestras, no band has gathered together so many great soloists at the same time. Sharing tenor solos with Lester Young, for instance, was Herschel Evans, a warmer, more romantic soloist than his partner; his work on *One o'clock jump* (he takes the first tenor solo), *Swinging the blues* (the second one this time) and *Blue and sentimental*, all to be found on (5), are splendidly lyrical. Most of the band's other soloists (Buck Clayton, Harry Edison, Dicky Wells, Lester Young, Vic Dickenson) are discussed under separate headings; all contributed outstanding solos to the band's recordings during those early years. The more extrovert trumpet solos were usually blown by Edison, while Clayton was responsible for most of the delicate, muted playing. *Fiesta in blue*, however, (7) and (10), features Clayton in a miniature 'concerto', using a plunger-mute as well as playing open. (The other tracks on (10), incidentally, are sextet performances from 1950, all of them duplicated on (11).) Another musician who took plenty of solos was Benny Morton, a trombonist who elevated ambiguity to the condition of art. Morton's smeared tone and almost whimsical phrasing (there are moments when he sounds like a brassier version of Pee Wee Russell) can be heard in a typically audacious solo in *Out the window* (3) and (4). When Herschel Evans died in 1939 (he was only 30 years old), his place was taken at one recording session by Chu Berry (Berry can be heard playing an obbligato behind Jimmy Rushing in *Evil blues* (5)); his permanent replacement, however, was Buddy Tate, a tenor player with a style very similar to Evans,

[31]

although not so inventive a soloist. Lester Young left the band at the end of 1940, and his successor was Don Byas, a musician with a talent for creating gentle, almost ruminative solos. Some of Byas's best playing occurs in *Harvard blues* (6) and *Something new* (9).

Probably the most worthwhile single LP drawn from this period is (5). (It includes, incidentally, three tracks – *John's idea*, *Texas shuffle* and *Blue and sentimental* – which are also on (3).) (6) contains splendid examples (made between 1939 and 1942) of the band performing blues of various tinges and bar-lengths, but also includes three tracks by the octet of 1950. (1) and (2) bring together some of Lester Young's greatest solos; nearly all the tracks, however, date from 1940, a time when the band was beginning to use more complex (and usually much duller) arrangements, so that the ensemble work occasionally lacks fire. From around 1941, in fact, until Basie disbanded his group in 1950, the orchestra was sometimes less impressive than the individuals playing it it. There were plenty of good soloists to be heard, among them Wardell Gray, Lucky Thompson, Emmett Berry, J. J. Johnson, Paul Gonsalves, Clark Terry and Illinois Jacquet, but the orchestrations were often commonplace. Examples of this period can be found on records (11) to (15). There were exceptions, of course, such as the spirited *Wonderful thing* (14), featuring some very dashing ensemble work.

In 1950, largely because of the precarious condition of the American music business, Count Basie formed a sextet (sometimes it was an octet), its front-line gathering together the oddly assorted talents of Clark Terry, Wardell Gray, Serge Chaloff and Buddy De Franco. Most recordings by this group were uneven in quality, with far too little heard from Terry and Gray, and with Basie himself sometimes playing in a curiously genteel fashion. (6), (10) and (11) contain typical performances. These were not, of course, the first recordings which Basie had made as leader of a small group. *Dickie's dream* and *Lester leaps in*, brilliantly informal, with inspired playing from Dickie Wells and Lester Young, were recorded by the Kansas City Seven, a detachment from the Basie orchestra, in 1939 and are included in (1). Four more performances (including the superb *Lester leaps again* and *After theatre jump*) were recorded in 1944 by a similar group, again calling itself the Kansas City Seven, and issued on 10 Mer MG25015; this LP has been deleted for several years.

In 1947 Basie organized a group which included Emmett Berry and Paul Gonsalves (Gonsalves was then playing particularly well) for two sessions. Three of the performances which resulted, including the vivacious *Backstage at Stuff's*, can be found on (13).

Count Basie's biggest popular success, however, has been achieved during the past decade, as leader of a band that maintains a phenomenally high standard of technical perfection but which sounds complacent much more often than it sounds inspired. This orchestra possesses competent soloists, men like Joe Newman, Thad Jones, Henry Coker, Al Gray, Frank Foster, Frank Wess and Billy Mitchell, but none who can be compared as creative performers with Lester Young, Dickie Wells, Buck Clayton and Herschel Evans. Not surprisingly, the arranger has assumed much greater importance than in the past. Two arrangers who have played an especially big part in shaping the sound and character of the present-day Basie orchestra are Ernie Wilkins and Neal Hefti, the former basing much of his work upon the twelve-bar blues, the latter very skilful at using the dynamic potentialities of an ensemble that can still sound tigerish when it wants to. But this orchestra had its genesis in a band which Basie organized in 1951, and which can be heard in *Little pony* (featuring a lengthy and inspired tenor solo by Wardell Gray) (12), *Nails* and *Howzit* (8) and *Beaver Junction* (12). Apart from (17) and (18), the work of various pick-up groups (Basie played the organ, Oscar Peterson the piano, on a few tracks), the remaining LPs all feature Basie's new band.

The most rewarding of these latter-day records are (19), (25) (actually made in Sweden, despite the title given the American LP), (27) (recorded while Eddie 'Lockjaw' Davis, a very colourful and dynamic tenor player, was working with the band) and (28). (27) is devoted to scores by Neal Hefti, (28) to orchestrations by Quincy Jones. (26) was recorded on-stage at the 1957 Newport Jazz Festival, the band being joined on some of the tracks by Lester Young, Jo Jones, Roy Eldridge and Jimmy Rushing. Joe Williams, Rushing's successor as singer with Basie, has a rich, flexible voice, but seems more at home in ballads than in blues. His rather melodramatic style, demonstrated on (22), is almost the antithesis of Rushing's gusty tenacity. Jimmy Rushing can be heard, incidentally, on 'The Sound of Jazz' – 12 Fon TFL5025. (A) 12 Col 1098, CS8040, recorded during rehearsals for an American TV jazz programme. On these tracks Basie leads an all-star ensemble, the outstanding soloist being Coleman Hawkins.

(1) LESTER YOUNG MEMORIAL ALBUM, Vol. 1 – 12 Fon TFL5064. (A) 2-12 Ep SN6031. *1936–40.*

(2) LESTER YOUNG MEMORIAL ALBUM, Vol. 2 – 12 Fon TFL5065. (A) 2-12 Ep SN6031. *1936–40.*

(3) JUMPIN' AT THE WOODSIDE – (A) 12 Br 54012. *1937–8.*

(4) BASIE'S BEST – 10 Br LA8589. *1937–9.*

(5) COUNT BASIE AND HIS ORCHESTRA – 12 Br LAT8028. (A) 12 Dec 8049. *1937–9.*

(6) BLUES BY BASIE – 12 Ph BBL7190 (*d*).(A) 12 Col CL901. *1939–50.*

(7) BASIE'S BACK IN TOWN – (A) 12 Ep LN3169. *1940–1.*

(8) COUNT BASIE – 7 Ph BBE12283. *1940–51.*

(9) COUNT BASIE CLASSICS – 12 Fon TFL5077. (A) 12 Col CL754. *1941–6.*

(10) COUNT BASIE – 7 Fon TFE17226. *1941–50.*

(11) ONE O'CLOCK JUMP – 12 Fon TFL5046. (A) 12 Col CL997. *1942–55.*

(12) COUNT BASIE – 7 Fon TFE17015. *1945–51.*

(13) THE COUNT – 12 Cam CDN120. (A) 12 Cam 395. *1947–9.*

(14) COUNT BASIE – 7 HMV 7EG8147 (*d*). (A) 12 RCA LPM-1112 (incl. extra tracks). *1947–50.*

(15) COUNT BASIE – 7 HMV 7EG8221 (*d*) (A) 12 RCA LPM-1112 (incl. extra tracks). *1947–50*

(16) BASIE RIDES AGAIN – (A) 12 Ver 8108. *1952.*

(17) COUNT BASIE SEXTET–10Col 33C9010.(*d*). (A) 12 Ver 8090. *1952.*

(18) THE COUNT AND OSCAR – 7 Col SEB10060. (A) 12 Ver 8090. *1952.*

(19) COUNT BASIE DANCE SESSION – 12 Col 33CX10007. *1953.* (A)[1]

(20) COUNT BASIE DANCE SESSION No. 2 – 12 Col 33CX10044. *1954.* (A).[1]

(21) BASIE – 12 Col 33CX10065. (A) 12 Ver 8103. *1954.*

(22) COUNT BASIE SWINGS, JOE WILLIAMS SINGS – 12 Col 33CX10026. (A) 12 Ver 8063. *1955.*

[1] NOTE: All the tracks on (19) and (20) can be found on (A) Ver 8018 (BASIE ROARS AGAIN) and (A) Ver 8104 (KING OF SWING). The distribution of the tracks, however, does not correspond to that on the British LPs.

(23) APRIL IN PARIS – 12 Col 33CX10088. (A) 12 Ver 8012. *1955*.

(24) BASIE'S BACK IN TOWN (with Ella Fitzgerald) – Col SEB10070. *1956*.

(25) BASIE WAS HERE – 7 Col SEB10083. (A) BASIE IN LONDON (with extra tracks) 12 Ver 8199. *1956*.

(26) BASIE AT NEWPORT – 12 Col 33CX10110. (A) 12 Ver 8243, 6024. *1957*.

(27) THE ATOMIC MR. BASIE – 12 Col 33SX1084, (S) SCX3265. (A) 12 Rou 52003, (S) SR52003. *1957*.

(28) ONE MORE TIME – 12 Col 33SX1183, (S) SCX3284. (A) Rou R52024, (S) SR52024. *1958–9*.

(29) CHAIRMAN OF THE BOARD – 12 Col 33SX 1224, (S) SCX3304. (A) Rou R 52032, (S) SR52032. *1959*.

RAY BAUDUC (1908)   *drums*

A fine drummer who has played mostly with Bob Crosby. Although a white musician he has managed more than most to get the crisp, driving and varied approach of drummers like Zutty Singleton and Baby Dodds, and it was partly due to his efforts that the Bob Cats were such a great little group.

(1) RIVERBOAT DANDIES (Bauduc and Lamare group) – (A) 12 Cap T-877. *1957*.

BILLY BAUER (1915)   *guitar*

Bauer is one of the very few contemporary guitarists to pull his weight in the rhythm section when he is not playing a solo. He is a remarkably intelligent jazzman whose helpful feeding of chords in just the right places spurs on even the most recalcitrant soloists. For several years a vital member of the Woody Herman Herd, Bauer has been associated with the Lennie Tristano school since the late nineteen-forties. With Tristano he has developed an affinity for the styles of Lee Konitz and Warne Marsh and it is with these two saxophonists, Konitz in particular, that the true value of his playing is most apparent. His guitar work is beautifully integrated with Konitz's alto on the two duets, *Indian Summer* and *Duet for saxophone and guitar* (1), while his presence in a pianoless rhythm section (3) means that he shoulders much of the harmonic responsibility. Suffice it to say that (3) is one of Lee Konitz's best appearances on record and is due in no small measure to the sensitivity of Bauer's

[35]

chordal interpolations. His sole album as leader is a superb showcase for his unique talents; it is an album which gets away from the stereotyped, run-of-the-mill LPs and gives evidence of having been carefully planned. *Blue mist* is a delightful, unaccompanied solo (he is assisted by piano, bass and drums on the other ten tracks) which is reminiscent of Django Reinhardt in places.

(1) CONCEPTION (various artists) – 12 Esq 32-052. (A) 12 Pre PRLP7013. *1951*.

(2) BILLY BAUER—PLECTRIST – (A) 12 Ver 8172. (Four titles each on Col SEB10061 and SEB10089.) *1956*.

(3) THE REAL LEE KONITZ – 12 Lon LTZ-K15147. (A) 12 Atl 1273. *1957*.

SIDNEY BECHET (1891-1959)   *soprano sax, clarinet*

Sidney Bechet is probably the only major soloist in jazz whose importance lies entirely in the music he created. He influenced hardly anybody (Johnny Hodges is almost a lonely exception), he inaugurated no trends, he really never led a band for very long. But he was an outsize soloist, a kind of Donald Woolfit of jazz, whose rhetorical playing, sometimes violent, occasionally sentimental, dominated any group he played in. His weaknesses and virtues were exaggerated by his choice of instrument, for the soprano saxophone, when played indifferently, can be either hideously strident or unbearably voluptuous. In Bechet's hands, however, it became a vehicle for that startling mixture of brashness and sensitivity, of nostalgia and genuine lyricism, which the musician poured into his solos. For Bechet was a very natural performer; even his vibrato, wider than that of anyone else in jazz, was the hallmark of a man who liked to play that way, who never worried about the correctness of his approach to music. Bechet's solos were predominantly melodic (there is little implication of harmony, never any ambiguity) and at his finest he was a superbly lyrical performer. Sometimes he descended into bathos, sometimes he fell back (particularly in later years) upon his own clichés; yet on the right day he could be a magnificently impassioned soloist, as majestic as Louis Armstrong, as intense as Charlie Parker. And like both those men, he too was a great blues player.

In New Orleans, Bechet had been known as a clarinettist, and he continued to play that instrument – although more and more sparingly – until the last years of his life. It was a pity he used the instrument so little, for it brought out a special eloquence in his music. He could manipulate his tone with great virtuosity, using a twist here, a deeper tinge there, to add expressiveness to his phrasing. And where Bechet's soprano playing disrupted most ensembles, his clarinet playing usually fitted in ideally. A good example of this can be found in the 1941 recording of *Egyptian fantasy* (issued on HMV 78, long ago deleted), where Bechet and Henry Allen establish a perfect balance in the front-line. As for his solo work on the clarinet, *Blues in thirds* (1), where he is accompanied by Earl Hines and Baby Dodds, must be counted among the greatest of jazz recordings.

The best of Sidney Bechet's early recordings were made with various Clarence Williams groups – either the Blue Five (*Wild cat blues, Kansas city moan*) or the Red Onion Jazz Babies (*Cake walking babies*) – but none is currently available. In 1932 Bechet and the trumpet-player Tommy Ladnier organized the New Orleans Feetwarmers, and three tracks recorded by this band – *Shag, Lay your racket* and the audacious *Maple Leaf rag* – are included in (1), while another title, *I've found a new baby*, can be found in GREAT JAZZ BRASS – a Camden LP. Throughout most of the 1930s Bechet worked in Noble Sissle's orchestra, and it is a group drawn from that band which he leads on *Blackstick, When the sun sets down south* and *Sweet patootie* (4), the first and second items being outstandingly good. *Blackstick* is also in ENCYCLOPAEDIA OF JAZZ, Vol. 2, on Br (A) Dec. (The other tracks on (4), incidentally, come from a French session made in 1956 and are of little interest). The performances on (2) are rather wishy-washy, while (3) is a set of quartet recordings made in 1947 (including a lithe version of *Buddy Bolden stomp*). The American LP includes, in addition, three tracks with Bob Wilber's Wildcats, also recorded in 1947. A performance of exceptional value – Sidney Bechet and Tommy Ladnier playing *Weary blues* and *Sister Kate* at a Carnegie Hall concert in 1938 – can be found in 'Spirituals to Swing' ((A) 12 Van 8523). And it was with an orchestra led by Tommy Ladnier that Bechet made his next outstanding recordings, *Really the blues* and *Weary blues*. The former is included in (A) 12 Fol 2811, while both items appear on 10 HMV DLP1110 (d). This latter LP, however, contains only second masters (both inferior) of these recordings and it is worth looking out for the old HMV 78s.

(5) and (6) include some of Bechet's most eloquent performances from this period. On the former is his 1939 version of *Summertime*, a recording which became unusually popular and made him begin featuring more of these rather florid performances. This LP also includes *Blue horizon*, while (6) contains *Pounding heart blues* and *Blues for Tommy*. It was around this time, too, that Bechet played on two important sessions – one with Jelly Roll Morton, the other with Louis Armstrong. On the Morton recordings (all were once available on HMV 78s) he was in spirited form, contributing a particularly venomous solo to *Oh, didn't he ramble*. The Louis Armstrong session produced four classic performances, with Armstrong and Bechet ideally counterpoising one another in *Coal cart blues*. All four tracks are available on 7 Br OE9287. In 1940 Bechet began recording again with his New Orleans Feetwarmers, the personnel of which varied considerably. (1) includes *Shake it and break it* (with a fine trombone solo by Sandy Williams), the slow, dragging blues *Nobody knows the way I feel*, and *Wild man blues*, all by this group. *Nobody knows* is also available on GREAT JAZZ REEDS – a Camden LP. On another Camden album (12 CDN-105, (A) 12 CAL-321), by the 'N.B.C. Chamber Music Society of Lower Basin Street', Bechet performs a good *Muskrat ramble*, not helped at all by a stodgy accompanying group. (7) and (8) contain tracks recorded with Muggsy Spanier in 1940, including (on (7)) a very exciting *China boy*. The other half of (8) was made at the same time as (15), the products of a session recorded in London in 1949 with the Humphrey Lyttelton band.

The finest recordings Bechet made during the 1940s, however – and probably the finest he ever made – are contained on (9), a superb collection of blues on which he was partnered by the clarinettist, Mezz Mezzrow. It is no exaggeration to describe such tracks as *Gone away blues* and *Out of the gallion* as classic performances, worthy to be ranked alongside Louis Armstrong's *Potato head blues* or *Knockin' a jug*. The adaptation of the New Orleans pattern to a front-line of clarinet and soprano sax produced an entirely fresh texture; there was too a perfect interior balance, Mezzrow and Bechet interweaving in some of the most intimate ensemble improvisation ever heard in jazz. On a couple of tracks (*Blood on the moon* and *Old school*) the group

[38]

was augmented by Hot Lips Page, who plays a fierce, biting lead. Although this LP contains the cream of these performances, there are a number almost as good which are not included, and many of these are still available in Britain on King Jazz 78s. These recordings include *Where am I?* (KJ3), *Perdido street stomp* (KJ4), *Chicago Function* (Parts 1 and 2) (KJ5), *Breathless blues/Groovin' the minor* (KJ6), *I'm going away from here* (KJ7), *I'm speaking my mind* (KJ8) and *Kaiser's last break/Delta mood* (KJ11).

On (10) Bechet plays agreeably enough in the company of Joe Sullivan, while (11) finds him leading a group that included Art Hodes and Wild Bill Davison, the latter sounding more relaxed than he usually does. These are good but not at all remarkable performances. Most of (12) is played by a similar band, this time with Jimmy Archey added on trombone and Joe Sullivan taking over from Hodes on a few tracks. The finest jazz here, though, occurs in two duets – *Bechet's fantasy* and *Old stack o' lee blues* – by Bechet and Albert Nicholas. (13) was recorded in Paris (where Bechet had been appearing in a jazz festival) and presents him in fiery soprano playing, with good drumming by Kenny Clarke. One of Bechet's finest solos, in *Cé mossieu qui parlé* (14), was also recorded in Paris, this time with Claude Luter's band, a French revivalist group. Luter's band is heard again in (16), a fairly good collection of its kind, with the emphasis upon virtuoso playing by Bechet, an emphasis which recurs on most of the records Bechet made with French groups. By now Bechet was living in France and enjoying exceptional fame and popularity there. His work over the next decade, however, was to suffer from his playing too much with inferior musicians. Probably Luter's band was the best of those which worked with him regularly. It is heard yet again on (24), by far the finest of the various concert recordings Bechet made in Paris, most of them distressingly bad. Apart from a rowdy version of *When the saints go marching in*, this LP contains plenty of good music, including luxuriant blues playing in *Sobbin' and cryin' blues*. By now Bechet was featuring himself more and more frequently in purplish versions of popular songs, as well as playing plenty of Creole tunes and little melodies (often with an Edwardian as well as a Creole tinge) that he wrote himself. (18) consists of performances in this category, although these were better than most, including well-controlled versions of *Jacqueline* and *September song*.

[39]

Much more virile jazz, however, can be found on (17), played by a trio consisting of Bechet, Lil Armstrong and Zutty Singleton. Bechet spent some months in the United States during 1953, and while there he recorded (19), (20), (21) and (22). On (19) he was teamed with Jonah Jones, a trumpet-player possessing the necessary quiddity to stand up to him. Their collaboration produced, among other good tracks, a moving performance of *Black and blue*. A year later Jonah Jones partnered Bechet once more (23), this time in Paris, and once again the music turned out well. (20) was recorded at a concert in Los Angeles, but a concert which caught Bechet at the peak of his form, supported by a very competent group in Bob Scobey's band. He plays well-poised solos in *On the sunny side of the street, St. Louis blues, Muskrat ramble* and *Summertime*. (21) and (22) were recorded with a group including Vic Dickenson, but Bechet was in poor health at the time and his playing lacked its usual fire.

As the years went on, Bechet's playing became more and more stereotyped. Instead of creating new solos, he would repeat his old ones (often very good ones, of course) note for note. This meant that much of his latter-day work sounded stale. During the last five years of his life, in fact, practically the only worthwhile playing Bechet achieved on records was done in the company of visiting American musicians, musicians who spurred him into improvising something new. One of these occasions produced (25), an LP on which Bechet performed with Sammy Price's Bluesicians, not a great band but a pretty good one, and including at least two exceptional soloists in Emmett Berry and Price himself. These are meaty performances, even if the ensembles get a bit messy here and there. (26) was recorded with the French pianist, Martial Solal, and a rhythm section which had Kenny Clarke and Al Levitt alternating on drums. Solal, a relatively modern pianist (he plays a little like Hank Jones), partnered Bechet surprisingly well. There are good solos here, but the overall level is uneven and it seems a pity that the material did not include any blues. Teddy Buckner, a forceful trumpet-player, very much in the Armstrong tradition, can be heard in (27) and (28). The former, a studio recording, with Kansas Fields on drums, is the superior LP. (28) (half of it recorded in Knokke, the other half in Cannes) has Vic Dickenson and Sammy Price as well, but the music is very disjointed, both Bechet and Buckner over-blowing badly at times.

[40]

(29) is Bechet's last recording, made at a concert in Brussels, the group also including Buck Clayton, Vic Dickenson and Kansas Fields. By this time, unhappily, Bechet seemed to have given up trying and his playing lacks boldness.

(1) SHAKE IT AND BREAK IT – 10 HMV DLP1042 (*d*). *1932–41.*
(2) SIDNEY BECHET – 7 Ph BBE12109 (*d*). (A) 12 Col CL836 (plus extra titles). *1938–47.*
(3) SIDNEY BECHET – 7 Ph BBE12357 (*d*). (A) 12 Col CL836 (plus extra titles). *1938–47.*
(4) THE SIDNEY BECHET STORY – (A) 12 Br BL54048. *1938–56.*
(5) JAZZ CLASSICS, Vol. 1 – (A) 12 BN 1201. *1939–47.*
(6) JAZZ CLASSICS, Vol. 2 – (A) 12 BN 1202. *1939–47.*
(7) BECHET-SPANIER BIG FOUR – 7 Mel epm-7-62. *1940.*
(8) BECHET-SPANIER/BECHET-LYTTELTON – 7 Mel epm-7-68. *1940–9.*
(9) REALLY THE BLUES – 12 Vog LAE12017. *1945–7.*
(10) BECHET-SULLIVAN QUARTET – 7 Tem EXA7. *1945.*
(11) SIDNEY BECHET AND HIS BLUE NOTE JAZZMEN, Vol. 2 – 10 Vog LDE086. *1945–9.* (A).[1]
(12) SIDNEY BECHET AND HIS BLUE NOTE JAZZMEN, Vol 1 – 10 Vog LDE025. *1946–50.* (A).[1]
(13) SIDNEY BECHET AND HIS FEETWARMERS – 10 Esq 20-058. *1949.*
(14) SOUVENIRS OF NEW ORLEANS – 7 Vog EPV1020. *1949.*
(15) BECHET-LYTTELTON – 7 Mel EPM-7-51. *1949.*
(16) SIDNEY BECHET – 12 Vog LAE12024. *1950–2.*
(17) NEW ORLEANS IN PARIS – 10 Vog LDE069. *1952.*
(18) SIDNEY BECHET – 7 Vog EPV1062. *1952–3.*
(19) SIDNEY BECHET AND HIS BLUE NOTE JAZZMEN, Vol. 3 – 10 Vog LDE127. *1953.* (A).[1]
(20) SIDNEY BECHET WITH BOB SCOBEY – 7 Vog EPV1026. *1953.*
(21) SIDNEY BECHET AT STORYVILLE, Vol. 1 – 10 Vog LDE132. (A) Four titles on 12 Sto 902. *1953.*
(22) SIDNEY BECHET AT STORYVILLE, Vol. 2 – 10 Vog LDE149. (A) Three titles on 12 Sto 902. *1953.*
(23) SIDNEY BECHET AND HIS VOGUE JAZZMEN – 10 Vog LDE119. *1954.*

[1] NOTE: A majority of the tracks on (11), (12) and (19) are contained on (A) 12 BN 1203 (GIANTS OF JAZZ, Vol. 1), 12 BN 1204 (GIANTS OF JAZZ, Vol. 2) and 12 BN 1207 (THE FABULOUS SIDNEY BECHET) respectively. In each case a number of additional tracks have been included.

(24) OLYMPIA CONCERT – 12 Vog LAE12003. *1954.*

(25) SIDNEY BECHET WITH SAMMY PRICE'S BLUESICIANS – 12 Vog LAE12037. (A) 12 Br 54037. *1956.*

(26) SIDNEY BECHET HAS YOUNG IDEAS – (A) 12 WP PJ1236. *1957.*

(27) 'BRAVO' – 12 Vog LAE12153. *1958.*

(28) FESTIVAL DE JAZZ, 1958 – 12 Vog LAE12168. *1958.*

(29) CONCERT Á BRUXELLES – 12 Nix NPL28006. *1958.*

BIX BEIDERBECKE (1903–31) *cornet, piano*

One of the legendary names of jazz, emerging from a fog of romantic nostalgia following an early death and an uncomfortable genius, Beiderbecke is one of the oddities of jazz history. He was not a hot musician in the Negro tradition and he never played in a really hot group – in fact if he had lived longer it would probably have become apparent that he was one of the most progressive musicians and he would have ended up happily and successfully playing alongside Charlie Parker. As it was he played before his time and we are left with a tantalizing glimpse of what could have been. His tone has a strange luminous quality and his solos follow a line that could only be the result of a harmonic development of the theme far more complicated and imaginative than the composer of the number or the band playing it could conceive. His recorded piano solo (4) with its Billy Mayerl type title and characteristics shows the lines on which his mind was working – the cooling down and Europeanizing of jazz which was in fact what pianists like Billy Mayerl and composers like Raymond Scott were doing. On the cornet he could only hint at these ideas because no one was there to supply the needed harmonies.

His exotic tone enlivened what would otherwise have been rather dull recordings with the Wolverines in 1924 (1), *Fidgety feet* and *Copenhagen* standing out as bustling Dixie-styled performances. Two sides, *I'm glad* and *Flock o' blues*, started the trend where Bix found a fellow-feeler in Frankie Trumbauer. The recordings of 1925 in the meantime with his Rhythm Jugglers, *Davenport blues* and *Toddlin' blues*, established a Bixian style (deleted Lon AL3543). 1927 was an important year. It included the recordings with Bix and his Gang, mostly from Paul Whiteman's orchestra, which notably included *At the jazz band ball* (2), *Jazz me blues* (2) and *Royal Garden blues* (2); the recordings with Trumbauer and his Orchestra, especially *Singin' the blues* (3) and *I'm coming Virginia* (3) – two of his best recordings; some recordings with Jean Goldkette for Victor, not at present available; and some recordings with Paul Whiteman's orchestra (4) where Bix occasionally shines forth. Later recordings with Trumbauer and Whiteman showed a falling off of jazz quality and oddities like *Barnacle Bill the sailor* with Hoagy Carmichael, although enlivened by a good Bix solo ('Great Jazz Brass') hardly do much to glorify the annals of jazz.

(1) BIX BEIDERBECKE AND THE WOLVERINES – (A) 12 Riv 12-123. Lon AL3532 and AL3543 (*d*). *1924–5*.

(2) THE BIX BEIDERBECKE STORY, Vol. 1 (BIX AND HIS GANG) – (A) 12 Col CL-844. 7 Fon TFE17059. *1927–8*.

(3) THE BIX BEIDERBECKE STORY, Vol. 2 (BIX AND TRAM) – (A) 12 Col CL-845. 7 Fon TFE17109, TFE17060. *1927–9*.

(4) THE BIX BEIDERBECKE STORY, Vol. 3 (WHITEMAN DAYS) – (A) 12 Col CL-846. 7 Fon TFE17061. *1927–9*.

BUNNY BERIGAN (1909–42)   *trumpet*

If Bix Beiderbecke is the most purely lyrical of white trumpet players, then his closest rival must certainly be Bunny Berigan. Both men died young (Beiderbecke at 28, Berigan at 31), both were keenly admired by their fellow musicians while living, both have been turned into something of a legend after their deaths. But although Berigan displays more than a sprinkling of Beiderbecke's lyrical approach in his solos, even to the extent of introducing a few Bix-like cadences, the structure of his playing derives from Louis Armstrong. Warm-toned, powerful, full of characteristic flourishes, his work is immediately recognizable.

Bunny Berigan was a member of Benny Goodman's first regular orchestra and plays one of his most famous solos on Goodman's 1935 recording of *King Porter stomp* (7 RCA RCX1019). In 1936 he moved across to Tommy Dorsey's orchestra, and can be heard on 7 RCA RCX1002 in *Marie* and *Song of India*, performances which include two more turbulent yet logical solos. He formed his own band in 1937 (the 'swing craze' was well under way by then and plenty of sidemen were starting out on their own), a band featured on (3), an EP which includes the 1937 version of Berigan's signature tune *I can't get started*. Berigan's own playing is masterly, but the band rarely lives up to his standards.

An earlier recording of *I can't get started* (with Artie Shaw on clarinet and Joe Bushkin on piano) was made in 1936 and is included in (1), together with *A melody from the sky* and *Rhythm saved the world*, from the same session. The tenor player on these and several other tracks was Forrest Crawford, a musician with an optimistic, impetuous style who seems to have disappeared from the jazz scene. The same LP has Berigan playing one of his finest solos in *Solo hop*, by Glenn Miller's orchestra. Two other tracks (*Dixieland shuffle* and *Let's do it*) are by a big band, but the remainder all feature jam session groups. The vocal choruses by Chick Bullock which adorned several of the original 78s have been deleted in the transfer to LP. (2) contains four titles recorded especially for release in Britain by a group that included Cliff Jackson (he takes delightful piano solos on every track), Eddie Miller and Edgar Sampson. Berigan plays poorly on *Blues* but improves on the other tracks, especially on *I'm coming Virginia*.

(1) TAKE IT, BUNNY! – 12 Ph BBL7086 (*d*). (A) 12 Ep LG3109. *1935–7*.
(2) BUNNY BERIGAN'S BLUE BOYS – 7 Par GEP8582 (*d*). *1935*.
(3) BUNNY BERIGAN – 7 RCA RCX1005. *1937*.

CHU BERRY (1910–41)   *tenor saxophone*

There was always an impetuous, slightly headlong quality about Chu Berry's playing. To the sound and pattern of Coleman Hawkins' style he brought a nervous excitement of his own. It is this which gives his work its main value and interest, for he was never a particularly inventive player; his rhapsodizing in slow tempos, for instance, lacked the imaginative power which unites Hawkins' essays in this genre. Chu, in fact, was a 'swinging' tenor player, using a light, dry tone and mainly concentrating upon the upper register of his instrument. In the early 1930s he worked for a time with Benny Carter's orchestra and was present at the sessions Spike Hughes recorded with this band in 1933. In several cases he split tenor choruses with Coleman Hawkins. Solos by Berry can be heard in *Fanfare*, *Music at midnight*, *Firebird* and *How come you do me* (12 Dec LK4173); on all except the last-named track, Chu takes the first solo, Hawkins the second. Three years later Chu Berry contributed

[44]

two outstanding solos to *Swing is here* and *I hope Gabriel likes my music*, by Gene Krupa's All Star Swing Band (7 HMV 7EG8111 (*d*), (A) 12 Cam 340). By this time he was working with Fletcher Henderson's orchestra, and can be heard playing brief but often exciting solos on this band's recordings, notably in *Stealin' apples* (Br 78, (*d*)).

In 1937 Chu Berry recorded two sessions with his Stompy Steve-dores. Eight tracks by this group (four with Hot Lips Page on trumpet) are included in (1), plus three more by the Cab Calloway orchestra, all with solos from Chu. The tenor player worked for Calloway from 1937 until his death (in a road accident) in 1941, and can be heard on many Calloway recordings, including a long, rhapsodic solo in *Ghost of a chance*, once released on a Par 78 but since deleted. Chu made two more sessions under his own name for (A) Com, in 1938 (with Roy Eldridge) and in 1941 (with Hot Lips Page), and these recordings were once available on (A) 12 Com 20024. When Herschel Evans died in 1939 Chu took his place on a Count Basie recording session and can be heard in a good solo on *Lady be good* (Br 78 (d)) and playing an obbligato behind Jimmy Rushing in *Evil blues* (12 Br LAT8028 (A) 12 Dec 8049). Finally, two of Berry's finest solos can be found in *Shufflin' at the Hollywood* ('Great Jazz Reeds', 12 Cam CDN-139 (A) 12 Cam CAL-339) and *Sweethearts on parade* ('Open House', 12 Cam CDN-138 (A) 12 Cam CAL-517), both with Lionel Hampton's orchestra. A minor curiosity (although it's also a good solo) is the improvisation he plays in *High Society*, also with Hampton's band, on 'Jivin' The Vibes' (12 Cam CDN129 (A) 12 Cam CAL-402).

(1) CHU – 12 Ph BBL7054 (*d*). (A) 12 Ep LG-3124. *1937–40*.

EMMETT BERRY (1915) *trumpet*

Just like any other sort of artist, the jazz musician tends either to erupt, briefly but gloriously, quite early on, turning the remainder of his career into a long anti-climax, or else he begins indifferently and slowly fumbles his way to success. Emmett Berry belongs to the latter group. He served a long apprenticeship with big bands, starting off in 1937 with Fletcher Henderson's orchestra and only completing it when he left Count Basie thirteen years later. Many of his early solos were disappointing (*Sweet and lovely* of 1941 on

[45]

EmArcy's TRUMPET INTERLUDE collection, for instance, is curiously unenterprising), but over the years Berry has gradually developed a style in which delicacy and strength are cunningly balanced. Louis Armstrong, Roy Eldridge, and Harry Edison seem to have been his exemplars. Some of his best solos can be found on tracks recorded with Johnny Hodges' little band between 1951 and 1954. And it was with that band, but with Charlie Holmes playing alto sax instead of Hodges and with the tenor-player, Al Sears, acting as leader, that he recorded *Berry well*, a trumpet feature carrying echoes of *Struttin' with some barbecue*, on 7 Par GEP8688. Berry takes another outstanding solo in *Nell don't wear no button up shoes*, made at the same session (in 1951) and issued on 7 Par GEP8681. 'Jo Jones Special', 12 Van PPL11002 (*d*), (A) 12 Van 8503, recorded in 1955, is notable for Berry's splendid work with the mute, as well as some luxuriant tenor playing by Lucky Thompson. Later that year Berry travelled to Europe with Sam Price's Bluesicians, and in Paris he took part in several sessions. He plays particularly well on the majestic *Blue Berry* ('Swingin' Paris Style', 12 Vog LAE12027) by Price's Bluesicians. His own LP (1) was recorded shortly afterwards. As well as presenting Berry in unusually good form, it displays the warm, resilient tenor playing of Guy Lafitte, one of the most original of the French jazz musicians. Another of Berry's best solos – a piquant, very fragile comment on *Love is here to stay* – is included in 'Trumpets All Out', 12 Lon LTZ-C15093, (A) 12 Sav 12096, an LP, made in 1956, on which he blows his trumpet alongside Harold Baker, Art Farmer, Ernie Royal and Charlie Shavers.

(1) EMMETT BERRY AND HIS ORCHESTRA – 10 Col 33S1107 (*d*). *1956*.

BARNEY BIGARD (1906)   *clarinet*
Stanley Dance, in a memorable phrase, once compared Barney Bigard to 'a falcon soaring against cliffs of brass'. He was writing, of course, about the clarinettist when he was a member of Duke Ellington's orchestra, for it is that period of his career which produced the finest music. The decorative element in Bigard's playing, the wide, looping phrases, the Noone-like swoops and runs, all the paraphernalia of the New Orleans clarinettist in fact, made a perfect foil to the heavy textures of Ellington's orchestrations. Among his best solos with the Ellington band are those in *Saratoga swing* (a

splendid example of his blues playing) (12 Cam CDN119, (A) 12 Cam 459), *Jack the Bear* (12 RCA RD27133, (A) 12 Vic LPM1715) and *Rocks in my bed* and *A portrait of Bert Williams* (12 RCA RD27134, (A) 12 Vic LPM1364). Three tracks on THE DUKE's MEN, an (A) Ep LP, are played by a small group drawn from the Ellington orchestra: as well as featuring some of Bigard's most supple playing (particularly in the languid *Clouds in my heart*) they contain solos by Cootie Williams. Many other Bigard-led performances are to be found on various LPs of assorted Ellington small groups. When the Ellington band was in Paris in 1939, Bigard played on four tracks recorded by the Rex Stewart Footwarmers (7 HMV 7EG8447), and these solos must rank among his very finest.

After leaving Duke Ellington in 1942 (after being with the band for fourteen years), Bigard played for a time with Kid Ory, then joined Louis Armstrong's All Stars. During all this period, however, his solos were timid and repetitive, never comparable to his work with the Ellington band. An exception is the leaping solo he recorded on *Lulu's mood*, by the Zutty Singleton Trio, 12 Cap T793 ('The History of Jazz', Vol. 1). Since he left the Armstrong group, Bigard has lived on the West coast, where he leads the band heard on (1), a group reputed to play very exuberant, easy-swinging jazz.

(1) JAZZ HALL OF FAME – (A) 12 Lib 3072. *1958.*

BLIND BLAKE (Arthur Phelps) (?–1932?)   *vocal, guitar*

Though no mean singer, it was as a guitarist that Blind Blake excelled. His highly developed technique enabled him to provide ideal accompaniments for blues singers and musicians alike, creating a considerable demand for his services at recording sessions. His singing, a little lacking in excitement, is in the style of the classic, rather than the country blues; it is a sound which may please but will rarely startle. The very strong element of ragtime made his blues playing a fascinating sound, always in perfect taste. But, alas, there is a sad lack of dynamics in his playing. This is very largely the reason for which one would hesitate to rank him with the few brilliant – there were many good ones – blues musicians/singers of all time.

(1) BLIND BLAKE – 10 JC JFL2001. *1926–9.*
(2) THE MALE BLUES, Vol. 3 – 7 JC JEL4.
(3) JOHNNY DODDS, Vol. 1 – 10 Lon AL3505 (d). *1928.*

(4) JOHNNY DODDS, Vol. 2 – 10 Lon AL3513 (*d*). *1928.*
(5) JOHNNY DODDS, Vol. 4 – 10 Lon AL3560 (*d*). *1928.*
(6) PIONEERS OF BOOGIE WOOGIE, Vol. 1 – 10 Lon AL3506 (*d*). *1929.*
(7) *Hey hey Daddy blues/Brownskin Mama blues* – 10 78 Tem R23 (*d*). *1927.*
(8) *C. C. Pill blues/Southern rag* – 10 78 Tem R40 (*d*). *1927.*

EUBIE BLAKE (1883) *piano*

A famous ragtime composer in his day who graduated to the entertainment world, being responsible for most of the music for two of the greatest coloured shows ever written; *Shuffle Along*, 1921, and *Chocolate Dandies*, 1924; also *Blackbirds of 1930*. It is a great shame that he has recorded so little as a pianist. One piano-roll track was available on HARLEM PIANO ROLL (10 Lon AL3553 (*d*)), an interesting collection, and that is about all. We can be doubly grateful for an EP (1) which shows what a fine and entertaining musician he was. Tracks like *Jubilee tonight* and *I'm just wild about Harry* are full of the old vaudeville spirit, with minstrel-style vocals by Noble Sissle, fine clarinet by Buster Bailey and joyful drumming by Panama Francis. *Eubie's boogie rag, Mobile rag* and *Sunflower slow drag* leave no doubt as to his effervescent talents as a pianist. (2) continues the saga.

(1) RAGTIME, Vol. 1 – THE FABULOUS PIANO OF EUBIE BLAKE – 7 TR JKP2008. *1958.*
(2) RAGTIME, Vol. 2 – THE FABULOUS PIANO OF EUBIE BLAKE – 7 TR JKP2014. *1958.*

ART BLAKEY (1919) *drums*

Since the late nineteen-forties jazz drummers seem to have concentrated on playing with more volume than before. Undoubtedly one of the loudest is Art Blakey, yet Blakey usually succeeds in avoiding boorishness by his quick and intelligent appreciation of the situations at hand. He is at his best in the company of strong soloists or accompanying percussive pianists such as Thelonious Monk and Horace Silver; he is at his worst behind weaker front-line men whose powers of invention soon crumble beneath the bombastic anarchism of Blakey in full flight. Nevertheless he is one of the most individual percussionists jazz has ever known with an unswerving dedication to the beat, boundless energy and a good sense of time. He has a tendency to dominate small groups and will sometimes throw in a crush roll to disrupt a soloist's line when he thinks a punctuation is required; similarly he will suddenly break into double time when supporting a member of the front line, even though the soloist has not indicated a desire to alter the metric pulse in this way. But these deviations from accepted practice have all helped to establish the Blakey method of drumming, a method which has been imitated frequently but never surpassed. Art has led some remarkably good groups in the past (and some singularly bad ones too), one of the best being the quintet he took to Birdland at the beginning of 1954. Blue Note BLP1521 and 1522 were recorded at the club and feature the quintet members (Clifford Brown, Lou Donaldson, Horace Silver, Curley Russell and Blakey) at peak form. Later in the same year the Jazz Messengers were formed, the first group comprising Kinny Dorham, Hank Mobley, Silver, Doug Watkins and Blakey; again Blue Note took their recording gear on location, this time to the Café Bohemia where they captured the best of the Messengers on two LPs, BLP1507 and 1508. Due to personnel changes the Messengers underwent a decline during which time Blakey took the opportunity of subjugating the new and weaker soloists, consequently fast tempos and lengthy drum solos became the order of the day as witness (4). A major part of this LP is devoted to a pretentious percussion display entitled *Ritual*, in the course of which the entire unit (Bill Hardman, Jackie McLean, Sam Dockery, Spanky DeBrest and Blakey) adds to the tub-thumping and tintinnabulations. With two changes of personnel, tenor saxist Johnny Griffin for McLean and pianist Junior Mance for Dockery, the Messengers made a much better LP (5) which enabled the listener to appreciate the true value of the soloists. Despite the album title, 'Hard Drive', the accent is on music played at much saner tempos with a consequent increase in solo quality, trumpeter Hardman in particular playing with poise and inventiveness. With Thelonious Monk sitting in for Mance this same personnel made an outstanding LP (6) in which the pianist quickly impressed his unique personality on the music; *Blue Monk* from this album is a noteworthy performance while the high-speed fingering of Griffin throughout is remarkable for its accuracy. (7) is an interesting experiment for Art is given the chance of driving a specially-assembled big band containing many men who have worked for him in the past. Some of the section playing is imperfect but the overall enthusiasm and uninhibited power of the ensemble recalls the exciting orchestras of Dizzy Gillespie. Without doubt Blakey is the most suitable drummer to accompany either Monk or Horace Silver. (3) features Thelonious playing a set of standard tunes with Art and Oscar Pettiford and the drummer's punctuations add much to Monk's solos. (1) finds Blakey backing up Horace Silver on his first trio recordings, underlining the pianist's inventions with suitably aggressive figurations; the same LP contains Art's stimulating unaccompanied drum solo *Nothing but the soul* which is kept to within the sensible limitations of three minutes. One side of (2) contains a quartet session by Miles Davis and it is on Monk's tune *Well you needn't* that Blakey rises to the occasion, punching home his fill-ins with force and accuracy.

(1) HORACE SILVER TRIO – (A) 12 BN BLP1520. (Eight titles on Vog LDE065.) *1952* and *1953*.

(2) MILES DAVIS, Vol. 2 – (A) 12 BN BLP1502. *1954*.

(3) THELONIOUS MONK TRIO – 12 Lon LTZ-U15071. (A) 12 Riv RLP12-209. *1956*.

(4) ART BLAKEY'S JAZZ MESSENGERS – 12 Vog LAE12096. (A) PJ 402. *1957*.

(5) THE JAZZ MESSENGERS – 12 Par PMC1084. (A) 12 Beth 6023. *1957*.

(6) JAZZ MESSENGERS WITH THELONIOUS MONK – 12 Lon LTZ-K15157. (A) 12 Atl 1278. *1957*.

(7) ART BLAKEY'S BIG BAND – 12 Par PMC1099. (A) 12 Beth 6027. *1957*.

BLUES AND FOLKSONG

It will be appreciated that in the field of Negro blues and folksong, sub-division is necessary in order to facilitate reference.

These divisions are:

(1) Country blues and folksong;

(2) City blues;

(3) Classic and jazz blues;

(4) Rhythm and blues;

(5) Gospel and spirituals;

(6) Worksongs, prison blues and prison spirituals.

[50]

Certain singers/musicians of outstanding ability have been listed alphabetically in the main body of this discography: Blind Lemon Jefferson, Leroy Carr, etc. Others may be found in collections which are accounted for in one or other of these separate divisions. While this method, though arbitrary, is thought to be the simplest for indicating a basic style, there must be some dissension over borderline cases. The reader is therefore advised to take the broadest possible view of a method which is intended for the guidance of the novice rather than the further education of the more experienced collector. Incorporation in the main body of this volume will depend upon quality, not quantity, of recordings available. This is the reason for which it is felt that Blind Willie Johnson – one EP – must be given priority over Ray Charles – 5 LPs. As a complete listing of currently available material would be impractical, it is hoped that inclusion in any part of this work will be accepted as an indication that the material is of some quality.

The records have all been selected from British and American sources but valuable material by Washboard Sam, Sonny Boy Williamson, Big Maceo Merriweather, Jazz Gillum and others, may be found on French labels, particularly on Fr RCA: a tribute to M. Hugues Panassié's perseverance.

It should be noted that much of the information contained was graciously supplied by Bill Broonzy.

COUNTRY BLUES AND FOLKSONG
The artists in capitals have main entries in the book.

Texas Alexander, *vocal* – incl. 12 Ph BBL7369.
Barefoot Bill, *vocal, guitar* – incl. 12 Ph BBL7369.
Lewis Black, *vocal, guitar* – incl. 12 Ph BBL7369.
BLIND BLAKE q.v. (Arthur Phelps).
Barbecue Bob (Robert Hicks), *vocal, guitar* – incl. 12 Ph BBL7369.
BIG BILL BROONZY q.v.
Bob Campbell, *vocal, guitar* – incl. 12 Ph BBL7369.
Texas Bill Day, *vocal, guitar* – incl. 12 Ph BBL7369.
SLEEPY JOHN ESTES q.v.
BLIND BOY FULLER q.v. (Fulton Allen).
JESSE FULLER q.v.
Georgia Slim, *vocal, guitar* – incl. 7 Jcl JEL2.

Georgia Tom (Thomas A. Dorsey), *vocal, piano* – incl. 7 Jcl JEL3.
BOBBY GRANT q.v.
Otis Harris, *vocal, guitar* – incl. 12 Ph BBL7369.
Buddy Boy Hawkins, *vocal, guitar* – incl. 10 Lon AL3535 (*d*), 7 Jcl
   JEL8.
King Solomon Hill (*see* JOE WILLIAMS).
John Lee Hooker, *vocal, guitar* – 10 78 Vog V2102. (A) 12 Riv 12-838.
   12 Aud AL1520.
LIGHTNIN' HOPKINS q.v.
Peg Leg Howell, *vocal, guitar* – incl. 12 Ph BBL7369.
Bo Weavil Jackson, *vocal, guitar* – 7 45 Jcl JDL127. *Why do you
   moan/Some scream High Yellow.*
Little Walter Jacobs, *vocal harmonica* – (A) 12 Chess 1428.
BLIND LEMON JEFFERSON q.v.
Big Bill Johnson (*see* BIG BILL BROONZY).
HUDDIE LEDBETTER q.v.
Kansas Joe McCoy, *vocal, guitar, mandolin* – incl. 12 Ph BBL7369.
   7 45 Jcl JDL81. *One more greasing/100 years.*
BROWNIE MCGHEE q.v.
MUDDY WATERS q.v. (McKinley Morganfield).
Stovepipe No. 1 (Sam Jones), *vocal, stovepipe* – incl. 12 Ph BBL7369.
Tallahassee Tight, *vocal, guitar* – incl. 12 Ph BBL7369.
TAMPA RED q.v. (Hudson Whittaker).
SONNY TERRY q.v. (Saunders Terrell).
Ramblin' Willard Thomas, *vocal, guitar* – incl. 7 Jcl JEL4.
BUKKA WHITE q.v.
JOSH WHITE q.v.
Henry Williams, *vocal, guitar* – incl. 12 Ph BBL7369.
JOE WILLIAMS q.v.
SONNY BOY WILLIAMSON q.v.

CITY BLUES

LEROY CARR q.v.
CHAMPION JACK DUPREE q.v.
Howlin' Wolf (C. Burnett), *vocal, harmonica* – 7 Lon REU1072.
CRIPPLE CLARENCE LOFTON q.v.
Memphis Slim (P. Chatman), *vocal, piano* – 10 78 Esq 10-319. (A)
   12 VJ LP1012.

LITTLE BROTHER MONTGOMERY q.v.
RED NELSON q.v.
JAMES ROBINSON q.v.
WALTER ROLAND q.v.
CHARLIE SPAND q.v.
SPECKLED RED q.v. (Rufus Perryman).
JIMMY and MAMA YANCEY q.v.

CLASSIC AND JAZZ BLUES

LaVern Baker, *vocal* – 12 Lon LTZ-K15139 (A) 12 Atl 1281. *1958.*
(A) 12 Atl 8002. (A) 12 Atl 8007
IDA COX q.v.
CHIPPIE HILL q.v.
LONNIE JOHNSON q.v.
Sara Martin, *vocal* – incl. 10 Lon AL3510. *1928 (d).*
Lizzie Miles, *vocal* – 7 Nix SLPY150; 7 Mel EPM7-55; 7 Col
SEB10088, incl. 7 7EG8178. *1929 (d);* (A) 12 Ck 1182/3/4. (A) 12
Cap T792.
Billie Pierce, *vocal, piano* – incl. 12 Ctr JGN1001. (A) 12 Ton 1. *1957.*
MA RAINEY q.v.
JIMMY RUSHING q.v.
BESSIE SMITH q.v.
Dinah Washington, *vocal* – 12 Mer MLP6519. *1943–53.*

RHYTHM AND BLUES

John Bennings, *vocal* – 10 78 Esq 10-376.
Piney Brown, *vocal* – 10 78 Esq 10-330.
RAY CHARLES q.v.
H-Bomb Ferguson, *vocal* – 10 78 Esq 10-372.
WYNONIE HARRIS q.v.
JOE TURNER q.v.
JIMMY WITHERSPOON q.v.

GOSPEL SONGS AND SPIRITUALS

The Drinkard Singers – 12 Col 33CX10112. (A) 12 Ver 8245. *1957.*
12 Lon LTZ-C15155. (A) 12 Sav 14013. *1958.*
The Five Blind Boys – 7 Vog EPV1106; incl. 12 Vog LAE12033.
The Golden Gate Quartet – 7 Col SEG7643 (d); 7 Col SEG7700 (d);

[53]

10 Col 33CSX9; 10 Fon TFR6009; 7 Col SEG7924; 12 Col 33SX1172; 12 Har 7018.

MAHALIA JACKSON q.v.

Professor Johnson, *vocal* – 7 Br OE9352. *1950*.

BLIND WILLIE JOHNSON q.v.

Rev. Kelsey, *preaching* – 7 Br OE9256.

SPIRIT OF MEMPHIS q.v.

SISTER ROSETTA THARPE q.v.

The Ward Singers, *vocal* – 12 Lon LZ-C14013. (A) 12 Sav 14001; 7 Lon EZ-C19024/33/34; 12 Lon LTZ-C15155. (A) 12 Sav 14013. (A) 12 Sav 14006; 12 Sav 14015; Sav 14020.

Clara Ward, *vocal* – 12 Lon LTZ-D15168. (A) 12 Dot 3138, 25138; Dot 3186, 25186.

WORKSONGS, PRISON BLUES AND PRISON SPIRITUALS

These listed under the collective heading for each LP. All are strongly recommended.

(1) 'MURDERERS HOME' – 12 Nix NJL11. (A) 12 Trd 1020.

(2) 'NEGRO PRISON SONGS' – 12 Fol FE4475.

(3) 'AFRO-AMERICAN SPIRITUALS, WORKSONGS, AND BALLADS' – 12 L.o.C. AAFS L.3.

(4) 'AFRO-AMERICAN BLUES AND GAME SONGS' – 12 L.o.C. AAFS L.4.

(5) 'NEGRO WORKSONGS AND CALLS' – 12 L.o.C. AAFS L.8.

(6) 'NEGRO RELIGIOUS SONGS AND SERVICES' – 12 L.o.C. AAFS L.10.

It is also advised that the enthusiast make himself familiar with the contents of the FOLKWAYS catalogue as it contains a quantity of pertinent material.

Finally, and most strongly recommended, is the magnificent series of recordings made at the Louisiana State Penitentiary in Angola, and issued by the FOLK-LYRIC RECORDING CO. of Baton Rouge, Louisiana. These are soon to be made available in Great Britain, on the COLLECTOR label.

CLAUDE BOLLING (1930)   *piano, arranger*

Earl Hines has been the obvious influence on pianist Claude Bolling, one of the best jazzmen France has produced since the war. Although associated for a time with traditional-style groups Bolling's love for jazz of all types has been obvious from the varied company he has kept on record. A 78 r.p.m. coupling made in Paris during 1950 (Vog V2373) pairs him with trumpeter Roy Eldridge on two trumpet-piano duets, *Fireworks* and *Wild man blues*, modelled on the Hines-Armstrong pattern but played with tremendous conviction. (1) was made during the visit of the Lionel Hampton band to Europe in 1953 and is one of the best examples of the true jam session on record. Bolling plays superbly and, like the French tenor saxist Alix Combelle who plays on some tracks, is easily the equal of the stylistically-varied American jazzmen. Claude does not actually play on (2), contenting himself to lead and arrange for the middle-period groups heard on the four tracks. The percussive piano work is by the accomplished Martial Solal while Roger Guerin and Fred Gerard are responsible for the trumpet solos. The most striking individualist on the date, however, is tenor saxist Guy Lafitte who plays well on *In the sun*, exhibiting his liking for the Coleman Hawkins-Ben Webster approach. Bolling's own admiration for Duke Ellington has been revealed on the records which he has made with his big band and it is unfortunate that none of these fine LPs has been made available outside France.

(1) LIONEL HAMPTON JAM SESSION – 12 Vog LAE12034. (A) 12 Con C3502. *1953*.

(2) CLAUDE BOLLING ALL STAR GROUPS – 7 Or EP7016. (A) 12 Bally LP12003 (with eight additional titles). *1956*.

SHARKEY BONANO (1904)   *trumpet, vocal*

An exuberant player who always manages to put a great deal of zest and attack into his group without being one of the top jazz trumpeters. The group on (4) plays with precision, polish and a happy sort of earthiness complemented by Lizzie Miles' vigorous vocals and Sam deKemel's extraordinary antics on a bugle. (1) is a quieter sample of his work.

(1) SOUTHERN COMFORT – (A) 12 Cap T266. 10 Cap (*d*) LC6531. *1949–50*.

(2) A NIGHT IN OLD NEW ORLEANS – 12 Cap T792 (*d*). (A) 12 Cap T792. *1950–54*.

(3) NEW ORLEANS CONTRASTS (with Paul Barbarin) – (A) 12 Riv 12-217. *1951*.

[55]

(4) MIDNIGHT ON BOURBON STREET – (A) 12 Cap T367. 10 Cap (*d*)
    LC6600. *1952.*
(5) RECORDED IN NEW ORLEANS, Vol. 1 (with Barbarin, Girard and
    Matthews) – 12 GTJ LAG12083. (A) 12 CTJ12019. *1956.*
(6) NEW ORLEANS DIXIELAND (with Pecora and Girard). (A) 12 Sou
    216.

WILL BRADLEY (1912) *trombone*

Bradley has led a variety of small jazz borderline groups, many of
them founding their fortune on the boogie woogie craze. Some of
these exhilarating and driving performances are to be found on (1).
(3) is a peculiar bastard sort of Dixieland showing how borderline
Bradley can be in spite of stalwarts like Rex Stewart and Bud Freeman.
The rest clearly show the sad tale of a could-be jazzman who never
found out where his allegiance lay.

(1) BOOGI WOOGIE – (A) 12 Ep LN-3115. *1940–1.*
(2) THE HOUSE OF BRADLEY – (A) 12 Ep LN-3196. *1940–1.*
(3) DIXIELAND JAZZ (with Bobby Byrne) – (A) 12 GA 33-310.
    7 TR2007 (JAZZ FOR SALE No. 2). *1948.*

RUBY BRAFF (1927) *trumpet*

A trumpet-player who improvises melodic, often rather dainty
solos, using a highly eclectic style, Ruby Braff came into prominence
during the 1950s. He has suffered a little from being over-praised,
one critic even going so far as to claim that the 'calm singing quality'
of his playing linked him with such great trumpet-players as Joe
Smith, Bunny Berigan and Frankie Newton. That is to go too far.
Braff is actually a very good musician, one with a genuine talent for
melodic invention, but just as his tone can sometimes grow too
sugary, too brilliant, his phrasing can also become too facile. Nevertheless, when he is playing at his best – as he does in (7), (8) and (9),
or even just capably – as in most of the other records listed below,
he is a lively and very lyrical performer.

Although (1) is an uneven LP it does contain four good tracks,
including a delicate version of *Fine and mellow*. (2), (3) and (4) are
duets by Braff and the pianist Ellis Larkins, a very sympathetic
partner, while (5) presents the trumpeter with Vic Dickenson and the
tenor-player Sam Margolis. (6) and (10) are recordings of tunes
associated with Billie Holiday and Bunny Berigan respectively, the

latter including some clarinet-playing by Pee Wee Russell. Pee Wee can also be heard in the Newport Festival LP (11), an exceptionally good performance, while 'Jazz at Storyville' (12 Lon LTZ-C15061, (A) 12 Sav 12034) presents earlier recordings by these two musicians. On (7) Braff plays with three different groups, one of them including Lawrence Brown and Coleman Hawkins; his work on this LP is outstanding. The Louis Armstrong influence upon Braff's playing, always a strong one, is revealed at its starkest in (8) and (9), where the trumpeter works with just a rhythm section, but a rhythm section containing that fine pianist Dave McKenna. (12) has Braff playing a set of his favourite tunes, including a good old one, *Lazy*. (13), by a larger group, has a few solos by Roy Eldridge and Vic Dickenson. Finally, on (14) Braff can be heard doing about as much as can be done with some rather unsuitable 'standards' (*Russian lullaby, Loch Lomond, Too-Ra-Loo-Ra-Loo-Ra*, etc.); probably the most interesting thing about this LP is that it allows us to hear Bob Brookmeyer at the piano, always a joyful thing.

(1) HUSTLIN' AND BUSTLIN' – 12 Vog LAE12051. (A) 12 Sto 908. *1951–4.*

(2) TWO PART INVENTION IN JAZZ – 10 Van PPT12010 (*d*). (A) 12 Van 8516. *1955.*

(3) TWO PART INVENTION IN JAZZ, Vol 2 – 10 Van PPT12022 (*d*). (A) 12 Van 8516. *1955.*

(4) TWO BY TWO – (A) 12 Van 8507. *1955.*

(5) RUBY BRAFF SPECIAL – 12 Van PPL11003 (*d*). (A) 12 Van 8504. *1955.*

(6) HOLIDAY IN BRAFF – 10 Lon LZ-N14022. *1955.*

(7) BRAFF! – 12 Ph BBL7130 (*d*). (A) 12 Ep LN-3377. *1956.*

(8) DANCING IN THE DARK – 7 HMV 7EG8311. (A) (plus extra titles) 12 ABC 141. *1956.*

(9) RUBY BRAFF QUARTET – 7HMV 7 EG8397. (A) (plus extra titles) 12 ABC 141. *1956.*

(10) HI-FI SALUTE TO BUNNY – (A) 12 RCA LPM 1510. *1957.*

(11) RUBY BRAFF OCTET AT NEWPORT – 12 Col 33CX10104. (A) 12 Ver 8241. *1957.*

(12) YOU'RE GETTING TO BE A HABIT WITH ME – (A) 12 Stereocraft RCS507. *1958.*

(13) EASY NOW – (A) 12 RCA LPM1966, (S) LSP1966. *1958.*

(14) BLOWING AROUND THE WORLD – (A) 12 UA UAL3045, (S)
6045. *1959.*

•

BOB BROOKMEYER (1929) *valve-trombone, piano*

Born in Kansas City, Bob Brookmeyer's style of trombone playing
is frequently the personification of relaxation. In fact the cool
approach is sometimes refined to such an extent that Brookmeyer's
solos induce sleepiness in certain listeners more quickly than sheep-
counting. When the conditions are right Bob can play thrilling,
inventive passages which are in perfect context, as witness his work
throughout (2) where he is teamed with Zoot Sims and a rhythm
section containing Jo Jones. His work with the Gerry Mulligan
Quartet alternated between drabness (when he tried to copy the
recorded solos of Chet Baker, presumably to satisfy audiences)
and genuine inspiration which offset the solo style of the leader.
Both (1), which was recorded at concerts in Paris, and (3), taped
at a club in Boston, contain good solos by Brookmeyer who
fits well into this instrumentation. His appearances with Stan
Getz were less impressive for although he instilled in Getz the
need for a more down-to-earth approach his own trombone playing was generally uninspired. On piano he is a much more
interesting soloist playing in a kind of whimsical Thelonious
Monk manner. (4) contains his keyboard version of *Truckin'*
which is delightful in every respect, while on the same LP he plays
piano with one hand and trombone with the other during the
course of *Don't be that way*. This LP together with (5) was made
during Brookmeyer's term of service with Jimmy Giuffre's Trio,
a gloomy, pseudo-folk-ridden unit which showed every sign of
breaking its tenuous relationship with jazz. (5), however, contains
none of the Giuffre melancholia and is perhaps Brookmeyer's best
record; guitarists Jim Hall and Jimmy Raney are perfectly in accord
with each other while Bob enjoys himself on both trombone and
piano, exhibiting more good humour than one normally associates
with his playing.

(1) GERRY MULLIGAN QUARTET – 12 Vog LAE12015. (A) 12 WP 1210.
1954.

(2) BOB BROOKMEYER-ZOOT SIMS – 12 Vog LAE12053. (A) 12 Sto
914. *1956.*

(3) GERRY MULLIGAN QUARTET – 12 Vog LAE12080. (A) 12 WP
1228. *1956.*
(4) TRADITIONALISM REVISITED – 12 Vog LAE12108. (A) 12 WP
1233. *1957.*
(5) THE STREET SWINGERS – 12 Vog LAE12147. (A) 12 WP 1239. *1957.*

BIG BILL BROONZY (1893–1958) *vocal, guitar*
'Big Bill was the last of those great singers with a "rooster-crow"
in the voice,' said Alan Lomax in 1958. His fanatical admiration of
Broonzy's work many of us feel to have been fully justified. Yet one
leading American in the field of blues research has, recently, written
a bitter attack on Broonzy in which he implies that this singer's
latter-day success was due to his imitation of Josh White. This
may well be incomprehensible to anyone who heard Broonzy
during his first British tour, in 1951. At this time his voice was keen
and bright as we had never heard it on record; this may well have
been his peak. Only on rare occasions has Broonzy come through
fully on disc but, despite this, there are quantities of his recordings
worth purchasing. His most consistent recording period – a rare
case of quantity and quality – was in the middle and late '30s when,
with small jump bands, or with pianists Josh Altheimer and Black
Bob, he produced such titles as *Mill man blues, Louise Louise blues* and
Just a dream, long since deleted from the catalogues.

Broonzy did not learn to play the guitar until he was well into his
twenties and, at first, was greatly influenced by Blind Blake, Blind
Lemon Jefferson and Lonnie Johnson. Fairly soon, however, he
developed a distinctive sound which, he claimed in later years, was
pure Mississippi; it was more purely Big Bill Broonzy. As an
instrumentalist he played fast numbers with an amazing swing,
assured and proudly masculine; his slow numbers were performed
with a strangely relaxed bitterness of sound.

But it was in the perfect blend of voice and guitar that Broonzy
achieved greatness. Whether over the measured patterns of *Blues in
1890* (4) (also called *Joe Turner blues*) and *Stump blues* (1), or the
free antiphonal phrasing of *Willie Mae blues* (3), Bill Broonzy's
voice dominated the performance. 'I make my guitar answer,' Bill
Broonzy once said, 'but I don't never let it talk at the same time as
me.'

[59]

On BACKWOODS BLUES Broonzy appears as Big Bill Johnson.

In using the listing below the reader may be helped by the knowledge that Mel EPM7-65 and Col SEG7674 are specially recommended. On Vog LAE12009 *Backwater blues* is labelled as *Big Bill blues*, while the master used for *John Henry* is inferior to the one used on Vog V2074.

(1) BIG BILL BROONZY – 7 Mel EPM7-65. *1951.*

(2) BIG BILL BROONZY – 7 Vog EPV1024. *1951.*

(3) BIG BILL BLUES – 12 Vog LAE12009. *1951–2.*

(4) *John Henry/Blues in 1890* – 10 78 Vog V2074. *1951.*

(5) *Big Bill Blues/Hey hey Baby* – 12 78 Vog V2075. *1951.*

(6) BIG BILL BROONZY SINGS THE BLUES – 7 Col SEG7674. *1956.*

(7) BIG BILL BROONZY SINGS THE BLUES, Vol. 2 – 7 Col SEG7790. *1956.*

(8) BIG BILL BROONZY – 12 Ph BBL7113. *1956.*

(9) SOUTHERN SAGA – 7 Nix NJL16. *1955.*

(10) BACKWOODS BLUES – 10 Lon AL3535 (*d*). *1931–2.*

(11) BLUES IN THE MISSISSIPPI NIGHT – 12 Nix NJL8. (A) 12 UA 4027. *1942.*

(12) BIG BILL'S BLUES – 12 Col WL-111.

(13) BIG BILL BROONZY'S STORY – 12 Fol FG3586. *1956.*

(14) COUNTRY BLUES – 12 Fol FS2326. *1956.*

CLIFFORD BROWN (1930–56)   *trumpet*

Clifford Brown was the most promising new trumpeter to arrive since Fats Navarro and Miles Davis. He died in a car accident at a time when he seemed to have reached some kind of maturity as a soloist and it is a matter for conjecture just how great a jazzman he would have become had he lived longer. He made some records in New York during the early part of 1953 before joining Lionel Hampton's big band. (1) is by the band which pianist Tadd Dameron was leading at Atlantic City during the summer of that year, a band which contained Gigi Gryce and Benny Golson as well as Brownie and Philly Joe Jones. *Theme of no repeat* is an excellent Dameron arrangement and includes a fine cup-muted solo from Brown. This was the group which Hampton 'raided' for talent at the instigation of Quincy Jones; Gryce, Golson and Brown were signed up by Lionel Hampton after one audition but Golson decided against making the European trip with Hampton. Jazz fans in Sweden had a chance to hear this remarkably talented group of musicians under Lionel's leadership at the beginning of the European itinerary, a band which contained amongst others Clifford Brown, Art Farmer, Quincy Jones, Gigi Gryce, Jimmy Cleveland, George Wallington and singer Annie Ross. Despite Hampton's orders some of the more outstanding soloists from the band, together with such Swedish jazzmen as Bengt Hallberg, Lars Gullin, Ake Persson, Jack Noren, etc., recorded in Stockholm and all the results reflect the bursting enthusiasm of these keen young men. Brownie plays a typically clean-toned, hot chorus on *Lover, come back to me* (1) and generally outshines the other soloists on the date. Moving on to Paris later that month the Hampton stars were plunged into a series of recording sessions which produced some of the most exciting jazz of the decade. With Gryce and Quincy Jones turning out score after score, Franco-American bands were continually assembling in the Paris studios of Vogue Records to record some memorable music. Both Gryce and Jones recognized the tremendous potential of Brown as a soloist and it was Gigi who gave him his full-scale showcase, *Brown skins* (2), one of the finest trumpet and band 'concertos' in jazz. A sextet made up of Gryce and Brown plus a Parisian rhythm section recorded a number of Gigi's tunes including *Salute to the Bandbox*, *Baby* and *Strictly romantic* (3), all of which show the incredible breadth of imagination and degree of technical control which was to mark all of Brownie's work on record. Under his own name Clifford recorded an album of standard tunes, mostly at ballad tempo (4) but with a hurricane version of Kern's *The song is you* included to show that the trumpeter was second only to his idol, Fats Navarro, so far as clean tonguing and accurate fingering were concerned. Back in New York after the tour Brown left hte Hampton organization and worked for a time with Art Blakey's new quintet at Birdland where the Blue Note company recorded the unit in February, 1954 (BLP1521 and 1522); then, in March, drummer Max Roach offered him a job in Hollywood. What was to become the Roach-Brown unit worked for a time on a temporary basis with casual sitters-in filling tenor, piano and bass positions. With Teddy Edwards and the late Carl Perkins helping out, the Roach-Brown quintet played at a concert for producer Gene Norman, who recorded the music for issue on LP (5);

this was the concert which produced Clifford's version of *Tenderly*, perhaps the most impressive of all his featured solos. A contract with the EmArcy label and the employment of Harold Land (tenor), Richie Powell (piano) and George Morrow (bass) as permanent members followed and the Roach-Brown unit proceeded from strength to strength. Several albums by this extrovert but inventive quintet were made in Hollywood, the first for EmArcy (6) containing the evocative *Parisian thoroughfare* written by Bud Powell and utilizing imitation traffic noises in the introduction and coda. In New York, towards the end of 1954, Clifford added sensitive obbligatos and solos to new albums by vocalists Sarah Vaughan (7) and Helen Merrill (8), these being the only examples on record of Brownie's great talent for working with ballad singers. Further records with Land still on tenor (9) preceded the important personnel change which brought Sonny Rollins into the unit. Working alongside Rollins seemed to bring out the best in Clifford and it is unfortunate that he made only two LPs with Sonny before his death. Both albums, the first recorded in Chicago (10), the second in New York under Rollins' name (11), indicate that Brownie had reached a new plane and he plays here with even greater confidence and control than before. Sonny's *Valse hot* (11), which is played throughout in 3/4 time, finds Clifford negotiating the unusual time signature with ease. His death, at the age of 25, was a severe blow to jazz for he was one of the most accomplished soloists of the school which showed that modern jazz could be as hot as any earlier style. After his death Brownie's friend, Benny Golson, composed the dedicatory *I remember Clifford* which has been recorded by many of the trumpeter's friends and admirers.

(1) TADD DAMERON ORCHESTRA – (A) 12 Pre PRLP7055. (Four titles on 10 Esq 20-044, remainder on Esq EP3 and EP4.) *1953.*

(2) GIGI GRYCE ORCHESTRA – 10 Vog LDE070. (A) 10 BN BLP5049. *1953.*

(3) GIGI GRYCE-CLIFFORD BROWN SEXTET – 10 Vog LDE048. (A) 10 BN BLP5048. *1953.*

(4) CLIFFORD BROWN QUARTET – 10 Vog LDE042. (A) 10 BN BLP5047. *1953.*

(5) CLIFFORD BROWN-MAX ROACH – 12 Vog LAE12036. (A) 12 GN GNP18. *1954.*

(6) CLIFFORD BROWN-MAX ROACH – 12 (A) 12 EmA 36036 (*d*). (Some titles on Mer MMC14041.) *1954.*

(7) SARAH VAUGHAN – (A) 12 EmA 36004. (Two titles on Mer YEP9507.) *1954.*

(8) HELEN MERRILL – (A) 12 EmA 36006. *1954.*

(9) CLIFFORD BROWN-MAX ROACH – (A) 12 EmA 36037 (*d*). (Some titles on Mer MMC14041.) *1955.*

(10) CLIFFORD BROWN-MAX ROACH – (A) 12 EmA 36070 (*d*). (Some titles on Mer MMC14041.) *1956.*

(11) SONNY ROLLINS PLUS FOUR – 12 Esq 32-025. (A) 12 Pre PRLP 7038. *1956.*

SANDY BROWN (1929)   *clarinet*

Outside of Pee Wee Russell and (in the right company) Mezz Mezzrow, it is hard to think of any clarinettist alive today who plays blues as convincingly as Sandy Brown. Johnny Dodds' jagged phrasing and Sidney Bechet's thick vibrato, his sharp melodic twists, have obviously helped to shape Sandy's playing, yet he has developed a style that is very much his own. In addition, he is an uncommonly adventurous musician, turning every solo into an act of discovery, running musical risks that less timid men avoid. Sandy Brown is, in fact, one of the very few British jazz musicians who can be ranked alongside the best Americans. During most of his career he has been closely associated with Al Fairweather, a fellow Scot, who plays trumpet on a majority of the records listed below.

(1) and (2) were made when Sandy Brown's band was nominally a New Orleans group, although already using 'High Life' rhythms and elbowing its way into 'mainstream'. (3) features seven guest instrumentalists, the best of whom are Dave Stevens (piano), Diz Disley (guitar), and Johnny Picard (trombone). Fairweather wrote all the themes, and he and Sandy play lively solos. Wally Fawkes and Sandy Brown, the former lyrical, the latter truculent, make an interesting contrast on (4) and (5). (6) is a really outstanding LP, every track a good 'original' with bright, supple playing by Brown and Fairweather. Adventurous solos can be found on (10 Nix NJL20) while (7) moves farther along the path of (6), again using plenty of 'originals', again blending the modern with the traditional. Sandy Brown also plays well on 7 Nixa NJE1037 (with groups led

by Dick Heckstall-Smith and Al Fairweather), as 'B. MacSandy' on a Stan Greig EP (7 Tem EXA90), and with the Al Fairweather quintet on two tracks of 10 Nixa NJT503, as well as popping up here and there (and always stealing the show) in 'Clarinet Jamboree' (12 Col 33SX1204).

(1) SANDY BROWN JAZZ BAND – 7 Tem EXA33. *1955.*

(2) SANDY BROWN JAZZ BAND – 7 Tem EXA49. *1956.*

(3) SANDY'S SIDEMEN – 12 Tem TAP3. *1956.*

(4) WALLY FAWKES-SANDY BROWN QUINTET – 7 Dec DFE6378. *1956*

(5) WALLY FAWKES-SANDY BROWN QUINTET – 7 Dec DFE6379. *1956.*

(6) McJAZZ – 12 Nix NJL9. *1957.*

(7) AL FAIRWEATHER AND SANDY BROWN ALL STARS – 12 Col 33SX1159. *1959.*

DAVE BRUBECK (1920)   *piano*

The words 'popular success' and 'Dave Brubeck' are synonymous in jazz and any jazz musician who makes a commercial success of his music must be prepared to face hostile criticism from his less successful colleagues. Actually Dave's acceptance is a little difficult to understand at first sight for he is not a particularly accomplished pianist. (He is less a master of his instrument than, say, Hank Jones or Al Haig while pianist Dick Marx has produced several LPs, notably 'Too Much Piano' on Cor LVA9005 (A) Br 54006, which seem more deserving of acclaim by the jazz-fringe than most of Brubeck's output). Where Dave has scored again and again is in his exploitation of hitherto neglected audiences in colleges and universities. In addition (and perhaps this should have been said first) he is completely sincere about his music and tries hard to give full value for money in the way of creativeness at every performance. The sight of an artist actually bringing an idea into existence before the audience's eyes is not new in jazz but Brubeck's demeanour gives credence to the act and, in so doing, draws the public into his confidence. In a way Dave's struggles at the keyboard give rise to a kind of audience-participation which is so often lacking in the cultivated boredom of expression practised by so many of his contemporaries. A further reason for his success is a genuinely musical one; alto saxist Paul Desmond has been part of all Dave's bands and the *rapport* existing between Brubeck and Desmond is almost unique in jazz. Starting his career at his home-town of San Francisco Dave formed an interesting Octet during the late nineteen-forties which paralleled the approach and instrumentation of Miles Davis's 'Capitol' band although Brubeck denied having heard of Davis's unit until some time after the dissolution of the Octet. (1) contains some interesting pieces played by the group, some arranged by Dave (*The way you look tonight* is his best effort) and some by the talented tenor saxist Dave Van Kreidt. There is evidence on the Octet titles that Brubeck found difficulty in swinging and the value of the group is due largely to (*a*) the unusual scores, and (*b*) the presence of such superior jazzmen as Van Kreidt, Dick Collins (trumpet) and Desmond. Out of the Octet came first the Trio (piano, bass and drums doubling vibes) and later the Quartet. (2) and (3) are perhaps the best of all the records by the earlier quartet; both were recorded at concerts and each hits a high inspirational level. (2) was taped at Oberlin University and, for some reason, finds the group operating under some kind of tension which adds considerably to the quality of the music. Desmond is particularly good on all the tracks but strikes greatest fire during his *The way you look tonight*. (3), recorded just before Christmas at the College of the Pacific, finds Brubeck in top form largely due to the excellence of the piano on which he played. *Laura* is a Debussyesque solo with the soft undertones of *Submerged cathedral* and forms a complete contrast with the hard-hitting *All the things you are* in which great use is made of a fugal idea. This latter track remains one of the best Quartet performances irrespective of date or personnel. As a composer Dave has produced a number of quite charming tunes two of which, *In your own sweet way* and *The Duke*, have found their way into the repertoire of Miles Davis. (4) includes both tunes in a set of piano solos titled Brubeck Plays Brubeck. In 1957 a significant personnel change brought in drummer Joe Morello, a vital, swinging musician as opposed to the capable but relatively uninspired time-keepers heard with previous editions of the Quartet. With the addition of Morello (and later, Gene Wright on bass) Dave's unit became a Quartet in the truest sense of the term with all four men contributing to the success of the music. (5) is made up of tunes from Walt Disney films and includes a most unusual treatment of *Someday my prince will come*, played as an exercise in time-signatures (3/4 against 4/4), a prelude to later experiments along the same lines. After touring Europe and Asia in the spring of 1958 Dave produced his Impressions of Eurasia album (6), a kind of musical sketch-book made up of themes inspired by the various countries visited during the tour. *Marble Arch* has a light and airy quality which forms an ideal setting for Desmond's lyricism. (7) is devoted to the music of Duke Ellington and was recorded at the 1958 Newport Jazz Festival. Apart from Desmond's solos this LP is of value in that it shows Brubeck to be capable of swinging in a forthright manner when the occasion demands.

(1) DAVE BRUBECK OCTET – 12 Vog LAE12008. (A) 12 Fan 3-239. *1950*.

(2) DAVE BRUBECK QUARTET – 12 Vog LAE12048. (A) 12 Fan 3-245. *1953*.

(3) DAVE BRUBECK QUARTET – 12 Vog LAE12110. (A) 12 Fan 3-224. *1953*.

(4) BRUBECK PLAYS BRUBECK – 12 Ph BBL7116. (A) 12 Col CL878. *1956*.

(5) DAVE DIGS DISNEY – 12 Fon TFL5017. (A) 12 Col CL1059. *1957*.

(6) IMPRESSIONS OF EURASIA - 12 Fon TFL5051. (A) 12 Col CL 1251. *1958*.

(7) DAVE BRUBECK QUARTET – 12 Fon TFL5059. (A) 12 Col CL1347. *1958*.

GEORGE BRUNIS (1900)   *trombone*

A driving, tailgate style trombonist who has been the impulsive force behind such bands as the New Orleans Rhythm Kings and Muggsy Spanier's Ragtime Band. His style is pugnacious and yet retains a mellow smoothness particularly in solos such as the one on the fine *Ugly chile* (A) Com 78 CMS546 (*d*). The discs under his own name are rather unsuccessful and unrepresentative, but there is plenty good Brunis about on record.

(1) DIXIELAND ALL STARS (with Pete Fountain) – 7 Tem EXA96. (A) 12 Sou 210. *1955*.

(2) DEEP IN THE HEART OF DIXIELAND – (A) 12 Dis 3009.

[66]

RAY BRYANT (1931) *piano*

Although he worked with such visiting stars as Charlie Parker and Miles Davis in his home-town, Philadelphia, it was not until Ray Bryant came to New York in 1956 that he began to gain some of the recognition due to him. Miles Davis was responsible for his first record date in 1955 (Esq 32-028, (A) Pre PRLP7034) when he took his place with an all-star group which made good use of the Bryant tune *Changes*. Subsequently he worked with singer Carmen McRae's accompanying trio and played on many record dates with such men as Sonny Rollins, Coleman Hawkins, etc. Ray lists Teddy Wilson amongst his favourites and, like Wilson, he possesses the ability to play sensitive, intelligent accompaniments as well as flowing, well-constructed solos. Although he became identified with contemporary-styled jazzmen at the outset he has since shown that he is capable of fitting in with almost any type and style of group, as indicated by his work with the Tiny Grimes-Coleman Hawkins unit (Esq 32-082, (A) Pre PRLP7138) and the Hal Singer-Charlie Shavers Quintet ((A) Pre PRLP7153). The titles on (1) are of interest largely through the efforts of that excellent jazz singer Joe Carroll, who performs with his customary exuberance and good humour; tenor saxist Seldon Powell is also on hand to make this a most enjoyable record. (2), by Art Blakey's drum-heavy ensemble, features Bryant to advantage on his own tune *Cubano chant* which is easily the best track on the LP. The trio heard on the eight titles comprising (3) is, in fact, the Carmen McRae unit (Bryant, Ike Isaacs on bass and Specs Powell on drums). This is in every way a delightful LP of jazz piano, ranging from the melodic, reflective *Golden earrings* to Bryant's powerful *Splittin'* (with Wright excelling himself as a master of brushwork) via John Lewis's moody *Django*. Clearly Bryant is one of the best and most adaptable of the newer pianists to gain prominence during the late nineteen-fifties and it is some mark of his care as a professional to note that his playing is consistent in its high quality.

(1) RAY BRYANT QUINTET – 7 Fon TFE17143. (A) 12 Ep 3272 (with extra titles). *1956*.

(2) ART BLAKEY PERCUSSION ENSEMBLE – 12 Ph BBL7196. (A) 12 Col CL1002. *1957*.

(3) RAY BRYANT TRIO – 12 Esq 32-066. (A) 12 Pre PRLP7098. *1957*.

[67]

TEDDY BUCKNER (1910)   *cornet*

Another case of a jazzman who became known in the swing era
bands, having played with Benny Carter, Lionel Hampton and
Horace Henderson, and then seemed to decide that his true love was
New Orleans jazz after all.

The result when he played with Ory, and since, leading his own
Dixieland groups, is an easy, clear and cantabile style of playing
combined with a professional attitude towards jazz. He is abetted
by a fine musician like Joe Darensbourg. The result is polished but
spirited jazz approaching the perfection of the Wilbur de Paris
group, and some fine Armstrong-based playing.

(1) TEDDY BUCKNER IN CONCERT AT THE DIXIELAND JUBILEE – 10
    Vog LDE175. (A) 12 DJ 503. *1955*.

(2) TEDDY BUCKNER AND HIS DIXIELAND BAND – 12 Vog LAE12026.
    (A) DJ 504. *1955*.

(3) TEDDY BUCKNER AND THE ALL STARS – (A) 12 DJ 507. *1956*.

(4) A SALUTE TO LOUIS ARMSTRONG – 12 Vog LAE12129. (A) 12
    DJ 505. *1958*.

TEDDY BUNN (1909)   *guitar*

If Lonnie Johnson was the most important jazz guitarist of the
1920s, Teddy Bunn filled a similar position during the next decade,
the years just before Charlie Christian revolutionized the whole
technique of jazz guitar playing. Bunn's single-string work is particularly nimble, while he can also perform the most moving slow
blues. Some of his best blues playing will be found on recordings
made in 1937 and 1938 with Jimmie Noone (*Four or five times*) and
Johnny Dodds (*Wild man blues, Melancholy blues*), 10 Cor LRA10018.
He plays equally fine solos in *If you see me comin'* and *Gettin' together*
(Mezzrow-Ladnier Quintet) and *Comin' on with the come on* (Mezz
Mezzrow orchestra) (1938) on 10 HMV DLP1110 (*d*). (This LP
contains 2nd masters, generally inferior, so it is worthwhile looking
for the old 78s.) Some of Bunn's wittiest playing occurs on the
records he made with the Spirits of Rhythm, with whom he worked
for a long period in the 1930s. With Leo Watson improvising his
audacious scat choruses, the Spirits of Rhythm were the best, the
gayest and most dextrous of all vocal groups. Their old 78 releases –
I Got rhythm/Rhythm is an outstanding coupling, issued on both Br

and Par but long-deleted – are well worth searching for. Teddy Bunn also recorded some solos for BN in 1939, but these are no longer available.

DON BYAS (1913)   *tenor saxophone*

The influence of Coleman Hawkins shaped the playing of most tenor saxophonists who took up their instrument during the 1930s. Don Byas was one of them, yet although his work still reflects Hawkins' opulent, rich-toned approach, he has adapted his style to embrace some of the modern developments. One of the best of Byas's early solos can be found in *Lafayette* ('Kansas City Jazz', (A) 12 Dec 8044), made by Hot Lips Page's band in 1940. In January of 1941 Byas replaced Lester Young in the Count Basie orchestra, staying with the band for the next two years, during which period he contributed some notable solos to the band's recordings, including *Harvard blues* ('Blues by Basie', 12 Ph BBL7190 (d),(A) 12 Col CL901) and *Something new* ('Count Basie Classics', 12 Fon TFL5077, (A) 12 Col CL754). Byas came to Europe with Don Redman's orchestra in 1946 and has stayed here ever since, spending most of his time in France. More and more he has come to specialize in playing slow ballads, a genre which reveals the scope of his virtuosity – his melodic inventiveness, his keen harmonic sense. Both (1) and (2) fall into this category, the former including a masterly performance of *The man I love*, the latter a lyrical *Over the rainbow*. (1) is actually the better record, for (2) – consisting entirely of slow ballads – soon becomes soporific. Byas partners the pianist Mary Lou Williams on (3), playing particularly well in the faster numbers, *O.W.* and *New Musical Express*.

(1) DON BYAS, HIS TENOR SAX AND RHYTHM – 10 Esq 20-005. *1951.*
(2) DON BYAS AND HIS RHYTHM – 7 Vog EPV1068. *1953.*
(3) DON CARLOS MEETS MARY LOU – 7 Vog EPV1042. *1953.*

DONALD BYRD (1932)   *trumpet*

It is regrettable that Donald Byrd, together with many of his contemporaries, arrived on the recording scene in time to be swept along with the increased sale of the long-playing record. His big band experience is limited but his technique is formidable. He seems always to be available for recording dates, and between July 1955 and

[69]

April 1958 he played on no less than fifty-nine twelve-inch LPs. Understandably, in the light of this output, his assets and liabilities have been revealed on many occasions while his powers of improvisation have been taxed beyond the limit. Despite the financial advantages of this quantity output the artistic drawbacks are many and most listeners have become wary of approaching a new Byrd LP for fear of hearing the same ideas merely rearranged in a different sequence. Clearly this is not Byrd's fault and it would be wrong to condemn him for becoming embroiled in a situation which has affected so many new jazzmen; it seems likely that during the lean years the only work he could come by was with the Prestige, Blue Note and Savoy record companies. Nevertheless, it is necessary to be extremely selective in one's choice of Byrd's LPs and to avoid, as far as possible, those albums which allow him to play lengthy solos which soon reveal his expected inadequacies of staying power. (Very few musicians in jazz can continue to create fresh ideas after two or three choruses.) Stylistically Byrd owes allegiance to Fats Navarro and Clifford Brown, but his lack of big band experience probably accounts for his small tone. He is heard in a series of interesting settings for five trumpets on (1) where his small sound is contrasted with the mellow richness of Joe Wilder and the varied personalities of Ray Copeland, Ernie Royal, and Idrees Sulieman. Although under his own name (2) is, in fact, by Art Blakey's Jazz Messengers with guest trumpeter Joe Gordon sitting in for some numbers. Gordon's cutting tone and crackling attack tends to place Byrd in an inferior position. (3) is virtually the Messengers again and is a better than average session of its type with Byrd in a thoughtful mood on some tracks. (4) and (5) are perhaps the best of the recommended records for here Byrd is placed in a more disciplined context by arranger Gigi Gryce; there are no long, aimless solos played with just rhythm accompaniment and it seems that, given the right kind of direction, Byrd could become a useful soloist. The Jazz Lab uses the same instrumentation as Miles Davis's 'Capitol' band in places and it is this full, cushioning ensemble which adds depth and richness to Byrd's persuasive version of Benny Golson's *I remember Clifford* (4).

(1) Top Brass – 12 Lon LTZ-C15013. (A) 12 Sav MG12044. *1955*.
(2) Donald Byrd's Jazz Group – 12 Esq 32-013. (A) 12 Tra LP4. *1955*.

(3) HORACE SILVER QUINTET – 12 Ph BBL7183. (A) 12 Ep LN3326.
    1956.
(4) THE JAZZ LAB – 12 Ph BBL7210. (A) 12 Col CL998. *1957.*
(5) THE JAZZ LAB – 12 Ph BBL7244. (A) 12 Col CL1058. *1957.*

C

LEROY CARR (1899–1935)   *piano, vocal*

With Leroy Carr anguish is transformed into poignancy. In a
short recording life – June 1928 to February 1935 – Carr made 126
sides, which, selling in considerable quantities, caused him to become
the most influential singer since Blind Lemon Jefferson. A moving,
but gentle singer, his blues had a fine lyricism which was sustained
throughout most of his recordings. His piano accompaniments were
pleasant, if a little static, but the blend which Carr achieved with his
guitarist, Scrapper Blackwell, was an outstanding factor in the
formation of City Blues. The unfortunate misunderstandings which
occasionally caused these two musicians to record separately, finally
broke up this most important partnership.

Leroy Carr's death, sometime in 1935, was greatly mourned and
at least three singers – Bill Gaither (Leroy's Buddy), Amos Easton
(Bumble Bee Slim) and Francis (Scrapper) Blackwell, close followers
of Carr's style – recorded tributes within a short time of his death.
This, Bill Broonzy said, was due to 'woman trouble', Carr having
been poisoned by the mistress with whom he had been living for
some years. Though he recorded in Chicago, Leroy Carr lived and
worked mainly in Indianapolis, an important Western blues centre;
his house-parties were noted for their gaiety. Since Carr's death,
little had been heard of Scrapper Blackwell until, in the early summer
of 1959, he started to play again in Indianapolis.

Carr's most famous song was *How long blues*, now part of
the standard jazz repertoire, which he recorded on five separate
occasions, with new lyrics. There is an extraordinary beauty in
his use of ordinary words; this is exemplified in his fine *Blues
before sunrise* and *Midnight hour blues* (1). Unfortunately, there is
only one example of Carr's 'two-beat' playing (*Barrelhouse woman,
No. 2* (3)) available in Britain, but this will serve to illustrate the

[71]

greater instrumental complexity of the duet, when performed in this style.

(1) Treasures of North-American Music, Vol. 1 – 7 Fon TFE 17051. *1932–4.*

(2) *Alki blues*/rev. The Hokum Boys – 10 78 JCL58.

(3) *Barrelhouse woman, No. 2/ I believe I'll make a change* – 10 78 JCL92.

BENNY CARTER (1907)   *alto sax, trumpet, arranger, bandleader*

The great jazz soloist can usually be distinguished from more normally talented musicians by his sense of poise. This quality of poise, of repose, is perhaps the most noticeable thing about Benny Carter's playing. In addition, of course, there is his conception of the solo as a total creation, not just a succession of exciting phrases propped against one another. The same concern with formal values, the same search for elegance, can be discovered in Carter's writing for jazz ensembles. His scores make little use of textures, they rarely blend brasses with reeds; instead one section is deployed against another. And when he is actually composing, Carter appears to conceive the melody first, then to arrange it, separating these two actions in a way that Duke Ellington (with whom the theme and its instrumental expression are more closely allied) would never do. Benny Carter's gift, in fact, is predominantly lyrical; he never attacks the emotions. Where Johnny Hodges is a romantic soloist, Carter's approach is classical; where Ellington explores a world of sound, Carter arranges shapely melodies.

As well as being one of the three great alto saxophonists in jazz, Carter also plays the trumpet. In fact he has often declared that the trumpet is his favourite instrument. An early example of his trumpet playing can be heard in *Out of nowhere*, a track on (A) 12 Fol 2809, recorded by the Chocolate Dandies in 1933; on another Chocolate Dandies recording (*Bugle call rag* (A) 12 Fol 2811) he plays a clarinet solo. Carter formed his first band in 1932, but this group, the Club Harlem Orchestra – one of the most subtle and stylish of jazz orchestras – was never commercially successful. Of (1) and (2), both by this orchestra, the former is the better, *Symphony in riffs* and *Devil's holiday* containing some of Carter's most dazzling scoring for saxophones. (2) is marred by the fact that Carter sings on three tracks, but again the orchestrations are masterly. When Spike Hughes visited the U.S. in 1933, he used Carter's band as the nucleus for his recording group. Carter's contributions to the Hughes records, however, were limited to a superb solo on *Pastoral* and a good one in *Sweet Sue* (SPIKE HUGHES AND HIS NEGRO ORCHESTRA, 12 Dec LK4173, (A) 12 Lon LL1387).

In 1936 Carter came to Europe. While in Britain (where he spent a year as staff-arranger with Henry Hall's B.B.C. Dance Orchestra) he recorded (3) using British musicians. Much of the playing is stilted (British jazz was still a puny infant in those days) but Carter takes some excellent solos on alto, trumpet and tenor sax. Some of Carter's best recordings from this period are unfortunately no longer available. These are the British Vocalion 78s which he made in Holland, his band including the British trombonist George Chisholm and (on records only) Coleman Hawkins. Carter also played on a session arranged by Coleman Hawkins (7 HMV 7EG8393), scoring *Crazy rhythm* and *Honeysuckle rose* for four reeds and taking an elegant solo on the former. On his return to the U.S. in 1939 he wrote another brilliant arrangement (*I'm in the mood for swing*) for a saxophone quartet on a Lionel Hampton recording date, also contributing notable solos to this track and to *Shoe shiner's drag* (both on JIVIN' THE VIBES, 13 Cam CDN129, (A) 12 Cam CAL402). None of the recordings which Carter made with the excellent bands he led during the early 1940s, however, is any longer available.

Carter's playing in the post-war years showed that he had been affected by the modern jazz movement. The details of his phrasing, for instance, although never the structure of his solos, owed something to Charlie Parker. It is particularly interesting, therefore, to hear him soloing immediately after Hodges and Parker on the 1952 *Funky blues* (JAM SESSION 12 Col 33CX10008 (*d*)). By this time Carter was no longer leading a regular band, but working as an arranger in Hollywood. Most of his playing had to be done on odd recording sessions. He is particularly eloquent in the company of Art Tatum and Louis Bellson on *Blues in B flat* (7 Col SEB10027 (*d*)), an exceptionally interesting performance because both Carter and Tatum rarely played simple unadorned blues. Tracks by this group can be found on Col SEB10062 and on two American LPs, MAKIN' WHOOPEE (12 Ver 8227) and THREE GIANTS (12 Ver 8013). *Blues in*

B flat and *Idaho*, incidentally, are contained in 12 Col 33CX10141 (THE ANATOMY OF IMPROVISATION) and 12 Col 33CX10115 (ART TATUM) respectively. Tracks on ALTO SAXES (12 Col 33CX10072, *1955*) consist of two performances with the Oscar Peterson Trio, most of them – apart from *A foggy day* – rather dull. During the same year (1955) Carter contributed some beautifully lucid solos to an otherwise disappointing LP by Billie Holiday VELVET MOOD (12 Col 33CX10064 (A) 12 Ver 8096). He also played good trumpet and alto solos on SESSION AT MIDNIGHT (12 Cap LCT6110, (A) 12 Cap T707), and turned out to be the star performer (despite the presence of Dizzy Gillespie and Bill Harris) on NEW JAZZ SOUNDS (12 Col 33CX10049 (*d*), (A) 12 Ver 8135).

(4), (5) and (6) all belong to the last few years, and demonstrate more clearly than any of the other records, just how much Carter's style has altered. His playing on (4), for instance, has a passion that was absent in the 1930s; it is closer, in fact, to the way Willie Smith was playing during those years than to his own work of that period. But one misses the sense of lyrical detachment, the purity and relaxation of those earlier solos. This is a pleasant LP, all the same, with goodish solos from Ben Webster. (6) presents another small group session, this time with Earl Hines, Leroy Vinnegar and Shelly Manne. The results are again a trifle disappointing, neither Hines or Carter really cutting loose at any time. And the trumpet solos both here and on (4) are just a bit too sweet, too much like inferior Charlie Shavers. (5) is by a big band, playing Carter's arrangements; it sags in between jazz and commercial big-band swing. Carter's alto-playing is immaculate, however, and some of the tracks (notably the 'originals') are excitingly scored.

(1) BENNY CARTER AND HIS ORCHESTRA – 7 Col SEG7691 (*d*). *1933*.
(2) SWING IT – 7 Col SEG7702 (*d*). *1933*.
(3) SWINGIN' AT MAIDA VALE – 12 Dec LK4221. *1936*.
(4) JAZZ GIANT – 12 Con LAC12188. (A) 12 Con 3555, (S) 7028. *1959*.
(5) ASPECTS – 12 Lon LTZ-T15169. (A) UA LP4017, (S) 5017. *1959*.
(6) SWINGIN' THE TWENTIES – 12 Vog LAC12225. (A) 12 Con B3561,
   (S) 7561. *1959*.

ALBERT CASEY (1915)   *guitar*
Although he rarely receives proper recognition (indeed, he now

seems to have vanished completely from the jazz scene), Albert Casey must be ranked among the finest of jazz guitarists. Mixing single-string work with rich chording and subtle changes, Casey has always imparted an infectious swing to his solos. There is strength as well as resilience in his playing. His influence can still be perceived at work in one or two younger guitarists, such as the remarkable Wes Montgomery. Because so much of his solo playing was concentrated upon the first string of his guitar, Casey at one time began using a B (second) string in the first string position, to give extra power. Subsequently he switched to an electric guitar. Most of Casey's solos are encountered on records by Fats Waller's gay little band, for Casey worked with Waller almost continuously from 1934 to 1943. He is featured at some length in Waller's 1941 recording of *Buck jumpin'* (never released in Britain), while among his most enticing short solos are those on *Black Raspberry Jam* (12 RCA RD27047), *Blue turning grey* (10 HMV DLP1017, (*d*)) and *Let's pretend there's a moon* (10 HMV DLP1118 (*d*)). Two old HMV 78s (both deleted) are worth looking out for: *Fats Waller's original E flat blues*, containing some outstanding single-string playing, and Frankie Newton's *Rompin'*. *How high the moon* on Capitol's HISTORY OF JAZZ, Vol. 4, is a rather nondescript performance by a Sextet that includes Willie Smith, Illinois Jacquet and Sid Catlett, while *Buck still jumps* comes out of 'Jazz Off The Air', a 10 Vogue LP (LDE007), of jamming by Roy Eldridge, Flip Phillips and a rhythm section. (The LP was issued in the U.S. on Esoteric J2 but has since been deleted.) This particular track, however, supplies a generous sample of Casey's playing.

SERGE CHALOFF (1923-57)   *baritone saxophone*

Although interest in the baritone saxophone has centred around Gerry Mulligan in recent years the work of the late Serge Chaloff should not be forgotten. Chaloff was the first musician to transcribe Charlie Parker's ideas for use on the larger saxophone and in order to do this it became necessary for him to play baritone faster than any of his predecessors. Throughout his life he retained his love for Parker's music and infused a gread deal of warmth and passion into his solos. (1) contains two good examples of Chaloff during his stay with Woody Herman; on *Four brothers* he is teamed with three

[75]

tenors (Stan Getz, Zoot Sims and Herbie Steward) and succeeds in keeping up with them in the solo routine. Al Cohn's *The Goof and I* on the same LP was written especially to feature Serge who receives the vital support of the full-bodied Herman ensemble. (2) is by a small group from a slightly later edition of Woody's Herd, a record which includes Cohn's excellent tune *The most* and Chaloff's fast-moving *Chickasaw* (based on the chords of *Cherokee*). (3) is made up of two previous ten-inch LPs made in Boston during 1954; the quintet side, with Russ Freeman on piano, is noteworthy for a particularly fine and relaxed *Easy Street* with Serge at his most lyrical. The band on the reverse contains musicians from Herb Pomeroy's orchestra and is more noteworthy for the writing and playing of the unique Dick Twardzick than for Chaloff's appearances. (4) was made in Hollywood with an inspired rhythm section (Sonny Clark, Leroy Vinnegar and Philly Joe Jones) and contains some of the best Chaloff solos on record. *Thanks for the memory* finds him at his most passionate while *All the things you are* shows that he could handle his instrument with the ease of a tenor.

(1) The Three Herds – 12 Ph BBL7123. (A) 12 Col CL592. *1947.*
(2) Serge Chaloff and The Herdsmen – 7 Esq EP203. *1949.*
(3) The Fable of Mable – 12 Vog LAE12052. (A), two 10 Sto LPs, LP310 and LP317. *1954.*
(4) Serge Chaloff Quartet – 12 Cap T742. (A) 12 Cap T742. *1956.*

RAY CHARLES (1932)   *vocal, piano, alto saxophone*

If his singing were even one half as good as his piano playing, there would be more to say about him as a vocalist. However, let us say that, despite the obvious excitement which he generates, the mixture of gospel-style vocal phrasing with banal blues lyrics is most unsatisfactory, if not positively objectionable. His piano playing, on the other hand, is remarkably fine and he is a most convincing blues musician. For this reason, we prefer The Great Ray (1) to all his other LPs; he does not sing a note on either side. Soul Brothers (2), with Milt Jackson, is also recommended.

(1) The Great Ray Charles – 12 Lon LTZ-K15134. (A) Atl 1259. *1956.*
(2) Soul Brothers – 12 Lon LTZ-K15146. (A) Atl 1279. *1957.*

[76]

(3) RAY CHARLES AT NEWPORT – 12 Lon LTZ-K15149, (S) SAH-
K6008. (A) Atl 1289, (S) S-1289. *1958.*
(4) YES INDEED! – 12 Lon HA-E2168. (A) Atl 8025. *1957–8.*
(5) THE GENIUS OF RAY CHARLES – 12 Lon LTZ-K15190. (A) 12 Atl
1312, (S) S-1312. *1959.*

CHRISTIAN CHEVALIER (1930) *piano, arranger*

Chevalier ranks with Gosta Theselius and Ken Moule as a leading
European arranger. He has absorbed the lessons of such men as Gerry
Mulligan and Bill Holman and his own big band EP (1) reflects the
work of the Americans. *B.S.O.P.* must be singled out for special
mention for it is one of the most successful showcases to have been
designed around a soloist – in this case tenor saxist Bobby Jaspar.
While in Europe at the end of 1955 and the beginning of 1956
trumpeter Chet Baker recorded some of Chevalier's compositions
for the French Barclay label (Felsted in Britain) and took a few of
Christian's scores back to America on his return. *Vline* (sometimes
misspelled *V-line* or *Vlyne*) was recorded by Baker's 'big' band
(actually a nine-piece unit) on Vog LAE12109, (A) WP 1229, but
despite the contrary information on the sleeve to this album *Not too
slow* and *Mythe* were composed and arranged by bass player Pierre
Michelot. In 1954 an all-star British group in London recorded
Chevalier's *Mountain sunset* (Vog LDE050) at a hurried and not
altogether successful session. Christian's own piano playing, which
may be heard in a few places on (1), is reminiscent of John Lewis's.
(1) CHRISTIAN CHEVALIER AND HIS ORCHESTRA – 7 Col SEG7675.
1956.

GEORGE CHISHOLM (1915) *trombone*

Of all the jazz soloists that Britain has produced, George Chisholm
is probably the most original as well as the most distinguished. It was
in the late 1930s that he came to London from Glasgow. Benny
Carter heard him and asked him to join the band he was taking to
Holland (Chisholm takes brusque but inventive solos on several
British Vocalion 78s – all deleted – by this group). *Rosetta* and
You'll always be mine on Decca SCRAPBOOK OF BRITISH JAZZ, Vols.
1 and 2, were made soon after his return in 1938. Chisholm's own
playing, stark in pattern, granular in texture, full of urgency, is
typical of his work at this time. The supporting group falls well

below his standard. Other Chisholm solos from this period can be found on 'Fats Waller in London, No. 2' (HMV 7 7EG8341). *Broadhurst garden blues* in SCRAPBOOK OF BRITISH JAZZ, Vol. 2, an uncommonly fine track, dates from the war-years and 1944, when Chisholm was a member of the R.A.F. Squadronaires. Since the war Chisholm's style has undergone some modification. It is still forth-right and completely unique, but there is an added smoothness, an extra urbanity. Examples of latter-day Chisholm can be heard on (1), an LP which presents the trombonist in the company of some of the better British jazz musicians, but always retaining artistic dominance. During the past decade Chisholm has been a very busy session-man, taking part in a vast number of recordings, yet on the right occasion he can still play solos that put him up among the very greatest jazz trombonists. One instance is his solo in *Blue interlude*, played by a group under the leadership of Bertie King, a fine West Indian alto player, on Nix NJT506 ('Mainstream At Nixa', Vol. 2).

(1) CHIS – 12 Dec LK4147 (*d*). *1956.*

CHARLIE CHRISTIAN (1919–40)   *guitar*

Charlie Christian did for the guitar (in his case, the electric guitar) what Coleman Hawkins had done for the tenor saxophone, Louis Armstrong for the trumpet, Jimmy Harrison for the trombone, a decade earlier. He gave it genuine status both as a solo instrument and as part of the jazz ensemble, turning it into a voice that could take its place in the front-line, alongside the trumpet or tenor saxophone. For the first time, of course, the new electric and amplified guitars had made it possible for guitarists to be heard. Up to then even the best guitarists, men like Lonnie Johnson, Teddy Bunn and Al Casey, had usually been condemned to playing in the rhythm section, only taking the occasional solo up at the microphone. Christian came into jazz at the moment when this technical change was under way, and he created a style, indeed a fresh place in the ensemble for the new instrument. In the process, he showed himself to be a musician of great originality, possessing a very sophisticated harmonic sense, a wonderful feeling for rhythm, and a genuinely adventurous imagi-nation. His solos (making great use of eighth-notes), have remained classic performances.

Most of Charlie Christian's recorded solos were made with Benny

Goodman groups between 1939 and 1941. A particularly splendid collection is on (3), containing not only *Gone with what wind, Seven come eleven, Air mail special* and *Solo flight* (this one with the Goodman Orchestra), but also extra 'takes' of Christian's solos, spliced in with the originals. It is interesting, too, to compare the casual, relaxed *Waitin' for Benny*, recorded while the musicians were waiting for Goodman to turn up, with the brilliant but chaste Sextet version of the same theme, *A smo-o-o-oth one*. The other main collection of Sextet recordings from this period, 12 Ph BBL7178, is no longer available, except in the U.S. ((A) 12 Col CL500); it is worth searching for a copy, however, as this LP includes such tracks as *Shivers, Stardust* and *Breakfast feud*. The last-named, incidentally, can also be found on 7 Ph BBE12189. *Rose room, Grand slam* and *I can't give you anything but love* are in 'All the cats join in', 12 Fon TFL5067, while *Poor butterfly* and *I've found a new baby* are included on 7 Fon TFE17079.

Five tracks by the Benny Goodman Sextet, recorded during a concert at Carnegie Hall in 1939, just after Christian had joined the group, can be found on 'Spirituals to Swing', (A) 12 Van 85234. (The guitarist is also heard playing with Count Basie's Kansas City Six.) Christian also plays an outstandingly good solo in Lionel Hampton's *One sweet letter from you* ('Open House', 12 Cam CDN-138, (A) 12 Cam CAL-517). But perhaps the most intriguing item of all is (1), taped by Jerry Newman during informal sessions at Minton's Playhouse in 1941. This is the way Christian played off the stand, sitting in with Joe Guy, Thelonious Monk and Kenny Clarke. (2) contains additional material taped at Minton's, together with some recordings made at the Uptown House.

(1) JAZZ IMMORTAL – 10 Vog LDE002. (A) Esoteric 548 (rev. Gillespie). *1941*.
(2) DIZZY GILLESPIE, CHARLIE CHRISTIAN, 1941 – (A) Cou 548. *1941*.
(3) CHARLIE CHRISTIAN WITH BENNY GOODMAN – 12 Ph BBL7172. (A) 12 Col CL-652. *1940–41*.

BUCK CLAYTON (1911)   *trumpet*

Most of the virtues of middle period (or 'mainstream') jazz are fairly neatly embodied in the playing of Buck Clayton, a musician who spent seven years (from 1936 to 1943) in Count Basie's trumpet section, and since then has preferred to work in the company of other ex-Basie musicians. Hugues Panassié once described Clayton's playing as having been inspired by Louis Armstrong, then by Joe Smith. Certainly it is easy to recognize the melodic structure Clayton inherited from Armstrong, and to see something of Joe Smith's wistful quality in many of his solos. But even in recording *West End blues* (2), after playing Armstrong's famous introduction and first chorus, Clayton turns the classic pattern to his own ends. Much of Clayton's solo playing with Basie, however, made use of mutes, which Clayton manipulated most expertly, his range extending from the rather theatrical (but admirable) solo in *Fiesta in blue* (7 Fon TFR17226, (A) 12 Ep LN3169), a 'concerto' designed to feature his playing, to the delicate filigree work in *Don't you miss your baby* (Br 78, (d)). Most of Clayton's best pre-war solos can be found on Basie recordings, but he also performed small miracles on several sessions by Billie Holiday, made during the same years. In 1949 he toured France, and while in Paris recorded (1) and some of the tracks on (2). The former is notable for *Blues in first* and *Blues in second*, two majestic pieces of blues-playing. (*Blues in first* is also included in (2).) Four years later Clayton returned to Europe. He led the Alix Combelle orchestra through a set of Basie-styled arrangements (3), and recorded most of the items on (2), including a splendid *Wrap your troubles in dreams*.

Commencing in the winter of 1953, Buck Clayton became the central figure in a number of jam session recordings (4), (5), (6), (7) and (8), featuring such soloists as Joe Newman, Urbie Green, Joe Thomas, Trummy Young, Sir Charles Thompson and – on (6), playing the most inspired clarinet solo of his career – Woody Herman. Ruby Braff, Benny Green, Coleman Hawkins and Buddy Tate also took part in (7), an LP marred by tape-splicing in *Jumpin' at the woodside*, which combines solos from sessions made five months apart. (9) and (10) are by a smaller group, with Vic Dickenson contributing witty trombone solos. (10) is an exceptionally pleasing record, devoted entirely to blues, with Clayton on his own in *Blues blasé*. (11) presents the band which came to Britain in 1959, caught here at about the peak of its form with the ensemble playing Buck's neat arrangements, and with good solos from Emmett Berry (he 'cuts' Buck on this session), Dicky Wells and the pianist, Al Williams.

Buck Clayton can be heard playing outstanding solos, of course, on records by many other groups apart from his own. It is, however, worth singling out one example, his beautifully designed solos (*Honeysuckle Rose* and *One o'clock jump*) on 10 Fon TRF6022, by the Benny Goodman Trio (with guests). Clayton has taken part in many of the sessions organized by Stanley Dance for Felsted, and he also plays well on 'Mainstream', 12 Lon LTZ-K15182, SAH6066, (A) 12 Atl 1303, in a group led by Vic Dickenson.

(1) BUCK CLAYTON QUARTET – 7 Vog EPV1101. *1949.*
(2) BUCK – 12 Vog LAE12032. *1949–53.*
(3) BUCK CLAYTON WITH ALIX COMBELLE'S ORCHESTRA – 10 Vog LDE140. *1953.*
(4) THE HUCKLEBUCK AND ROBBINS NEST – 12 Ph BBL7032. (A) 12 Col CL548. *1953.*
(5) HOW HI THE FI – 12 Ph BBL7040 (*d*). (A) 12 Col CL567. *1953–4.*
(6) BUCK CLAYTON JAM SESSION – 12 Ph BBL7068. *1954.*
(7) JUMPIN' AT THE WOODSIDE – 12 Ph BBL7087 (*d*). (A) 12 Col CL701. *1954–5.*
(8) ALL THE CATS JOIN IN – 12 Ph BBL7129 (*d*). (A) 12 Col CL882. *1956.*
(9) BUCK CLAYTON SPECIAL – 12 Ph BBL 7217. *1957.*
(10) BUCKIN' THE BLUES – 12 Van PPL11010 (*d*). (A) 12 Van 8514. *1957.*
(11) SONGS FOR SWINGERS – 12 Ph BBL7317, (S) SBBL533. (A) 12 Col CL1320, (S) CS8123. *1958.*

AL COHN (1925) *tenor, baritone saxophones*

Although he did not play on the Woody Herman recording of that name, Al Cohn must be considered one of the original *Four brothers*. Like Zoot Sims, Stan Getz, Herbie Steward, etc., Cohn turned to Lester Young for his inspiration but unlike most of his contemporaries he arrived at a thicker, darker tone. For some years he lagged behind his colleagues as a soloist, lacking that quality of presence which marks the jazz individualist. On the session which brought together five similar-styled tenors – Getz, Sims, Cohn, Allen Eager and Brew Moore – Al is the weakest soloist and sounds like an enervated version of Zoot Sims (1). In 1950 he made his first quartet records (2), a date with George Wallington, Curley Russell and Tiny Kahn. Despite the inadequacies of the recording it is possible to appreciate that Cohn has finally emerged as a true soloist; in fact *How long has this been going on* is a mature solo worthy of a more experienced jazzman. Paralleling his work as an instrumentalist has been his career as a composer and arranger. He did some writing for the 1947 Woody Herman Herd, including Serge Chaloff's feature *The Goof and I*, but he blossomed forth in this field during the early nineteen-fifties when he seemed to be turning in scores for record dates of all descriptions. He became as active an arranger in New York as Shorty Rogers had become in Hollywood. Cohn's connexions with RCA Victor led, inevitably, to several dates under his own name, the most representative of which is (3). Here he guides a medium-sized band containing such soloists as Joe Newman, Billy Byers, Gene Quill, etc., through a series of arrangements which occasionally reach a peak of originality and never fall below Cohn's high standard of professionalism. Other dates for RCA included outright attempts to recreate the Kansas City Seven feeling, a session with strings (the acme of respectability) and a 'workshop' album in which Cohn pitted his tenor against a brass choir. Some of Al's best writing has been in less adventurous surroundings, however. He wrote for and played with the big bands of Larry Sonn (Cor LVA9040, (A) Cor 57057) and Elliot Lawrence (Vog LAE12071, (A) Fan 3236). In the latter album, recorded on location at Atlantic City, Cohn reaches new heights as a soloist with his moody, expressive *Alone together*, replacing the vocalist for whom this arrangement was originally written; his warm tone and emotional approach disproves effectively the misleading charges that post-war stylists are capable only of cerebral improvisations. Cohn's success as a writer is due in no small part to his continuing desire to be an instrumentalist as well; the musician who functions in both capacities works from a much broader palette of experience. As a soloist Al has been paired off on a number of occasions with the stylistically similar Zoot Sims to excellent effect. (4) finds them together, creating mellow, two-tenor jazz on seven tracks while the eighth, *Two funky people*, is a kind of contemporary Mezzrow-Bechet duet with Al and Zoot both playing clarinets. On a number of record dates Cohn has played baritone in a brash, somewhat coarse-toned manner and bumps his way through *There will never be another you* (HMV 7EG8367, (A)

ABC LP115) in an engaging manner backed by a sympathetic rhythm section.

(1) THE BROTHERS - Esq 7 EP134. (A) 12 Pre PRLP 7022 (with additional titles). *1949.*

(2) AL COHN QUARTET - (A) 12 Sav 12048. (Four titles, with two alternative takes, first issued on now-deleted Pro 10 LP 3002. Available in Britain on Esq 78 r.p.m.: *Groovin' with Gus/ Let's get away from it all,* 10-213, *Infinity/How long has this been going on?* 10-366.) *1950.*

(3) AL COHN AND HIS ORCHESTRA - HMV 10 LP DLP1107. (A) 12 RCA LP LJM1024 (with two extra titles). *1955.*

(4) AL AND ZOOT - Cor 12 LP LVA9074. (A) 12 Cor 57171. *1957.*

NAT 'KING' COLE (1917)   *piano*

Before Nat Cole virtually gave up playing the piano in order to concentrate upon his singing, he was regarded as an unusually incisive and inventive jazz pianist. His style, based upon Earl Hines' playing, had a very individual lightness and delicacy about it. A couple of his most sprightly solos, in fact, can be found on two Lionel Hampton tracks, *Blue because of you* (12 Cam CDN-138, (A) CAL517) and *Jack the bellboy* (7 RCA RCX1004), both recorded in 1940. He can also be heard playing alongside Lester Young on four tracks of (A) Score SLP4019 (*1942*) and on the whole of (A) Ver 8164 (*1950*). *I want to be happy* (*1950*), is also included in Vol. 1 of 'The Jazz Scene' (10 Col 33C9007, (*d*)). (1) brings together some of the best tracks made by the King Cole Trio, including *Honeysuckle rose*, also available 'Encyclopaedia of Jazz, Vol. 3.' Nat Cole sings on (2), but the LP is notable for solo playing by Stuff Smith, Harry Edison, Willie Smith and Juan Tizol.

(1) IN THE BEGINNING - 12 Br LAT8123. (A) 12 Dec 8260. *1940-1.*

(2) AFTER MIDNIGHT - 12 Cap LCT6133. (A) 12 Cap W782. *1956.*

BILL COLEMAN (1904)   *trumpet*

No trumpet player soars through the upper register with such a suggestion of ease as Bill Coleman. Mobility is the essence of his style and rarely does he pause longer than an instant upon a single note. Lightness and elegance, in fact, are the virtues of Coleman's music.

[83]

He made some records with Fats Waller's Rhythm in 1934 and 1935 (one of his best solos with that group – in *I'm a hundred per cent for you* – is included on 12 RCA RD27047, (A) 12 RCA LPM1246), but his most inspired playing seems to be that on recordings made when he was in Europe just before the war. 'Dicky Wells in Paris' (12 HMV CLP1054 (*d*)) contains *Hangin' around Boudon*, blues-playing of unusual beauty, and *Between the devil and the deep blue sea*, one of his most exciting performances. Other outstanding solos occur in *Japanese sandman* and *Sweet Sue*. When Coleman returned to Paris after the war he tried for a time to adapt his playing to the modern style, but with disastrous results. By the time he made the three EPs listed below he had reverted to his normal manner. Although none of these items could be called outstanding, all of them contain good solos, not only from Coleman but also from that excellent French tenor-player, Guy Lafitte.

(1) BILL COLEMAN IN PARIS – 7 Col SEG7645 (*d*). *1955*.

(2) METRO JAZZ – 7 Col SEG7684 (*d*). *1955*.

(3) BILL COLEMAN AND HIS ORCHESTRA – 7 Col SEG7722. *1956*.

ORNETTE COLEMAN (1930)   *alto saxophone*

On the sleeve to his first LP Coleman is quoted as having a 'real control of pitch'. On first hearing him play, however, the listener is likely to reach an opposite conclusion. Coleman appears to be doing his best to strike out along a new line in jazz in his search for 'human' sounds but so far as he has been less successful than, say, John Coltrane. Ornette's apparent disregard for correct harmony falls strangely on ears attuned to more conventional music and his use of quarter tones in a group containing a fixed pitch instrument incapable of producing quarter tones – the piano – leads to some effects which are frankly discordant. The alto saxist extemporizes in such a reckless manner in places that one begins to doubt if he has complete control over his instrument. Yet the tunes themselves, all Coleman originals, are played with such accuracy in the ensemble statements that Ornette's mastery of his instrument is not in doubt; it is simply that in giving himself the maximum harmonic and melodic freedom he sounds like a musician carrying out warming-up exercises. The trouble seems to lie in Coleman's environment for although his four colleagues are in sympathy with his aims, they themselves play in a much more orthodox manner. In short, Coleman's first LP fails because none of his sidemen are tuned in on the same wavelength so far as improvisation is concerned. There is not one track on this LP which measures up to *Intuition* by Lennie Tristano's Sextet (Cap EAP1-491), a work in which six musicians created a completely free improvisation with no preconceived chord sequences, melody line or even time signature. As yet Ornette Coleman's music is too undisciplined to be judged in this fairly orthodox context but it seems likely that he will gradually convert more musicians to his way and presumably do away with a piano in his future groups.

(1) SOMETHING ELSE! THE MUSIC OF ORNETTE COLEMAN – 12 Vog LAC12170. (A) 12 Con C3551. *1958.*

BUDDY COLLETTE (1921)   *flute, clarinet, saxophones*
Versatility is the watchword so far as Buddy Collette is concerned. He has made records using almost every known reed and woodwind instrument and proved himself to be the master of many. Although he was active in Los Angeles jazz circles as early as the middle-forties it was not until he joined drummer Chico Hamilton's quintet in 1955 that he gained prominence. His subsequent replacement by Paul Horn coincided with a lowering of standards and it is true to say that Hamilton's quintet has never fulfilled the promise it showed when Buddy was a member. (1) is the first Hamilton LP and contains some typically excellent work from Collette who shines on alto and plays cool, Getz-like tenor. He never quite comes up to expectations on either of his own LPs (2) and (3) although both feature sufficient solos by Buddy on flute, clarinet, alto and tenor to show that on the three first-named instruments he ranks with all but the very best in the field. ((2) is noteworthy if only for the presence of such under-rated professionals as Jewel Grant, Gerald Wilson, Ernie Freeman and Dave Wells, all of whom have been active in the Los Angeles area for some years but who seldom get a chance to play on a jazz date.) *Johnny walks*, which occupies one side of (4), is a graceful and flowing alto solo, perhaps the best he has ever recorded. On (5) Buddy plays flute in the company of three other flautists (Bud Shank, Paul Horn and Harry Klee) throughout an LP which soon degenerates into boredom due to the lack of variation. To add insult to injury the sleeve fails to identify any of the flute solos.

(1) CHICO HAMILTON QUINTET – Vog 12 LAE12039. (A) 12 WP 1209.
1955.

(2) BUDDY COLLETTE – Vog 12 LAC12090. (A) 12 Con C3522. 1956.

(3) BUDDY COLLETTE – Vog 12 LAC12092. (A) 12 Con C3531.
1956.

(4) BUDDY COLLETTE – HMV 7 7EG8356. (A) 12 ABC LP179 (with
eight additional titles). 1957.

(5) SWINGING SHEPHERDS – Mer 12 MMB12001. (A) 12 EmA 36133.
1958.

JOHN COLTRANE (1926)   *tenor saxophone*

In his determined attempts to hit on an original style John Coltrane
has passed uneasily through some difficult years. His strident shoutings
proved indigestible to many listeners during the trial period but when
he eventually found satisfaction it became clear that he was the most
individual tenor saxist since Stan Getz. The effect of Miles Davis
(with whom he has played – with one or two breaks – since 1955)
on Coltrane has been responsible for a certain amount of relaxation
at a time when the tenor player's work threatened to degenerate
into empty fury. (1), by Davis's quintet, finds John in excellent form
and reveals his sometimes-obscured love for melody; despite the
hard-edged tone and the scooping approach his solo on *You're my
everything*, for example, is passionate and sincere. The first date
under his own name (2), is not wholly successful due to the presence
of two lesser front-line men (Sahib Shihab and Johnny Splawn,
playing baritone and trumpet respectively) on some tracks although
the tracks by Coltrane and rhythm only – *Violets for your furs* and
While my lady sleeps in particular – give more than a hint of the tenor
saxist's potential. (3) and (4) are extensions of the formula for here
Coltrane is supported solely by the Red Garland Trio. Both LPs are
recommended and the superiority of one over the other is largely
a matter of personal preference. (3) contains a furious, up-tempo
Soft lights and sweet music, a splendid ballad reading of *You leave me
breathless* and a fine *Bass blues*. (4) has a rocket-assisted *Russian lullaby*
(some lullaby this) as well as a beautifully developed *Good bait*. (5),
released under the enjoyably misleading title 'Mainstream '58' (one
in the eye for the pigeon-holers) is by a quintet which, with Wilbur
Harden on flügelhorn, sounds like a second-carbon of the Miles

[86]

Davis group. Coltrane is in full control of the situation here and shoulders the heaviest solo load backed well by Tommy Flanagan's flowing piano.

(1) MILES DAVIS QUINTET – 12 Esq 32-068. (A) 12 Pre PRLP7129. *1956.*

(2) COLTRANE – 12 Esq 32-079. (A) 12 Pre PRLP7105. *1957.*

(3) JOHN COLTRANE – 12 Esq 32-091. (A) 12 Pre PRLP7123. *1957.*

(4) SOULTRANE – 12 Esq 32-089. (A) 12 Pre PRLP7142. *1958.*

(5) MAINSTREAM '58 – 12 Lon LTZ-C15159. (A) 12 Sav 12127. *1958.*

KEN COLYER (1928) *cornet, vocal, guitar*

A staunch, even fanatical, supporter and lover of New Orleans jazz, Colyer has modelled himself and his band on the traditional model, playing abrupt and economical clichés, applied to a wide repertoire of standards, pops and ragtime. Once, finding himself with a rather streamlined, polished and threatening-to-be-commercially successful band on his hands he beat a righteous retreat back to the harsh lands of true jazz. This excellent record (2) contained some music that marked the beginnings of British equality in jazz with some of the white American bands, a neat concise music with skilful musicians like Chris Barber and Monty Sunshine in which setting Colyer's pleasant but not very powerful playing shows up to a wonderful advantage. *Isle of Capri* is a remarkably nimble and exciting track while *Harlem rag* and *La Harpe Street* have a cheerful ragtime atmosphere, cleanly and pleasingly caught. Unfortunately Colyer also sings on one track.

Back to the Delta (3) and back to the holy creed, the next LP was a comparatively rough affair. It also contained three tracks on which Colyer, in his inimitable Cockney style, sang three traditional songs. With some good support from Alexis Korner, Bill Colyer and Micky Ashman, these tracks were almost a great success, in spite of the callow singing. Two tracks from a London Festival Hall traditional jazz concert were included on 12 Dec LK4088. The rest of the Colyer recordings for Decca have remained in the proper groove with two exceptions. One a rather horrible record made in Hamburg and one an exceptionally good record of four authentic ragtime numbers (11), in which the band seems to justify its style and approach with maximum effect. The concise, jerky pattern of ragtime is

[87]

caught technically and in spirit with great exactitude, and the crisp almost abrupt playing is entirely suited to the music. This EP is one of the best that a British band has ever made.

(1) KEN COLYER IN NEW ORLEANS – 10 Vog LDE161 – 7 Vog EPV1102. *1953*.

(2) NEW ORLEANS TO LONDON – 10 Dec LF1152. *1953*.

(3) BACK TO THE DELTA – 10 Dec LF1196. *1954*.

(4) AND BACK TO NEW ORLEANS, Vol. 1 – 7 Dec DFE6268. *1955*.

(5) AND BACK TO NEW ORLEANS, Vol. 2 – 7 Dec DFE6299. *1955*.

(6) SKIFFLE GROUP – 7 Dec DFE6286. *1955*.

(7) CLUB SESSION – 12 Dec LK4178. *1956*.

(8) SKIFFLE GROUP, No. 2 – 7 Dec DFE6444. *1957*.

(9) KEN COLYER AND HIS OMEGA BRASS BAND – 10 Dec LF1301, 7 Dec DFE6435. *1957*.

(10) COLYER PLAYS STANDARDS – Dec 12 LK4294. *1958*.

(11) THEY ALL PLAYED RAGTIME – 7 Dec DFE6466. *1958*.

(12) COLYER IN HAMBURG – 10 Dec LF1319. *1958*.

(13) COLYER SKIFFLE GROUP IN HAMBURG – 7 Dec DFE6563. *1958*.

EDDIE CONDON (1905)   *guitar, banjo*

Condon's musicianly activities are in the strictly limited field of rhythm guitarist and banjoist and in his early recording days he did this important but unlimelighted job with some creditable results, as heard on the sides with Billy Banks, with Fats Waller on *Harlem fuss* and *The minor drag*, and on his own great 1933 recordings where he actually gives a distinctive bouncing kind of rhythm instantly recognizable as his. Since then his ambitions as a musician have declined and his activities with the guitar are usually confined to carrying it on to the platform and carrying it off again. His main activities now are as a jazz promoter and wise-cracking master of ceremonies. He has tackled the very difficult task of keeping Chicago jazz and jazz musicians alive. His best efforts in this line were on the 1939 Chicagoan recordings with Kaminsky, Gowans, Russell, Freeman and Sullivan (1) and on occasional sides made between 1944 and 1947 which produced the occasional gem like *Down among the sheltering palms* (2) notable for Pee Wee Russell's wonderful solo.

Chicago style musicians are an unhappy lot. They try to show their vigour and inspiration by wild overblowing which generally produces discordant and harsh noises, they are completely without the Negro's easy relaxation, and they have no deep inspiration. The total result of numerous Condon sessions since this time, is an occasional flash, a lot of noise and very little that one can label as lasting music. Sessions like (14) are frankly horrible.

(1) EDDIE CONDON AND HIS CHICAGOANS—CHICAGO JAZZ ALBUM (with McPartland and Wettling) – 12 Br LAT8042 or 7 Br OE9152. (A) 12 Dec DL8029. *1939.*

(2) JAM SESSIONS AT COMMODORE – (A) 12 Com 30006. *1940–3.*

(3) CONDON À LA CARTE – (A) 12 Com 30010. *1940–3.*

(4) IVY LEAGUE JAZZ – (A) 12 Dec 8282. *1944–7.*

(5) A NIGHT AT EDDIE CONDON'S – (A) 12 Dec 8281. *1944–7.*

(6) WE CALLED IT MUSIC – 10 Br LA8542. *1947.*

(7) JAM SESSION COAST TO COAST (with Rampart Street Paraders) – (A) Col SL-547.

(8) JAMMIN' AT CONDON'S – 12 Ph PBL7031. (A) 12 Col CL-616. *1954.*

(9) BIXIELAND – 12 Ph BBL7109. (A) 12 Col CL-719. *1955.*

(10) EDDIE CONDON'S TREASURY OF JAZZ – 12 Ph BBL7131. (A) 12 Col CL-881. *1956.*

(11) AT NEWPORT (with Louis Armstrong) – (A) 12 Col CL-931. *1957.*

(12) THE ROARING TWENTIES – 12 Ph BEL7227. (A) 12 Col CL-1089. *1957.*

(13) EDDIE CONDON IS UPTOWN NOW – 12 MGM C768. (A) 12 MGM 3651. *1958.*

(14) DIXIELAND DANCE PARTY – 12 Lon LTZ-D15158. (S) SAH-D6014 (A) 12 Dot 3141, (S) 25241. *1958.*

EDDIE COSTA (1931) *piano, vibes*

At a time when so many contemporary pianists seem to be losing the use of their left hands, it is refreshing to hear the invigorating style of Eddie Costa. Costa drives hard in a brittle, percussive manner and is the possessor of a considerable technique; more important, perhaps, is his ability to swing all the time, irrespective of material or tempo. (1) is one of his earliest records on which he is accompanied by bass player Vinnie Burke and drummer Nick Stabulas. *Get happy,* transcribed to the minor, is played for the most part below middle C and is something of a *tour de force*. *Sweet and lovely*, on the same LP, is a graceful vibes solo lacking some of the intensity of Eddie's piano work. In recent years Costa has been much in demand for New York recording dates and has enlivened a number of otherwise drab sessions. His buoyant style adds life to a number of guitarist Tal Farlow's technically-perfect but otherwise glib albums. It is Costa's playing which saves (2), recorded at the 1957 Newport Festival, from mediocrity for the Costa-led rhythm trio is hampered by two particularly uninspiring soloists in Rolf Kuehn, clarinet, and Dick Johnson, alto. Eddie plays vibes throughout (3), an album devoted to six tunes from the show *Guys and Dolls*. He negotiates the differing time signatures on *Luck be a lady* (from 6/8 to 4/4 in every chorus) and plays with great charm and elegance on *I've never been in love before*. Although Milt Jackson seems to be the major influence on vibes, Costa's solo style closely resembles Vic Feldman. On the British issue of (3) – as three separate EPs – no personnel information is given on any of the sleeves or labels and it is as well to know that the fine rhythm section which assists Costa throughout comprises Bill Evans, Wendell Marshall and Paul Motian on piano, bass and drums respectively.

(1) EDDIE COSTA-VINNIE BURKE TRIO – (A) 12 Jub LP1025. *1956*.
(2) EDDIE COSTA—AT NEWPORT – 12 Col 33CX10108. (A) 12 Ver MGV8237. *1957*.
(3) EDDIE COSTA QUARTET – (A) 12 Cor CRL57230, six-title LP split into three EPs for British issue; Cor FEP 2018, 2019 and 2020. *1958*.

IDA COX (1889) *vocal*

Though she could never match Bessie Smith's voice, Ida Cox was always well in the running. Whether this was because her lyrics were of an unusually high standard, such as in *Fogyism* (1), is hard to tell. Her voice, more sleazy than Bessie's, added a rough edge to her singing which is most attractive. She was popular from her very first recordings in 1923, and the 1930s saw her touring the South with her own tent show. In 1939 she came to New York to appear in the Spirituals To Swing concerts and recorded in that year, and in 1940 (her last session), with groups which included Hot Lips Page, Red

Allen, J. C. Higginbotham, Ed Hall, James P. Johnson, Charlie Christian and Lionel Hampton. However, the trumpet players most closely associated with her were Tommy Ladnier and Joe Smith. *Misery blues* (2) and *Last mile blues* (3) are among her best recordings and the oddly assorted accompanying group on *Deep sea blues* (5) and the other 1939 titles, are worthy of a proper hearing.

(1) KING OLIVER PLAYS THE BLUES – 10 Lon AL3510 (*d*). *1928.*
(2) IDA COX SINGS THE BLUES – 10 Lon AL3517 (*d*). *1923–8.*
(3) *Last mile blues/I can't quit that man* – 10 78 Par R2837 (*d*). *1940.*
(4) THE GREAT BLUES SINGERS – 10 Lon AL3530 (*d*). *1927–46.*
(5) IDA COX – 7 Fon TFE17136. *1939.*

BOB CROSBY (1913) *bandleader, vocal*

A rather undistinguished singer himself, in 1935 he took over the Ben Pollack orchestra and made a series of recordings with a big band that were rather remarkable for the amount of hot improvised feeling obtained by a group of that size. This was largely due to a number of very fine white jazz musicians within the band – Billy Butterfield, Yank Lawson, Muggsy Spanier, variously amongst the trumpets, Warren Smith and Floyd O'Brien amongst the trombones, Irving Fazola and Matty Matlock on clarinets, Eddie Miller and Gil Rodin on saxes, pianists like Bob Zurke and Jess Stacy, Bob Haggart on bass and Ray Bauduc on drums. At various times a small unit from the band containing various permutations of these musicians made some sprightly Dixieland sides under the name of the Bob Cats.

The orchestra is well represented on an LP (1) with recordings ranging from 1936 to 1956. Delightful early numbers like *The old spinning wheel* of 1937, *Smokey Mary* of 1939, *Ja da* of 1940 and *Tin roof blues* of 1942 with fine Jess Stacy and Floyd O'Brien solos. On (2) are two of the orchestra's best-known recordings (along with recordings by other swing bands of the period) *Dogtown blues* and *South Rampart Street parade* made in 1937.

The Bob Cats are well represented on a further LP (3) which has a good cross-section of their work. Outstanding are the exhilarating *March of the Bob Cats* and *Mournin' blues* as well as *Slow mood*, which is an Eddie Miller feature, *Big foot jump* featuring Bob Zurke and *I hear you talking*, a happy quartet number featuring Miller, Zurke, Haggart and Bauduc. Later recreations, resuscitations and

[91]

hi-fi-ations on Coral, Columbia and Capitol, although sprightly, are not worth twopence when compared with the originals.

(1) BOB CROSBY 1936–1956 – 12 Cor LVA9045. (A) 12 Cor 57089. *1936–56.*

(2) FIVE FEET OF SWING (with Jimmy Dorsey, Dorsey Bros., Glen Gray, Chick Webb) – 12 Br LAT8037. (A) 12 Br DL8045. *1937.*

(3) BOB CROSBY'S BOB CATS – 12 Br LAT8050. (A) 12 Dec DL8061. *1937–40.*

(4) THE BOB CATS BALL – (A) 12 Cor 57005. *1937–40.*

(5) BOB CROSBY IN HI-FI – (A) 12 Cor S7068. *1950s.*

(6) BOB CROSBY'S BOB CATS – 12 Cap T293. (A) 12 Cap T293. *1950s.*

(7) BOB CATS BLUES – (A) 12 Cor 57060. *1950s.*

(8) BOB CATS ON PARADE – (A) 12 Cor 57061. *1950s.*

(9) BOB CROSBY'S BOB CATS IN HI-FI – 12 Cor LVA9083. (A) 12 Cor 57170. *1957.*

(10) THE BOB CROSBY SHOW – (A) 12 Col CL-766. *1950s.*

(11) SOUTH PACIFIC BLOWS WARM – (A) 12 Dot 3136. *1950s.*

D

PETE DAILY (1911)   *cornet*
A musician with a clear easy style that produces uncomplicated, unexceptional but rather pleasing Dixieland music with no particular depth. Occasional moments of vulgarity mar some of the recordings, but most of them are musicianly and bounce along very nicely.

(1) DIXIELAND JAZZ BATTLE, Vol. 1 – 10 Br LA8515 (*d*). *1945.*

(2) PETE DAILY'S DIXIELAND BAND – 10 Cap LC6525 (*d*). (A) 12 Cap T183. *1947–9.*

(3) DIXIE BY DAILY – 10 Cap LC6603 (*d*). (A) 12 Cap T385. *1949–52.*

(4) JAZZ BAND BALL (with Murphy, Lewis and Ory) – (A) 12 GTJ 12005. *1947.*

TADD DAMERON (1917)   *piano, arranger*
Composer of such jazz standards as *Ladybird* and *Good bait*, Tadd Dameron must be placed in the forefront of the modern jazz arrangers. He was the first man to grasp the fundamentals of the

[92]

Parker–Gillespie music and use it as an orchestral style. He was responsible for the highly individual sound of the big Gillespie band, deploying his unique voicing of the reeds against the hard-hitting brass. A great discoverer of talent, however young and immature, it is thanks mainly to Dameron that men such as Fats Navarro and Clifford Brown were given a start in their careers. Tadd's own (recording) bands have usually sounded rough and under-rehearsed but the moving spirit behind the music has been apparent in every bar. (1) is by the fine little band Dameron led at Atlantic City during the summer of 1953, a band which contained Clifford Brown, Gigi Gryce and Philly Joe Jones. Brownie takes a fine cup-muted solo on the haunting *Theme of no repeat*, while Jones is impressive on his own showcase (written by Tadd) *Philly JJ*. For a man whose own technique is limited, Dameron's piano work on *Dial B for beauty* is surprisingly professional. (2), like (1), has the elusive Dameron sound in the ensemble (hot, crackling trumpeter, in this case Kinny Dorham, and lead alto with a wide vibrato) and again features a lesser-known jazzman of note. Here it is the tenor saxist Joe Alexander, whose urgent playing makes sense on *Delerium*. *Fontainbleu* is the main work, a completely written-out descriptive piece dedicated to the French palace which the eight-piece band interprets with feeling if not great accuracy. Trombonist Henry Coker's big moment occurs when he is given *Flossie* as a shop-window for his wares; he needs no second bidding and makes an excellent job of things. (3) is by a quartet (John Coltrane, Tadd Dameron, bass and drums) and the pairing of Coltrane and Dameron leads one to wish that the two might have recorded more frequently together. Coltrane has a great understanding of Tadd's music and it is a little unfortunate that the somewhat casual approach could not have been replaced by a larger group playing Tadd's arrangements of these six original tunes.

(1) TADD DAMERON BAND – 10 Esq 20-044. (A) 12 Pre PRLP7055 (with four additional, non-Dameron titles). *1953*.
(2) TADD DAMERON BAND – 12 Esq 32-034. (A) 12 Pre PRLP7037. *1956*.
(3) MATING CALL (QUARTET) – 12 (A) 12 Pre PRLP7070. *1956*.

JOHNNY DANKWORTH (1927) *alto saxophone*
One of the first European jazzmen to assimilate the new jazz style

fostered by Parker and Gillespie, Johnny Dankworth was the leader of a remarkable septet during the early 'fifties. The Dankworth Seven sounded at times like a scaled-down Miles Davis 'Capitol' band although the leader's writing gave the group individual characteristics. Unfortunately none of the original Seven records – featuring Don Rendell, Jimmy Deuchar and Bill LeSage – is now available on microgroove (they were all recorded for Jazz Parade/ Vogue or Esquire) and Dankworth is represented by his latter-day and musicianly big band. (1) contains two of John's alto solos with band accompaniment, solos which seem to reflect Benny Carter as much as Charlie Parker, plus the original and very clever parodies *Experiments with mice* and *Big jazz story*. The former is particularly funny and has the Dankworth band turning in creditable imitations of Gerry Mulligan, Glenn Miller, Stan Kenton, Sauter-Finnegan, Benny Goodman, etc., all strung together by John's narration. The new instrumentation, which made its appearance during 1957, is heard on four tracks of (2); here, a five-man unit comprising trumpet, tenor, alto, trombone and baritone, takes the place of the expected reed section giving the ensemble a distinctive sound. The remaining tracks on the LP are by small groups drawn from within the ranks of the big band and are features principally for Dickie Hawdon's exciting, Clifford Brown-like trumpet and Laurie Monk's trombone. (3) is the best example of the Dankworth band currently available and captures the in-person excitement on some numbers: *Swingin' the blues*, a head arrangement, builds steadily to a climax and has the band blowing with gay abandon while *Stardust* is a fine showcase for the breathy, Chu Berry-like tenor of Danny Moss.

(1) JOHNNY DANKWORTH ORCHESTRA – 7 Par GEP8697. *1953*, *1954*, *1956* and *1957*.

(2) JOHNNY DANKWORTH ORCHESTRA – 12 Par PMC1043. (A) 12 Ver 20006. *1957*.

(3) JOHNNY DANKWORTH ORCHESTRA – 12 Par PMC1076. *1958*.

COW COW DAVENPORT (1894–1955)   *piano, vocal*

A fine blues pianist and boogie woogie exponent, composer of *Cow Cow boogie* made popular by Ella Fitzgerald and Ella Mae Morse. His style was primitive, driving, rough, winning by its honesty and feeling. Some sides from the Riverside/London LPs are now deleted but two fine tracks are available on PIANO JAZZ, Vol. 1 (12 Cor LVA9069, (A) 12 Br 54014). Two of his finest recordings on which he only sings are worth finding on a deleted Br 03509 – *That'll get it/Don't you loud mouth me* – with Sammy Price on piano, and others.

MILES DAVIS (1926)   *trumpet*

At a time when most young trumpeters hitched themselves to the Gillespie star, Miles Davis emerged with a style which owed nothing to Dizzy. Miles' reserved, almost static sound was first heard on record with Charlie Parker and his playing provided an ideal foil for Bird's flashing brilliance. In 1948 he was elected leader of a co-operative nine-man band which worked for just two weeks but whose records, for Capitol, have had a considerable effect on the course of subsequent jazz development. Where most musicians were intent merely on digesting Parker's *solo* style and using it as a means in itself, Davis, together with Gil Evans, John Lewis and Gerry Mulligan took Bird's playing as a means towards an end and developed a low-temperature ensemble sound dependent on scored passages and used to offset solos by Miles, Mulligan, Lee Konitz, Jay Jay Johnson and Kai Winding. The importance of this unit cannot be overstressed; from it came a number of lasting effects including the use of french horn and tuba to give depth and colour to an ensemble. The arrangements were tailored to suit the individual members of the band, in the same way that Duke Ellington has always written with certain soloists in mind; moreover, the arrangers were themselves inprovising jazzmen. (1) is a record which should be a part of any contemporary jazz library, not only as an example of Davis, Mulligan, Konitz, etc., but as a kind of textbook illustrating the most intelligent use of jazz instruments. From the days of his epoch-making band until his sudden 'acceptance' following his appearance at the 1955 Newport Jazz Festival Davis existed in comparative obscurity; were it not for occasional record dates made with pick-up groups there would be little or no evidence to indicate the direction of the trumpeter's development during this period. Despite some initial set-backs – and (2) is a particularly sad set of titles by a band which includes Benny Green, Sonny Rollins and John Lewis, all sounding full of woe – Miles was working on his technique, attempting to extend his range yet maintain the full, mellow tone at all times. In addition he was constantly on the look-out for any new avenues of development, either for a group style or as a means of individual expression. A skirmish with the Lennie Tristano school led to nothing (3) but a date under his own name with men of his own choice (4) produced some virile, driving jazz (Art Blakey was on drums) as well as well-poised ballads such as *Paper moon* and *My old flame*. Here, Rollins' style is unformed with technical drawbacks in evidence during every chorus but the potential value of his work is considerable. Miles acts as leader in every sense and hits on a number of worthwhile ideas which he develops to logical conclusions. His three dates for Blue Note, spread over a period of two years, have been issued in their entirety on two LPs (5) and (6); the first session, with Jay Jay Johnson, Jackie McLean and Kenny Clarke, produced a sombre *Dear old Stockholm* (the Swedish folk-song which Stan Getz first adapted as a jazz vehicle), a romping *Donna* (the same tune as *Dig* on (4) incidentally) and two probing trumpet and rhythm tracks *Yesterdays* and *How deep is the ocean*. A year later a more muscular sounding sextet, kicked along by Art Blakey's drumming, produced six memorable tracks, the high spots being the hard-hitting *Kelo* and the adaptation of Bud Powell's piano solo, *Tempus fugit*. The final Blue Note date featured a quartet (Miles, Horace Silver, Percy Heath and Blakey) playing a bright, swinging kind of jazz. Monk's tune *Well you needn't* has some masterly drumming (Blakey has a tendency to impress his personality on a group's style) and a tongue-in-cheek imitation of Thelonious himself. At the other end of the scale Miles' wispy reading of Richard Rogers' *It never entered my mind* is played with muted reserve and a general air of introspection. (7) revolves around the arrangements of Al Cohn (who, together with Zoot Sims, played tenor on the date) and strikes a nice balance between lightly scored ensembles and extended solo passages; John Lewis's piano adds the right kind of foundation to Miles' fragile statements. (8) collates two quartet and one quintet date and includes the prototype versions of Davis' *Tune up* and *Four*. Davey Schildkraut's sharp, Parkerized alto is effective on *I'll remember April*, a track on which Miles plays with great confidence and communicative warmth. The sextet heard on (9) is truly an all-star gathering for it comprises Miles, Lucky Thompson, Jay Jay Johnson, Horace Silver, Percy Heath and Kenny Clarke. The extended versions of *Blue 'n'*

[96]

boogie and *Walkin'* are minor classics for all six men happen to be on form and hit on a productive mood from the first bar. One side of (10) consists of two takes of the ten-minute duration *Bags groove* from the argumentative session held on Christmas Eve, 1954; the first take contains what must be one of Miles' very finest solos on record, a solo which builds steadily to a peak of creativity and tends to overshadow the superlative work of Milt Jackson who comes on after Davis has finished. The reverse side of this LP is made up of a 1954 date with a much-improved Sonny Rollins and that wholly compatible rhythm section, Horace Silver, Percy Heath and Kenny Clarke. With a playing time of forty-seven minutes (10) is a bargain for the genuine collector. In 1955 Davis formed his quintet which remained *in toto* for eighteen months. Partnering Davis in the front line was tenor saxist John Coltrane whose early struggles were rewarded by the ultimate discovery of his own highly individual style. (11), (12), (13) and (14) are by the quintet (Davis, Coltrane, Red Garland, Paul Chambers and Philly Joe Jones) and it is difficult to place them in order of perfection, so high is the general standard. Never before has Davis sounded so confident nor so inspired; clearly the quintet was designed to his own specification with the rhythm section performing in an unorthodox but very effective manner, Garland accents the first and third beats, Chambers plays a kind of running solo and Jones busies himself with all kinds of rhythmic patterns superimposed on the basic metre. (12) has a number of ballads played with warmth and sentiment; Coltrane is particularly impressive on *You're my everything* from this LP. (13) contains a moving *'Round about midnight* and a breathtaking *Ah-leu-cha* during the course of which Jones manages to play the melody on his drums. (15) adds Cannonball Adderley's alto to the quintet but the effect is nullified by the fact that Adderley, who relies almost entirely upon a slippery interpretation of Charlie Parker, is below the artistic level of his fellows. *Straight no chaser* from this LP is the outstanding track; during the course of his solo Garland block-chords the whole of Davis' original solo from *Now's the time*, recorded in 1945 with Bird. (16) is a more adventurous programme which seems to show the effect of Gil Evans on Miles. Scales in place of chord progressions are used as a basis for improvisation while *All blues* uses a 6/8 time signature throughout. Bill Evans plays piano in place of Garland, bringing to the group a poised, calm effect which is complemented by the smooth rhythmic continuity of Jimmy Cobb who drums in place of Philly Joe Jones. The two LPs which Davis made in collaboration with arranger Gil Evans ('Miles ahead' and 'Porgy and Bess') are discussed under the Gil Evans entry.

(1) MILES DAVIS ORCHESTRA – 12 Cap T762. (A) 12 Cap T762. *1949* and *1950*.

(2) MILES DAVIS ORCHESTRA – (A) 12 Pre PRLP7025. Three titles on 10 Esq 20-091. *1951*.

(3) LEE KONITZ SEXTET – 12 Esq 32-052. (A) 12 Pre PRLP7013. *1951*.

(4) MILES DAVIS SEXTET – 12 Esq 32-062. (A) 12 Pre PRLP7012. *1951*.

(5) MILES DAVIS, Vol. 1 – (A) 12 BN BLP1501. *1952* and *1953*.

(6) MILES DAVIS, Vol. 2 – (A) 12 BN BLP1502. *1952*, *1953* and *1954*.
    NOTE: Two of the sessions on (5) and (6) are contained in 10 Vog LDE028 and LDE064

(7) MILES DAVIS ALL STARS – 10 Esq 20-021. (A) 12 Pre PRLP7025 (with additional titles). *1953*.

(8) BLUE HAZE – 12 Esq 32-088. (A) 12 Pre PRLP7054. *1953* and *1954*.

(9) MILES DAVIS ALL STAR SEXTET – 10 Esq 20-062. (A) 12 Pre PRLP7076 (with additional tracks). *1953*.

(10) BAGS GROOVE – 12 Esq 32-090. (A) 12 Pre PRLP7109. *1954*.

(11) MILES DAVIS QUINTET – 12 Esq 32-021. (A) 12 Pre PRLP7014. *1955*.

(12) MILES DAVIS QUINTET – 12 Esq 32-048. (A) 12 Pre PRLP7094. *1956*.

(13) MILES DAVIS QUINTET – 12 Phi BBL7140. (A) 12 Col CL949. *1956*.

(14) MILES DAVIS QUINTET - 12 Esq 32-068. (A) 12 Pre PRLP7129. *1956*.

(15) MILES DAVIS SEXTET – 12 Fon TFL5035. (A) 12 Col CL1193. *1958*.

(16) MILES DAVIS SEXTET – 12 Fon TFL5072. (A) 12 Col CL1355, (S) CS8163. *1959*.

WILD BILL DAVISON (1906) *cornet*

One of the white horn players who started in Chicago in the 1930s and later came under the Condon management. His name is well merited; he plays an often exciting and driving kind of music which invariably, at some point in the proceedings, declines into vulgar noise-making, the natural resort of the non-Negro musician who cannot achieve his excitement through rhythmic subtlety and flow.

(1) MILD AND WILD – (A) 12 Com 30009. *1943.*

(2) ALL STAR STOMPERS – 10 Vog LDE020. *1947.*

(3) SWEET AND HOT – 12 Lon LTZ-U15068 (*d*). (A) 12 Riv 12-211. *1947.*

(4) JAZZ AT STORYVILLE – 10 Lon LZ-C14020. (A) 12 Sav 12035. *1951.*

(5) WILD BILL DAVISON BAND – 10 Mel MLP501. *1952.*

(6) DIXIELAND AT STORYVILLE – 10 Vog LDE134. *1954.*

(7) RINGSIDE AT CONDON'S – (A) 12 Sav 12055. 10 Lon LZ-C14004 and LZ-C14024. *1955.*

(8) WITH STRINGS ATTACHED – 12 Ph BBL7104. (A) 12 Col CL-983. *1956.*

(9) DIXIELAND (with Bill Stafford) – (A) 12 Reg 6026. *1957.*

BUDDY DE FRANCO (1923)   *clarinet*

Immaculate is a word which describes De Franco's work almost to perfection; his severest critics would probably qualify such a description with the adjectives 'cold' and 'empty'. It is certainly true that there is little warmth in Buddy's work, but the same might be said of almost all clarinettists who have chosen to work in the modern idiom. Perhaps the flute is better suited to contemporary jazz. Most of Buddy's records feature him with a small group and in many cases the supporting musicians provide the greatest jazz interest. (1) has some typically clean, smooth clarinet solos played with almost frightening competence, but it is the work of Kenny Drew (piano), Jimmy Raney (guitar) and Art Blakey (drums) which tends to steal the thunder. The same story might be told of dozens of De Franco recordings and it is not proposed to mention any of the other LPs and EPs in similar vein. (2) rings the changes in that a vocal group and conga drummer (Sabu Martinez) are added to the quartet. Martinez and Blakey take over on the lengthly *Star of Africa* to the almost complete exclusion of Buddy, the two drummers turning in the kind of performance they did earlier for Blue Note under the title *A message from Kenya*. (3) is part of a series of 'Tatum-plus' pairings which Norman Granz conceived and although Buddy tends to play a little cautiously in places, there are ample indications that he and Tatum might have made some outstandingly brilliant performances had Art lived longer. De Franco was one of the very, very few soloists whose instrumental command equalled that of the pianist. (4) is entitled 'Buddy De Franco Plays Benny Goodman' and is just that, although Buddy makes no attempt to sound like BG in his solos. This is the best De Franco record to be made available in Britain and features fine solos from all concerned (De Franco, trumpeter Don Fagerquist, the late Carl Perkins on piano, guitarist Barney Kessel, tenor saxist George Auld and vibraphonist Vic Feldman. Leroy Vinnegar, Stan Levey and Bob Neel are also present).

(1) BUDDY DE FRANCO QUARTET – 10 MGM 112. (A) 12 MGM 3396 (with four additional titles). *1952.*

(2) BUDDY DE FRANCO – 10 Vog LDE077. (A) 12 GN GNP103. *1953.*

(3) TATUM – DE FRANCO – 7 Col SEB10101. (A) 12 Ver 8229 (with additional titles). *1956.*

(4) BUDDY DE FRANCO OCTET – 12 HMV CLP1215. (A) 12 Ver 2089. *1957.*

WILBUR DE PARIS (1900) *trombone*

Just as some great contemporary painters, writers and classical musicians work within an old tradition to produce lively art with a contemporary appeal, so do certain jazzmen find that their sympathies lie within the area of New Orleans jazz and make this the basis of their style. Simply to copy and revive New Orleans jazz is nothing more than one of those circus acts we have mentioned elsewhere. But to add personality, form, new compositions, and technical skill to the older forms, keeping them alive and kicking is an acceptable offering. Wilbur de Paris emphasizes his awareness of this task by calling his music *New* New Orleans jazz. He plays, he says, 'exactly as the earlier players would be playing if they were alive today.' This is well born out by the pioneer jazzmen who make up the nucleus of his band on recent recordings. Beside himself, his brother Sidney de Paris and the late Omer Simeon, all of whom played with pioneer jazz groups in the 1920s, he uses some younger musicians

[100

in sympathy with the style but without needing to create artificially the archaic brays and out-of-tuneness of certain revival creeds.

The band has its critics who are horrified at the use of the banjo and later the mouth-organ, but a crisp rhythm is the basis of New Orleans jazz. It emphasizes a crispness of thought that typifies the group. There is a clear organic shape to their performances that is lacking in so much jazz, the kind of clearly anticipated formal movement and completion that one detects in a classical work like the Beethoven violin concerto, not merely a hotchpotch, random movement but a logical development from end to end. This, plus a technical excellence which leads to a clear statement in the playing, seems to be the point where the Wilbur de Paris band achieves more than many other American bands and their British counterparts who so often fail to give a performance any shape. Even the rhythm is used as an integral part of the performance rather than a mere metronomic nuisance in the background, only there to maintain a strict tempo. Their best LP was the second one to appear in this country (2) including three excellent consecutive performances in *Hot lips*, *Yama Yama man* and *Flow gently, sweet Afton* and the well-thought-out *Madagascar* which followed the highly successful *Martinique* (1), the first of a series of jazz experiments with West Indian rhythms – a highly successful series too although they would probably not amuse musical purists. On this first recording (1) there was also a very successful recording of *The pearls* which stood out as a hint of the immaculate stylization to come and makes an interesting comparison with Morton's own recordings of this composition. The third LP (3) was a concert performance and cannot be compared for quality or finish with the others but still achieves a high standard, including another of the M series, *Majorca* and some very pleasing tracks – *Juba dance* featuring Omer Simeon, *Wrought iron rag*, an unusual *Sister Kate* featuring Wilbert Kirk on harmonica, *Banjoker* featuring Lee Blair and a rollicking *Piano blues* for Sonny White. The next LP (4) is the least interesting as far as the band is concerned but is a wonderful record for followers of, Jimmy Witherspoon whom it features. The next LP (5) was a surprise as it featured tunes by Cole Porter. It is not entirely successful but has its moments as in a delightful *Wunderbar* mainly featuring the harmonica. It did draw some warm praise, however, from a British modern jazzman who hadn't believed up till then that such a group of old-timers could manipulate such harmonies. In a very exciting LP (6) the band returned to some jazz classics and brought them up in a most commendably snappy manner including *Muskrat ramble*, *High society* and *Panama rag*, mixing them happily with some new tunes. (7) follows in the same vein.

(1) NEW ORLEANS JAZZ – 10 Fel EDL87010. (A) 12 Atl 1233. (S) S-1233. (MARCHIN' AND SWINGIN' – 4 tracks added.) *1952.*

(2) NEW NEW ORLEANS JAZZ – 12 Lon. LTZ-K15024. (A) 12 Atl 1219. *1955.*

(3) AT SYMPHONY HALL – 12 Lon LTZ-K15086, (S) SAH-K6016. (A) 12 Atl 1253, (S) S-1253. *1956.*

(4) NEW ORLEANS BLUES (with Jimmy Witherspoon) – 12 Lon LTZ-K15150. (A) 12 Atl 1266. *1957.*

(5) PLAYS COLE PORTER – 12 Lon LTZ-K15156. (A) 12 Atl 1288. *1958.*

(6) SOMETHING OLD, NEW, GAY, BLUE – 12 Lon LTZ-K15175, (S) SAH-K6060. (A) 12 Atl 1300, (S) S-1300 *1959.*

(7) THAT'S A-PLENTY – 12 Lon LTZ-K15192, (S) SAH-K6079. (A) 12 Atl 1318, (S) S-1318. *1959.*

JIMMY DEUCHAR (1931)   *trumpet*

The late Fats Navarro has been the biggest influence on the style of trumpeter Jimmy Deuchar whose precise articulation and controlled playing was a feature of the original Johnny Dankworth Seven. His broad tone and tasteful lyricism is well suited to the ballads on (1) of which *The folks who live on the hill* is particularly memorable. Although most of his records have been with small groups of his own choosing, the rare instances of Deuchar soloing with a big band point to his all-round experience, as witness *Summertime* with Jack Parnell's Orchestra (Par PMD1053). (2) features him in the triple role of soloist-arranger-composer, playing in the company of such preferred associates as Tubby Hayes, Derek Humble, Ken Wray and Vic Feldman but it is (3) which shows Jimmy at his best. One side is devoted to four tunes from *Pal Joey* played by a quintet containing Tubby Hayes on baritone; the reverse comprises Deuchar originals, including the noteworthy *Heather mist* on which Derek Humble, Ken Wray, Harry South and the leader are inspired to produce their best solos of the day.

[102]

(1) JIMMY DEUCHAR QUARTET – 7 Esq EP53. *1954.*
(3) JIMMY DEUCHAR ENSEMBLE – (A) 12 Con C3529. (Four titles on
Tem LAP2, remainder on Tem TAP4.) *1955* and *1956.*
(3) PAL JIMMY – 12 Tem TAP20. *1958.*

VIC DICKENSON (1906) *trombone*
A great and versatile musician with a pungent wit that makes him
the Fats Waller of the trombone. He follows the imaginative path
of players like Dicky Wells and Benny Morton and is equally at
home in traditional or mainstream groups. Buried for years in the
big orchestras of Calloway, Hopkins, Basie, Carter and others, he
came to light in 1954 with a fine series of recordings for Vanguard
under his own name and since then has become very rightly popular
and has been heard to good advantage in many small-group recordings, notably the Felsted recordings under Dicky Wells' name.
It can safely be said that all his records are worth having for all
maintain a high standard of musicianship and intelligence.
(1) VIC DICKENSON SEPTET, Vol. 1 – 10 Van PPT1200. (A) 10 Van (d)
VRS8001. *1954.*
(2) VIC DICKENSON SEPTET, Vol. 2 – 10 Van PPT12005. (A) 10 Van
(d) VRS8002. *1954.*
(3) VIC DICKENSON SEPTET, Vol. 3 – 10 Van PPT12015. (A) 10 Van
(d) VRS8012. *1954.*
(4) VIC DICKENSON SEPTET, Vol. 4 – 10 Van PPT12019. (A) 10 Van
(d) VRS8013. *1954.*
*The 4-10 (A) Vanguards (d) have been replaced by 2-12 records
Van 8520 and 8521. 1954.* (SHOWCASE).
(5) VIC'S BOSTON STORY – (A) 12 Sto 920. *1957.*
(6) MAINSTREAM – 12 Lon LTZ-K15182, (S) SAH-K6066. (A) 12
Atl 1303, (S) S-1303. *1958.*

BABY DODDS (1894-1958) *drums, washboard*
Probably the best and most imaginative of the New Orleans
drummers with the possible exception of Zutty Singleton. Gave
great drive to any group he played with and drummed with a
constantly varied approach. Recorded with Johnny Dodds, King
Oliver, Sidney Bechet and on many classic jazz sessions.
(1) TALKING AND DRUM SOLOS – (A) 10 Fol FJ-2290.

(2) BAND AND DRUM SOLOS – (A) 10 Am D-2.

(3) BRASS BAND – (A) 10 Am D-1.

(4) DRUM DEMONSTRATIONS – (A) 10 Am D-3.

JOHNNY DODDS (1892-1940)   *clarinet*

With the exception of Sidney Bechet, no one made the clarinet a more powerful means of jazz expression than Johnny Dodds. When it is considered that he played and held his own in small jazz groups with trumpeters like Louis Armstrong, George Mitchell and Natty Dominique and trombonists like Kid Ory, we can understand the necessity for and the cause of this powerful approach. When a clarinet is played hard it takes on a strong vibrato, complains now and then in squeaks and honks and an occasional overtone, producing piercing and angular top-register playing and rich and plummy low-register playing. These are the main characteristics of Dodds' clarinet music. He has the direct approach of Armstrong to jazz in that his approach is straightforward and often sticks close to the melody while he has the technique and imagination to produce some often surprising and ambitious variations. The one thing that neither lack is consistent drive, power and imagination coupled with an ebullient and good-humoured approach to the music. A classical musician would have to get used to Dodds' 'ugly' tone (comparing it with the purer tone of Noone for example), but to the jazz-trained ear it seems a natural sound because it was so much a part of the jazz we were brought up on and has become the model for 75 per cent of the would-be revivalists.

Once more, we have to comment, at this stage that much of the better Dodds has disappeared with the change-over of the Victor label from EMI to Decca, where a disregard of jazz practically amounting to an anti-jazz bias now almost completely blocks any sensible or responsible policy of jazz reissues. You will have to search the second-hand shops for a magnificent LP containing the July 1928 sides (HMV DLP1073). Much of the earlier Dodds has disappeared with London LPs AL3505, 3513, 3555 and 3560 (1) and many fine 78s have disappeared with the Vocalion series (V1008, V1025, V1032, etc.). But there is still much of value remaining: the great New Orleans Wanderers and New Orleans Bootblacks sides of July 1926 – *Perdido Street blues, Gatemouth, Too tight,* and *Papa dip*

[104]

included (2), and many of the recordings listed under Louis Armstrong will be found to be equally useful as examples of Dodds at his greatest. The sides with his Black Bottom Stompers although a hard and unsympathetically recorded series are full of powerful jazz and are included on (3) with two delightful quartet sides, *Forty and tight* and *Piggly wiggly* featuring Herb Morand on trumpet.

After many years of silence Dodds recorded again in 1938, producing a magnificent set of recordings on which Charlie Shavers played some unexpectedly tasteful and subdued trumpet: *Wild man blues, 29th and Dearborn, Melancholy* and *Blues galore* (4). Two final sides made in 1940 and in the New Orleans album (LAT8146), which most collectors will want anyway for Armstrong reasons, were comparative failures.

(1) New Orleans Clarinet – (A) 12 Riv 12-104. (Material included on deleted AL3505, etc.) *1926–8.*

(2) Johnny Dodds with Kid Ory – 12 Ph BBL7136. (A) 12 Ep LN-3207. *1926–8.*

(3) Johnny Dodds, Vol. 1 – 10 Cor LRA10025. *1927–9.*

(4) Jimmie Noone and Johnny Dodds – 10 Cor LRA10018. *1938.*

ARNE DOMNERUS (1924)   *clarinet, alto saxophone*

Stalwart of many jazz sessions held in Stockholm, Arne Domnerus has altered his manner of playing, chameleon-like, to keep pace with his changing hero-worship. Commencing along well-established Benny Carter lines he made an abrupt swerve in the direction of Charlie Parker in 1949 (he played with Parker at the first Paris Jazz Fair). Next on the list was Lee Konitz, who visited Sweden in 1951. Lee's visit resulted in Arne's switch to the angular approach and cold, clarinet-like tone of the Tristano-school saxophonists. This was followed by a process of settling down and the final emergence of the natural Domnerus style, a pleasing, big-toned alto sound containing elements of the three previous periods. Arne has been heard on many post-war Swedish jazz records both as leader and as sideman with such men as Quincy Jones, James Moody, Lars Gullin, Bengt Hallberg, etc.; a fine pair of titles dating from 1951 was released in Britain on Overseas HMV and in America on Victor LP (both now deleted) and it is worth trying to get hold of a second-hand copy of *Party for Pres/Old black magic* on which the Domnerus alto is backed by a rhythm section. (1) contains four titles with Arne plus the Bengt Hallberg Trio (the reverse of the LP is by the trio minus Domnerus), a quartet of pleasing Hallberg originals all of which have excellent contributions from the alto saxist.

(1) BENGT HALLBERG QUARTET – 10 Esq 20-014. (A) 10 Pre PRLP145. *1952.*

TOMMY DORSEY (1905–56)   *trombone*

It is unfortunate that Tommy Dorsey's latter-day fame as the leader of a very commercial band should have obscured his early reputation as a jazz musician. He was, after all, in his best work, one of the handful of white musicians whose playing caught the relaxation of the better Negro performers. He started out by copying Miff Mole; then, like Jack Teagarden, he took Jimmy Harrison for his model. In 1934 Tommy and his brother Jimmy formed the Dorsey Brothers orchestra. 'Dixieland Jazz 1934–5' (12 Br LAT8256, (A) 12 Dec 8631) contains eleven tracks by this group, the music rather stilted apart from Dorsey's trombone solos. In 1935 Tommy organized his own group. He took as his signature tune a pop-song of the day, *I'm getting sentimental over you* (1) and (2), and began, more and more, to feature himself in solos that exploited his sweet tone and smooth technique. During the late 1930s and early 1940s his band included such fine musicians as Bunny Berigan, Bud Freeman and Dave Tough, the greatest of the white drummers, while Dorsey himself could still play good jazz when he wanted to. (1) and (4) both contain *Song of India* and *Marie*, with fine Berigan solos, also Sy Oliver's 1944 arrangement of *Opus No. 1*. Of the many (A) RCA LPs by this Dorsey band, one of the best is (3), which includes four tracks by the Clambake Seven, a Dixieland unit drawn from the orchestra.

(1) YES INDEED – (A) 12 RCA LPM1229. *1935–44.*
(2) TOMMY DORSEY – 7 RCA RCX1023. *1935–49.*
(3) TRIBUTE TO TOMMY DORSEY, Vol. 1 – (A) 12 RCA LPM1432. *1936–41.*
(4) TOMMY DORSEY – 7 RCA RCX1002. *1937–44.*

CHAMPION JACK DUPREE (1910)   *vocal, piano*

An earthy singer and violent pianist, Jack Dupree was once a professional boxer. He decided to become a full-time blues artist in the early '40s and his series of recordings for OKeh were proof of his quality. The sessions made for Joe Davis, in 1946, were less satisfactory, musically, but they produced one of Dupree's hit numbers, *Fisherman's blues* (1). He went on recording sporadically, from then on, but not much was heard of him until his latest LP, 'Blues From the Gutter', which cannot be considered really satisfactory. In fact, shortly before the LP was made, he did have some success with a single called *Strollin'*, a version of which is incorporated in the LP. The accompaniment, here, is thunderously heavy and it is astounding that Dupree's singing comes through so clearly. The best track is *Going down slow* (2).

(1) *Fisherman's blues/County jail special* – 10 78 Vog B16. (A) 10 78 JDvs5103 (d). *1946*.

(2) Blues From The Gutter – 12 Lon LTZ-K15171. (A) 12 Atl 8019. *1959*.

E

ALLEN EAGER (1927)   *alto, tenor saxophones*
    Allen Eager is usually bracketed with Stan Getz, Zoot Sims, Al Cohn and the other 'Brothers' but unlike his fellows, he has never played with Woody Herman. His appearances on record have been comparatively few although he is greatly admired by all post-Lester Young saxophonists. (1) finds him in the company of Getz, Cohn, Sims, Brew Moore and a rhythm section where the stylistic similarity of the five front-liners is quite remarkable. Eager shares the lengthy *Mulligan's too* with baritone saxist Gerry Mulligan and emerges as the best soloist on the date. He again steals the scene on (3) where his lucid contributions stand out in the lack-lustre settings designed around the faltering trumpet of Tony Fruscella. During a stay in Paris Allen played on a date featuring American, French and British jazzmen (4) and is heard to best advantage on the moody *Illusion*. Back in America the following year he worked around New York for a time and appeared on record with a stellar and wholly compatible saxophone section (5). Teamed with Lee Konitz, Zoot Sims, Al Cohn and Gerry Mulligan, Eager makes noteworthy

contributions on both alto and tenor on a record which is spoiled only by the out-of-context guitar of Freddie Greene.

(1) THE BROTHERS – 7 Esq EP134. (A) 12 Pre PRLP7022. *1949.*

(2) GERRY MULLIGAN ALL STARS – 12 Esq 32-014. (A) 12 Pre PRLP 7006. *1951.*

(3) TONY FRUSCELLA – 12 Lon LTZ-K15044. (A) 12 Atl 1220. *1955.*

(4) JAZZ INTERNATIONAL – 12 Vog LAE12029. *1956.*

(5) GERRY MULLIGAN SONG BOOK – 12 Vog LAE12128. (A) 12 WP 1237. *1957.*

JON EARDLEY (1928)   *trumpet*

Although inactive, musically, since 1957 Jon Eardley is remembered for the eighteen months he spent with Gerry Mulligan's quartet and sextet. During this period he appeared on three of Gerry's LPs and on each showed himself to be a warm-blooded soloist with considerable potential. He partners Mulligan ideally on the completely spontaneous *Blues going up* (Vog LAE12006, (A) 12 WP 1201), hitting a peak of telepathic anticipation towards the end. On the same record he plays a sober, rather moving part on *Little girl blue*. On his first album to be released in Britain (1) he is hampered by some ineffectual tenor work from his front-line partner, J. R. Monterose, but overcomes the shortcomings long enough to play a noteworthy solo on *Hey there*. An additional point of interest is the inclusion of two Tadd Dameron themes, *Sid's delight* and *If you could see me now*; the former indicates an unabashed admiration for the late Fats Navarro. The Septet LP (2) finds him in the distinguished company of Zoot Sims and Phil Woods; there is a Mulliganesque flavour to the arrangements and a general improvement in Eardley's instrumental control. Both records are recommended particularly in view of the fact that Eardley seems to have given up music, at least temporarily.

(1) JOHN EARDLEY QUINETT – Esq 10 20-074. (A) 10 Pre PRLP207. *1955.*

(2) JON EARDLEY SEPTET – Esq 12 32-040. (A) 12 Pre PRLP7033. *1956.*

HARRY EDISON (1915)   *trumpet*

The trouble with Harry Edison is that one hears too much of him. Because of his technical brilliance, he is constantly in demand at recording studios, with the result that his tight, muted tone, his favourite clichés, his habit of starting a solo with a single, repeated note, all these become much too familiar. None of this would matter if Edison had a resourceful imagination, but his kind of trumpet-playing – a kind very successful in the right context, as it was in the Count Basie band – is exuberant rather than imaginative, buoyant instead of lyrical. Edison's virtues, in fact, are those of a sturdy rather than an adventurous soloist. As far as style goes, he stands – like Roy Eldridge – between the swing men and the modernists, but his playing is less fantastic, more down-to-earth, than Eldridge's. He can be fierce, he can be delicate (after all, his nickname is 'Sweets'); most of all, though, he can swing – in a very direct, impassioned way.

Edison spent twelve years with Count Basie and he can be heard on many of the band's recordings. Among his best solos are those in *Panassié stomp*, *Swingin' the blues* and *Texas shuffle*, all available on 12 Br LAT8028, (A) 12 Dec 8049. His finest playing on record, though, must be the eight choruses in *Pennies from heaven* (1), a beautifully integrated solo building up to a natural climax. Almost as good is the solo in *September in the rain*, on the same LP. Otherwise Edison's recordings maintain a scrupulous level of competence, enhanced or marred by the quality of his companions. Buddy Rich's drumming, for instance, takes up too much space on (2). (3) is helped by the solos, both luscious and blustering, of Ben Webster. (4), (5), (6) and (7) contain more good tenor-playing, this time by Jimmy Forrest, a robust yet tasteful soloist. (The tune labelled *Pussy willow* on (4), incidentally, has quite a different melody from that bearing the same title on (5). It comes off a completely separate session, anyway.) On (8) Edison leads the same group as on (4), with Buck Clayton added, and it is Clayton and Jimmy Forrest who make the running.

(1) SWEETS AT THE HAIG – 10 Vog LDE118. (A) 10 WP 4 (d). *1953.*
(2) BUDDY AND SWEETS – 12 Col 33CX10080. *1955.*
(3) SWEETS – 12 Col 33CX10087. (A) 12 Ver 8097. *1956.*
(4) THE SWINGER – 12 HMV CLP1277. (A) 12 Ver 8295. *1958.*
(5) THE ORIGINAL HARRY EDISON – 7 Col SEG7914. (A) 12 Rou 52023. *1958.*
(6) FOUR SWEETS – 7 Col SEG7934. (A) 12 Rou 52023 *1958.*
(7) SWEETENINGS – 7 Col SEG7947. (A) 12 Rou 52023. *1958.*
(8) HARRY EDISON SWINGS BUCK CLAYTON – 12 HMV CLP1321. (A) 12 Ver 8293, (S) 6016. *1959.*

ROY ELDRIDGE (1911)   *trumpet*

Roy Eldridge forms one of the links (another, and earlier, link is
Henry Allen) that join the older generation of trumpet-players with
the modernists. The structure of Eldridge's playing reflects the
influence of Louis Armstrong (just listen to (8) or to the duets with
Claude Bolling (4)) while his loose, multi-noted melodic lines point
the way to Dizzy Gillespie. A virtuoso performer, Eldridge at his
best is capable of creating marvellously light and lyrical solos. At his
worst, however – and he must be the most uneven of all important
jazz soloists – he will slip into tasteless displays of technique. A few
of these even mar some of the records listed below.

Swingin' on that Famous Door, made in the 1930s by the Delta Four,
features lithe, exciting playing, available on (A) Coral's THE STORY
OF JAZZ, CJE100. (1) contains a couple of splendid solos in *Wabash
blues* and the slow, Armstrong-like *Rockin' chair* (this track is actually
by Eldridge with the Gene Krupa orchestra), but *After you've gone*
is a noisy tear-up. *The Gasser*, in ENCYCLOPAEDIA OF JAZZ, Vol. 3,
is a not particularly distinguished recording from the early 1940s.
(2), (3), (4) and (5) were all made when Eldridge was in Europe.
(2) includes *I remember Harlem*, which has some of his finest blues
playing; (3) is excellent, except for one track (*Oh shut up*); while (4)
presents Eldridge and the French pianist, Claude Bolling, in trumpet
and piano duets that carry echoes of Louis Armstrong and Earl Hines.
The highspot of (5) is Eldridge's version of *Echoes of Harlem* (originally
devised by Duke Ellington for Cootie Williams); otherwise this EP
is devoted to Eldridge's singing and trumpet acrobatics.

Dale's wail, a beautifully coherent performance, is contained in
(6), the trumpeter being accompanied on this LP by an Oscar Peterson
group. More duets – this time by the unusual combination of trumpet
and drums (played by Alvin Stoller) – turn up on (7); half the tracks
are good, half bad. (8), however, is one of Eldridge's most satisfying
latter-day records. It presents him leading Eddie Barefield, Benny
Morton, Dick Wellstood, Walter Page and Jo Jones through a set
of rather hackneyed Dixieland tunes. The ensemble playing is a
trifle stodgy but the solos bite home. *Trumpet blues*, a fast blues with
adroit playing by Eldridge on THE ANATOMY OF IMPROVISATION
(12 Col 33CX10141, (A) 12 Ver 8230), has been extracted from an
otherwise disappointing LP – ROY AND DIZ (12 Col 33CX10025 (*d*)).

More good solos by Eldridge can be heard in JAZZ GIANTS '56 (12 Col 33CX10054 (*d*), (A) 12 Ver 8146), KRUPA AND RICH (12 Col 33CX10040, (A) 12 Ver 8069), DRUMMER MAN by Gene Krupa's orchestra (12 HMV CLP1087 (A) 12 Ver 2008) and JAM SESSION NO. 5 (12 Col 33CX10067).

(1) ROY ELDRIDGE – 7 Ph BBE12102 (*d*). *1937–41.*
(2) ROY ELDRIDGE AND HIS LITTLE JAZZ – 7 Vog EPV1019. *1950.*
(3) ROY ELDRIDGE AND HIS LITTLE JAZZ – 7 Vog EPV1073. *1950.*
(4) ROY ELDRIDGE-CLAUDE BOLLING – *Fireworks/Wild man blues* – 78 Vog V2373. *1950.*
    A selection of these tracks (2), (3) and (4) is on (A) Dial 304 (*d*).
(5) THE HEAT'S ON – 7 Esq EP195. (A) (plus other titles) 12 Pre 114 (*d*). *1951.*
(6) ROY ELDRIDGE QUINTET – 10 Col 33C9005 (*d*). (A) (plus other titles) 12 Ver 8089. *1953.*
(7) THE EXCITING ROY ELDRIDGE – 7 Col SEB10100. *1955.*
(8) ROY ELDRIDGE AND THE CENTRAL PLAZA DIXIELANDERS – 7 Col SEB10085. (A) (plus other titles) 12 Ver 1010. *1956.*

DUKE ELLINGTON (1899)   *composer, pianist, bandleader*
Jazz history rarely splits up quite so neatly as critics would like it to do. In the case of Duke Ellington, however, the foremost composer of jazz and the leader of its greatest orchestra, a separate phase of his career seems to have coincided with each of the last four decades. The 1920s saw Ellington leading a band of brilliant individual musicians, their solos given unity by his arrangements, arrangements comparable in their function to those which Jelly Roll Morton wrote for his Red Hot Peppers. In the 1930s Ellington took on status as a composer, becoming more and more concerned with problems of form and harmony, developing sophisticated textures. The 1940s saw an increase in the rhythmic power of his music, a simplification of some elements, the complication of others, and the creation of more extended works. The 1950s have been less adventurous, Ellington's music rather jogging along within patterns he has already defined, often relying more upon the virtuosity of individual soloists than upon the orchestral strength of the band. But throughout each of these periods Ellington's orchestra and music have preserved a strong central identity. The musicians may have changed (except for the

[111]

indestructible Harry Carney, the monolithic Johnny Hodges), but the sound of the ensemble, the conventions of the solos (the use of wa-wa mutes, for instance), these have persisted. Duke Ellington has always been a very practical musician, aware of the concessions that must be made to keep a band like his solvent and successful, perhaps even using these restrictions as a framework for his imagination, and he once summed up the nature of his achievement in a single sentence. Somebody asked him how he would define a successful performance, to which Ellington replied: 'Being at the right place, doing the right thing, before the right people, at the right time.'

The first record listed below (1) is of very little musical interest. The scoring is primitive, the majority of the solos – apart from the trumpet and trombone work of Bubber Miley and Charlie Irvis – merely crude. Miley, of course, is a key-figure in Ellington's early music, the greatest of the 'growl' trumpet-players, a superb performer of blues. Miley's use of mutes produced the bizarre tones, the savage eruptions, which are so much a feature of his style, grotesqueries which fit completely into his solo conceptions, to some extent shaping and guiding their melodic lines. Another Ellington performer whose playing, like Miley's, could be called dramatic rather than lyrical, was the trombonist Tricky Sam Nanton, a musician equally expert at handling mutes to obtain subtle shades of meaning. It was the violent repertoire of Miley and Nanton which caused night-club audiences in the 1920s to imagine they were listening to 'jungle' music. In fact, Ellington's compositions have always been indisputably European in harmony and form, closer to the Methodist hymnal than to African music. (*Black and tan fantasy*, as a matter of fact, one of the classics of the 'jungle' period, is really a variant upon the popular religious ballad, *The holy city*.) Arthur Whetsel was the other trumpet-player, never exactly a jazz soloist but a musician whose pale, wistful tone was the perfect vehicle for stating many of Ellington's slow themes. The clarinettist was first of all Rudy Jackson, then another New Orleans musician, Barney Bigard, whose fluent, rococo style proved ideal when deployed against the heavy textures which Ellington started using in the 1930s. Otto Hardwicke, using rather an oily tone, was the alto soloist until Johnny Hodges joined the orchestra in 1928. Hodges, of course, in one of the three great alto-players (the other two are Charlie Parker and Benny Carter) and his work is discussed in greater detail in another part of this book. Finally there was Harry Carney, adding the deep voice of his baritone saxophone to the ensemble and also performing curiously agile solos. These men, together with Ellington himself, were the soloists during the first stage of the band's career. They are the musicians heard in (4) and on most tracks of (2), (3) and (5). There are classic performances to be found on these recordings, including the original versions of *East St. Louis Toodle-Oo* and *Mood indigo* (2), *Rockin' in rhythm* and *Black and tan fantasy* (3), *Hot and bothered* and *The Mooche* (5). Another track from this period, one that features superb trumpet playing by Bubber Miley, is *Creole love call*, included, quite inexplicably, on (16), an LP otherwise devoted to recordings made in the 1940s. (8), incidentally, contains another version of *Mood indigo*.

When Bubber Miley left, his place was taken by Cootie Williams (q.v.). Cootie was not a 'growl' trumpet-player when he joined Ellington, but he soon became a specialist in this genre, although performing in a lighter, less intense style than Miley's. This was the band which played on the other tracks of (2), (3) and (7), this was the band which Duke Ellington led at the Cotton Club, the Harlem night-club (although for 'whites only') where he made his reputation as a bandleader. (7) is a particularly valuable LP, containing such outstanding recordings as *Saratoga swing*, *Stevedore stomp* and *Jungle nights in Harlem*. Also on this LP is the longer of the two versions of *Creole rhapsody* which Ellington recorded in 1931. *Creole rhapsody* was an important work in Ellington's development as a composer, his first stretch outside the three-minute form which had previously restricted his writing. The version on (7), however, is inferior to that on (3), being padded out with irrelevant out-of-tempo passages and lacking the conciseness and tension of the earlier, and shorter, recording. As performed on (3), *Creole rhapsody* ranks among Ellington's masterpieces, taut and beautifully self-contained, and it symbolizes his new status. Here, almost for the first time in jazz, the soloists were subservient to the imagination of a composer. It was the climax of a trend in Ellington's music which had steadily been growing stronger throughout the preceding four or five years.

By 1931 the Ellington orchestra was a subtle instrument, with

Ellington able to conceive a score, knowing exactly how each soloist would approach it. 'Duke sure loves his brass,' said Fred Guy once. Certainly the brass section dominated Ellington's composition during the early 1930s, yet already he was blending instruments together – scoring for combinations of brass and woodwinds, rather than writing for separate sections all the time, the common practice of most arrangers during that period. (9), (10) and (11) present good examples of the band at this time, while the 1934 recording of *Solitude* – Ellington's first hit-song – is contained in (8). New solo voices were joining the band, in the persons of Lawrence Brown, a trombonist with a smooth, very sensual tone, and Ivie Anderson, easily the finest singer that Ellington ever used, a singer with a cool, curiously restrained style that now sounds unusually modern. Rex Stewart, a master of tricky, half-valve playing but also a trumpet-player with a wide variety of styles, joined a little later, in 1935. (9) contains such beautiful performances as *Blue tune* (splendidly voiced for the brass), *Bundle of blues*, *Drop me off at Harlem* (one of Ellington's most delightful themes) and *Slippery horn* (featuring the trombone section). (10) was recorded at the Chenil Galleries in Chelsea, during the Ellington band's tour of Britain in 1933; it includes fine performances of *Harlem speaks* and *Hyde Park*. It is worth pointing out here, incidentally, that many fine recordings made by Ellington for the American Victor company (available nowadays to RCA in Britain, but at that time released on HMV 78s) have never been reissued. These include *Echoes of the jungle*, *It's a glory*, *Bugle call rag* (a very personal interpretation), *Daybreak express*, *Dear old Southland* (with a fine Hodges solo), *Stompy Jones*, *Blue feeling*, *Rude interlude* (an outstanding example of Ellington's use of texture) and *Dallas doings*, all recorded between 1931 and 1934. Until Victor and RCA get around to reissuing these performances, it is worth searching for copies of the old 78s.

The recordings on (11) belong to the second half of the 1930s and include *Reminiscing in tempo*, Ellington's most extended work up to that time, originally spread over two 10-in. 78s. (It is important to note, by the way, that while this work is complete on the U.S. release, only half of it – the first two sections – were included on Phi BBR8086. British collectors, therefore, should either get the American LP or look for the old Br 78s.) In many ways *Reminiscing in tempo* was by no means as revolutionary as *Creole rhapsody* had been (it is little more than a passive, fairly melancholy tone-poem, a charming but fragile work), and it is hard to understand why it provoked such an uproar at the time, Ellington then being accused of 'going high-brow' and 'deserting jazz'. On the whole, though, 1935 and 1936 were not vintage years for Ellington's music, although he did record a few outstanding performances. One was *Showboat shuffle*, a musical picture of a Mississippi stern-wheeler; it is worth searching for the Br and Voc 78s. At this time, too, Ellington began writing short 'concertos' for various soloists in his band, the two most successful being *Clarinet lament (Barney's concerto)* and *Echoes of Harlem (Cootie's concerto)* (Br and Voc 78s (*d*)). At the same time, as if responding to the fact that jazz was turning into 'swing', the Ellington orchestra began to achieve remarkable rhythmic integration, swinging as a whole band rather than as brass and reeds above a rhythm section. One of the most uninhibited of Ellington's recordings, *In a jam* (also known as *Dinah's in a jam*), belongs to this period, containing a superb chase-chorus between Johnny Hodges and Cootie Williams, their solos contrasted yet interlocking. It was released originally on a Voc 78 and has not been reissued. (13) contains performances made during a period of transition, a period when Ellington was moving away from the heavy, often static scoring of the early 1930s towards the more dynamic, swinging patterns of his 1940 band. He was also beginning to re-record some of his older compositions, and this LP includes new versions of *East St. Louis Toodle-Oo*, and *Prologue to the black and tan fantasy* (the other half, the *Fantasy* itself, has been omitted), as well as such gay tracks as *The gal from Joe's, Braggin' in brass* and *Portrait of a lion*. Also worth mentioning at this point is (6), an unusually good anthology of Ellington recordings, including both the *New East St. Louis Toodle-Oo* and the *New black and tan fantasy*, and ranging from the 1928 version of *The Mooche* up to Ellington's 1947 recording of *Don't get around much any more*.

With (14), (15) and (16) we arrive at what was certainly Ellington's greatest orchestra, a band which included such veterans as Cootie Williams, Rex Stewart, Tricky Sam Nanton, Lawrence Brown, Barney Bigard, Johnny Hodges and Harry Carney, but was now augmented by the tenor saxist, Ben Webster (q.v.), the trumpet-

[115]

player, Ray Nance (who replaced Cootie Williams in 1940) and that wonderful bassist, Jimmy Blanton. The inclusion of Blanton in the rhythm section really changed its whole character, for he produced a lighter, much less rigid swing than any of his predecessors. Blanton was a great virtuoso, and although he enjoyed only a very short career (he died in 1942, aged only 21), he transformed the whole technique of bass playing in jazz. Ben Webster brought to the Ellington band a talent that could be alternately rugged or tender, and his presence among the reeds gave that section a strength which encouraged Ellington to write for it more frequently. Ray Nance, more or less unknown when he joined Ellington, soon developed into one of the band's finest soloists – indeed, he still is. He possesses a broad, shining tone and an easy, legato style of playing; whenever it is needed, too, he can perform 'growl' solos in a style that is more ferocious than Cootie's. His violin-playing, however, has very little to do with jazz. Another addition to the Ellington orchestra was Billy Strayhorn, who began collaborating with Ellington in 1939, writing many arrangements for the band and also playing the piano occasionally on records and at concerts. Strayhorn's influence upon Ellington's music has probably been mixed, for while he can concoct such delightful scores as *Take the 'A' train* and *Clementine*, he is also capable of writing rather pretentious near-pastiches of European impressionist music. There is little to choose between (14) and (16). The former includes (in addition to the 1927 *Creole love call*) such items as *Jack the bear*, *Ko-Ko*, *Concerto for Cootie*, *Harlem air shaft* and *Across the track blues* – all among Ellington's finest performances, as well as the 1944 recording of *Black, brown and beige*, a shortened version of an extended work. This version, however, includes the gay *West Indian dance* and *Emancipation day* in addition to *Work song*, *Come Sunday* and *The blues*. (16) contains *Cotton tail* (with aggressive playing by Ben Webster), *Portrait of Bert Williams*, *All too soon*, *Sepia panorama*, *In a mellotone*, *Take the 'A' train*, *Just a-sittin' and a-rockin'*, *Perdido* and nine other equally good tracks. *Take the 'A' train* is also included on (12), an EP that contains *Sidewalks of New York*, featuring some of Nanton's best trombone playing.

By the time (17) was recorded, the Ellington orchestra had seen the departure of Rex Stewart, Barney Bigard, Tricky Sam Nanton (he died in 1946) and Ben Webster, and the arrival of Harold Baker,

Jimmy Hamilton, Tyree Glenn and Al Sears. This is a pleasant set of performances, stressing the soloists rather than the orchestra, but only *H'ya Sue*, with fine playing by Hodges and Tyree Glenn (who took over Nanton's range of solos), can be classed among Ellington's better work. The *Liberian Suite* (18), consisting of five dances prefaced by *I like the sunrise*, its maudlin lyric sung in a sentimental fashion by Al Hibbler, was also recorded at this time. For the most part, the work is only as good as the soloists. Much more adventurous scoring can be found in *Tone parallel to Harlem*, made four years later but also included in (A) (18). (It was, incidentally, issued as part of 12 Ph BBL7003, an LP since deleted.) (19) is by a small group from the Ellington orchestra, recorded during a period when Willie Smith had taken Johnny Hodges' place in the band, and soon after Cat Anderson, Paul Gonsalves and Louis Bellson had joined it. By a curious paradox, Bellson, a white man, was the finest drummer Ellington has ever had, although his particular virtues emerge more clearly when he is heard with a big band (as on (20)). This LP, however, includes some remarkable 'growl' trumpet work by Cat Anderson in *Cat walk*, a muscular, swinging alto solo on *Caravan* by Willie Smith, and some gusty tenor-playing by Paul Gonsalves, a musician with more harmonic sense than melodic inventiveness. (20) contains Betty Roche's long scat vocal in *Take the 'A' train* (together with hurried tenor-playing by Gonsalves) and, on the back, a new version of *The Mooche*.

(21), an LP of Ellington playing piano solos, backed up by Wendell Marshall and Butch Ballard, together with (22), (23) and (24), inaugurates the Capitol period, a time when the band was presented in rather brassy and flamboyant performances. Typical of this period is the ornate and rowdy scoring of *Things ain't what they used to be* (23). Rather better are *Frivolous Banta* (22), *Kinda Dukish* (24) and *Satin Doll*. But the outstanding performances of the Capitol period occur in (25), an LP containing such items as *One o'clock Jump*, *In the mood*, *Flying home*, *Stomping at the Savoy* and *Honeysuckle rose*, all scored by either Buck Clayton, Dick Vance or Jimmy Hamilton, and Ellington's own *Rockin' in rhythm*, *Happy-go-lucky local*, and *Black and tan fantasy* (a rather theatrical version, with Ray Nance playing the famous solo), all interpreted with great verve and enthusiasm. By this time, of course, Clark Terry had joined the orchestra and Quentin Jackson was playing the 'growl' trombone solos. Terry has been a particularly valuable soloist, his work consistently lyrical and often very witty. By the time Ellington recorded (26) (he had by now moved away from Capitol), Johnny Hodges was back in the reed section and Jimmy Woode and Sam Woodyard were playing bass and drums respectively. The band, in fact, had acquired the appearance it presented when touring Britain in 1958. (26), as it happens, is one of Ellington's most delightful recordings in recent years, a journey through some of his earlier compositions, using the original arrangements of such pieces as *Jack the bear*, *Creole love call*, *Stompy Jones* and *Ko-Ko*, as well as presenting a few new ones, in *Unbooted character*, *Lonesome lullaby* and *Upper Manhattan medical group*.

Paul Gonsalves' marathon tenor solo in *Crescendo and Diminuendo in blue* was, according to most eye-witnesses, the zenith of Duke Ellington's appearance at the 1956 Newport Jazz Festival. But (33), an LP recorded at that event, shows that in fact this was the least rewarding part of Ellington's performance. The finest things to be found here are Hodges' playing in *Jeep's blues* and the middle section (*Blues to be there*) of the *Newport Festival Suite*, otherwise a rather patchy work. It is a great shame, incidentally, that a deformed version of *Crescendo and Diminuendo in blue* should become so popular while the fine 1937 recordings of these two pieces still remain out of the catalogue. 'A Drum is a Woman' (28) was composed by Duke Ellington for a television ballet. The work has its moments of gaiety, particularly in *Hey, Buddy Bolden* and in one or two of the songs, but on the whole it must be classed among Ellington's more ephemeral compositions. Next Duke Ellington and his orchestra accompanied Ella Fitzgerald in half of her performances (one LP in each set) of 'The Duke Ellington Songbook', (29) and (30). On the whole this was an uneasy partnership, neither Ella nor the band sounding at their best. (30) is the better of the two sets, for it includes a short suite, 'A portrait of Ella', and a rocking performance of *E & D blues*, with Johnny Hodges playing a nearly miraculous solo. With 'Such sweet thunder' (31), Ellington produced his finest work of the 1950s, a series of short pieces, each related to a theme or character in one of Shakespeare's plays. *Half the fun*, a sensuous evocation of Cleopatra's barge drifting down the Nile, is the most successful track, but *Up and down* (with picaresque Clark Terry and Nance, for once, playing his violin aptly), *Madness in great ones* (harnessing the dizzy talents of

Cat Anderson), and *Lady Mac* (moving in well-disguised waltz-time) are all outstanding.

(32) presents expanded versions of the *Work song* and *Come Sunday* sections of *Black, brown and beige* (Ellington seems to have dropped the 'Three Dances'); they are expanded, however, only in the sense of becoming longer, for nowhere does Ellington really elaborate or transform the themes. Mahalia Jackson, that magnificent gospel-singer, sings on *Come Sunday*, but there is a distressing lack of conviction about this partnership. Her voice is also wasted in a mediocre setting of the *Twenty-third Psalm*. (33) contains, among other things, a flamboyant version of *El Gato* (featuring Cat Anderson), over-ripe Hodges on *Multicoloured blue*, a witty flügelhorn solo by Clark Terry in *Juniflip*, and a satisfying trumpet-violin duet, *Mr. Gentle and Mr. Cool*, between Harold Baker and Ray Nance. But this LP (another one recorded at the Newport Festival) is a light-weight affair, although it includes an interesting duet between Harry Carney and Gerry Mulligan (*Prima Bara Dubla*). Duke Ellington and his Spacemen – Clark Terry, Jimmy Hamilton (on clarinet), Paul Gonsalves, the three trombonists and the rhythm section – are heard in (34), mainly notable for a lilting performance of *Jones*; apart from Terry's solos, though, this is a disappointing LP. So is (35), a set of deliberately light-hearted but still rather boring performances of tunes like *Who's afraid of the big bad wolf?* and *The donkey serenade*. Ellington's music for 'Anatomy of a Murder' (36) is a very slight group of pieces, most of them animated only by the playing of individual soloists. (37) was obviously recorded with stereo in mind, for it starts off with nine percussionists tapping and hammering away. *Tymperturbably blue*, again with massed percussion, is pleasant, and there is some gritty singing by Jimmy Rushing on another track, but the only real meat in this LP are the first three sections of *Toot suite*.

So far this survey of Ellington's records has rather overlooked the important role which Ellington plays as a pianist, both within the ensemble and in solos. In his way he is as remarkable a band pianist as Count Basie, playing exactly enough (but never too much) behind the soloists, ideal at linking one sequence of a piece with another, able, when he wants to, to amplify the rhythm section. Ellington's solo-playing is represented on very many records by his orchestra; it can also be heard in (20), already mentioned, and in (38), where he and Johnny Hodges perform with a group of non-Ellington musicians. It is only Ellington's rather vinegary solos that really justify the first side of this LP, but in the other half both he and Hodges give a classic performance of *Weary blues*, while *St. Louis blues* is almost as good. Ellington's work here falls somewhere in between that of Willie 'The Lion' Smith and Thelonious Monk, a delectable situation for any pianist to be in.

(1) THE DUKE—1926 – 10 Lon AL3551 (*d*). *1926.*

(2) DUKE ELLINGTON AND HIS FAMOUS ORCHESTRA, Vol. 1 – 10 Vog Cor LRA10027. All except two tracks incl in (A) 12 Br 54007. *1927–31.*

(3) DUKE ELLINGTON AND HIS FAMOUS ORCHESTRA, Vol. 2 – 10 Vog Cor LRA10028. All except two tracks incl in (A) 12 Br 54007. *1927–31.*

(4) DUKE ELLINGTON – 7 Fon TFE17117. *1928.*

(5) SALUTE THE DUKE – 7 Col SEG7575 (*d*). *1928–39.*

(6) THE MUSIC OF DUKE ELLINGTON – (A) 12 Col CL558. *1928–49.*

(7) DUKE ELLINGTON AT THE COTTON CLUB – 12 Cam CDN119. (A) 12 Cam 459. *1929–31.*

(8) CARAVAN – 7 RCA RCX1022. *1930–45.*

(9) JAZZ COCKTAIL – 10 Col 33S1044 (*d*). *1932–6.*

(10) THE DUKE IN LONDON – 7 Dec DFE6376. *1933.*

(11) BLUE LIGHT – 10 Ph BBR8086 (*d*). (A) (plus extra titles) 12 Col CL663. *1934–9.*

(12) DUKE ELLINGTON ORCHESTRA – 7 RCA RCX1006. *1934–45.*

(13) A BLUES SERENADE – 10 HMV DLP1172. *1937–9.*

(14) IN A MELLOTONE – 12 RCA RD27134. (A) 12 Vi LPM1364. *1940–2.*

(15) THE DUKE AND HIS MEN – (A) 12 Vic LPM1092. *1940–2.*

(16) AT HIS VERY BEST – 12 RCA RD27133. (A) 12 Vic LPM1715. *1940–6* and *1927.*

(17) DUKE ELLINGTON ORCHESTRA – 10 Ph BBR8044. *1947.*

(18) LIBERIAN SUITE – 10 Ph BBR8060 (*d*). (A) (plus *Tone parallel to Harlem*) 12 Col CL848. *1947–51.*

(19) DUKE ELLINGTON'S CORONETS – 10 Vog LDE035. *1951.*

(20) DUKE ELLINGTON ORCHESTRA – 7 Ph BBE12002. *1952.*

(21) THE DUKE PLAYS ELLINGTON – 12 Cap LC6670 (*d*). (A) 12 Cap T477. *1953.*

(22) DANCE TO THE DUKE – 7 Cap EAP1004. (A) 12 Cap T637. *1953-4.*
(23) DANCE TO THE DUKE – 7 CapEAP-2-637. (A) 12 Cap T637. *1953-4.*
(24) DANCE TO THE DUKE – 7CapEAP-3-637. (A) 12 CapT637. *1953-4.*
(25) ELLINGTON 55 – 12 Cap LCT6008 (*d*). (A) 12 Cap T521. *1954.*
(26) HISTORICALLY SPEAKING – 12 Par PMC1116. (A) 12Beth 60. *1956.*
(27) ELLINGTON AT NEWPORT – 12 Ph BBL7133. (A) 12 Col CL934. *1956.*
(28) A DRUM IS A WOMAN – 12 Ph BBL7179. (A) 12 Col CL951. *1956.*
(29) ELLA FITZGERALD SINGS THE DUKE ELLINGTON SONGBOOK, No. 1– 12 HMV CLP1213/4. (A) 12 Ver 4008/2. *1956.*
(30) ELLA FITZGERALD SINGS THE DUKE ELLINGTON SONGBOOK, No. 2– 12 HMV CLP1227/8. (A) 12 Ver 4009/2. *1956.*
(31) SUCH SWEET THUNDER – 12 Ph BBL7203. (A) 12 Col CL1033, (S) CS8091. *1956-7.*
(32) BLACK, BROWN AND BEIGE – 12 Ph BBL7251, (S) SBBL506. (A) 12 Col CL1162, (S) CS8015. *1958.*
(33) NEWPORT 1958 – 12 Ph BBL7279, (S) SBBL526. (A) 12 Col CL1245, (S) CS8072. *1958.*
(34) THE COSMIC SCENE – 12 Ph BBL7287. (A) 12 Col CL1198. *1958.*
(35) AT THE BAL MASQUE – 12 Ph BBL7315, (S) SBBL543. (A) 12 Col CL1282, (S) CS8098. *1958.*
(36) ANATOMY OF A MURDER – 12 Ph BBL7338, (S) SBBL514. (A) 12 Col CL1360, (S) CS8166. *1959.*
(37) ELLINGTON JAZZ PARTY – 12 Ph BBL7324, (S) SBBL516. (A) Col CL1323, (S) CS8127. *1959.*
(38) BACK TO BACK – 12 HMV CLP1316. (A) 12 Ver 8317, (S) CS6055. *1959.*
(39) FESTIVAL SESSION – 12 Ph BBL7355, (S) SBBL556. (A) 12 Col CL1400, (S) CS8200. *1959.*

SLEEPY JOHN ESTES (?–1951?)   *vocal, guitar*
    The great blues singers were never limited by regional styles, they enveloped the entire race. And, while eccentricity is not essential to greatness, individual personality is implicit in such achievement. But, of course, there are great eccentrics and, among blues singers, there has been no greater eccentric than Sleepy John Estes. He is reputed to have come, variously, from Georgia, Tennessee, Carolina,

and Texas (Texas, according to Bill Broonzy). His first recording session was in September 1929 and he made 17 sides – 2 were un-issued – by the end of May 1930. His voice was broad and fluent and the records were made more exciting yet by the tense mandolin playing of Yank Rachel. After the last session nothing was heard of him for four years.

In those four years something must have happened. When he recorded again, in 1934, he had completely altered his style; from being very good he had changed to greatness. Now, however, his voice strained and sobbed till the words of his songs were almost unintelligible. He created many of his blues with almost unbearable tension, as though he must break down with the next stanza. The effect was increased by contrast with his solid guitar playing and the impeccable sound of Noah Lewis's harmonica. From 1934 to 1941 – his last session – he retained this eccentricity of delivery, though he proved, as on the 1937 recording of *I ain't gonna be worried no more*, ((A) Dec7414) that he could still sound gay. There are but three sides of his music available in Britain and it would be exceedingly difficult to overestimate their value to the genuine 'amateur' of country blues.

(1) *Drop down Mama/Married woman blues* – 10 78 Bro3562. *1934*.
(2) *Working man blues* – incl on 12 RCA RC24002. *1941*.

PEE WEE ERWIN (1913)   *trumpet*

There is no question of Pee Wee Erwin being a great jazzman. He is a competent run of the mill professional musician who finds it profitable to play Dixieland jazz. Neither has he any obvious design in mind as to the shape and sound of his band. Hence the unconnected and variable performances to be found on the records listed here, which we include in order to give Dixieland its fair coverage in the book. It also points out some interesting morals – notably that even such a low-rating type of jazz as Dixieland can still be played well and badly by fair and good musicians respectively. (1), for instance, is a fine example of pure emptiness, a group of disinterested musicians trying to be jolly about a lot of music that might as well have not been recorded. (2) is a bunch of not very well-known musicians who obviously enjoy the music, and though at times rough, they give a wonderfully big full sound and play an interesting selection of material. Not profound music but happy, melodic and at times good. (3), on the other hand, is a dismal failure by several standards, for although it has a galaxy of names like Dickenson, Bailey, Hopkins, Wettling and Hinton, it ends up by doing nothing. Most of these musicians are better occupied in other fields and they never show any likelihood of knitting together into the compact group that good Dixieland demands. So who does such a record please? – probably not even its sponsors, who won't make a lot of money out of it. We have discussed these three unimportant records because they typify the commercial approach to jazz. The big record companies go on releasing a steady stream of them while they refuse to let any of the gold-mine of proven great jazz, which they keep locked to all eager diggers, be released. The situation seems likely to remain like this until the great bubble of this precarious boom in any sort of record is pricked and burst.

(1) DIXIELAND AT THE GRANDVIEW INN – 12 Lon HA-A2009. (A) 12 Cad 1011. *1957.*

(2) OH PLAY THAT THING – 12 Lon LTZ-T15153, (S) SAH-T6011. (A) 12 UA 4010, (S) UA S-5010. *1958.*

(3) ACCENT ON DIXIELAND – (A) 12 Ur 1202. GOLDEN ERA OF DIXIE-LAND JAZZ – 12 Gal GLP347. *1958.*

(4) MISTER DIXIELAND – (A) 12 AL 1502. *1959.*

GIL EVANS (1912)   *piano, arranger*

Without doubt Gil Evans is the most important jazz arranger to have arrived since the war. He has been touted as Duke Ellington's 'replacement' and while such a claim is fatuous in the extreme it is certainly true to say that the quality of Gil's work ranks second only to that of the Duke. His handling of the Claude Thornhill orchestra, a superior dance band which reached its peak just after the war, gave more than an indication of his potential, as witness such 1946 and 1947 Thornhill recordings as *Anthropology, Robbin's nest* and the beautiful *Sunday kind of love,* all of which were arranged by Evans. The sound of the Thornhill band, with its tuba and french horns, appealed strongly to trumpeter Miles Davis who enlisted the aid of Evans, Gerry Mulligan and John Lewis in the quest for a jazz group style based on Evans' tonal conception. The result is jazz history and the two-week life of the Davis band bore no relation to the lasting influence which it was to have. (1) contains eleven of the twelve

[123]

titles which the group recorded including the outstanding *Boplicity*, a
superlative Evans arrangement of a tune written by Davis. Unac-
countably Capitol omitted the twelfth track, *Darn that dream* with a
vocal by Kenny Hagood, from the LP reissue, a lapse which is all the
more regrettable since Evans was responsible for this arrangement too.
The band's instrumentation (trumpet, trombone, alto, baritone,
french horn, tuba and rhythm) provided a replica of the Thornhill
ensemble on a smaller scale, a wide range of tone colours being
made available to the arranger. Davis's trumpet, Mulligan's baritone,
Jay Jay Johnson or Kai Winding's trombone and the flawless but cold
alto of Lee Konitz were placed in superior yet totally sympathetic
settings. Apart from a memorable *You go to my head*, written for a
Teddy Charles-led band (2), Evans was relatively inactive in jazz
until an inspired decision by Columbia Records resulted in a second
Gil Evans-Miles Davis collaboration (3). This is perhaps the best of
all Evans' work on record; seldom has any arranger, irrespective of
style or period, succeeded in designing his orchestrations to fit the
personality of the featured soloist so well. Davis's trumpet and
flügelhorn playing is heard at its best and in places Evans has transcribed some of Miles' typical phrases for use by the full ensemble.
The result is some of the greatest and most cohesive jazz on record.
A few months later Evans recorded a further album (4), this time with
a smaller band which might be considered the logical successor to the
Miles Davis unit of 1948. Using two trumpets got over the previous
difficulty of the burden which fell on Miles – who had complained
that the task of playing both lead and solo roles was too exacting for
one man – while the inclusion of a bass trombone in place of tuba
gave greater flexibility in the lower register. Evans himself played
piano in a spare but engaging style and the solo star was Steve Lacey,
perhaps the first soprano saxist in jazz who does not sound like Sidney
Bechet. The music is of a very high quality although the concept of
the LP differs from that of (3). (4) is, quite simply, a very superior
small jazz group playing superlative arrangements while (3) is a big
band subservient to the inspired solo work of one man. (5) echoes (3)
in the sense that there is only one soloist of note, Julian Adderley,
and the writing by Evans (which spans the jazz library from *St. Louis
blues* to *Bird feathers*) is designed accordingly. Adderley, a Parker-
derived alto-saxist with little individuality in small bands, answers

[124]

the challenge magnificently and it is due largely to his efforts that the LP ranks second only to (3). (6) again teams Davis and Evans, this time on an LP devoted to the music of Gershwin's *Porgy and Bess*. Although less consistent in quality than (3) there are some moments of even greater brilliance such as Miles' wistful interpretation of *Summertime* against Evans' moody background and the tense, nervous drumming of Philly Joe Jones, beautifully offset by the ensemble in *Gone*.

(1) MILES DAVIS AND HIS ORCHESTRA – 12 Cap T762. (A) 12 Cap T762. *1949*.

(2) TEDDY CHARLES TENTET – 12 Lon LTZ-K15034. (A) 12 Atl 1229. *1956*.

(3) MILES DAVIS ORCHESTRA – 12 Fon TFL5007. (A) 12 Col CL1041. *1957*.

(4) GIL EVANS AND TEN – 12 Esq 32-070. (A) 12 Pre PRLP 7120. *1957*.

(5) GIL EVANS ORCHESTRA – 12 Vog LAE12173. (A) 12 WP 1246. *1958*.

(6) MILES DAVIS ORCHESTRA – 12 Fon TFL5056, (S) STFL507. (A) 12 Col CL1274, (S) SCL1274. *1958*.

DON EWELL (1916)   *piano*
A pianist who harks back to the older models for his inspiration, particularly Jelly Roll Morton and the ragtime pianists with a flavouring of Johnson/Waller technique. His playing is slightly artificial but robust and pleasantly melodic. His best recording is (4).

(1) DON EWELL'S PIANO JAZZ – 7 GTJ EPG1167. *1947*.

(2) EWELL PLAYS KING OLIVER – 12 Tem TAP7. *1952–3*.

(3) WITH MAMA YANCEY – 10 Tem LAP7. *1955*.

(4) MUSIC TO LISTEN TO DON EWELL BY – 12 GTJ LAG12131. (A) 12 GTJ12021. *1956*.

F

AL FAIRWEATHER (1927)   *trumpet*
In 1953 Al Fairweather travelled from Edinburgh to London with the clarinettist Sandy Brown. He has stayed in London ever since, and for a large part of that time has played alongside Sandy. After

starting out in the Louis Armstrong tradition, Fairweather has gradually broadened his style, a touch of Ruby Braff's tone and phrasing creeping in here and there, even – judging by (3) – of Miles Davis. He began by acting as a foil, although a very resourceful and sympathetic one to Sandy Brown's clarinet playing, but his solo work has latterly taken on a much stronger identity. *I'm in the market for you, Chinatown, my Chinatown, Save it pretty mama, Last minute blues,* were all recorded with Sandy Brown in 1956. (Nix 10 NJT503 and 7 NJE1037). (1) is a little self-consciously 'mainstream' perhaps, but with competent solos from Tony Coe (alto), Red Price (tenor) and Fairweather himself. Sandy Brown plays adventurously on (2) and this LP also contains an impressive trumpet solo in *Big Bill.* The mixing of modern and traditional elements reaches a climax, however, in (3), a very ambitious LP, featuring ingenious scoring and brisk solos from George Chisholm, Sandy Brown and three alto-players – Joe Harriott, Tony Coe and Bruce Turner.

(1) FAIRWEATHER FRIENDS – 12 Nix NJT511. *1957.*
(2) AL FAIRWEATHER AND SANDY BROWN ALL STARS – 12 Col 33SX1159. *1959.*
(3) AL'S PALS – 12 Col 33SX 1221. *1959.*

ART FARMER (1928)   *trumpet*

The death of Clifford Brown in 1956 resulted in the title 'Most promising new trumpeter' being passed to Art Farmer. Farmer has lived up to the title and although he has played on many, many records, he has never turned in a bad or even mediocre performance. Tonally he is close to Miles Davis but his harmonic and linear conceptions differ and there should be no danger of the two trumpeters being confused in a blindfold test. Art works within his own capabilities and never attempts to overreach himself during his solos; in short he is one of the most poised musicians jazz has known. He made his first records with the late Wardell Gray (1) out in California at the beginning of 1952; one of the titles from the date, *Farmer's market,* was composed by Art and achieved a certain amount of fame later when Annie Ross added words to the melody. Moving east to New York as a member of Lionel Hampton's thrilling band during the summer of 1953 Farmer made his first records as leader (2) on a session which featured some of his fellow Hampton soloists; the arrangements were by Quincy Jones (who played piano on the session) and Gigi Gryce. All seven musicians were completely in accord and the four titles serve as a superior introduction to the tremendous talents which resided within the Hampton ranks at that time. After a hectic programme of recording in Paris and Stockholm during Lionel's 1953 tour of Europe (see also under Clifford Brown) Farmer left Hampton and worked in New York with assorted small bands. (3) is by a pick-up group (Farmer on trumpet, his twin brother Addison Farmer on bass, pianist Wynton Kelly and drummer Herbie Lovelle) but the cohesion seems to indicate that it was a regular quartet of long-standing. There is ample evidence here of Farmer's growing maturity as a ballad player (*Autumn nocturne, Alone together* and *I walk alone*) and as a confident technician on the up-tempo numbers (*Gone with the wind*, played at hurricane pace, Beaufort Scale 9). His control and accurate pitching is a joy to hear on such a lovely song as *Autumn nocturne* while the very choice of material shows that he has tried to get away from the over-played numbers. The rhythm section is near perfect with Lovelle playing with that combination of drive, low volume and good taste which is so well suited to Farmer's style. A more disciplined atmosphere pervades (4) which is by a quintet which Farmer co-led with Gigi Gryce. Again the material – all originals this time – is fresh and unhackneyed, several of Gryce's tunes getting right away from the established thirty-two bar song form. Farmer's engaging lyricism is matched all the way by the wholly delightful keyboard work of Duke Jordan who wrote *Forecast*, the only non-Gryce number of the set. On (5), Farmer is heard solo on all six tracks by Quincy Jones' big band; on each appearance he is muted, as Jones explains, 'to emphasize his wonderfully distinctive melodic lines.' Taking away the warm beauty of Farmer's tone makes it easier to concentrate on *what* he plays rather than *how* he plays, and it is patently obvious that his solo construction is extremely intelligently conceived. A very successful quartet date – and perhaps the best of Farmer's LPs currently available – will be found on (6). The Hank Jones-Addison Farmer-Roy Haynes rhythm team provides an ideal background which combines smooth professionalism and an extrovert sense of swing (Haynes' drumming is as alert and masterful as ever); again the programme is made up of largely unusual material which includes one number by the esoteric composer George Russell. Farmer accepts the challenge implicit in such writing and rises to the occasion with a magnificent solo passage. Towards the end of 1958 Farmer joined Gerry Mulligan's quartet and it was obvious at once that his trumpet was the best foil for Mulligan's baritone since the earliest days of the first quartet. (7) is a highly recommended collection by the Farmer-Mulligan unit with some intriguing interplay between the two horns. Mulligan's predilection for bearing down on the beat and Farmer's equal and opposite one for constructing flowing phrases which skim across the normal breaks in phrase patterns makes for some stimulating contrasts.

(1) WARDELL GRAY MEMORIAL, Vol. 2 – 12 Esq 32-023. (A) 12 Pre PRLP7009. *1952.*

(2) ART FARMER SEPTET – 12 Esq 32-042. (A) 12 Pre PRLP7031. *1953–4.*

(3) ART FARMER QUARTET – 10 Esq 20-051. (A) 10 Pre PRLP193. *1954.*

(4) ART FARMER QUINTET – 12 Esq 32-037. (A) 12 Pre PRLP7017. *1955.*

(5) QUINCY JONES ORCHESTRA - 12 HMV CLP1162. (A) 12 ABC149. *1956.*

(6) ART FARMER QUARTET – 12 Vog LAC12197. (A) 12 Con C3554. *1958.*

(7) GERRY MULLIGAN QUARTET – 12 Ph BBL7320. (A) 12 Col CL1307. *1958–9.*

WALLY FAWKES (1920) *clarinet*

Wally Fawkes has always been a clarinettist within the lyrical tradition of New Orleans jazz, an elegant, self-assured, gently urbane musician. On (3) and (4) he is teamed with Sandy Brown, essentially a blues player, a clarinettist with a tougher, more intense approach. The conflict is a stimulating one. (1) and (2) are by the Fawkes-Turner Sextet, the two ex-Lyttelton musicians trying to recapture the instrumental balance of the old Jimmy Noone Apex Club Band. Pleasant but rather tame. (5) presents Wally Fawkes' Troglodytes playing a set of tunes made famous by Billie Holiday. Too many fluffs spoil the jazz. Only the pianist, Lennie Felix, does himself justice. Much, much better is (6), Fawkes playing a good *Flook's*

Fancy and Spike Mackintosh blowing a meditative trumpet solo on
Talk of the town.
(1) TAKIN' IT EASY, Vol. 1 – 7 Dec DFE6192. *1954.*
(2) TAKIN' IT EASY, Vol. 2 – 7 Dec DFE6193. *1954.*
(3) WALLY FAWKES-SANDY BROWN QUINTET – 7 Dec DFE6378. *1956.*
(4) WALLY FAWKES-SANDY BROWN QUINTET – 7 Dec DFE6379. *1956.*
(5) FAWKES ON HOLIDAY – 10 Dec LF1312. *1958.*
(6) FLOOK DIGS JAZZ – 7 Dec DFE6600, STO123. *1959.*

IRVING FAZOLA (1912–1949)   *clarinet*

A white musician of great polish and easy technique; his style based
on the Noone tradition without that extra heat that one would get
from a Negro musician. Whatever he played was done with good
taste and pleasing fluency. Recordings under his own name made in
1945 have not been issued on LP, but he is to be heard on Bonano's
High society (78 Par R2825 (d), (A) Col 35678 (d)), with Bob Crosby
especially *March of the Bob Cats* (12 Br LAT8050, (A) Dec 8061) and
Five Point blues (78 Dec F7152 (d), (A) Dec 2108 (d), and Muggsy
Spanier on *Hesitating blues* (10 Br LA8567).
(1) NEW ORLEANS EXPRESS (with George Hartman) – 12 Em A
    EJL1264. (A) 12 Em A 36022. *1945.*

VICTOR FELDMAN (1934)   *vibraphone, piano, drums*

Although he started his musical career wearing a millstone marked
'child prodigy' around his neck, Vic Feldman has remained remarkably level-headed and succeeded in proving that he is one of the very
finest jazzmen Europe has produced. Even before his emigration to
America – where he worked with Woody Herman for a time – in
1955 Victor had an impressive career on record including some with
that British jazz giant, Tommy Pollard, on piano. Just prior to Vic's
departure he did a number of 'farewell' sessions for both Tempo
and Esquire labels in London. (1) is by a septet containing the contrasting trumpets of Jimmy Deuchar and Dizzy Reece and the
unusual but wholly compelling piano of the great Tommy Pollard.
Victor's vibes caress the melody of *Sunshine on a dull day* (Feldman
plays ballads almost as well as Milt Jackson and Lionel Hampton)
and turns in some beautiful passages on the after-hours *When.* (2) is

by a specially assembled big band made up principally of Victor's jazz club associates; both Ronnie Scott and Dizzy Reece acquit themselves well in their solos. (3) is by virtually the same line-up although these titles were recorded almost eighteen months later during Feldman's first holiday back in Britain. The rich-toned bass of Lennie Bush, playing patterns and lines in place of simply choosing notes from the roots of the chords, the fierce crackling trumpet of Dizzy Reece and the accurate lead-work of Bobby Pratt, all these help to make this into a highly recommended LP. During the eighteen-month period between the big studio band recordings it seems apparent that Victor had gained a great deal of personality and solo presence. These two indefinable qualities crop up on both (4) and (5), two LPs recorded in Los Angeles. (4) is principally a showcase for bassist Leroy Vinnegar, (5) is a fantastic display of vibes playing (and piano work on some tracks) supported solely by bass (Scott La Faro) and drums (Stan Levey). *Bebop*, from this LP, must be one of the fastest, most agile performances ever done on the vibes in jazz. (4) is of interest not only for Feldman (who adds a lush quality to the music during *Would you like to take a walk?*) but also for the underappreciated Gerald Wilson (trumpet) and Teddy Edwards (tenor).

(1) VIC FELDMAN SEPTET – 10 Tem LAP5. Three tracks on (A) 12 Con C3541. *1955.*

(2) VIC FELDMAN BIG BAND – 7 Tem EXA29. Three tracks on (A) 12 Con C3541. *1955.*

(3) VIC FELDMAN BIG BAND – 12 Tem TAP12. *1956* and *1957.*

(4) LEROY VINNEGAR SEXTET – 12 Vog LAC12136. (A) 12 Con C3542. *1957.*

(5) THE ARRIVAL OF VIC FELDMAN – 12 Vog LAC12172. (A) 12 Con C3549. *1958.*

LENNIE FELIX (1920)   *piano*

Lennie Felix is an eclectic but discriminating pianist, at his best when his playing reflects the work of his favourite musicians, men like Tatum, Hines, Waller and Wilson. But he is far from being just an imitator of these pianists; instead, he uses their styles as a vehicle for his own ideas – and that he has plenty of ideas can be proved by comparing the two 'takes' of *Pennies from Heaven* (1), both completely different in mood and tempo. (1), in fact, is easily the best of these two LPs. On (2) Felix was joined by one or two guests, including that adroit alto-player Tony Coe; but two of the tracks feature a 'jangle-piano' and Felix also turns in a very unconvincing blues. Much better Felix solos can be found on 10 Col 33S1146 ('Salute to Satchmo'), by Nat Gonella and his Strong Arm Men. Tony Coe again sounds imperturbable and Gonella plays with a warm, flexible tone and rather on-the-beat phrasing.

(1) THAT CAT FELIX – 10 Nix NJT1514. *1958*.
(2) CAT ON A HOT TIN PIANO – 10 Col 33S1144. *1959*.

MAYNARD FERGUSON (1928) *trumpet, trombone*

For years something of an *enfant-terrible*, due to his regrettable predilection for soaring into the stratosphere at the drop of a mute, Maynard Ferguson emerged as the leader of a fine band during the late nineteen-fifties. Solo excesses apart, Ferguson's tremendous technical command makes him an ideal man to have in a trumpet section for his staying-powers are considerable. A great deal of his earlier work on record is barely worthy of comment for he seemed only to be capable of screeching in the dog-whistle frequency-range when solo time came around. With the advent of his own regular band, however, he appears to have sobered down somewhat and now he uses his formidable lung and lip qualities more sparingly. (1), titled 'A Message From Newport', although it was not actually recorded at the Newport Jazz Festival, is a good introduction to the band and its soloists. Much of the credit must go to the arrangers, notably Slide Hampton who also plays trombone with Ferguson, who have created some excellent scores for what is, in fact, a relatively small 'big' band. *Frame for the blues* is a noteworthy exercise in which the sense of climax is used with intelligence. (2) is by much the same personnel but the programme is slanted deliberately at a wider audience. This does not detract from the jazz interest, particularly on such tracks as *Don'cha go way mad* (a Jimmy Mundy composition which started life as an instrumental for Illinois Jacquet under the title *Black velvet*) and *BJ's back in town*. (3) was recorded on location at Birdland and finds the band in good spirits as it roars through such items as Miles Davis's *Oleo* and a number of Benny Golson's arrangements. Frankie Dunlop's lively drumming is noteworthy as is the strident alto of Jimmy Ford.

[131]

(1) MAYNARD FERGUSON ORCHESTRA – 12 Col 33SX1146. (A) 12
   Rou R52012. *1958*.
(2) MAYNARD FERGUSON ORCHESTRA – 12 Col 33SX1173. (A) 12
   Rou R25058. *1958*.
(3) MAYNARD FERGUSON ORCHESTRA – 12 Col 33SX1210. (A) 12
   Rou R52027. *1959*.

ELLA FITZGERALD (1918) *vocal*

Ella Fitzgerald has become something of an institution, a symbol of
the heights to which pop-singing can rise, although she is far from
being a pop-singer in the normal sense of that term. Ella's exuberant,
optimistic voice moves through a song rather as a jazz musician might
do, sometimes lingering over the melodic line, at other moments
indulging in dramatic swoops and dives. She is an artist, in fact,
who has succeeded in making the most of two worlds, the world of
popular songs (but always the best ones) and the world of jazz. It
was Benny Carter who discovered Ella Fitzgerald (he heard her
singing at an amateur talent contest in Harlem), and who recommended her to Chick Webb. Her earliest recordings (one, *A-Tisket,
A-Tasket*, can be found on (1)) were made with the Webb orchestra.
When the drummer died in 1939, Ella took over the band herself for
a time, and she can be heard singing with it on (2). (1) actually
presents Ella with a very varied collection of groups, including
Louis Jordan's Tympani Five, the Mills Brothers and the Delta
Rhythm Boys. Her singing in those early years (particularly her pre-
war singing) now sounds a little gawky, a little involved in its period,
when compared with the astonishing nonchalance of her later work.
   By the 1950s Ella had reached maturity as a singer, and one of her
very finest recordings is (3). On both this and (4) she is partnered by
the pianist Ellis Larkins, a remarkably skilful accompanist. (5)
contains several of Ella's excursions into scat-singing (digressions
which are anathema to some of her warmest fans but send others
into ecstasies), including *Flying home*, *How high the moon* and (with
the technique slightly changed) *Ella hums the blues*. (6), (10) and (11)
suffer a little from the fact that Armstrong was never quite at ease
on these sessions (the supporting musicians suit Ella's style much
better). (7) and (8) present Ella accompanied on half the tracks by
Duke Ellington's orchestra, on the other half by a small group that

includes Stuff Smith and Ben Webster. The latter are far superior, Ella sounding wonderfully relaxed. (9) and (12) are concert performances, splendidly done, with Ella's most dazzling display of scat-singing to be found on the latter LP.

Many of Ella Fitzgerald's finest recordings actually belong to the field of popular music, rather than to jazz. On them she is often accompanied by orchestras with string sections and with no elements of jazz in their arrangements. The series of 'songbooks' (with the exception of the Duke Ellington ones) belong in this category, Ella usually sounding rather more subdued, placing the emphasis upon the words rather than upon her interpretation of the melodies. These LPs comprise 'The Cole Porter Songbook' (2 vols.) (12 HMV CLP1083/4, (A) Ver 4001/2), 'The Rodgers and Hart Songbook' (2 vols.) (12 HMV CLP1116/7, (A) 12 Ver 4002/3), 'The Irving Berlin Songbook' (2 vols.) (12 HMV CLP1183/4, (A) 12 Ver 4019/20) and 'The George and Ira Gershwin Songbook' (5 vols.) (12 HMV CLP1338/9. CLP 1347/8 and CLP1353; CSD1293/3, CSD1299/300 and CSD1304; (A) 12 Ver 4024/5/6/7/8). Two volumes of 'Ella and Louis sing "Porgy and Bess" 'are on 12 HMV CLP1245/6, (A) 12 Ver 4011/2. Finally, a couple of really outstanding albums are 'Like Someone in Love' (with Stan Getz playing occasional tenor solos) (12 HMV CLP1166, (A) 12 Ver 4004) and 'Ella Sings "Pal Joey" ' (7 HMV 7EG8327), including the full-length version of *Bewitched, bothered and bewildered*.

(1) ELLA AND HER FELLAS – 12 Br LAT8223. (A) 12 Dec 8477. *1938–51*.

(2) ELLA FITZGERALD SOUVENIR ALBUM – 10 Br LA8581. *1940–1*.

(3) ELLA SINGS GERSHWIN – 10 LA8642. (A) 12 Dec 8378 (incl extra titles). *1950*.

(4) SONGS IN A MELLOW MOOD – 12 Br LAT8056. (A) 12 Dec 8068. *1954*.

(5) LULLABIES OF BIRDLAND – 12 Br LAT8115. (A) 12 Dec 8149. *1954–5*.

(6) ELLA AND LOUIS – 12 HMV CLP1098. (A) 12 Ver 4003. *1956*.

(7) DUKE ELLINGTON SONGBOOK, No. 1 (2 vols.) – 12 HMV CLP1213/4. (A) 12 Ver 4008/2. *1956–7*.

(8) DUKE ELLINGTON SONGBOOK, No. 2 (2 vols.) – 12 HMV CLP1227/8. (A) 12 Ver 4009/2. *1956–7*.

(9) ELLA AT NEWPORT – 12 Col 33CX10100. (A) 12 Ver 8234. *1957.* (rev. Billie Holiday).

(10) ELLA AND LOUIS AGAIN – 12 HMV CLP1146. (A) 12 Ver 4017. *1957.*

(11) ELLA AND LOUIS AGAIN, No. 2 – 12 HMV CLP1147. (A) 12 Ver 4018. *1957.*

12) AT THE OPERA HOUSE – 12 Col 33CX10126. (A) 12 Ver 8264, (S) 6026. *1957.*

(13) LOUIS AND ELLA SING 'PORGY AND BESS', Vol. 1 – 12 HMV CLP1245. (A) 12 Ver 4011/2, (S) 6040/1. *1959.*

(14) LOUIS AND ELLA SING 'PORGY AND BESS', Vol. 2 – 12 HMV CLP1246. (A) 12 Ver 4011/2, (S) 6040/2. *1959.*

BUD FREEMAN (1904) *tenor saxophone*

He has the unusual attribute, in jazz, of playing the saxophone so that it sounds just like a saxophone, pure and simple. The result has often been that he also sounds just like a palais-de-danse musician trying to improvise a jazz solo. Like many of the Chicagoan, Condon-faction musicians he gained an almost magical power from the wave of enthusiasm and inspiration that engulfed these men in the late twenties and early thirties. Perhaps also, in those days, there was a little more interest in what was to be played on a recording and they shaped their solos carefully to have full effect in a three-minute session. Nowadays, let loose for minutes on end to fill up an LP, some of these musicians sound a little thin and uninspired. Freeman's great moments are to be found on the Condon recordings of *The eel, Home cooking* and *Tennessee twilight* made in 1933 and with his Summa Cum Laude Orchestra on recordings made for Bluebird (1) and American Decca (deleted Br LA8526) and on the Columbia recordings with his Famous Chicagoans made in 1940, (2). (4) tries to repeat these days with only moderate success, while (5) has some unambitious tracks particularly those where he is accompanied by Dave Bowman and a rhythm section. The ideas occasionally wear thin, but there are some light and melodious moments.

(1) A STRING OF SWINGIN' PEARLS (with Manone, Condon, Trumbauer, Gifford, Stacy) – (A) 12 Vic LPM-1373. *1939.*

(2) CHICAGO STYLE – 7 Fon TFE17082. BUD FREEMAN AND HIS ALL-STAR JAZZ – (A) 12 Har 7046. *1940.*

(3) JAZZ FOR SALE, NO. 1. THE BUD FREEMAN TRIO – 7 TR JKR8021.
(A) CHICAGO STYLE (also Bradley, Byrne) – 12 GA 33-313.
1946.
(4) MIDNIGHT AT EDDIE CONDON'S – 12 EmA EJL1257. (A) 12 EmA
36013. *1955.*
(5) NEWPORT-NEWS – 12 Lon LTZ-N15030. (A) 12 Beth 29. *1956.*
(6) CHICAGO AUSTIN HIGH SCHOOL JAZZ IN HI-FI – (A) 12 Vic
LPM1508. *1957.*

BLIND BOY FULLER (Fulton Allen) (1903–1940) *vocal, guitar*
One of the most successful singers during the middle and late
1930s, Blind Fuller died of kidney trouble in the summer of 1940.
A fine guitarist, he had an excellent feeling for the pace of backing
melodies. His singing was raw and guttural and blended well with the
finer texturing of his instrumental accompaniments. Sonny Terry
worked as his harmonica player for a time before 1940 and Brownie
McGhee, his most successful follower, also toured with him. *Step it
up and go* was one of his biggest hits and his dancing, on stage, gave
an additional impetus to his public appearances. It was in his honour
that Bill Broonzy recorded *Jivin' Mr. Fuller blues* while Fuller returned
the compliment with *Jivin' Big Bill blues.* Fuller's death was a very
definite loss to the blues, for he was still quite a young man.
(1) *When you are gone* – incl. 12 Ph BBL7369. *1940.*

JESSE FULLER (1896) *vocal, 12-string guitar, harmonica, fotdela*
This folk singer, often reminiscent of Barbecue Bob, has been
living on the West Coast for many years. Brought up mainly in
Georgia, his blues playing is considerably influenced by the styles
which he heard around Atlanta in the early part of this century.
His voice is clear and hard – virtually no vibrato – and his recording
of *John Henry* (2), played with a knife-blade on open tuning, is one
of the best he has made. He plays a high-hat cymbal and foot-operated
bass (fotdela) which he invented; a one-man band in the idiom of jug
music.
(1) JESSE FULLER – 12 GTJ LAG12159. (A) 12 GTJ 12031. *1953.*
(2) WORKING ON THE RAILROAD – 10 Top 10T59. *1955.*

G

ERROLL GARNER (1921)   *piano*

Of all the newer jazz pianists Erroll Garner has the most distinctive and readily identifiable style. His schizophrenic approach, in which the left hand lags behind the beat, has been copied by a host of lesser artists but Garner's style is so personal that it makes a dangerous model to follow. He is reportedly unable to either read or write music, a fact which obviously has no effect at all on his ability to create valid and lasting jazz. Unlike so many of his contemporaries his concept of the piano is orchestral, rather in the manner of the older 'stride' pianists, and he combines spread chords with a fast technique to give the effect of a gigantic machine which is capable of producing music. It would be wrong, however, to describe his playing as mechanical for the singular turns of phrase are unique. On (3), recorded at a 'Just Jazz' concert in Hollywood, he backs up a superb tenor solo by Wardell Gray on *Blue Lou* before launching himself headlong into a long passage in which he never once allows the audience's attention to wander. Some of the playing is so intricate (phrases overlap each other, some are spread out then telescoped into a smaller number of bars to make up a kind of musical mosaic pattern) that on first hearing the listener might be excused for thinking that the pianist has lost his place in the chorus. Without doubt *Blue Lou* is one of Garner's finest performances and it is significant that the only other solos which approach it for sheer musicianship were also recorded at a public concert (5). This LP was taped at Carmel, California, and is strongly recommended to jazz enthusiasts irrespective of their own stylistic preferences. In fact Garner's playing knows no pigeon holes apart from the all-embracing one which decrees that jazz must swing. A number of his records verge dangerously close to the cocktail lounge style (probably deliberate in some cases) when Erroll allows himself to coast through a ballad at slow or medium tempo but such moments are absent from both (4) and (6) which are composed of *solos*. (It is necessary to italicize the term in order to stress the absence of bass and drums.) (4), first recorded for the Dial label in Hollywood, contains two copy-book Garner lessons in the romping *Frankie and Johnny* and *Play piano*

[136]

play. (7) is by Erroll and a big studio band, a not particularly exciting formula aimed presumably at a less discerning audience; the high spot, however, is the unveiling of Erroll's catchy and charming little tune *Misty*, a melody which seems to be a natural outgrowth of the pianist's style. (8) – actually two records – is a largely disappointing album based on the questionable gimmick of recording a series of tunes with French or Parisian title associations. Erroll simply does not swing at all in places (some of the material is wholly unsuited for the purpose) and he was further ill-advised to try to play the harpsichord on a few tracks. It is apparent at once that this completely uninhibited pianist needs years of practice before he will be in a position to turn in worthwhile performances on this historic keyboard instrument.

(1) PENTHOUSE SERENADE – 12 Lon LTZ-C15125. (A) 12 Sav 12002. *1945–9*.

(2) SERENADE TO LAURA – 12 Lon LTZ-C15126. (A) 12 Sav 12003. *1945–9*.

(3) THE BEST OF GENE NORMAN'S JUST JAZZ – 12 Vog LAE12001. *1947*.

(4) ERROLL GARNER – 12 Vog LAE12209. (A) 12 Roo 2213. *1947*.

(5) ERROLL GARNER TRIO – 12 Ph BBL7106. (A) 12 Col CL883. *1955*.

(6) ERROLL GARNER SOLOS – 12 Ph BBL7226. (A) 12 Col CL1060. *1957*.

(7) OTHER VOICES – 12 Ph BBL7204. (A) 12 Col CL1014. *1956* and *1957*.

(8) PARIS IMPRESSIONS – (two records). 12 Ph BBL7313 and BBL7314. (A) 12 Col C2L9. *1958*.

STAN GETZ (1927)   *tenor*

Although he has been singled out as the very epitome of 'cool' jazz Stan Getz is, in fact, one of the most accomplished of soloists whose records show that he can fit in with almost any contemporary style. Taking Lester Young as his basic influence Stan has travelled along a route of his own, adding different tonal qualities, acquiring non-Young characteristics and generally shaping his own career as an individualist. He is now one of the few really original and distinctive voices in jazz. Associated for some years with Woody Herman and the *Brothers* (Zoot Sims, Herbie Steward, Al Cohn, etc.) Getz finally made his break with Woody following the success of the Herd's lovely *Early Autumn* recording which featured Stan's melodic and tasteful tenor. Since the beginning of 1949 he has worked almost exclusively with small bands of his own (he made a brief excursion into the field of studio band work in 1952) as well as taking part in some JATP tours. (1) is a highly recommended collection of a dozen quartet tracks made during his most poised and relaxed period. In all cases the supporting groups are hand-picked (one of Stan's favourite pianists, Al Haig, is present on eight of them) so that there is a cohesive quality to the music. (1) contains the much-discussed *Too marvellous for words* as well as the introverted *My old flame*; throughout the course of the programme Stan's tone is hard-edged and clear even when he infringes on the alto register. (2) commemorates a visit to Sweden and finds Stan in the ideal company of pianist Bengt Hallberg (Lars Gullin joins in on baritone for two of the tracks). Hallberg's graceful, melodic keyboard style complements Getz to perfection and the result is jazz surrounded by an ethereal aura. Back in America a few months later Stan assembled a quintet for a booking at the Storyville club in Boston; this scratch date brought into being one of the finest quintets of his career with Al Haig, Jimmy Raney, Teddy Kotick and Tiny Kahn fusing their talents to form one of the best rhythm sections of recent years. Fortunately this ephemeral personnel's music was captured on tape ((3) and (4)) and while the recording balance might not be perfect throughout, it does not detract from the enjoyment of the music. With such a rhythm team behind him Stan is inspired; gone are the plaintive sighs at slow tempo and in their place is a forceful, virile style which sweeps rhythm section and listener along in its wake. Late in 1952 Getz was signed as a recording artist by Norman Granz and after a few sessions using the expected tenor-plus-rhythm formula Stan decided to form a new unit with Bob Brookmeyer's valve trombone partnering his tenor in the front line. (5) – actually two records – is the best example of this unit on record. Three of the sides were recorded on-stage at the end of a cross-country tour and the listener is able to witness the group getting into its stride as the evening proceeds. Brookmeyer's playing is very dull in places but his presence (together with that of pianist Johnny Williams) seems to have inspired Getz who swings hard on Johnny Mandel's *Pernod* and Al Cohn's *Tasty pudding*. Although Brookmeyer's work with Getz on record is gloomy he seemed to instil a greater obligation to the beat into the tenor saxist's personality. When Stan made up a hastily improvised quintet during a JATP concert (6) with Jay Jay Johnson his extrovert swing made him the most virile soloist in the group. Jay Jay's trombone makes an ideal foil for Getz here as they charge their way through such up-tempo material as *Crazy rhythm*; despite the exciting atmosphere, however, the tenor saxist is able to introduce a change of mood with his subtle reading of the ballad *It never entered my mind*. In many ways this LP (6) is one of the best Getz has ever made although the general standard of his work on record is so high that it is difficult to draw comparisons. As an example of the maturity which Getz achieved during the middle 'fifties (7) is revealing for it is perhaps the most down-to-earth session on which he has played. Guitarist Herb Ellis leads a unit comprising Getz, Roy Eldridge, Ray Brown and Stan Levey through a programme of blues and it is Getz who digs deepest into the spirit of the material. In fact, Stan is responsible for constructing the background riffs during the guitar solos while the more forthright Eldridge is content to tag along behind. (8) is by another wholly compatible quartet (Getz, Lou Levy, Leroy Vinnegar and Stan Levey), a setting which provides Stan with the foundations for some inspired solo work. His version of *Like someone in love* is the definitive one in jazz while his masterly use of the stop-time sections of *Blues for Mary Jane* and *How about you?* could not be bettered. It would be extremely difficult to decide whether (6) or (8) is the best Getz LP in the current catalogues. (9) was made in Chicago (and was actually the last record date Stan made in America before settling in Europe in the spring of 1958) with a Chicago rhythm section and, unfortunately, the lifeless, faltering trumpet of Chet Baker who has seldom sounded more enervated. It is Getz who saves the day, turning *Jor-du* (on which Baker has the good sense not to play) into something of a *tour de force*.

(1) STAN GETZ COLLATES – 12 Esq 32-011. (A) 12 Pre PRLP7002. *1949* and *1950*.

(2) STAN GETZ IN SWEDEN – 10 Esq 20-007. (A) 12 Roo 2207 (with four additional titles). *1951*.

(3) STAN GETZ QUINTET, Vol. 1 – 12 Vog LAE12158. (A) 12 Roo 2209. *1951.*

(4) STAN GETZ QUINTET, Vol. 1 – 12 Vog LAE12199. (A) 12 Roo 2225. *1951.*

(5) GETZ AT THE SHRINE, Vols. 1 and 2 – 12 Col 33CX10000 and 33CX10001. (A) 12 Ver 8188-2 (two records). *1954.*

(6) GETZ AND JAY JAY AT THE OPERA HOUSE – 12 Col 33CX10127. (A) 12 Ver 8265. *1957.*

(7) NOTHING BUT THE BLUES – 12 Col 33CX10139. (A) 12 Ver 8252. *1957.*

(8) THE STEAMER – 12 HMV CLP1276. (A) 12 Ver 8294. *1957.*

(9) STAN MEETS CHET – 12 HMV CLP1292. (A) 12 Ver 8263. *1958.*

TERRY GIBBS (1924) *vibes*

Most of Terry Gibbs' work on record is marked by a tremendous vitality and a tendency to play too many notes. His effervescent spirit has resulted in a type of jazz which is swinging but superficial, a description which might be applied with equal truth to the greater output of Oscar Peterson. However, two sessions stand out from the considerable number of releases under Gibbs' name. (1) is devoted to tunes by Duke Ellington (and Billy Strayhorn) and is played by a well-integrated quartet comprising Pete Jolly (piano-accordion). Leroy Vinnegar and Gary Frommer. Although Gibbs exceeds his normal standard in his own solos (he plays vibes, xylophone and marimba incidentally) it is Jolly who contributes most to the un-doubted success of the record. His intelligent use of a synthetic-sounding instrument gives the group a big sound and it seems unlikely that a more swinging version of *Caravan* exists on record. (2) is by the big band which Terry formed in the spring of 1959 and contains the pick of Hollywood's jazzmen. Basically the personnel is the same as that of Bill Holman's orchestra (Cor and HMV/Andex) and, although the chosen programme is designed deliberately to embrace such well-established favourites as *One o'clock jump, Midnight sun,* etc., the group gives more than an indication of its potential. Lovers of such extrovert orchestras as the Woody Herman Herd and Chubby Jackson's big band will enjoy the hard-hitting brass and the bursting enthusiasm of all concerned with Gibbs' exciting project.

(1) TERRY GIBBS QUARTET – (A) 12 EmA 36128. (Eight titles, of which

four apiece will be found on Mer YEP9503 and YEP9511. *1957*.

(2) TERRY GIBBS ORCHESTRA - 12 Mer MMC14018. (A) 12 Mer MG20440. *1959*.

DIZZY GILLESPIE (1917) *trumpet*

Although the names Dizzy Gillespie and Charlie Parker are usually bracketed together in a discussion of contemporary jazz history if was Parker who contributed the major share in the development ot the new style. By comparison Gillespie has always had his roots deeper in the previous swing era and, unlike Parker, has always had an acute awareness of publicity values. It was Dizzy who started the 'bebop' fads, the beret, the ool-ya-koo language, the dark glasses and the goatee beard. It was Dizzy who saw the commercial possibilities of the new music and who decided to launch a new band on the crest of the bop wave. This has, in no way, ever detracted one iota from Gillespie's tremendous value as a jazz musician; it is simply an indication that Parker's single-mindedness of purpose and total dedication to music probably lost him thousands of dollars which he might have earned had he possessed the business outlook of Gillespie. Dizzy's first band, formed in 1944, never recorded, but his second big band made several sides for the old Musicraft label. (1) contains the best of these, together with some small group tracks featuring Dizzy with Parker, Sonny Stitt, Dexter Gordon, Milt Jackson, Al Haig, etc. The bursting spirit of this fine band comes through in several places as witness the lip-searing trumpet section work on the frantic *Things to come*, the rolling *Our delight*, Ray Brown's bass on *One bass hit* and Gillespie's fantastic technique during his solos. A later edition of the band may be heard on (2), now deleted from the British catalogues but well worth obtaining second-hand. The irrepressible spirit is still present, added to which are the exciting rhythms of the Cuban bongo drummer Chano Pozo who augmented the band personnel until his untimely death in January, 1949. John Lewis's *Two bass hit*, a showcase for Al McKibbon, has become better known in recent years under the more respectable title *La ronde*; Tadd Dameron's *Good bait* has become a jazz standard while *Oo-pop-a-da*, with its unison vocal by Gillespie and Kenny Hagood, set the style for future scat excursions. (2) consists of studio-made recordings;

[141]

(3), by the same band, was taped at a concert and the 'in-person' excitement is apparent from the opening bars of *Emanon*, the first number. The band builds to fever pitch in places with Teddy Stewart and Chano Pozo thrashing away in the rhythm section; *Manteca* (a Cuban word meaning 'lard') develops along jungle lines complete with ensemble chants and percussion fireworks. Clearly there has never been another band in jazz to match the unbridled zeal of this Gillespie orchestra. The section work was seldom perfect but the flaring enthusiasm for the new jazz style made technical perfection a thing of lesser importance. When Dizzy was forced, due to economic pressure, to disband in 1950 jazz lost an important collective voice. Shortly after the break-up Gillespie made an album with strings (4) which not only showcased his beautiful tone and technique but still remains the best example of the marriage between soloist and scored background. Johnny Richards was responsible for the arrangements and the tunes – *Lullaby of the leaves*, *Alone together*, *What is there to say* amongst them – were picked with care. Following the failure of his big band Dizzy led a number of ephemeral small units, some of which were brilliant and some well below the form expected from a musician of Gillespie's stature. *The champ*, included in (5), created a stir when it was first released for it brought home to many listeners that the new jazzmen could play hot and exciting small-band jazz with the accent on the beat rather than on some subtle, shifting rhythm which subjugated the 4/4 structure beneath a complexity of patterns. Art Blakey drove the band hard and fast, an atmosphere to which Dizzy, Budd Johnson, Jay Jay Johnson and Milt Jackson responded with obvious enjoyment. In retrospect *The champ* represents a kind of turning point, a shift in emphasis away from the introvert 'cool' style to the brash, straight-down-the-middle brand of jazz which gave rise to such red-blooded groups and the Jazz Messengers and its various offshoots. Subsequent Gillespie small bands have featured a style of music which veers between the JATP excitement of *The champ* and the smut-laden atmosphere of the music hall. Both extremes, together with a great deal of in-between ground, are represented on (7) and (8), the former recorded at a Paris concert, the latter at a Paris studio. Mary Lou Williams' tune *In the land of Oo-bla-dee*, sung by Joe Carroll on (8), is typical for it contrasts humour (the lyric by Milt Orent is a neat twist on an old fairy-tale)

[142]

and first-class jazz (Dizzy plays a magnificent solo after the vocal) over a virile, swinging rhythm section. The concert tracks (7) have a great deal of built-in atmosphere, some stage 'business' and a roaring vaudeville spirit in places. Yet Dizzy is still capable of turning in fine solos under these conditions as he proves so conclusively on (7) with his thoughtful treatment of *They can't take that away from me*. The beautiful trumpet tone is heard to even greater advantage on the ballads and blues recorded in Paris the previous year (6); Gillespie's *Sleepytime down south* makes no concessions to Armstrong and is a warm, personal treatment. In the summer of 1953 Dizzy signed a contract with Norman Granz and it was Norman who conceived the idea of pairing Gillespie with his boyhood idol, Roy Eldridge. The two resultant LPs, (9) and (10), have their faults – there is a lack of imagination in the arrangements although the two trumpet and rhythm instrumentation is, of necessity, limited – but the point is driven home that both Roy and Diz are giants in their field and that, stylistically, there is much in common. (11) is a welcome return to the big band format, if only a studio assembled group; with Dizzy at the helm and with Buster Harding in charge of the arranging the orchestra finds no difficulty in creating a good impression on *Cool eyes*, *Hob nail special* and *Pile driver*. (12) is by the Modern Jazz Sextet, a unit created in the studio for one session only. Gillespie partners Sonny Stitt (playing alto) for the first time on record since 1945 while the John Lewis, Skeeter Best, Percy Heath, Charlie Persip rhythm team is ideal. A moving *Blues for Bird* and a sprightly *Tour de force* show off the capabilities of the two front-line men (and indicate that both have developed as soloists since those old Musicraft sides incidentally); in the now-to-be-expected *Ballad medley* Dizzy plays a thoughtful version of *How deep is the ocean?* drawing on John Lewis's sensitive keyboard work for added inspiration. (13) contains the major part of a session by the big band which Dizzy used on his U.S. State Department-sponsored world tour. Unfortunately the date seems to have been carried out under hectic conditions leaving the engineers no time to balance the band properly; in addition no more than one take of each number was done. Nevertheless, the roaring spirit of the orchestra comes across and there are some effective solos from Phil Woods (alto), Joe Gordon (trumpet on *Night in Tunisia*) and Dizzy himself. (14) includes further titles from the same session

[143]

but the best tracks come from a later date with a slightly altered personnel. *Stablemates* is one of Benny Golson's tunes (Golson plays tenor in the sax section of the Gillespie band) and the imaginative way in which Benny uses the ensemble calls to mind the work of the great Tadd Dameron. (15) contains another Golson score in *Whisper not*, a swinging *Left hand corner* and a suitably moody *Jor-du*. It is regrettable that Gillespie was unable to keep the band together, despite the dedicated enthusiasm of all concerned, for it was one of the very few nurseries for new talent during the late 'fifties. Too many of the younger soloists have rocketed to fame with a recording contract and a couple of LPs but few of them have had the benefit of big band experience simply because the number of big bands has been reduced to rather less than a handful. The Gillespie orchestra gave prominence and help to Lee Morgan and Phil Woods, to name only two of the newer men who passed through the ranks; when Dizzy paid off his men for the last time at the beginning of January, 1958, it was the end of an era. Since that time Gillespie has toured as a soloist or worked with small groups. (16), a highly recommended LP incidentally, presents the nucleus of the unit he brought to Europe late in 1959 and includes the bluesy piano work of Junior Mance. Gillespie plays with restraint and is particularly memorable during his muted solos.

(1) Dizzy Gillespie Orchestra – 12 WRC R29. (A) 12 Sav 12020. *1945, 1946.*

(2) Dizzy Gillespie Orchestra – 10 HMV DLP1047. (Most of these titles plus some additional ones on (A) 12 Vic LJM1009.) *1946–9.*

(3) Dizzy Gillespie Orchestra – 10 Vog LDE076. (A) 12 Gene Norman Presents LP23. (The two extra titles on LP23 come from an earlier concert held in Paris.) *1948.*

(4) Dizzy Gillespie With Strings – 10 Vog LDE033. (A) 12 Sav 12110 (with additional non-string tracks). *1950.*

(5) Dizzy Gillespie Sextet – 7 Vog EPV1094. (A) 12 Sav 12047 (with additional sextet tracks). *1951.*

(6) Dizzy Gillespie Orchestra – (A) 12 Atl 1257. (Five titles issued on 78 rpm in Britain on Esq and Fel but now deleted.) *1952.*

(7) Dizzy Gillespie Orchestra – 10 Vog LDE039. (A) 12 Roo 2214 (with additional tracks from the same concert). *1953.*

(8) Dizzy Gillespie In Paris – 10 Vog LDE135. (A) 10 Con 2504.
1953.
(9) Roy and Diz, Vol. 1 – 12 Col 33CX10025. (A) 12 Ver 8109.
1954.
(10) Roy and Diz, Vol. 2 – 12 Col 33CX10084. (A) 12 Ver 8110.
1954.
(11) Dizzy Gillespie Orchestra – 7 Col SEB10075. (A) 12 Ver 8178
(with additional titles). *1954.*
(12) Modern Jazz Sextet – 12 Col 33CX10048. (A) 12 Ver 8166.
1955.
(13) World Statesman – 12 Col 33CX10077. (A) 12 Ver 8174.
1956.
(14) Dizzy in Greece – (A) 12 Ver 8017. *1956* and *1957.*
(15) Birks Works – (A) 12 Ver 8222. *1957.* Note : Eleven tracks
from (14) and (15) were combined for British issue on 12
Col 33CX10144. *1957.*
(16) Have Trumpet Will Excite – 12 HMV CLP1318. (A) 12
Ver 8311. *1959.*

BENNY GOODMAN (1909) *clarinet*

Despite the fact that Benny Goodman is a remarkably gifted
clarinettist, it is likely that his main contribution to jazz has really
been as a kind of impresario, the leader of various small groups
which have displayed the brilliance of such musicians as Teddy
Wilson, Lionel Hampton, Charlie Christian and Cootie Williams.
Goodman himself, although technically a virtuoso, has never been
in quite the same class as those musicians – judged from the standpoint of jazz playing. A critic once described Goodman as grappling
with a tune rather than playing around with it, a comment that has a
grain of truth in it and helps to explain the lack of relaxation in much
of his work. There also often seems to be a lack of emotion in his
playing, a detachment not compensated for by any outstanding display
of formal inventiveness. It was not always thus. Some of Goodman's
earliest recordings (collected on (1)) are remarkably spirited, almost
intense. Two tracks – *Clarinetitis* and *That's a plenty* – recorded with
piano and drums in 1928, show the strong influence that Frank
Teschemacher had upon this young clarinettist. Other performances
included here are a 1929 *Muskrat ramble* (with Wingy Manone, Bud

Freeman and Joe Sullivan), a couple of tracks with Jimmy McPartland (*Blue*, *Wolverine blues*), a group of pieces by Red Nichols' Five Pennies, Adrian Rollini's *Davenport blues*, and two tracks by the Venuti-Lang All Stars (*Someday sweetheart* and *Farewell blues*). These last two items, along with *Beale street blues* and *After you've gone*, boasting fine Teagarden vocals and trombone playing as well as outstanding Goodman solos, can be found on 7 Br OE9468. Other exceptionally spirited solos by Goodman during this period occur in *Dallas blues* and *Royal garden blues* by Ted Lewis's band (7 Ph BBE12106). A particularly attractive set of performances can also be found on (2). The British EP (now deleted) included *Texas tea party, I gotta right to sing the blues, Ain't cha glad* and *Dr. Heckle and Mr. Jibe*, all with singing and playing by Teagarden; in addition, the U.S. release has several more items by the Goodman-Teagarden band, including two which contain the first vocal choruses Billie Holiday ever sang on record, and a couple of tracks by the Charleston Chasers, one being the famous version of *Basin Street blues*.

But it was the orchestra which Benny Goodman organized in 1935, with its arrangements written by Fletcher Henderson, with Gene Krupa behind the drums and Bunny Berigan in the trumpet section, which thrust him into sudden popularity. It was the first time that any band playing jazz had been successful upon this scale. Earlier bands – the Casa Loma orchestra, for instance, and the Dorsey Brothers – had tried and failed. Goodman's success produced, in its turn, a host of imitators, most of them basing their performances upon his. 'Swing', in fact, had arrived. The band which Goodman led during the last half of the 1930s can be heard on records (3) to (11); there is, not surprisingly, a good deal of overlapping between the British LPs and the American LPs. *King Porter stomp*, one of Goodman's earliest recordings with the big band, featuring a fine Henderson arrangement and including one of Bunny Berigan's best solos, is contained on (5) and (10). Harry James, who joined the band a little later, is heard playing his trumpet in *Life goes to a party* (3) and (11). Perhaps the finest soloist, once Berigan had left the orchestra, was Jess Stacy, a pianist with a sharp, staccato touch; he is heard at his best in *Big John special* (3), while another track on that LP, *Wrappin' it up*, has some elegant alto playing by Dave Matthews. By the time that both these tracks were made Krupa had left the band, being replaced by Dave Tough, easily the finest white drummer of his generation and an inspiration in this particular rhythm section.

Meanwhile Benny Goodman had begun featuring a trio and and quartet, using Teddy Wilson, Lionel Hampton and Gene Krupa, in addition to himself. Jelly Roll Morton had done something very similar in the late 1920s, but that was on records, whereas Goodman presented his small groups in the flesh as well. Some of Wilson's most subtle playing, in fact, can be found on these trio and quartet recordings. Good examples are included in (4) and on (9) (*After you've gone*) and (7) (*Lady be good, Stomping at the Savoy*), while many others crop up in records (12) to (18). (12), (13), (16), (17) and (18) all consist of 'air-shots' (recordings made from broadcasts) and feature both the big band and the small groups. (18) is of special interest, for it contains a track – *AC-DC Current* – by the 1940 Sextet, with Charlie Christian playing guitar. (14) and (15) were recorded at the Carnegie Hall concert of 1938; in addition to tracks by the Goodman band (including a splendid impromptu solo by Jess Stacy at the end of *Sing, sing, sing*) and the small groups, there are solos from Johnny Hodges, Count Basie, Cootie Williams, Harry Carney, Lester Young and Buck Clayton. Another set of concert performances can be found on the 'Spirituals to Swing' LP ((A) 12 Van 8523/4), including some Sextet tracks dating from 1939, just after Charlie Christian had joined the group.

It is Charlie Christian (q.v.) whose playing dominates most of the small group recordings which Goodman made between 1939 and 1941. In 1940 Cootie Williams also joined Goodman, and the combination of these two musicians, plus Goodman himself and some surprisingly inspired tenor-playing by Georgie Auld, produced a large number of outstandingly good tracks. The two most important collections of these are (20) and (21), but (23) includes *Rose room, Grand slam* and *I can't give you anything but love*, (25) *Poor butterfly* and *I've found a new baby*, and (26) *Breakfast feud* (a track also found on both (20) and (21)), all of these made by groups that include Charlie Christian and sometimes Cootie Williams as well. Goodman himself seemed to play better in this kind of company; certainly some of his best solos can be found on these recordings. Meanwhile the Benny Goodman orchestra had undergone changes. It had a new pianist – first Fletcher Henderson, then Mel Powell, and included a fine trombonist in Lou McGarity, a musician with a forthright but highly inventive style (he takes an exceptionally good solo on a sextet track, *If I had you* (23)). As well as Fletcher Henderson, whose health was beginning to fail, Eddie Sauter was writing arrangements for the band, and a selection of scores by these men can be heard on (19) and (24), while more big-band tracks are contained in (22). After the departure of Lionel Hampton in 1940 and Cootie Williams in 1941, and after the death of Charlie Christian, the character of the Goodman Sextet changed. It became more amiable, less fiery. Performances by the later sextet (usually containing either Mel Powell or Teddy Wilson, with perhaps Red Norvo on vibes) can be found in (21), (23), (25) and (26), while (27) is entirely devoted to sextet recordings – pleasant but not at all extraordinary – by a group including Norvo and Wilson.

(28) and (29) contain some of the small group recordings that Goodman made for Capitol in 1947. As well as some good solos by Goodman himself, many of these contain brisk piano playing by Jimmy Rowles. (30) brings together the original Goodman Trio – Goodman, Wilson, Krupa – playing a benefit concert for Fletcher Henderson in 1951, with guest stars in the persons of Buck Clayton (who plays superbly on two tracks), Johnny Smith and Lou Mc-Garity. (31) is, by comparison, a rather run-of-the-mill affair, by a sextet that included Terry Gibbs. 'The Benny Goodman Story,' the filmed biography (or what the scenario writers chose to call by that name) of the clarinettist and bandleader, appeared in 1955, provoking a flood of records by both Goodman himself and various groups led by ex-sidemen. Of particular interest are the sound-track recordings, one LP (32) being by the big band (including Stan Getz, Urbie Green and Teddy Wilson), while (33) contains a number of trio and quartet tracks. During the last few years, unfortunately, Goodman has produced very few records that could be called outstanding – indeed some have been unusually dull. One exceptionally good one, however, is (34), including some fine piano playing by Russ Freeman (with both the big band and the quintet) and with Goodman in his liveliest form for quite a long time.

(1) B.G. 1927–34 – 12 Cor LVA9011. (A) 12 Br 54010. *1928–34*.
(2) BENNY GOODMAN ORCHESTRA – 7 Col SEG7606 (*d*). (A) (plus other titles) 12 Col CL821. *1931–5*.

(3) THIS IS BENNY GOODMAN – (A) 12 RCA LPM1239. *1935–8.*

(4) BENNY GOODMAN TRIO-QUARTET-QUINTET – (A) 12 RCA LPM1226. *1935–8.*

(5) THE GOLDEN AGE OF BENNY GOODMAN – (A) 12 RCA LPM1099. *1935–8.*

(6) THE GOLDEN AGE OF SWING – (A) 5-12 RCA LPT6703. *1935–9.*

(7) STOMPING AT THE SAVOY – 7 RCA RCX1033. *1935–6.*

(8) SING, SING, SING – 7 RCA RCX1026. *1935–7.*

(9) BENNY GOODMAN – 7 RCA RCX1009. *1935–8.*

(10) AND THE ANGELS SING – 7 RCA RCX1019. *1935–9.*

(11) BENNY GOODMAN – 7 RCA RCX1036. *1937–8.*

(12) BENNY GOODMAN JAZZ CONCERT, No. 1 – 12 Ph BBL7009 (*d*). (A) 3-12 Col CLCL817/8/9. *1937–8.*

(13) BENNY GOODMAN JAZZ CONCERT, No. 2 – 12 Ph BBL7010 (*d*). (A) 3-12 Col CL817/8/9. *1937–8.*

(14) CARNEGIE HALL JAZZ CONCERT – 12 Ph BBL7000. (A) 2-12 Col OSL160. *1938.*

(15) CARNEGIE HALL JAZZ CONCERT – 12 Ph BBL7001. (A) 2-12 Col OSL160. *1938.*

(16) BENNY GOODMAN TREASURE CHEST, Vol. 1 – 12 MGM C805. (A) MGM 3788. *1938–9.*

(17) BENNY GOODMAN TREASURE CHEST, Vol. 2 – 12 MGM C807 (A) MGM 3789. *1938–9.*

(18) BENNY GOODMAN TREASURE CHEST, Vol. 3 – 12 MGM C810. (A) MGM 3790. *1938–40.*

19) BENNY GOODMAN PRESENTS FLETCHER HENDERSON ARRANGEMENTS – (A) 12 Col CL524. *1939–40.*

(20) CHARLIE CHRISTIAN WITH BENNY GOODMAN – 12 Ph BBL7172. (A) Col CL652. *1939–41.*

(21) BENNY GOODMAN SEXTET – 12 Ph BBL7178 (*d*). (A) 12 Col CL500. *1939–45.*

(22) BENNY GOODMAN AND HIS ORCHESTRA – (A) 12 Col CL534. *1939–45.*

(23) ALL THE CATS JOIN IN – 12 Fon TFL5067. *1939–46.*

(24) BENNY GOODMAN PRESENTS EDDIE SAUTER ARRANGEMENTS – 12 Ph BBL7043 (*d*). (A) 12 Col CL523. *1940–1.*

(25) BENNY GOODMAN – 7 Fon TFE17079. *1940–51.*

(26) FAMOUS GOODMAN DATES, No. 1 – 7 Ph BBE12189. *1941–5.*

(27) Benny Goodman Sextet – 10 Fon TFR6006. *1945.*

(28) Mostly Sextets – (A) 12 Cap T668. *1947.*

(29) Benny Goodman Combos – (A) 12 Cap T669. *1947.*

(30) Benny Goodman Plays For Fletcher Henderson Fund – 10 Fon TFR6022. (A) (plus extra titles) 12 Col CL516. *1951.*

(31) The New Benny Goodman Sextet – (A) 12 Col CL552. *1952.*

(32) Benny Goodman Story, Vol. 1 – 12 Br LAT8102. (A) 12 Dec 8252. *1955.*

(33) Benny Goodman Story, Vol. 2 – 12 Br LAT8103. (A) 12 Dec 8253. *1955.*

(34) Happy Session – 12 Ph BBL7318, (S) SBBL539. (A) 12 Col CL1324, (S) CS8129. *1958.*

DEXTER GORDON (1923) *tenor saxophone*

Although he was prominent on record during the first five or six years after the war, Dexter Gordon's appearances of late have been regrettably few. His duets with Wardell Gray set the style for a whole range of two-tenor 'battles' although none of the copies approached the quality of the original. Dexter's swinging, elbowing style has had a considerable influence on the work of many newer soloists – John Coltrane amongst them – although few have equalled his length of line or sense of humour. His presence on (1) turns what might otherwise have been a mediocre date into a sparkling affair; Conte Candoli and Frank Rosolino rise above themselves in the front line, spurred on by Gordon's probing solos. Lou Levy, Leroy Vinnegar and Stan Levey (a fine rhythm section which has backed Stan Getz on record) adds fuel to the fire and when Dexter steps to the front for his sixteen-chorus solo on the pulsating *Stanley the steamer* the temperature reaches near-boiling point.

(1) This Time The Drum's On Me (Stan Levey Sextet) – 12 Par PMC1086. (A) 12 Beth 37. *1955.*

BOBBY GRANT (unknown) *vocal, guitar*

Bobby Grant's *Nappy head blues* (1) is of such exceptional quality that, though nothing is known about him, it was necessary to give him an individual entry. This magnificent voice, rising over a whined guitar accompaniment has some of the qualities which distinguished Leadbelly. *Lonesome Atlanta blues* (1), though credited to Grant, could

[150]

well be by another singer, so great is the difference in weight of voice.

(1) BACKWOODS BLUES – 10 Lon AL3535 (d). *1927*.

WARDELL GRAY (1921–55)

tenor saxophone

Although the Lester Young influence was present in the style of Wardell Gray there was also a robustness of tone not normally associated with Young admirers. Wardell's career paralleled that of Charlie Parker (they worked together in the Earl Hines band for a time) and although the tenor saxist was not an adventurous innovator he was nevertheless a soloist of a very high order. Unlike so many of his contemporaries he could build constructively over innumerable choruses without resorting to the use of trick effects to sustain his listener's attention. *One o'clock jump* (1) is a good example of Wardell playing in public with a group which includes Erroll Garner, Howard McGhee and Vic Dickenson; it is Gray who opens the solo sequence and creates the correct atmosphere with a long, flowing solo. *Blue Lou*, on the same record and from the same concert, is perhaps Wardell's finest performance for his imagination is both matched and inspired by the playing of Erroll Garner. (2) couples titles made at two quartet dates, the first held during the AFM recording ban in 1948 (*Stoned*, a twelve-bar later recorded as *Bedlam* with Benny Goodman, and a thinly disguised *Idaho* under the name *Matter and mind*), the second dating from June 1950. It is this second session which produced the superlative *Easy swing*, a relaxed example of Wardell's unmatched ability to swing. The two volumes of the Wardell Gray Memorial ((3) and (6)) contain all the material which he recorded for the Prestige label; (3) comprises the products of three different sessions including the prototype version of *Twisted*, later adapted by singer Annie Ross as the basis for some expert 'vocalese'. (6) is of a slightly lower standard (but is still strongly recommended); one side is occupied by two lengthy transcriptions from a club session with Wardell's fellow tenor-man Dexter Gordon and the then-Basie trumpeter Clark Terry. The reverse is by a small group which Gray led for a short time in 1952; *Sweet and lovely* and *Lover man*, like *Easy living* on (3), show that apart from his talent for forceful, uncompromising swing, Wardell could also transform ballad material in a manner rarely equalled by any other post-war soloist.

[151]

During 1950 and 1951 Gray was with Count Basie's Sextet (and with the big band which Count formed, unsuccessfully, in April 1950). His natural sense of swing and strong individuality made it clear at once that Wardell was ideally suited to the Basie organization. It is regrettable he made relatively few records with Count although he was prominently featured on a handful of sides. With the full band he added his own personal comments to Buster Harding's extrovert *Nails* (4) and had a special number, *Little Pony* (5), built around him by arranger Neal Hefti who took a riff created by alto saxist 'Pony' Poindexter and expanded it to full-length proportions. With the sextet Gray's half-chorus on *Little white lies* (4) measures up to the best of his previously made small-group records. During the late nineteen-forties Wardell was a member of Benny Goodman's band and may be heard on a number of now-deleted Capitol singles, notably *Having a wonderful wish*, *Hucklebuck* (both with the full band), *Oo-bla-dee*, *Bedlam* and *Blue Lou* (all with Goodman's Sextet). At the time of his death, under mysterious circumstances, he was working with Benny Carter's orchestra.

(1) THE BEST OF GENE NORMAN'S 'JUST JAZZ' – 12 Vog LAE12001. *1947*.

(2) WARDELL GRAY QUARTET – 7 Vog EPV1064. *1948* and *1950*.

(3) WARDELL GRAY MEMORIAL, Vol. 1 – 12 Esq 32-016. (A) 12 Pre PRLP7008. *1949, 1950* and *1953*.

(4) COUNT BASIE AND HIS ORCHESTRA – 10 Ph BBR8036. (A) 10 Ep LG1021. Tracks containing Gray solos, *1950* and *1951*.

(5) COUNT BASIE AND HIS ORCHESTRA – 12 Fon TFL5046. (A) 12 Col CL997. Tracks containing Gray solos, *1950* and *1951*.

(6) WARDELL GRAY MEMORIAL, Vol. 2 – 12 Esq 32-023. (A) 12 Pre PRLP7009. *1950* and *1952*.

JOHNNY GUARNIERI (1917) *piano*

One of the dangers of copying other great jazzmen, even as a joke, and there can surely be no more serious reason for doing it, is that your own talents are apt to get forgotten. Guarnieri is a very fine pianist – he would have to be to copy Basie and Waller so faithfully – but one is led to wonder why he should waste so much talent and time in doing this, unless he was very uncertain of his own capabilities. His own style is easy, swinging, and has elements in it which could have led to a great personal popularity if he had persisted with it. He is a fine technician and his playing is always pleasantly entertaining.

The first recording session under his name for the Savoy label gave him distinguished company including Lester Young and Billy Butterfield, playing *These foolish things* and *Exercise in swing*, two good performances, and two remarkable take-offs, *Salute to Fats* and *Basie English*, all obtainable on (1) or as part of a Lester Young LP (Lon 12 LTZ-C15132, (A) 12 Sav 12068). His next sessions for Savoy, a series of fine piano solos accompanied by Slam Stewart and Sammy Weiss have long been deleted in America (10 Sav MG15007) and never issued in England; neither have his 1946 Majestic recordings become available after their original 78 issue.

Of late his talents have been appearing more frequently on LPs. A highly successful selection of Duke Ellington numbers, including some of the popular items and a few rarer ones like the delightful *Scattin' at the Kit Kat* (2), all fine re-creations of Ellington's tunes, interesting to compare with Thelonious Monk's less respectful reshapings. A pleasing album of Will Hudson and Eddie de Lange numbers (3), two light-hearted and entertaining Victor albums (4), (5) and an album of his own compositions (6) all show him as an excellent if not particularly profound pianist.

(1) THE JOHNNY GUARNIERI SWING MEN – 7 Lon EZ-C19018. *1944.*
(2) THE DUKE AGAIN – 12 Cor LVA9044. (A) 12 Cor 57086. *1956.*
(3) THE SONGS OF WILL HUDSON AND EDDIE DE LANGE – 12 Cor LVA9049. (A) 12 Cor 57085 (*d*). *1956.*
(4) CHEERFUL LITTLE EARFUL – (A) 12 Cam CAL-345. *1957.*
(5) SIDE BY SIDE – (A) 12 Cam CAL-391. *1957.*
(6) JOHNNY GUARNIERI PLAYS JOHNNY GUARNIERI – (A) GC 3020. *1958.*

LARS GULLIN (1928)   *baritone saxophone*

For a European jazzman to win an American popularity poll is something of an honour, even if popularity polls are no real guide to artistic ability. Sweden's Lars Gullin came to the notice of the American jazz public through his records released on the Prestige (and later EmArcy) label. Not only is he one of the finest baritone saxists in jazz but his talents extend to composition and arrangement; he has the ability to write unusual material which combines jazz and Scandinavian folk music elements. Like many European jazzmen he leaned heavily on American ideas, so far as basic group conception was concerned, during the early stages of his career. (1) is a good LP by a band using an instrumentation modelled on that of Miles Davis's Capitol band (in Lars' case, trumpet, tenor, french horn, alto, baritone and rhythm). *Smart Alec* and *Smooth breeze* from this LP are outstanding in their way. (2), made two months later, is a frank copy of the then new Gerry Mulligan quartet although Lars' group replaces Chet Baker's trumpet by a more virile trombone (Ake Persson). *You blew out the flame in my heart* is the track which comes closest to achieving the closely-knit texture of the original. A quartet instrumentation of greater originality is heard on (3) where Gullin's singing baritone is teamed with guitar, bass and drums for four fine tracks. An extension of the formula is presented on (4) in which a four-piece front-line (trombone, clarinet, tenor and baritone) makes exemplary use of a quartet of Gullin originals. In many ways these are the best available recordings by the baritone saxist for they combine good solos with mature, intelligent writing of a very high order. In more recent years Gullin appears to have been relatively inactive, musically, and his absence from record has been regrettable for his earlier work indicated that he was already in world class as an instrumentalist.

(1) LARS GULLIN BAND – 10 Esq 20-019. (A) 10 Pre PRLP144. *1952.*
(2) LARS GULLIN QUARTET – 10 Esq 20-015. (A) 10 Pre PRLP151. *1953.*
(3) LARS GULLIN QUARTET – (A) 10 EmA 26041. (Two titles apiece on 7 Esq EP49 and EP79.) *1954.*
(4) LARS GULLIN SEPTET – (A) 10 EmA 26044. (Two titles apiece on 7 Esq EP77 and EP78.) *1954.*

H

BOBBY HACKETT (1915)   *cornet, trumpet*
When Bobby Hackett arrived in New York in 1937 he was hailed by jazz critics as 'a second Bix'. His playing, making much use of rubato, certainly owed a great deal to Beiderbecke. Since the war, however, his style has moved closer to Louis Armstrong's. Some of Hackett's finest recordings were made in the late 1930s, mostly with

groups assembled by Eddie Condon for (A) Commodore. Examples of this period can be found on (1), also on one track (*I'm coming Virginia*) of 'Benny Goodman Carnegie Hall Jazz Concert' (1938), 12 Ph BBL7000, (A) 12 Col CL-814. Most of these performances contain vivacious clarinet solos by Pee Wee Russell. For a time Hackett worked as guitarist with Glen Miller's orchestra; he also played the cornet solo in Miller's *String of pearls*, 7 RCA RCX1003. Bobby Hackett has appeared on a number of post-war Eddie Condon LPs, as well as making a quantity of records – many of them 'cocktail music' rather than jazz – under his own name. (4) is by the regular band he was leading in 1957; although basically a Dixieland group, this band performs quite adventurous arrangements, written by Dick Cary.

(1) THE HACKETT HORN – (A) 12 Ep LG-3106. *1938–40*.

(2) TRUMPET ARTISTRY OF BOBBY HACKETT, NO. 1 – 7 Ph BBE12177. *1950*.

(3) TRUMPET ARTISTRY OF BOBBY HACKETT, NO. 2 – 7 Ph BBE12178. *1950*.

(4) GOTHAM JAZZ SCENE – 12 Cap T857. (A) 12 Cap T857. *1957*.

(5) JAZZ ULTIMATE (with Jack Teagarden) – 12 Cap T933. (A) 12 Cap T933, (S) ST933. *1957*.

(6) THE BOBBY HACKETT QUARTET – (A) 12 Cap T1235, (S) ST1235. *1959*.

AL HAIG (1923) *piano*

Haig ranks second in importance, after Bud Powell, so far as contemporary jazz piano is concerned. His tasteful, logical and always lyrical playing brings to mind the elegance of Teddy Wilson and it is singularly unfortunate for the enthusiast (*a*) that relatively few records of Haig are currently available and (*b*) that Al's influence on newer pianists is not strongly marked. (Hank Jones is one of the few present-day pianists to reflect the melodic Haig approach.) Al may be heard on some of Stan Getz's best records (q.v.), notably the Storyville albums, and Getz cites Haig as one of his all-time favourite accompanists. (1) contains Al's best up-tempo solo on *Go* (harmonically *The way you look tonight*) where he receives the sterling support of Max Roach who is very much on-form throughout the session. (2) presents the trio (Haig, Tommy Potter and Roy Haynes) which

[155]

worked with both Stan Getz and the Charlie Parker With Strings unit during 1949 and 1950; *Opus caprice* (a familiar line on the *I got rhythm* chords) is an engaging track which demonstrates Al's facility and gentlemanly sense of swing. (3) and (4) were made at the same sessions and were amongst the last records taped by Haig before his semi-retirement. Both are strongly recommended principally for a moving *Round about midnight* on (3) and an unusual treatment of *Royal garden blues*, with some beautiful ballad interpretations on (4).

(1) Fats Navarro Quintet – 7 Esq EP13. (A) 7 Pre PREP1321. *1949.*

(2) Al Haig Trio – 7 Esq EP76. (A) 7 Pre PREP1328. *1950.*

(3) Al Haig Trio – 10 Vog LDE092. *1954.*

(4) Al Haig Trio – 12 (A) Cou CPT551. *1954.*

EDMOND HALL (1901)   *clarinet*

A dignified and professional musician who, at the same time, has not found an individual enough style to rank among the very best clarinettists. Although a New Orleans musician, he has none of the New Orleans roughness or, at the other extreme, the Creole sweetness; in fact his hard style is often nearer to that of a white musician. He became widely known as a result of his tours with the Armstrong All Stars in which group he fitted rather uncomfortably. His predilection is towards a routine sort of jazz which produces some pleasant but rather uneventful records.

(1) Blue Note Jazzmen – 7 Vog EPV1164. *1940s.*

(2) Jazz at The Savoy Café – 10 Lon LZ-C14005. *1949.*

(3) Sounds of Jazz – 7 Fon TFE17076. *1957.*

(4) Petite Fleur – 12 Lon LTZ-T15166. (A) 12 UA4028, (S) 5028. *1958.*

(5) Rumpus on Rampart Street – 12 TR 35/050. (A) Rae-Cox 1120. *1959.*

BENGT HALLBERG (1932)   *piano*

One of the most accomplished of all European jazz pianists, Hallberg startled the critics when he was first heard on record with Stan Getz (q.v.); Bengt was eighteen at the time yet he played like a seasoned veteran. Since then he has maintained this high standard of graceful, delicate keyboard jazz, a kind of modern Teddy Wilson with a more brittle touch. Although his playing seems to lack the superficial drive which characterizes the work of lesser soloists it is nevertheless valid and swinging. Time and again Hallberg has shown that jazz piano need not degenerate into the honk-and-stomp pattern if it is to have drive. His flexible lines are intensely lyrical and are played with clarity due to Bengt's considerable instrumental command. One side of (1) is devoted to four gentlemanly trio performances which include Gish White's *Cynthia's in love* (theme music from the film *The Snows of Kilimanjaro*) and *The things we did last summer*. The remaining pair are Hallberg originals and demonstrate the flair Bengt has for composing attractive tunes of quality and character; the descending phrase idea of *Zig zag* has an Ellington-like simplicity which, when transcribed for the full Johnny Dankworth band (BBC broadcast devoted to jazz in Europe, early in 1959), became an astonishingly good orchestral vehicle. (2) is also made up of trio tracks in which the accent is placed on music with a broader appeal (*The touch of your lips*, *Where or when*, etc.); the surprise is the unaccompanied *Little man you've had a busy day* which is modelled very closely on Art Tatum's singular style. (3) is the second Getz-Hallberg meeting on record, a pairing which again pays dividends handsomely. The continuity between piano and tenor solos sounds almost prearranged although in fact it is the natural outcome of artistic affinity. If the Hallberg and Getz passages were played on the same instrument they would sound like the creative work of one man.

(1) BENGT HALLBERG TRIO – 10 Esq 20-014. (A) 10 Pre PRLP145. *1952.*

(2) BENGT HALLBERG TRIO – 7 Ph BBE12208. (A) 12 Ep 3375. *1956.*

(3) STAN GETZ IN STOCKHOLM – (A) 12 Ver 8213. *1956.*

CHICO HAMILTON (1921) *drums*

After impressing the jazz world at large with his polished brush-work and firm beat (played with the minimum of volume) on Gerry Mulligan's first records, Chico Hamilton decided to form his own band in the summer of 1955. Gathering about him the greatly talented Buddy Collette (who played almost every known type of reed instrument), guitarist Jim Hall, bassist Carson Smith and the non-jazz musician Fred Katz on 'cello, Chico launched the group with (2),

[157]

half of which was recorded 'live' at a club in Long Beach, California. Collette provided most of the memorable moments with his lovely alto tone, his Getz-like tenor, faultless flute and warm clarinet. (3) was recorded in the studio about six months later and while there is a general tightening of the group sound there are also some signs of a *laissez faire* attitude beginning to creep in. The signs become reality with (4), a pale, spineless collection of tunes from *South Pacific*, played with all the guts and drive of a band at a suburban Kardomah café. A much better demonstration of Hamilton's considerable talents as a smooth, swift-moving drummer will be found on (1), ten tracks by an instrumentation comprising Chico, guitarist Howard Roberts (on six tracks), guitarist Jim Hall (on three tracks) and bassist George Duvivier. *Skinned strings* from this LP is a remarkable demonstration of the *rapport* which exists between Hamilton and Duvivier for this is an entirely extemporized bass-drums duet. Had Hamilton retained in his quintet the amount of jazz feeling apparent on (1) there is no reason to doubt that he would still be leading one of the better small groups of the day but the gradual diminution of talent has resulted in a kind of watery 'in-between' music of little value.

(1) CHICO HAMILTON TRIO – 12 Vog LAE12077. (A) 12 WP 1220. *1953, 1954* and *1955.*

(2) CHICO HAMILTON QUINTET – 12 Vog LAE12039. (A) 12 WP 1209. *1955.*

(3) CHICO HAMILTON QUINTET – 12 Vog LAE12045. (A) 12 WP 1216. *1956.*

(4) CHICO HAMILTON QUINTET – 12 Vog LAE12127. (A) 12 WP 1238. *1958.*

LIONEL HAMPTON (1913)   *vibraphone*

The vibraphone had no real identity in jazz until Lionel Hampton came along. Red Norvo was already playing the xylophone, but it was Hampton who transformed the more resonant vibraphone into an instrument capable of being used for jazz solos. In one way the vibraphone was ideal for Hampton's particular talents. Being percussive it responded to the intensely rhythmic aspect of his playing, while at the same time remaining capable of expressing his most delicate melodic inventions. And Hampton is an artist in whom these two aspects – the rhythmic and the melodic, the exuberant and the sensitive – are curiously joined. He can, without any apparent sense of incongruity, move from the brashest piece of riffing, with his band roaring behind him, and without a pause begin creating a fragile, intensely subtle improvisation.

The earliest Hampton solos are found on recordings by the Benny Goodman Quartet and Sextet made between 1936 and 1940. But all the time he was working for Goodman, Hampton was also making a series of remarkable record sessions under his own name, drawing both upon soloists from the Goodman band and upon such musicians as Chu Berry, Benny Carter, Cootie Williams, Nat Cole, Johnny Hodges, Ben Webster, Coleman Hawkins, Herschel Evans, Rex Stewart and many others. (1), (2) and (3) contain a selection of tracks from these sessions, including items by all the musicians mentioned above. The level in each case is exceptionally high. *Don't be that way* and *Shufflin' at the Hollywood* also belong to this period, the former, on RCA's GUIDE TO JAZZ, including one of Johnny Hodges most famous solos, the latter on Camden's GREAT JAZZ REEDS, featuring Chu Berry on tenor sax.

The big band which Lionel Hampton formed in 1940 can be heard on (4), a set of fairly rowdy performances, including *Flying home*. Hampton's big band went in for excitement rather than subtlety, but at least it rarely failed to swing. (5) contains tracks made when Hampton was in Paris in 1953, recorded at a party given by the Hot Club of France. A varied group of musicians took part, including Mezz Mezzrow, Jimmy Cleveland and Alix Combelle, but it is Hampton who dominates the LP, being in particularly inspired form. The Vogue issue, incidentally, omits *Blue Panassié*, one of the best tracks, and originally included in an earlier 10 Vog LP, LDE043.

The Apollo Concert on (6) is ostensibly by the Lionel Hampton band. In fact the band only appears on the final track, the rest of the LP being devoted to Hampton playing solos in his most sensitive manner. (7), incidentally, is an EP excerpted from (6). (8) presents Hampton with an Oscar Peterson group, performing fragile, rather chaste versions of *Midnight sun* and *Our love is here to stay*, but doing nothing else very surprising. (9), (10) and (11) are fairly uninhibited tracks, noisy yet genuinely vigorous, by the big band, this time a group very similar to that which toured Britain in 1956. Particularly worthwhile are *Midnight sun* on (9), and the medium-paced, rocking blues, *Pig ears and rice* on (11). (10) is marred by indifferent singing on one side.

Although (12) has been deleted, it is worth searching for, because it contains some of the finest playing that Hampton and Teddy Wilson have committed to record in recent years. *Moonglow* is a model of intimate jazz playing, while Hampton really surpasses himself in the fifteen superb choruses he plays in *I got rhythm*. (13) was made at the same session but is slightly less exciting. Both titles on this EP are included on (15) a fairly all-round collection of tracks made during the late 1950s by both small groups and the big band. (14) exhibits Harry Edison in a fairly spirited mood (he plays particularly well in *Verve blues*), and has graceful solos by Hampton but rather too much piano embroidery by Art Tatum, not always the ideal man to have in an ensemble of this kind.

(1) JIVIN' THE VIBES – 12 Cam CDN129. (A) 12 Cam CAL-402. *1937–9.*

(2) OPEN HOUSE – 12 Cam CDN138. (A) Cam CAL-517. *1937–40.*

(3) LIONEL HAMPTON – 7 RCA RCX1004. *1937–40.*

(4) HAMP'S BOOGIE WOOGIE – 10 Br LA8527. *1942–6.*

(5) JAZZ TIME PARIS – 12 Vog LAE 12034. (A) 12 Con 3502.[1] *1953.*

(6) APOLLO HALL CONCERT – 12 Ph BBL7015 (d). (A) 12 Ep 3190. *1954.*

(7) LIONEL HAMPTON – 7 Ph BBE12017. *1954.*

(8) THE HIGH AND THE MIGHTY – 12 Col 33CX10146. (A) 12 Ver 8117, 8228. *1954.*[1]

(9) LIONEL HAMPTON BIG BAND – 7 Col SEB10025. (A) 12 Ver 8019. *1955.*

(10) BIG BAND, No. 2 – 7 Col SEB10045. (A) 12 Ver 8019. *1955.*

(11) BIG BAND, No. 3 – 7 Col SEB10092. (A) 12 Ver 8019. *1955.*

(12) GENE KRUPA-LIONEL HAMPTON-TEDDY WILSON – 12 Col 33CX-10027 (d). (A) 12 Ver 8066 (d). *1955.*

13) STROLLIN' ALONG – 7 Col SEB10086. *1955.*

[1] NOTE: The selection of titles on (A) Con 3502 differs from that on Vog LAE12034 but does include *Blue Panassié*. (8) consists of tracks taken from both (A) Ver 8117 and 8228.

(14) LIONEL HAMPTON AND HIS GIANTS – 12 Col 33CX10063. (A) 12
    Ver 8170. *1955.*
(15) THE GENIUS OF LIONEL HAMPTON – (A) 12 Ver 8215. *1955.*

WYNONIE HARRIS   *vocal*
A singer in the unabashed tradition of the blues shouters, the
obviously unabashable Wynonie Harris performs with enthusiasm for
his subject matter. He is, in fact, one of the best R & B singers with
a gravel-scored voice to match his compulsive swing.
(1) WYNONIE 'MR. BLUES' HARRIS – 7 Vog EPV1103.

JIMMY HARRISON (1900–31)   *trombone*
During the fifteen years that he played the trombone, Jimmy
Harrison evolved a style which has influenced most of the musicians
who have followed him. It was, in every sense, an act of liberation,
for until then the trombonists – even the best of them, like Kid Ory
and George Brunies – had been restricted to very functional tasks.
Miff Mole had begun to use a softer tone and more subtle phrasing,
but it was left to Harrison – who had listened to Louis Armstrong
in 1922 and been transformed by the experience – really to take the
trombone out of the ensemble and make it as supple and expressive a
solo instrument as the trumpet, clarinet or saxophone. Harrison's
solos are simple, concise and lyrical in mood, performed with a
warm, sensitive tone. He and Dicky Wells probably rank as the
greatest of jazz trombonists. Unhappily, most of the recordings
which contain Harrison's finest solos are no longer available. These
include *St. Louis shuffle* and *Variety stomp* by Fletcher Henderson's
orchestra (10 HMV DLP1066 (*d*)), *The boy in the boat* and *Walk that
thing* by Charlie Johnson's Paradise Band (7 HMV 7EG8131 (*d*)), and
Bugle call rag by the Chocolate Dandies ((A) 12 Fol 2811). It is,
however, worth searching for these, and also for such long-deleted
78s as Chick Webb's *Heebie Jeebies/Soft and sweet* (Br), Fletcher
Henderson's *Fidgety feet* (Br) and the Chocolate Dandies' *Dee blues*
and *Bugle call rag* (Par).

HAMPTON HAWES (1928)   *piano*
Although he may be described, loosely, as a Bud Powell admirer,
Hawes plays a kind of jazz which sounds like a literal translation of

Charlie Parker from alto to keyboard. In addition there are overtones of Oscar Peterson not only in the fast, accurate fingering but also in the relentless drive. Hamp is an expert performer of the blues, irrespective of tempo, and usually includes two or more twelve-bars in his programme. His first twelve-inch LP (2) finds him in typically effervescent form, driving hard on the up-tempos, playing ballads with not too much saccharine in the mixture and bringing to the blues an admixture of nervous tension and deep-seated sincerity. (3) and (4) are almost as good although the playing tends to lack the same feeling of urgency in places. (5) – which is actually three separate LPs – was made in one night and shows a remarkably high standard throughout the course of the one hundred and fourteen minutes combined playing time. Guitarist Jim Hall gets in some telling statements and there are few bass and drum passages thrown in to disrupt the piano and guitar work. Although made under unsuitable conditions (a noisy crowd and low-fidelity recording) (1) has been included on the strength of *All the things you are*, a piano and trumpet (Shorty Rogers) duet aided by bass and drums. Hawes' firm resolution of ideas, brittle touch and extrovert swing are punched home by Shelly Manne's drums and the in-person atmosphere actually helps in the creation of some good jazz.

(1) HOWARD RUMSEY'S LIGHTHOUSE ALL STARS – 12 Vog LAC12120. (A) 12 Con C3508. *1953*.
(2) HAMPTON HAWES TRIO – 12 Vog LAC12056. (A) 12 Con C3505. *1955*.
(3) HAMPTON HAWES TRIO – 12 Vog LAC12081. (A) 12 Con C3515. *1955–6*.
(4) HAMPTON HAWES TRIO – 12 Vog LAC12091. (A) 12 Con C3523. *1956*.
(5) ALL NIGHT SESSION – 12 Vog LAC12161, LAC12162 and LAC12091. (A) 12 Con C3545, C3546 and C3547. *1958*.

COLEMAN HAWKINS (1904)   *tenor saxophone*

Most people still look upon the saxophone as being somehow symbolic of jazz. 'The wailing of muted saxophones,' in fact, was more than just a gaffe by a novelist of the Jazz Age, those years when women mislaid their waistlines and Royalty played the drums. Sometimes wailing, certainly never muted, the saxophone crept into jazz during the rose-coloured 1920s and grew up with that decade. Without any tradition to act as guide, however, the instrument lacked soloists at a time when the trumpet and clarinet, for instance, had many virtuosi. Johnny Hodges and Benny Carter eventually gave the alto saxophone a lyrical grace, while the soprano became a vehicle for Sidney Bechet's aggressive genius. But it was Coleman Hawkins who took up the tenor – the unwieldliest of the three – and gave it a real status in jazz. Up to that time the instrument – shallow-toned and rather sluggish – had been used only for adding sentimental trimmings. Hawkins endowed it with shape and colour, and in the process he also created a generation of young soloists, among them Ben Webster, Chu Berry and Herschel Evans, all of whom copied his approach.

Coleman Hawkins himself denies that he was the first man to play jazz on the tenor sax ('There was Happy Cauldwell in Chicago and Stomp Evans out of Kansas City. They were playing like mad'), but he does admit his playing had uniqueness. Not at first, though. His early solos with Fletcher Henderson's orchestra (he joined the band in 1922) were awkward and uncertain. Three or four years had to pass before a distinct musical personality began to emerge. By 1927, however, his style was becoming defined, and records such as *Fidgety feet*, *Clarinet marmalade* and *Sensation* (all on deleted Br 78s) contain solos which are recognizably his work. In 1929, when he recorded *Hello Lola* and *One hour* with Red McKenzie's Mound City Blue Blowers (GREAT JAZZ REEDS; 12 Cam CDN-139. (A) 12 Cam CAL-339), Hawkins was already a mature soloist. *Hello Lola* has a few traces of the slap-tonguing and staccato phrasing so fashionable with saxophonists during the 1920s, but there is also a new boldness, the solo swings powerfully all the time it is unfolding; it is alert, poised against the beat. The rhapsodic manner, however, has probably been Hawkins' most individual contribution to jazz improvisation and *One hour* is a masterpiece of this genre, a careful exploration of mood as well as theme. Other good solos from the same period can be found in Fletcher Henderson's *Sugar foot stomp* (one of the best versions is included in 'Guide to Jazz', (A) 12 RCA LPM1393; another is on a deleted Br 78) and *Just blues* ('Harlem Jazz', 10 Br LA8565 (d)).

It is probable that Coleman Hawkins reached the zenith of his artistry – or at least the first fine blossoming of it – between the autumn of 1932 and his departure for Europe in the spring of 1934. At this point his music was exquisitely balanced, a perfect blend of the lyrical and the dramatic. To this period belong his solos on the Spike Hughes recordings (12 Dec LK4173), solos which rank among his very finest work, especially those in *Sweet sorrow blues*, *Arabesque*, *Nocturne* and *Donegal cradle song*. During that year Hawkins also recorded *It's the talk of the town* and *I've got to sing a torch song*, both featuring his tenor playing at some length, with Fletcher Henderson's orchestra (7 Col SEG7630 (*d*)). These performances stem logically from *One hour*, with the technique taken a stage further; both are sensuous in texture, extremely romantic in atmosphere. Around this time Hawkins also made some Br 78s (long deleted) as co-leader of a group known as 'Henry Allen-Coleman Hawkins and their orchestra'. *Dark clouds* and *You're gonna lose your gal* contain particularly turbulent playing. Equally worthwhile, although more meditative in character, is Hawkin's work in *Heartbreak blues*, on Par 78 (*d*), by a group under his sole leadership. Hawkins spent five years in Europe altogether, from 1934 until 1939, and during that period he made a fairly large number of records, although mostly in the company of inferior musicians. Some of the finest were recorded with The Ramblers, a Dutch orchestra; these included *Chicago*, *Meditation*, *Netcha's dream* and – a splendid example of Hawkins at his opulent best – *A strange fact*. All were originally released on Dec 78s and have not been reissued. (1) contains a rather patchy version of *Stardust*, made in France in 1935, with the tenor player accompanied by Django Reinhardt and Stephane Grappelly, the latter playing the piano. *Crazy rhythm* and *Honeysuckle rose*, however, two of the finest recordings of Hawkins' entire career, are included in both (1) and (2). Benny Carter wrote arrangements for the quartet of saxophones (the other two were played by Frenchmen, André Ekyan and Alix Combelle) and he and Hawkins take solos of exceptional quality. Four months later Hawkins performed as a guest soloist with a group drawn from Benny Carter's orchestra (one he was then leading in Holland) on four titles recorded in Amsterdam, taking an outstanding solo in *My buddy* (Voc 78 (*d*)). By now a new element was perceptible in Hawkin's style. Just as big bands were beginning to lean more and more heavily upon riffs (influenced, no doubt, by the vigorous

[164]

example of Count Basie's orchestra), so Hawkins set out to get similar rhythmic effects – mostly in the faster numbers – by the reiteration of short, insistent phrases. The choppier melodic line produced by this method was more dramatic in impact, but it also meant that a solo lost some of its wider proportions.

When Coleman Hawkins returned to the United States it was to find that he now had a rival – Lester Young, a tenor player whose pale tone and oblique, angular phrasing represented the antithesis of Hawkins' approach. Not at all daunted, however, Hawkins proceeded to make his most famous recording, *Body and soul* (1), a solo performance that exerted a great influence upon his fellow musicians. Other good solos from this period include those in *The Sheik of Araby* (1) and *My blue heaven* (on RCA's GUIDE TO JAZZ). Throughout the first half of the 1940s Hawkins continued to work with musicians of the swing period, and those years saw him record such fine performances as *How deep is the ocean* (on ENCYCLOPAEDIA OF JAZZ, Vol. 3) and *Blue changes* ((A) Coral's STORY OF JAZZ), as well as *Make believe* and *On the sunny side of the street* (Mer MMB12013, REEDS THAT MATTER), two of his finest solos, the latter track also including solos by Tab Smith, Don Byas and Harry Carney. More good playing by Hawkins can be found in *Just one more chance* (and other tracks from the same session) by The Jazz Giants (actually a group under the leadership of Cozy Cole) on 10 EmA EJT751 (d). (It should be noted that on this LP the tracks by The Jazz Giants have suffered from editing, so that several solos by Joe Thomas and Trummy Young are missing. Collectors are advised to look for the original 78s.)

In 1944 Hawkins started using modern jazz musicians, both in his regular group (Thelonious Monk was one musician who worked for him) and on record sessions. His own playing also began to incorporate certain elements of modern jazz phrasing, not so much in the structure of the solos as in their details. It was not a radical change, for Hawkins' harmonic instinct, always keen, had been well ahead of his period, while his actual style of playing – the way he laid short phrases next to long ones, even some of his accenting – had a certain amount in common with Charlie Parker's. *Stuffy* (on Capitol's HISTORY OF JAZZ, Vol. 4), recorded with a group that included Howard McGhee and Sir Charles Thompson, is a good example of

[165]

Hawkins' work at this time. So are (4), on which he plays alongside Miles Davis, Kai Winding and Hank Jones, and (3), where his group included Fats Navarro, J. J. Johnson, Milt Jackson, Max Roach and (once again) Hank Jones. The best tracks on the latter EP, however, are Hawkins' solo features, *You go to my head* and *Cocktails for two*, both ravishing performances. One of Hawkins' more unconventional recordings, the unaccompanied solo, *Picasso*, was made in 1948 for Norman Granz's albums, THE JAZZ SCENE. The following year Hawkins returned to Europe, where he recorded (5), an EP containing a splendidly lyrical version of *Sophisticated lady*. (A fine slow blues, *Bean's talking again*, also made at this session, was only issued in France.) *Platinum love* and *There's a small hotel* (both on ANATOMY OF IMPROVISATION), both very concise performances, were made by a group containing that fine pianist, Al Haig.

The first half of the 1950s was, to a large extent, a period when Hawkins suffered neglect, his style of playing thoroughly out of fashion. The few LPs he made during those years feature him in gushing solos, accompanied by strings or some other unsuitable background. On (6), however, a very mixed set of tracks, the majority of them rhapsodic but uninspired, there are two adventurous performances of *I can't get started* and *If I could be with you* (the same tune as *One hour*). Not until (7), in fact, was an LP properly devoted to Hawkins' playing, and on this his work ranges from rhapsodic solos (*Think deep* and *Laura*) to tracks like *Juicy fruit* and *Sanctity*, where Hawkins sounds even grittier than the hardest of the neo-bop school of tenor players. Taken as a whole, this is an exceptionally rewarding LP, with Hawkins handsomely supported by J. J. Johnson, Hank Jones and the trumpeter, Idrees Sulieman. (8) presents the tenor player in an amiable but rather desultory set of performances, nearly all of them solos on 'standards'. On (9) Hawkins and Ben Webster can be heard playing together, an exciting and audacious partnership. Hawkins has the harder sound, the more garrulous style, but as far as inspiration goes there is little to choose between the two musicians. Apart from the rather brash *Blues for Yolande*, all these tracks are rewarding. More highly inventive playing by Hawkins is contained in (10), an LP recorded by the British jazz critic, Stanley Dance, on which Hawkins performs with a group that includes Buck Clayton and Hank Jones. All the tracks are good, especially the 11-minute

[166]

Bird of prey blues, with its seventeen full-blooded tenor choruses. About this time Hawkins also recorded a session with a group led by the guitarist Tiny Grimes ('Blues Groove', 12 Esq 32-082, (A) 12 Pre 7138). Even some rather epicene flute playing cannot destroy the robustness which Hawkins lends this record. (11) was also made with Tiny Grimes, this time under Hawkins' name and with Charlie Shavers on the session. Once again it demonstrates how Hawkins is currently bringing a singular hardness and explosiveness to his playing. It acts as a further reminder that he is really the progenitor of such *avant-garde* tenor players as Sonny Rollins and John Coltrane, musicians noted for their muscular, rather beefy eloquence. To hear Hawkins actually playing alongside Coltrane, as he does in 'Monk's Music', (A) 12 Riv RLP12-242, by the Thelonious Monk Septet, is an intriguing experience, rather like watching Jack Hobbs batting with Peter May.

(1) COLEMAN HAWKINS ALL STARS – 10 HMV DLP1055 (*d*). *1935–46*.

(2) COLEMAN HAWKINS ALL STARS – 7 HMV 7EG8393. *1937*.

(3) BEAN AND THE BOYS – 7 Esq EP192. *1946*.

(4) COLEMAN HAWKINS – 7 Vog EPV1147. *1947*.

(5) COLEMAN HAWKINS – 7 Vog EPV1021. *1948*.

(6) THE HAWK TALKS – 12 Br LAT8242. (A) Dec 8127. *1952–3*.

(7) THE HAWK FLIES HIGH – 12 Lon LTZ-U15117 (*d*). (A) 12 Riv 12-233. *1957*.

(8) THE GENIUS OF COLEMAN HAWKINS – 12 HMV CLP1293. (A) 12 Ver 8261. *1957*.

(9) BLUE SAXOPHONES – 12 Col 33CX10143. (A) 12 Ver 8327, (S) 6066. *1957*.

(10) THE HIGH AND MIGHTY HAWK – 12 Fel FAJ7005, SJA2005. (A) 12 Fel 7005. SJA2005. *1958*.

(11) HAWK EYES – 12 Esq 32-102. (A) 12 Pres 7156, (S) S7156. *1959*.

FLETCHER HENDERSON (1898–1952)

piano, arranger, bandleader

It is sad that so few recordings by Fletcher Henderson's orchestra are now available (there is no complete LP or EP still in the current catalogues), for this band not only created a body of fine music but it also played an important role in jazz history. It was the first of the big bands, a link between the three-part improvising of the New Orleans

[167]

groups and the sections of five brass and four reeds playing from written arrangements. Most of the early orchestrations which the Henderson band performed were the work of Don Redman (who played alto sax in the band), and they exploited the antiphonal 'call-and-response' pattern, a device very common in Negro gospel singing, a device, in fact, going right back to African tribal music. There was, oddly enough, considering Redman's later compositions, little attempt at creating tone-colouring, apart from frequent passages scored for a trio of clarinets. It was this pattern of scoring which Henderson developed during the 1930s (he did not start writing himself until 1933) and which he used in his arrangements for the Benny Goodman band, arrangements which set the style of most of the 'swing bands' of the late 1930s.

The earliest tracks on (1) are of little more than academic interest, the orchestrations little different from those used by commercial white bands of the period, the solos (apart from Charlie Green's robust trombone playing) diffuse and faltering. *Mandy make up your mind* (1), *Copenhagen* and *Money blues* (on (A) 12 Fol Jazz, 2807/8), however, all contain solos by Louis Armstrong, who was then working with the band in New York, solos that stand out from the period background with remarkable clarity, sounding as fresh as if they had been played yesterday. By 1926 the scores were taking on crispness and a more formal structure; by comparison with most of the tracks on (1), in fact, *St. Louis Shuffle* and *Variety stomp* (2) represent a great advance. These two recordings also contain a couple of the finest solos ever recorded by Jimmy Harrison, one of the greatest trombonists in jazz. Harrison is discussed more fully elsewhere, as are Joe Smith and Tommy Ladnier, the other outstanding soloists in the band at this time. Unhappily many of Henderson's finest performances of the late 1920s, records such as *Hot mustard*, *The stampede*, *Clarinet marmalade*, *Fidgety feet* (this has a superb Jimmy Harrison solo), *Snag it* and *Livery stable blues*, have not been reissued and can only obtained by searching for the 78 releases (all of them deleted years ago). Most of these items contain outstanding solos by Ladnier, Smith and Harrison.

Around 1930 the Henderson band began to undergo frequent changes in personnel. Ladnier and Smith were replaced by Rex Stewart and Bobby Stark, and later on Henry Allen took over from

Rex. A succession of trombonists moved in and out of the band –
Benny Morton, Claude Jones, J. C. Higginbotham, Sandy Williams,
Dicky Wells. Things were more settled in the reed section, even
though the lead alto chair seemed to be filled in turn by Benny
Carter and Hilton Jefferson. Buster Bailey was still there; he had been
there, in fact, ever since 1924, while Coleman Hawkins had joined
Henderson a year before that. Hawkins had now attained artistic
maturity and his work between 1930 and 1933 (when he left to go to
Europe) – probably his greatest period – revealed a consistently high
level of inspiration. The solo which climaxes the 1931 *Sugar foot
stomp* (RCA's GUIDE TO JAZZ) is a good example of his playing at this
time, beautifully poised, dramatic and yet highly lyrical. Another
notable solo can be found in *Just blues* (HARLEM JAZZ (*d*)), while two
of his earliest essays into rhapsodic, very sensuous improvising are
included in (3) – *I've got to sing a torch song* and *It's the talk of the
town*.

Although (4) was issued under Horace Henderson's name, the band
is actually that of his brother Fletcher. This EP, as it happens, contains
a fierce solo from Henry Allen (in *Old Man River*) and one of Dicky
Wells' most audacious pieces of improvising (in *Rhythm crazy*). By
now Henderson had begun writing arrangements himself, and two of
his best scores – *Wrappin' it up* and *Down South Camp meetin'* were
included in (5), a set of tracks by the 1934 band. In this band Hawkins
had been replaced by Ben Webster (his first replacement was Lester
Young, who was found to be 'not enough like Hawk'), but Henry
Allen was still in the trumpet section. *Shoe shine boy* (on RCA
RCX-1027), however, is by a later and less interesting band, although
it included such fine sidemen as Chu Berry, Joe Thomas and Roy
Eldridge.

In 1957, as part of the programme at the Great South Bay Festival
on Long Island, a group of ex-Henderson musicians (including
J. C. Higginbotham, Benny Morton, Dicky Wells, Coleman
Hawkins, Ben Webster, Emmett Berry and Joe Thomas), under the
leadership of Rex Stewart, performed some of Henderson's old
scores. This band – The Henderson All Stars – later went into a
recording studio, with the result that 'Cool Fever', the name given to
this set of re-creations, has been released on (A) 12 Ur UJ1212,
USD2012. While it is never possible to recapture the genuine

[169]

excitement of the past, these performances are quite creditable, with some good solos and enthusiastic (if sometimes shaky) ensemble work.

(1) BIRTH OF BIG BAND JAZZ – 10 Lon AL3547 (d). *1923–8.*

(2) FLETCHER HENDERSON AND HIS CONNIE'S INN ORCHESTRA – 10 HMV DLP1066 (d). *1927–33.*

(3) FLETCHER HENDERSON AND HIS ORCHESTRA – 7 Col SEG7630 (d). *1933.*

(4) HORACE HENDERSON ORCHESTRA – 7 Par GEP8614 (d). *1933.*

(5) MEMORIAL ALBUM – (A) 10 Dec DL6025 (d). *1934.*

WOODY HERMAN (1913)   *clarinet, alto*

Commencing his band-leading career fairly innocuously, Herman took over the Isham Jones unit before the war and featured some pleasant music under the by-line 'The band that plays the blues'. A combination of circumstances (the parallel developments of Parker and Gillespie, the coincidental assembling of a personnel in which youth and spirit were the watchwords, and an indefinable quality which seemed to spell success from the start) created a Herman-led band during the late war years which was to become known in later years as the First Herd. For sheer excitement this orchestra ranks second only to the later Dizzy Gillespie group. Dave Tough was on drums, adding fuel to a fire already stoked into glowing white heat by the whip-cracking trumpet section. Tough was one of the truly great jazz drummers, an adaptable musician capable of fitting in with the styles of Dixieland bands, Chicago outfits, large orchestras and the *avant-garde* music of Charlie Parker. It is Dave who may be heard punching home the brass figures on *Caldonia* ((1) and (2)) and churning up a great surging beat behind Flip Phillips and the ensemble on *The good earth* ((1) and (2)). His death in 1945 brought in another fine percussionist, in fact one of the most accomplished big band drummers in jazz, Don Lamond. Lamond's vitality and distinctive 'bomb dropping' became a unifying feature of subsequent Herman Herds up until 1949 when he left to join Harry James. Herman's five trumpets (Sonny Berman, Conrad Gozzo, Shorty Rogers, Pete Candoli and Cappy Lewis), his distinctive trombone soloist Bill Harris and warm-toned, inventive tenor saxist Flip Phillips all added their considerable weight to make up a band which is still looked upon as a high-water mark in Woody's career. With Ralph Burns writing ambitious, extended works such as *Summer sequence* and *Lady McGowan's dream* (1) the Herd went from strength to strength until it disbanded at the beginning of 1947. Six months later Herman was preparing another fine band, this time with a very high percentage of soloists (Stan Getz, Zoot Sims, Serge Chaloff, Herbie Steward, Shorty Rogers, Ernie Royal, etc.). Three tracks by this powerful Second Herd will be found on (2) including the famous Jimmy Giuffre composition *Four brothers* which became a term of identification for the post-Lester Young style of tenor playing adopted by Woody's reed soloists. (3) presents fundamentally the same personnel in a well-balanced programme ranging from the exquisite *Early Autumn* (containing one of Stan Getz's best and most famous solos) to the frantic, scat-sung *Lemondrop* by way of an engaging *Tenderly* – played in 3/4 time – and the roaring *More moon* featuring Gene Ammons on tenor. Always a nursery for new jazz talent, Herman's bands have been noteworthy for soloists whose styles reflect the contemporary development trends. (4) consists of tracks recorded originally for Herman's own Mars label by the Third Herd, a unit containing Bill Perkins and Arno Marsh on tenors, Urbie Green and Carl Fontana, trombones, and the talented Nat Pierce on piano. Much of the earlier Herds' spirit is recaptured in the swinging *Stompin' at the Savoy* and *Blue Lou*. Woody himself, whose reedy clarinet and sugary, Hodges-like alto style have remained unchanged throughout the history of his famous bands, has continued to feature himself in the role of vocalist on occasional Louis Jordan-type rhythm and blues numbers. (5) brings to the fore some new soloists in the persons of Richie Kamuca on tenor and the Chicago-born Cy Touff on bass trumpet. Horace Silver's *Opus de funk* is presented in orchestral form and there is a sprightly *Cool cat on a hot tin roof* with Woody bounding in on clarinet, riding on top of the opening riff. (6) is a very successful studio re-creation of some earlier Herman hits by a band containing a high percentage of ex-Woody sidemen. Al Cohn is responsible for most of the tenor solos and there is a memorable *Caldonia* with an addition made to the well-known lip-searing trumpet passage. Bob Brookmeyer was given the unenviable task of creating the trombone solo on *Bijou* and succeeds in turning in an exemplary chorus which is in no way a copy of the earlier Bill Harris version. Subsequent Herman bands have been short-lived and it is unfortunate that the outstanding Anglo-American Herd – with its superb all-British sax section – which toured Britain at the beginning of 1959 made no records.

(1) SUMMER SEQUENCE – 10 Fon TFR6015. (A) 12 Harmony 7093. *1945–7.*

(2) THE THREE HERDS – 12 Ph BBL7123. (A) 12 Col CL592. *1945–7, 1953* and *1954.*

(3) WOODY HERMAN – (A) 12 Cap T324. Eight titles on 10 Cap LC6560, remainder on 7 Cap EAP1026. *1948–50.*

(4) MEN FROM MARS – (A) 12 Ver 8216. Some titles on 10 Lon H-APB1014 and H-APB1018. *1952–4.*

(5) ROAD BAND – (A) 12 Cap T658. Issued in Britain as three 7 EPs: Cap EAP1009, EAP 2-658 and EAP3-658. *1955.*

(6) THE HERD RIDES AGAIN – 12 TR 35/038. (A) 12 Everest 5003. *1958.*

EDDIE HEYWOOD (1914)   *piano*

Heywood is a real mainstreamer of jazz piano, falling somewhere between the Hines-Wilson school and the art of Tatumery. A fine, swinging pianist with technique to spare and enough tricks of his own to have a really recognizable style. After playing with Benny Carter he started forming his own small groups. His recordings of the 1944 period include some really unusual and fine solos in sides made with great jazzmen like Hodges, Nance, Byas, Hawkins, Manne, Dickenson and others. Some of these are collected on (1). A growing sophistication is noted on 1945 sides made for American Decca (2), (3). Just as he was becoming really well known he had to retire from music with paralysis of the hands. In 1950 he was able to start playing again and made a number of commercial albums which are by no means all jazz but are worth listening to, particularly (8) which shows just how worthwhile some good rhythm and jazz feeling can make an LP which primarily sets out to be good music.

(1) FEATURING EDDIE HEYWOOD – (A) 12 Cor 57095. *1943–4.*

(2) LIGHTLY AND POLITELY – (A) 12 Dec 8202. *1945.*

(3) SWING LOW SWEET HEYWOOD – (A) 12 Dec 8270. *1945–6.*

(4) PIANORAME – (A) 12 MGM 3093.

[172]

(5) EDDIE HEYWOOD – (A) 12 MGM 3260.
(6) EDDIE HEYWOOD – (A) 12 EmA 36042.
(7) THE TOUCH OF EDDIE HEYWOOD – (A) 12 Vic LMP-1466.
(8) CANADIAN SUNSET – 12 RCA RD-27041. (A) 12 Vic LPM-15299.
(9) THE KEYS AND I – (A) 12 Vic LPM-1900.
(10) EDDIE HEYWOOD AT TWILIGHT – (A) Ep LN-3327.
(11) BREEZIN' ALONG WITH THE BREEZE – (A) 12 Mer MG20445.
1959.

J. C. HIGGINBOTHAM (1906)   *trombone*

A once progressive musician who did much to change jazz trombone playing but who now tends to be a forgotten man of jazz. It was remarkable to hear how his long, flowing phrases, and powerful, swinging tone altered a band like King Oliver's when he replaced Ory on some of the recordings made in 1928. While he was with Luis Russell from 1929–31 he recorded two classic sides under his own name *Give me your telephone number* and *Higginbotham's blues* (available on a long-deleted Par 78 R2799), the latter being really worth having, if a copy can be discovered. Later recordings with Red Allen show him at a peak in his career. He demonstrated a remarkable flexibility, rather as Armstrong does on trumpet, without any loss of power or majestic serenity. His recent recordings with Allen and others show absolutely no trace of the creative genius of his great days.

BERTHA CHIPPIE HILL (1905–50)   *vocal*

If it were only for her recording, with Louis Armstrong and Richard M. Jones, of *Trouble in mind* (Chicago, 1926), Chippie Hill deserves all the recognition which has lately been granted to her work. A contemporary of Bessie Smith, she was a more attacking singer than Bessie, shocking with the bite of her delivery, rather than thrilling with her beauty of voice. After disappearing for some fifteen years, she was recorded again in 1946 and was getting regular work as a singer when she was killed by an automobile in New York. Her last session, in April 1946, is notable for the fine piano accompaniment by Montana Taylor, and the revitalization of her singing.

(1) THE GREAT BLUES SINGERS – 10 Lon AL3530 (*d*). *1927–46.*

EARL HINES (1905)   *piano, vocal*

Both in terms of his own achievement and of influence, without regard to styles and periods, Earl Hines is one of the greatest, probably *the* greatest of all jazz pianists. His style comes from the Harlem school. He added to it a new power and a new dimension. He broke away from the mathematical phrasing that had been inherited from rag-time, the regularity of the blues – the piano being an old-established instrument tended to be least progressive in jazz styling in the early bands. Instead he began to phrase like a trumpet or clarinet, a flexible, flowing style, he even introduced an artificial vibrato such as a wind instrument naturally has because he sensed that a controlled vibrato can itself give rhythm to a single note. He used the whole range of the piano more often, constantly varying tone, volume, pitch and rhythm. Think back to his solo on Armstrong's *West End blues*. How many other pianists at that time were using such a graceful, delicate and intricate approach to piano playing. It is hard to realize now just how great the influence of Hines has been.

Of all jazz artists it is true to say that recordings give only a partial idea of their work, but it seems particularly true of Hines. Not a single record he has made gives any idea of his playing in the flesh, its monumental strength and its flexibility, and the constant stream of improvisation, for less than almost any other pianist does he rely on a set routine.

His 1928 solos made for the QRS label have always been talked of but they have very rarely been available except on some Hot Record Society 78s. Usually our first taste of Hines as a soloist is on his OKeh recordings of *Caution blues*, *A Monday date*, *57 varieties* and *I ain't got nobody*, all available on (1) together with a number of later tracks.

For the next few years Hines appeared on record with his orchestra which he led for twelve years at the Grand Terrace Club in Chicago from 1928. The only track from these early days is *Grand piano blues* on Great Jazz Pianists (12 Cam CDN-118, (A) 12 Cam CAL-328) recorded in 1929. A series of recordings for American Decca included some excellent sides like *Maple Leaf rag*, *Sweet Georgia Brown* and *Japanese sandman* (on deleted Brunswick 78s, 01928, 01995, 02131 and 02286). From the 1939–40 period came exhilarating sides like *Piano man*, *Father steps in* and *Grand Terrace shuffle* on a now deleted HMV 10 DLP1132.

[174]

Some 1946 sides on (2) and (3) are not up to the standard of the Victor recordings for the band plays in an idiom which doesn't entirely complement Hines' own work. Nevertheless there is a great deal of excitement in these tracks. Four sides made in 1947–8 are available on (4) where Hines plays with a fine swinging quartet. Some are also on (5). Four solo sides, *Fine and dandy, Honeysuckle rose, Snappy rhythm* and *Boogie Woogie on St. Louis blues*, made in Paris in 1949 (6), are good tracks but fail to convey quite all of Hines' powers. Better are a number of sides that may be found on Esquire 78s made between 1949 and 1950 for the French Royal Jazz label.

Hines at his best is to be heard on a series of American Columbia recordings (1) made one Monday morning in 1950. These are all gems – *Rosetta, When I dream of you, You can depend on me, Diane, Velvet moon, I hadn't anyone 'till you, These foolish things, Deed I do*, together with the earlier sides make up a record that anyone interested in jazz piano should have.

Two more sessions of light-hearted music get nearer to the real Hines. The first on which he plays Fats Waller numbers (9), is a highly enjoyable affair full of good melody. The next (11) gets down to some work with a mixed bag of popular songs. The nearest to a life-size Hines performance, however, is to be found on (12), one of the finest piano records to have been issued in recent years. Here Hines is given time to work up to a climax in which his terrific power, subtlety and technique are fully illustrated.

(1) EARL 'FATHA' HINES – 12 Ph BBL7185. (A) 12 Fan 3238. *1928–50.*

(2) OH FATHER – (A) 12 Ep LN-3223. *1933–8.*

(3) EARL HINES AND HIS ORCHESTRA – 7 Vog EPV1050. *1946.*

(4) EARL HINES AND HIS ORCHESTRA – 7 Vog EPV1059. *1946.*

(5) MIDNIGHT IN NEW ORLEANS – 7 MGM EP-573 (*d*). *1947–8.*

(6) EARL HINES QUINTET – 7 Vog EPV1144. *1949.*

(7) EARL HINES TRIO – 7 Vog EPV1160. *1949.*

(8) THE INCOMPARABLE EARL 'FATHA' HINES – 12 Gal GLP316. *1953.*

(9) EARL HINES PLAYS FATS WALLER – 12 Vog LAE12067. (A) 12 Fan 3217. *1955–6.*

(10) EARL 'FATHA' HINES SOLOS – (A) 12 Fan 3238. *1955.*

(11) PARIS ONE NIGHT STAND – 12 Ph BBL7222. (A) 12 Ep LN-3501. *1957.*

(12) EARL'S BACKROOM (also Cozy Cole) – 12 Fel FAJ7002, (S)
SJA7002. *1958*.
(13) EARL HINES HIS PIANO AND ORCHESTRA – 7 Par GEP8563 (*d*).
1953.

ART HODES (1904) *piano*

A white musician who has managed to avoid the tendency of
many white pianists to play a cocktail kind of jazz to replace the
natural vigour and swing of Negro jazz. Instead he went to the sources
of jazz and steeped himself in the blues. The result is that his recordings
are replete with the Negroid feeling, a sad, lugubrious, rolling sort of
music in which Hodes himself sets the atmosphere and mood, doing
nothing particularly imaginative or original, but keeping emotional
control of the music. There is rarely anything frivolous about a
Hodes session. One of his best-known recordings is *Georgia cakewalk*
made in 1942, a bright Dixieland performance in no way typical of
his work (on Br INTRODUCTION TO JAZZ). A curious but moving
series of recordings for Blue Note (1) and (2) are all collectors' items.
One of the most interesting tracks is *Blues 'n' booze* (1) which features
Max Kaminsky in an unusually ferocious mood.
(1) ART HODES' BACK ROOM BOYS – 10 Vog LDE174. (A) 10
BN BLP7021 (*d*). *1944–5*.
(2) ART HODES' BLUE NOTE JAZZ MEN – 7 Vog EPV1087. *1945*.
(3) CHICAGO JAZZ STYLE – (A) 12 Mer 20185.

JOHNNY HODGES (1907) *alto saxophone*

Whether heard on records or in the flesh, Johnny Hodges always
conveys a sense of infallibility. Institutions like the Bank of England
or the Rock of Gibraltar seem brittle by comparison. Hodges
continues to play just as he did when he joined the Duke Ellington
orchestra in 1928, creating the same kind of rococo patterns, although
perhaps with a softer, more ingratiating tone. One can criticize
certain aspects of his performances – his fondness for slithery, rather
sentimental solo features, or the blandness that has crept into his
playing during the past decade – but his stature remains unchallenge-
able. Hodges, in fact, is one of the great jazz musicians, an easy,
graceful soloist who has never been known to sacrifice his purity of
tone and line for cheap emotional fervour. He is also, as it happens,

[176]

one of the very few saxophonists to be directly influenced by Sidney Bechet; he and Bechet share in common a fondness for long, flowing melodic lines, for the same kind of ornamental cadences. During his thirty-two years – on and off – with the Ellington orchestra, Hodges has contributed many solos to its recordings, too many to be dealt with here in any detail. It is worth pointing out, though, that among the recordings currently available there are outstanding Hodges solos to be found in *Cotton Club stomp* and *Saratoga swing* (12 Cam CDN119, (A) 12 Cam 459), *Hyde Park* (7 Dec DFE6376), *The gal from Joe's*, *Gypsy without a song* and *Portrait of a lion* (10 HMV DLP1172), and *Hy'a Sue* (12 Ph BBR8044).

In 1938 Johnny Hodges began recording with his own small group, normally using musicians from the Ellington band. It is this group which can be heard on (1) and (2). The trouble about (1) is that every track has a vocal chorus and none is worth hearing. In complete contrast, (2) contains a couple of classic jazz performances in *Krum elbow blues* (with splendid, snarling trumpet from Cootie Williams) and *Jeep's blues*, a number Hodges still features today. On *Rent party blues*, incidentally, Hodges plays the soprano saxophone, keeping a firm grip upon that skittish instrument. The various Hodges-led groups on a Philips and two (A) Ver LPs ELLINGTON SIDEMEN also belong to this period. *Prelude to a kiss* becomes a little gooey but the other tracks are all worthwhile, particularly the ebullient *The jeep is jumping*. Three more of the small-band tracks, *Queen Bess*, *Squatty Roo* and *Things ain't what they used to be*, are included in GREAT ELLINGTON SOLOISTS (10 HMV DLP1025 (d)), all of them outstandingly good. *On the sunny side of the street* on (A) Coral's STORY OF JAZZ, is actually by the Eddie Heywood Trio (in this case Hodges, Heywood and Shelly Manne), recorded in 1944, one of the very many versions Hodges has made of this tune. (3) reflects the changes which had taken place in the Ellington band during the 1940s. Taft Jordan plays trumpet on one side, Harold Baker on the other. This is good but not at all remarkable music. (4) and (5) were made while the Ellington band was in Paris in 1950; (5) including the double-length *Last legs blues*.

(6) to (9) all belong to a period when Johnny Hodges was leading a regular band of his own, during his longest absence from the Ellington orchestra. This band included, at various times, such

[177]

valuable talents as Emmett Berry, Lawrence Brown, Ben Webster and Harold Baker. Hodges could never shake off his Ellington background, however, and most of these performances have their share of Ellington harmonies or voicing, while the best ones are generally of tunes associated with the Ellington band. That is why (9) is outstanding, although the level of the others is very high. (10) was recorded after Hodges' return to the Ellington orchestra; the full band, in fact, can be heard throughout one side, while the other tracks – the best ones, actually – are played by a small group. Outstanding are the relaxed, twelve-minute *Texas blues* and Billy Strayhorn's intriguing tune, *Snibor*. Both Clark Terry and Ray Nance play trumpets (the latter violin as well) on (11), another small-group recording. The only poor track here is a rather arty *Ballade for very sad and very tired lotus eaters*, but this is compensated for by a fresh-sounding version of *Take the 'A' Train* and an interesting, if slightly academic, performance of *Black and tan fantasy*, with Clark Terry taking the famous solo. (12) has Hodges leading the full Ellington band (except for Ellington himself) through a set of arrangements which recall the pre-war years (*Waiting for Duke*, for instance, has many echoes of *The gal from Joe's*). This LP, in fact, is rather more nostalgic than the others, and also suffers from some over-sugary playing by Hodges on *Bouquet (of roses)*. (13) has Hodges and Duke Ellington performing in the company of non-Ellington musicians (including Harry Edison and Jo Jones). The material is a collection of blues of varying tinges and bar-lengths. On the first side Hodges sounds too bland to be true (although Ellington contributes some vinegary piano solos) but the two men make their version of *Weary blues* into a minor jazz classic, while *St. Louis blues* is nearly as good.

Johnny Hodges has recorded comparatively little away from the Ellington orchestra or the circle of Ellington musicians. Among the few solos of his which can be found on other records, however, are three exquisite contributions to Lionel Hampton tracks – *Buzzin' around with the bee* (12 Cam CDN129, (A) 12 Cam 402), *On the sunny side of the street* (7 RCA RCX1004) and *Don't be that way* (12 RCA RC24002, (A) 12 RCA LPM1393). A curiosity (well, more than that, for the Hodges solo is handsomely poised) is the 1952 recording of *Funky blues* (12 Col 33CX10008 (d)), on which Hodges, Charlie Parker and Benny Carter all play solos.

[178]

(1) Prelude To A Kiss – 7 HMV 7EG8329. *1938*.
(2) Johnny Hodges – 7 Fon TFE17233. (A) (plus other titles) 12 Ep LN3105. *1938-9*.
(3) Johnny Hodges – 10 Vog LDE011. *1947*.
(4) Johnny Hodges – 7 Vog EPV1018. *1950*.
(5) Johnny Hodges – 7 Vog EPV1079. *1950*.
(6) Meet Mr. Rabbit – 7 Col SEB10105. *1951-2*.
(7) Johnny Hodges – 7 Col SEB10006 (*d*). *1951-2*.
(8) In A Tender Mood – 10 Col 33C9051 (*d*). *1952-4*.
   Most of the tracks on (7) and (8) are on (A) 12 Ver 8149.
(9) Memories of Ellington – 12 Col 33CX10008 (*d*). (A) 12 Ver 8180. *1954*.
(10) Ellingtonia '56 – 12 Col 33CX10055. (A) 12 Ver 8145. *1956*.
(11) Johnny Hodges With The Ellington All Stars – 12 Col 33CX10098. (A) 12 Ver 8203. *1956*.
(12) The Big Sound – 12 Col 33CX10136. (A) 12 Ver 8271. *1957*.
(13) Back to Back – 12 HMV CLP1316. (A) 12 Ver 8317. *1959*.

BILLIE HOLIDAY (1915-59) *singer*

The classic blues reached their consummation in the art of Bessie Smith, achieving in her singing their most highly conscious and dramatic form. Billie Holiday, a girl who grew up during the 1930s, took the cosmopolitan popular songs of her time and moulded them into significance. For Bessie Smith the poetry was already in her songs; Billie Holiday had to create it. She did so by the slant of her voice, the curve of her phrasing. Her method was to reduce the melody of a song to its basic elements, then to reconstruct it, moulding the line to suit her interpretation of the lyric. It was significant that Billie Holiday's favourite accompanist (an accompanist as ideally suited to her as Joe Smith was for Bessie Smith) was Lester Young, for her manner of singing had much in common with his tenor-playing. Both artists were fond of lagging a little behind the beat; both thought the words of a song important (Lester Young believed that a soloist should always know the lyrics of the ballad he was playing). In her singing Billie Holiday was an intuitive performer, guided by the logic of emotion, and in that fact lay the hazards of her art. Where singers like Ella Fitzgerald and Sarah Vaughan can nearly always be sure of giving a reasonably good performance, precisely

[179]

because their approach is partly formal, Billie Holiday, when her inspiration failed her, had to fall back on mannerisms. This, and the fact that her voice deteriorated sadly as the years went by, made much of her latter-day work distressing to hear. For it was never possible, even on her worst recordings, to listen to Billie Holiday with detachment. She always sounded a completely alive woman, her voice trapped between tenderness and pain.

Because her art was so intimate, Billie Holiday sang at her best in the company of a small jazz group. This was the kind of backing she received on early records by her own group and with Teddy Wilson's orchestra. Examples of this period – her greatest period – can be found on (1) to (5). Billie began using Lester Young on sessions when she was working with Count Basie's orchestra, and the conjunction of her voice and his tenor saxophone produced such wonderful performances as *Easy living*, *I must have that man* and *Foolin' myself* (1). (Two other tracks with Lester – *A sailboat in the moonlight*, *Me myself and I* – are included on the American LP.) *Billie's blues*, made in 1936, with Bunny Berigan in the accompanying group, can be found on both (2) and (3), while a version of *Summertime*, recorded at the same session, is included in 'Four From "Porgy and Bess"' (the other three performances are by non-jazz artists) on 7 Fon TFE17192. An earlier example of Billie Holiday's singing – her very first appearance on record, in fact – is contained in 'The Vintage Goodman', (A) 12 Col CL821, on which she sings *Your mother's son-in-law* and *Riffin' the Scotch*, while a memento of the year she spent singing with Artie Shaw's band can be heard on 12 RCA RD27065, (A) 12 RCA LPM1570 – *Any old time*. By 1939, however, Billie Holiday had become a solo artist, and it was in that year that she recorded *Strange fruit* (5), a song that will always be associated with her; indeed it is one of her most moving performances. On the same LP is the richly sensuous blues, *Fine and mellow*.

The use of a string orchestra as a background to Billie Holiday's singing can be found on several tracks of (6). There is a certain drop in tension, a loss of dramatic impact, but her recording of *Crazy he calls me* still remains extremely effective, a performance curiously innocent and free of the cynicism one finds in much of this singer's work. *Porgy*, sung with just a piano accompaniment, is also included on this LP and is among Billie Holiday's greatest recordings. There is some duplication of tracks between (7) and the EPs (9) and (10). The last-named two are superior to (11), (10) containing a fine performance of *The blues are brewin'*. Many of Billie Holiday's concert recordings made around this time are disappointing; an exception is (12), the singer giving compelling performances of *Trav'lin light*, *Strange fruit*, *Billie's blues* and *Body and soul*, among other songs. (13) suffers from a rather brash accompaniment but includes a wry-sounding *Detour ahead* and *Rocky mountain blues*. During the 1950's Billie Holiday's voice deteriorated alarmingly, and this became apparent on many of her later LPs. All the same there are still odd tracks in 'Lady in Satin' (12 Fon TFL5032, (A) 12 Col CL1157) and 'Billie Holiday' (12 MGM C792, (A) MGM E3764) where her singing takes on an anguished beauty, rather as Charlie Parker's playing does in *Lover man*. But at least one of Billie Holiday's last records, (14), presents her singing with a clarity and freshness reminiscent of her earlier days. She was accompanied here (as she is again on (15)) by a small jazz group, including Harry Edison, Ben Webster and Jimmy Rowles. *Fine and mellow* on 12 Fon TFL5025, (A) 12 Col CL1098, (S) CS8040, recorded during the following year at a rehearsal for the TV show, 'The Sound of Jazz', also caught the singer in an inspired moment.

(1) TEDDY WILSON AND BILLIE HOLIDAY – 10 Ph BBR8061 (*d*). (A) (plus extra titles) 12 Col CL637. *1935–8*.

(2) LADY DAY – 7 Fon TFE17010. *1936–7*.

(3) BILLIE HOLIDAY – 10 Col 33S1034 (*d*). *1936–40*.

(4) BILLIE HOLIDAY – 10 Ph BBR8032 (*d*). (A) 10 Col 6163 (*d*). *1937–42*.

(5) BILLIE HOLIDAY – (A) 12 Com 30008. *1939–44*.

(6) LOVER MAN – 10 Br LA8676 (*d*). (A) (plus extra titles) 12 Dec 8702. *1944–9*.

(7) THE BLUES ARE BREWIN' – (A) 12 Dec 8701. *1944–9*.

(8) THE LADY SINGS – (A) 12 Dec 8215. *1944–50*.

(9) LADY DAY, Vol. 1 – 7 Br OE9172. *1944–6*.

(10) LADY DAY, Vol. 2 – 7 Br OE9199. *1945–9*.

(11) LADY DAY, Vol. 3 – 7 Br OE9251. *1949–50*.

(12) BILLIE HOLIDAY AT JAZZ AT THE PHILHARMONIC – 10 Col 33C9023 (*d*). *1946*.

(13) BILLIE HOLIDAY – 7 Vog EPV1129. *1951*.

[181]

(14) Songs For Distingue Lovers – 12 Col 33CX10145. (A) 12
Ver 8257, (S) 6021, 8197. *1956*.[1]
(15) All Or Nothing At All – (A) 12 Ver 8329. *1956–7.*

LIGHTNIN' HOPKINS (1912) *vocal, guitar*

Since the death of Big Bill Broonzy, Lightnin' Hopkins has
been heard more regularly. Though he prefers to remain around
Houston his recently recorded LPs have brought him more into the
foreground of the blues. A singer with immense vitality, Hopkins
makes up his blues as he goes along. He started to record in the middle
'40s and, from this period, his *Abilene blues* (Aladdin 3096) is a most
impressive song. Of his recent recordings the Folkways LP (1) is
quite astounding in its quality and is most strongly recommended.
His voice, slightly nasal yet broad-toned, is flexible, far more so, in
fact, than his guitar playing. This has been highly praised but tends to
become over-fussy and, occasionally, lacks firmness. While his
singing appears to be getting even better, his guitar playing is less
masculine than it was ten years ago. He has made about 200
records.
(1) Lightnin' Hopkins – 12 Fol FS3822. *1959.*
(2) The Rooster Crowed In England – 12 77 LA12-1. *1954–9.*
(3) Lightnin' Hopkins Strums The Blues – 12 Sco SLP4022.
c. 1948.
(4) Lightnin' Hopkins, Country Blues – 12 Tra TLP1035. *1959.*

ARMAND HUG (1910) *piano*

Although claimed as a shining light of New Orleans jazz, Hug
betrays very little of the earthiness and blueness of the jazz of his
native town. He plays rather in a hardened and popularized Jess
Stacy manner with occasional lapses into pseudo ragtime. His recordings are all bright and breezy and eminently suited for what might
be called jazz-tinged background music.
(1) Recorded in New Orleans, Vol. 2 (with Wiggs, Pierson and
Pecora) – 12 GTJ LAG12141. (A) 12 GTJ 12020. *1956.*
(2) With the New Orleans Dixielanders (with Miller) – (A)
12 Sou 221. *1957.*

[1] Note: (14) contains all the tracks on (A) Ver 8257 and four titles from
8197.

SPIKE HUGHES (1908)   *bass, composer, bandleader*

Spike Hughes was active in jazz for only about four years, yet in that brief period he achieved a great deal. At the time he started most British jazz musicians were still under the spell of Red Nichols, Miff Mole and the other members of the New York white school. Only a few years earlier Fred Elizalde had actually brought over Adrian Rollini, Fud Livingston and Chelsea Quealy to play in his band at the Savoy Hotel. ('Jazz at the Savoy', 10 De LF1277, contains recordings made in 1927 and 1928 by this pioneering group.) Not surprisingly, Spike Hughes' earliest records (by his 'Decca Dents') were filled with echoes of the Five Pennies. (1) belongs to this period, made when Jimmy Dorsey was in Britain with the Ted Lewis band. *The mooche* (on Decca's SCRAPBOOK OF BRITISH JAZZ, Vol. 1, (A) London) represents an early dabbling in Ellington material; by the time *Doan' you grieve* (on Vol. 2) was recorded, however, Hughes was writing very Ellingtonian scores for a thirteen-piece band. But the climax of Spike Hughes' jazz career was reached in 1933, when he visited the U.S., where he made a series of recordings, using Benny Carter's orchestra (with guest stars added). Some of Hughes' scores were perhaps a little too complex to swing easily, yet most of the performances on (2) reach an extraordinarily high level. Nothing more exquisite than *Arabesque*, for instance, with Coleman Hawkins playing one of his most opulent solos, could be found in the 1930s anywhere outside Duke Ellington. Yet the recordings are probably most valuable because they contain some of Dicky Wells' greatest solos, together with superb playing from Chu Berry, Henry Allen (he takes a ravishing solo in *Sweet sorrow blues*), Coleman Hawkins and Benny Carter, and masterly drumming by Sid Catlett. 'I left jazz behind me at the moment when I was enjoying it most,' wrote Hughes eighteen years later, 'the moment when all love-affairs should end.'

(1) SPIKE HUGHES' THREE BLIND MICE WITH JIMMY DORSEY – 7 Dec DFE6377. *1930*.

(2) SPIKE HUGHES AND HIS NEGRO ORCHESTRA – 12 Dec LK4173. (A) 12 Lon LL1387 (*d*). *1933*.

J

MAHALIA JACKSON (1911)   *vocal*

Not only the greatest Gospel singer of our day, one might well be justified in saying that she is the finest Negro singer of our day, Mahalia Jackson is a supremely passionate performer. Her broad, soaring voice embraces all the religious fervour of the American Negro and her steadfast refusal to perform 'sinful' songs has only served to increase her following which appears to grow daily. The control which she exercises in all registers, enables her to create a completely mobile sound, full of dynamic ornamentations and perfectly gauged nuancing of ostenato notes. The words, here, are of considerable importance, and Mahalia Jackson sings with a passion which bears down on them till all sentimentality vanishes. Her phrases, gradually becoming more elaborate during her performance of a song, have the rhythmic impact of a great New Orleans trumpet lead and she generates a swinging beat, as propulsive as the best of jazzmen. She has modified her singing over the years and, where she had incredible vigour, she now has also majesty. Yet it is the majesty of supreme passion, the majesty of pure beauty.

(1) MAHALIA JACKSON – 10 Vog LDE005.
(2) MAHALIA JACKSON – 7 Vog EPV1125. *1947–50.*
(3) MAHALIA JACKSON – 7 Ph BBE12069. *1954.*
(4) NEWPORT 1958 – 12 Ph BBL7289. (A) Col CL1244. *1958.*
(5) MAHALIA JACKSON – 7 Ph BBE12229.
(6) MAHALIA JACKSON, Vol. 1 – 7 TR JKR8006.
(7) GREAT GETTIN' UP MORNING – 12 Ph BBL7362.
(8) BLESS THIS HOUSE – (A) 12 Col CL899.
(9) JUST AS I AM – 12 TR 30/006. (A) 12 Apo 479.
(10) SWEET LITTLE JESUS BOY – (A) 12 Col CL702.
(11) THE WORLD'S GREATEST GOSPEL SINGER – (A) 12 Col CL644.

MILT JACKSON (1923)   *vibraphone, piano*

The vibraphone is an exacting taskmaster. It requires a perfectionist to extract from it a good jazz sound and Milt Jackson is one of the very few soloists to have achieved success on the instrument since Lionel Hampton popularized it in the early 'thirties. Milt's tone suffered badly in the hands of the recording engineers at the beginning and on most of his early releases he sounds as if he is using a set of broken bottles in place of a normal keyboard. Nevertheless he manages to get across an impression of competence and quality with his beautifully phrased improvisations. It is unfortunate that the low-fidelity reproduction mars (1) for Milt takes part in a charming trio performance (with Hank Jones and Ray Brown) on the Debussy-like *Night music*. It was during this same period – 1947 – that Jackson played on some of Thelonious Monk's provocative works for Blue Note, an association which was renewed with considerable success four years later. (2) finds Milt sketching phrases across Monk's acrid chords and hitting a rare level of empathy with the esoteric pianist on *Criss cross*. The quartet which Jackson formed in 1951 developed into the Modern Jazz Quartet when Milt relinquished his leadership in favour of a co-operative partnership. (3) represents the group before reorganization and before the personnel became stabilized; Ray Brown alternates with Percy Heath on bass while Al Jones replaces Kenny Clarke on four titles. The music is loose and swinging with the accent firmly placed on Jackson's solos; there are no attempts at extended improvisation or at widening the boundaries of jazz and the group sticks to three-minute versions of such tunes as *Bluesology*, *Round about midnight*, etc. With the responsibility of leadership taken out of Milt's hands the policy of the quartet underwent a subtle change and the reader is referred to the John Lewis section for a discussion of the Modern Jazz Quartet albums. Away from the MJQ Jackson has made several LPs both as leader and as sideman. One of his best appearances was with the Miles Davis-led jam session in the Prestige studio on Christmas Eve, 1954. Certain extra-musical events before the date caused an atmosphere which nevertheless resulted in some top-level performances from all five men. Jackson is inspired on both released takes of his own tune *Bags' groove* (4) although the even higher standard attained by Miles Davis, who precedes Milt, tends to lessen the impact of the vibes choruses. (5) is, in many ways, the best and most consistent record under Jackson's leadership. The personnel is actually that of the MJQ with Horace Silver in place of John Lewis. Silver's harder, more brittle touch and down-to-earth swing bring out the best in Milt who romps through his own blues *Stonewall* and plays with

[185]

lyrical assurance on *Moonray, Wonder why* and *My funny valentine*. Silver does not allow the vibraphonist to lie back and coast through the ballads at half power; the piano interjections prod the soloist in a way that John Lewis invariably fails to do. (6) was supervised by the French pianist Henri Renaud (who also played on the date) and has some good, direct statements from Milt as well as worthwhile solos by Jay Jay Johnson, Al Cohn and Renaud, the latter by no means outclassed in the 'all star' surroundings. (7), (8) and (9) are saved from mediocrity by the presence of Lucky Thompson on tenor; Jackson has a tendency to produce interminable choruses on standard material phrasing in a hesitant 'I-am-being-subtle' manner which soon induces boredom. At the other end of the scale is (10), a too obvious attempt to hit on an earthy, basic mood by a group of sophisticated soloists which includes the overrated Ray Charles. (11) is even more disappointing for it is little better than good quality tea-shop music complete with twittering flute and a subdued rhythm section which plays with the care and desire to please of a new Athaneum club member on his first trip to the bar.

(1) HANK JONES – 10 Vog LDE006. *1947*. (Remaining seven tracks by various artists.)

(2) THELONIOUS MONK QUINTET – (A) 12 BN BLP1509. (Eight titles on 10 Vog LDE044.) *1951*.

(3) MILT JACKSON QUARTET – (A) 12 Sav MG12046. (Eight titles on 10 Lon LZ-C14006, remaining four on 7 Lon EZ-C19019.) *1951* and *1952*.

(4) MILES DAVIS ALL STARS – 12 Esq 32-090. (A) 12 Pre PRLP7109. *1954*.

(5) MILT JACKSON QUARTET – 12 Esq 32-009. (A) 12 Pre PRLP7003. *1955*.

(6) HENRI RENAUD ALL STARS – 12 Vog LAE12046. *1954*.

(7) MILT JACKSON – 12 Lon LTZ-K15064. (A) 12 Atl LP1242. *1956*.

(8) MILT JACKSON QUINTET – 12 Lon LTZ-C15074. (A) 12 Sav MG12070. *1956*.

(9) MILT JACKSON QUINTET – 12 Lon LTZ-C15091. (A) 12 Sav MG12080. *1956*.

(10) SOUL BROTHERS – 12 Lon LTZ-K15146. (A) 12 Atl LP1279. *1956*.

(11) BAGS AND FLUTES – 12 Lon LTZ-K15177. (A) 12 Atl LP1294. *1957*.

[186]

HARRY JAMES (1916) *trumpet*

Harry James is now enjoying what is virtually his second career as a jazz musician. His first reputation was won twenty years ago, as a trumpet-player in Benny Goodman's orchestra between 1936 and 1939. His playing with Goodman was often flamboyant and his best solos were usually reserved for more informal occasions, such as the 1937 session at which he recorded *Blue mood* (*Just a mood* in the U.S.) in an ensemble completed by Red Norvo, Teddy Wilson and John Simmons (it was issued first as a Dec 78, then on Par, but is now deleted), or the time he made *Shoe shiner's drag* and *I'm in the mood for swing* with Lionel Hampton in 1938, both to be found in 'Jivin' The Vibes' (12 Cam CDN-129, (A) 12 Cam CAL-402). But when he formed his own band in 1939 it rapidly became a background for either displays of technical acrobatics or else sentimental vapourings. Now James has worked his passage back to respectability by leading one of the most exhilarating big bands of the present day. Most of its scores have been written by Ernie Wilkins, so it is scarcely surprising that the band's general character is not unlike Basie's. Far and away the best of James' soloists is the alto-player, Willie Smith. Smith also leaves his impress upon the reed section, leading it with authority and making it sound a little like the old Lunceford saxophone team. James himself is still liable to lapse into the vulgar flourish or two, or to let sentiment seep into his tone, but when he plays in his Louis Armstrong style he sounds quite satisfying. Most important of all, this band is enthusiastic about its music, which may be why it sometimes sounds more inspired than the Basie orchestra in its cuter moments. All the LPs are worth hearing, although (4) and (5) are probably the best. The themes are better on the former, the band swings more on the latter.

(1) MORE HARRY JAMES IN HI-FI – 12 Cap LCT6107. (A) 12 Cap W712. *1955–6.*

(2) WILD ABOUT HARRY – 12 Cap LCT6146, SLCT6146. (A) 12 Cap T874, ST874. *1957.*

(3) THE NEW JAMES – 12 Cap T1037, ST1037. (A) 12 Cap T1037, ST1037. *1958.*

(4) HARRY'S CHOICE – 12 Cap T1093, ST1093. (A) 12 Cap T1093, ST1093. *1958.*

(5) Harry James' New Swinging Band -- 12 MGM C795. (A)
12 MGM E3778, SE3778. *1959*.

BLIND LEMON JEFFERSON (1897–1931)   *guitar, vocal*

At a time when there were many fine blues singers, several of them even great singers, the greatest to have been recorded was Blind Lemon Jefferson. He, says Alan Lomax, was responsible for giving formal definition to the blues, for crystalizing the twelve-bar stanza. This statement may not appear to account for the original eight- and sixteen-bar themes, yet, in a broad sense, it is true. The enormous influence which Jefferson has exerted on blues singers over the past forty years, cannot easily be over-estimated, and only one other singer, Leroy Carr, has come near to him in this respect. It is a sign of Jefferson's greatness that he completely transcended the limitations of regional style, creating melodic patterns which were to influence singers in rural and urban areas. The anguish with which Jefferson imbues many of his performances – *Prison cell blues* (1) is an excellent example – creates an almost unbearable tension which persists after the sound has ceased. His average recordings are of such high quality that a sub-standard song by Jefferson would still be acclaimed as an extremely fine performance from most other singers. Heavy walking bass patterns under ostenato singing, soon accepted as a basic method of performance, were complemented by slides and rapid runs in the treble register; all were given a peculiar sonority by his steel guitar. Jefferson did not always keep to strict eight- or twelve-bar lengths, though the basic harmonic structure of the blues (tonic, subdominant, dominant) is used in almost all his recordings.

Of the 87 sides which Jefferson recorded between 1925 and 1930, 28 have been issued in Britain. This unusually high proportion of British releases, includes some of his best records, amongst which are *Bad luck blues* (3), *Long lastin' lovin'* (4), *Shuckin' sugar blues* (2) and *One dime blues* (9). Most of these have, unfortunately, been deleted but six sides are still available in the Jazz Collector catalogue.

(1) Anthology of American Folk Music – (A) 12 Fol FP251/3.
(2) Folk Blues of Blind Lemon Jefferson – 10 Lon AL3508 (*d*). *1926–9*.
(3) Penitentiary Blues – 10 Lon AL3546 (*d*). *1926–9*.

(4) BLIND LEMON JEFFERSON SINGS THE BLUES – 10 Lon AL3564 (d).
  1927–9.
(5) THE MALE BLUES, Vol. 5 – 7 JC JEL8. *1926.*
(6) *Jack o'diamond blues/Chock house blues* – 10 78 JC L103. *1926.*
(7) *Shuckin' sugar blues/Rabbit foot blues* – 10 JC L91. *1926.*
(8) *Weary dog blues/Change my luck blues* – 10 78 TemE R38 (d). *1927.*
(9) *Gone dead on your blues/One dime blues* – 10 78 TemE R54 (d). *1927.*
(10) *Lock step blues/Hangmen's blues* – 10 78 TemE R39 (d). *1928.*
(11) CLASSIC FOLK BLUES – (A) 12 Riv 12-125. (This LP contains a
  selection of tracks from (2), (3) and (4).)

BUDD JOHNSON (1910)   *tenor saxophone*

Budd Johnson straddles two decades of jazz. He was not only a
member of Louis Armstrong's band back in 1933, he also sat alongside Dizzy Gillespie and Charlie Parker in Earl Hines' orchestra ten
years later. In fact it was Johnson, or so the legend runs, who urged
Hines to introduce the modernists into his band. Not that many
traces of modern jazz can be found on (1), a set of tracks by the Budd
Johnson Quintet and Septet. The only tinge of the modern idiom
comes from Johnson's own tenor sax when it echoes the phrasing of
Lester Young, and from the incisive piano playing of Ray Bryant
(on three tracks). Bryant is the best soloist in the quintet, Vic
Dickenson the star of the Septet. It's pleasant but not distinguished
music. Rather more interesting are 'Skin Tight and Cymbal Wise',
12 Col 33SX1076, and 'Entente Cordiale of Jazz', 7 Col SEG7715,
the products of a session organized by Arvell Shaw in 1956, with
arrangements written by Johnson and the French pianist André
Persiany, both of whom also play on the records. Vic Dickenson is the
outstanding soloist but there is also lyrical playing by Taft Jordan
and bold, cutting solos from Johnson himself. Some of the finest
Johnson is to be found on BEN WEBSTER AND ASSOCIATES (HMV).
(1) BLUES À LA MODE – 12 Fel FAJ7007, SJA2007. (A) 12 Fel FAJ7007,
  SJA2007. *1958.*

BUNK JOHNSON (1879–1949)   *cornet*

We shall never know what Bunk Johnson sounded like in his early
days before jazz recording had become a full-scale industry. He
played with Buddy Bolden and led the historic Eagle Band. After

the triumphs of his youth he disappeared from jazz for nearly forty years, only to be dragged out by the merciless enthusiasm of the jazz revival of the 1940s. Except that he probably had more power and accuracy, he probably played in the same style as we hear on his revival records, a short-phrased choppy style, extremely economical and at times almost bare, an approach very much favoured by the New Orleans players. By the time Johnson recorded in the 1940s his drive and inspiration had gone though it is still obvious that he was the best musician in most of the bands he led and his playing sounded sweet and musical against the brashness of Jim Robinson and of George Lewis.

The first recordings in 1942 were rough and sour, yet full of the spirit of enjoyment and hilarity that has always made this kind of jazz an acquired taste. A little of it is exhilarating, but after a while its persistent lack of subtlety and imaginative ideas becomes boring. It is unfortunate that so many British and American revival bands based themselves on such models for they copied the clichés and the faults without enlivening the music by a natural jazz sense. Bunk Johnson played with such a band when he recorded with the Yerba Jazz Band in 1943. The hectic and harrowing results on (1) will only appeal to those with eardrums like elephant hide.

A great mass of recordings for American Music made in 1944 are spoken of with reverence and show the music gradually gaining form and power as the veteran players begin to knit together again with some of their old confidence. A deliberate attempt at archaism in the old marching-band style prefaced a series of better recorded titles which show the band at its peak performance. The titles on (3) include the best that Johnson made, especially *Tishomingo blues* on which a remarkably in-tune band knits together to give an exciting, moving and powerful performance. The other three titles were *Maryland my Maryland, Alexander's Ragtime Band* and *You always hurt the one you love*. The 1945 Victor recordings which followed maintained this standard; most of these are at present unavailable. Some pleasing solos by Johnson accompanied by Don Ewell and Alphonse Steele were followed by a series of recordings for Columbia (4) in which Johnson mixed the ragtime tunes he loved so much with some popular songs. Quaint is probably the best word to describe these 1947 sessions; they certainly have considerably more charm than most of Bunk Johnson's but they are also very erratic. The final recordings for Commodore (5) show a rather tired Bunk and a general falling-off.

(1) BUNK JOHNSON AND THE YERBA BUENA JAZZ BAND – 10 GTJ LDG110. (A) 12 GTJ 12024. *1943.*
(2) BUNK JOHNSON'S JAZZ BAND – 7 Esq EP181. *1945.*
(3) BUNK JOHNSON AND HIS NEW ORLEANS BAND – 7 Br OE9257. *1945.*
(4) BUNK JOHNSON BAND – 12 Ph BBL7231. (A) 12 Col CL-829 (*d*). *1947.*
(5) BUNK JOHNSON AND HIS NEW ORLEANS BAND – (A) 12 Com. 30007. *1948.*

DINK JOHNSON (unknown)   *drums, piano*
    Dink Johnson is one of the rare vintages of jazz, a special liqueur to be brought out after the brandy and coffee of other traditional jazz pianists. His recordings have only appeared on some rather scarce American Music 78s, 515, 516 (made in 1945), and 523, 524, 525 and 526 (made in 1947). Dink, who was a brother-in-law of Jelly Roll Morton, was a pianist who had humour, personality and the spirit of jazz and ragtime in his soul. He was no great shakes technically but his recordings are so uniquely enjoyable and delightful that it is hard to imagine anyone who likes jazz not getting a great kick out of them. It is old-time, rough and ready stuff but the good-humoured spirit of the player comes through so forcibly that for once the finer points really don't matter. *The Stella blues, Las Vegas stomp* and *Frisco dreams* are unforgettable.

JAMES P. JOHNSON (1894-1955)   *piano*
    A skilful pianist who helped to establish the swinging piano style which has become known as Harlem piano simply because it was developed in that area. There is a lot of ragtime melody with most of the ragtime phrasing characteristics taken out, a process that Jelly Roll Morton had started a long time before. A rather finnicky player, almost too sensitive to be entirely within a jazz tradition, he does occasionally play early Harlem cocktail piano. But he is also capable of playing energetic stride piano with swing and intensity perhaps only equalled by Pete Johnson when he plays in a similar vein. His

mode of expression was carried on by pianists like Fats Waller, Ralph Sutton and some other lesser players, but he never had the same great influence as the more masculine and definite style which Earl Hines created on the same lines. His was clearly a solo style, introverted and meditative and could never fit successfully into a large band. Johnson at his most emphatic is to be found in his accompaniments to blues singers as with Rosetta Crawford on *I'm tired of fattening frogs* and *Double crossin' papa* (Br 03461, (A) Dec 7584 (*d*)) and *Stop it Joe* with its magnificently swinging intro, *My man jumped salty on me* (Vog V1002, (A) Dec 7657 (*d*)) made in 1939. A number of early transcriptions from piano rolls (1) show Johnson in an early stage of development, nearer to the ragtime idiom, and his own delicate style not yet fully realized. Some of his more filigree work is to be found on solos like *Riffs* and *Feelin' blue* and on *You've got to be modernistic* and *Jingles*, these last two available on two tracks of Cor LRA10022 – *Barrelhouse Piano. 1930.* Five fine but badly recorded tracks on (3) are overshadowed by two great LPs (4) recorded in 1944, a selection of Fats Waller tunes and (5), even more successful, a selection of his own works including definitive recordings of *Old fashioned love* and *Carolina shout.* Half of an LP Harlem Party Piano (2) contains some more tracks made in 1927, four mature sides well worth having particularly as the reverse side of the records is occupied by Luckey Roberts, and (6) is an example of a great accompanist with a not so great singer.

(1) REDISCOVERED EARLY SOLOS – (A) 12 Riv 12-105. 10 Lon AL3511, AL3540 (*d*). *1921–7.*

(2) HARLEM PARTY PIANO (with Luckey Roberts) – 10 Lon HB-U1057 (*d*). *1927.*

(3) JAMES P. JOHNSON – 7 Tem EXA65. *1944.*

(4) FATS WALLER FAVOURITES – 10 Br (*d*) LA8622. (A) 10 Dec (*d*) DL5228. *1944.*

(5) DADDY OF THE PIANO – 10 Br (*d*) LA8528. (A) 10 Dec (*d*) DL5190. *1944.*

(6) W. C. HANDY BLUES – 12 Fol FG-3540. *1945.*

JAY JAY JOHNSON (1924) *trombone*

If Bud Powell is the Charlie Parker of the piano then Jay Jay Johnson is Parker on trombone. He was first in his particular field, bringing a hitherto unknown agility to the instrument and has continued to lead the pack for a decade and a half. Jay Jay's smooth-as-satin tone and limitless technique enable him to translate his ideas into tangible form with complete assurance. After some years of big-band experience – including the orchestras of both Benny Carter and Count Basie – Johnson moved into the select circle of jazzmen who have topped popularity polls all over the world at a time when they were either unemployed musically or found difficulty in getting jobs with ephemeral club groups. (1) contains four titles by a small band made up of some musicians from the then current Illinois Jacquet outfit (Johnson and pianist John Lewis) plus Kinny Dorham and Max Roach from the Parker quintet. Johnson gets a peculiarly french-horn-like sound (although this may be due in part to the recording balance) and the date is memorable principally for the John Lewis score *Elysses*, a mature piece of writing which makes the sextet sound like a medium-size band. (2) was made five months later by a quintet (Jay Jay, Sonny Stitt on tenor, Lewis, Roach and Nelson Boyd); again it is Lewis's arrangement – this time of the lovely *Afternoon in Paris* – which provides the highlight although the strength of Stitt's tenor solos and the delicate tracery of Johnson's work gives the group a good feeling of contrast. Two takes of the twelve-bar *Blue mode* are included and it is noticeable that the trombonist's solos are not radically different in concept, an indication of the care and rehearsal which goes into Jay Jay's playing. Lewis and Johnson are together again on (3) which is also recommended for the youthful enthusiasm of Clifford Brown, here playing on one of his first record sessions. Lewis's *Sketch one* is an admirable performance of a score which warrants expansion by a larger group while Jay Jay's own emphatic *Turnpike* is ideally suited to the occasion. With just the rhythm section behind him the trombonist turns in a faultless *It could happen to you*, a model of taste, tone and technique. During 1954 Johnson teamed up with trombonist Kai Winding to form the Jay and Kai quintet. This unusual instrumentation led to some fine small-band records of which (4) is perhaps the best. The ballads are played superbly, the two trombones hitting a high level of creativity on *Dinner for one please James* and *We'll be together again*. In the theme statement of *Don't argue* Jay Jay and Kai play alternate bars and succeed in sounding like one instrument, so closely linked are their styles. *Bags' groove*, always a good vehicle for the more extrovert type of jazzmen, has a typically excellent Johnson solo with carefully considered climaxes. (5) is a highly recommended LP by Jay Jay and a well-integrated rhythm section (Tommy Flanagan, Paul Chambers and Max Roach); although the general formula is casual Johnson's intelligent approach to a record date never allows the interest to sag as he intersperses originals with such unusual numbers as *Cry me a river* and *Be my love*. Although (6) was issued under Sonny Rollins' name it is the trombonist who seems to take charge of the date whenever he is given a chance to solo. His brash, swinging solos over a percussive rhythm section containing both Horace Silver and Art Blakey (Thelonious Monk plays on two tracks) have more attack and guts than usual. Everyone plays well on (7) but it is Stan Getz who tends to overshadow Johnson although both front-line men strike fire on every track; it is simply that Getz achieves a more exciting atmosphere in his solos and the LP is warmly recommended for both Johnson and the tenor saxist.

(1) TROMBONE BY THREE – 12 Esq 32-036. (A) Pre 12 PRLP7023. *1949.* (Four tracks by Johnson, remainder by Bennie Green and Kai Winding.)

(2) SPJ JAZZ – 12 Esq 32-049. (A) 12 Pre PRLP7024. *1949.* (Five tracks by Johnson, remainder by Sonny Stitt-Bud Powell.)

(3) JAY JAY JOHNSON – 10 Vog LDE124. (A) 12 BN BLP1505 (with additional titles from other sessions). *1953.*

(4) JAY AND KAI – 10 Esq 20-045. (A) 12 Pre PRLP7030. *1954.* (Remaining titles on Pre PRLP7030 by Bennie Green.)

(5) FIRST PLACE – 12 Fon TFL5005. (1) 12 Col CL1030. *1957.*

(6) SONNY ROLLINS, Vol. 2 – (A) 12 BN BLP1558. *1957.*

(7) GETZ AND JAY JAY AT THE OPERA HOUSE – 12 Col 33CX10127. (A) 12 Ver 8265. *1957.*

LONNIE JOHNSON (1894)   *vocal, guitar*

It is surprising to find that people will argue as heatedly over Johnson's singing, as they will over his playing. Surprising because he is occasionally classed as a good blues singer, whereas his delivery reminds the writer more of an Irish tenor. He is, however, a notably fine guitarist who has, at times, provided magnificent accompaniments for difficult singers. One thinks immediately of the 22 solo accompaniments which he provided for Texas Alexander between 1927 and 1930. On these he must have followed bar by bar for Alexander rarely performed in the same way twice running. *When you get thinking* (1) shows how well this combination worked and the result testifies to Johnson's sense of melody. But his greatest successes came in the field of jazz and it is here, with Ellington and Armstrong, that Lonnie Johnson shines. His duets with Ed Lang are also of great interest and tend to confirm the opinion that jazz, rather than country or city blues, was Johnson's real metier.

(1) BLUES FELL THIS MORNING – 12 Ph BBL7369. *1929.*
(2) LONESOME ROAD – 7 Par GEP8635. *1947–8.*
(3) LONNIE'S BLUES – 7 Par GEP8663. *1947–8.*
(4) LONNIE'S BLUES, No. 2 – 7 Par GEP8693. *1947–8.*
(5) *Jelly roll baker/Drunk again* – 10 78 Vog V2015.

PETE JOHNSON (1904) *piano*

Pete Johnson might be called one of the modern boogie woogie pianists, if not in time then in approach. After the early primitive-styled blues players came the classic boogie woogie period led by Jimmy Yancey, Pinetop Smith and Meade Lux Lewis. They established the formal precision boogie which Pete Johnson took over to become one of the finest of them all. He adds to the raw material of boogie something of the mobile, springy rhythm of the Harlem pianists and plays a fine stride piano in their style himself. His early Solo Art recordings on Riverside and London (AL3549) are now deleted as are his *Goin' away blues/Roll 'em Pete* (Par R2672) and his well-known *Basement boogie/Death ray boogie* (Br 03292). Also his exhilarating duets with Albert Ammons except for *Boogie woogie jump* on GREAT JAZZ PIANIST – 12 Cam CDN-118, (A) 12 Cam CAL-328. Fortunately we still have a good LP of his work (1) which includes a fine *Answer to the boogie* and two of his swinging pieces *Mr. Freddie blues* and *Lights out mood*. A concert performance of 1950 catches him in a jovial mood (3) but the recording is rather poor, and two Vogue 78s are worth having (V2032 and V2019 recorded in 1947). But perhaps some of the finest work Pete Johnson has done is as accompanist to the blues-shouter Joe Turner. The two seem to urge one another on to greater excitement and inspiration and the complementary duets are very satisfying. An Atlantic album (4)

[195]

is almost as worth having for Johnson as for Turner with an exhilarating *Roll 'em Pete, How long blues* and *Morning glories* while (4) is
even more of a duet on equal terms (5).

(1) BOOGIE WOOGIE MOOD – 10 Cor LRA10016. (A) 10 Br BL58041
   (*d*). *1944*.
(2) ROLL 'EM BOY – 7 TR JKR8009. *1947*.
(3) PETE JOHNSON IN CONCERT – 7 Vog EPV1039. *1950*.
(4) THE BOSS OF THE BLUES (JOE TURNER) – 12 Lon LTZ-K15053.
   (A) 12 Atl 1234. *1956*.
(5) JOE TURNER WITH PETE JOHNSON – (A) 12 EmA 36014. *1950s*.
(6) JAZZ PIANO (also ERROLL GARNER) – (A) 12 GA 33-321. *1950s*.

BLIND WILLIE JOHNSON (1900?–1949)   *vocal, guitar*

The role of the itinerant singer in the Southern United States was
threefold. He was expected to provide music, entertainment in
general, and to act as a travelling newspaper. That, at least, was the
role of the itinerant blues singer. The gospel singer, however, was
more restricted. It was his mission to bring religion, and the greatest
of the street gospel singers, far greater in fact than any other on
record, was Blind Willie Johnson.

In this great singer one hears the strange fusion of Methodist and
Baptist hymns with age-old musical traditions of the West African
Negro. (It is interesting to note that there are men in Nigeria and
Ghana who, today, sing in a style very closely approaching that of
Blind Willie Johnson.) The complete unity of *Dark was the night* (1),
wordless yet totally explicit, is, in a way, the ultimate manifestation
of Johnson's greatness. The sympathy of sound between guitar and
voice has never, in the music of the American Negro, been closer
than it is here. Johnson hums, the guitar notes synchronize with his
voice. Then he sings lead and the guitar answers him. The guitar
takes the lead and Johnson answers. The miraculous control of tone
and timing make it one of the greatest records ever heard of this
music. But Johnson was well aware of words and, through his learning
of biblical texts, often used them with greater accuracy than his
contemporaries. Though he sang mainly in the hoarse throaty
tradition of the gospel singers, Johnson was capable of introducing
amazing sweetness of tone, creating vividly contrasting textures in
one song. The second voice is that of his wife, Angeline Johnson.

[196]

The records which he made all testify to his greatness as a singer and as a musician. His use of different tunings for different songs was just one more manifestation of his instinctive knowledge and feeling for the traditions upon which was grounded his supreme artistry. We may say with absolute certainty, that Blind Willie Johnson never made a *good* record; his worst was magnificent. Between 1927 and 1930 he made thirty sides, all for Columbia, and something of his story was revealed in a Folkways LP (2).

(1) BLIND WILLIE JOHNSON – 7 Fon TFE17052.
(2) THE STORY OF BLIND WILLIE JOHNSON – 12 Fol FA3585.

JONAH JONES (1909) *trumpet*

There is a toughness, a pugnacity, about Jonah Jones' best work which those people who know this musician only from his latter-day Capitol recordings will not credit him with possessing. Hugues Panassié once described Jonah Jones as swinging 'the most next to Louis Armstrong and Tommy Ladnier'. This statement may have rather exaggerated Jones's stature, but at least Panassié came nearer to the truth than those critics who thought of the musician as a 'comic trumpet-player' – largely because he played for a long time in Stuff Smith's boisterous little group and later on worked for Cab Calloway. Some of Jonah Jones' earliest and best solos, as a matter of fact, can be found on long-deleted 78s by Stuff Smith's Onyx Club Boys, including *You're a viper*, *Tain't no use* and *It ain't right*, all released in the 1930s on British Vocalion. The trumpet-player based his style upon Louis Armstrong's – not the Armstrong of the Hot Five and Seven so much as the virtuoso of the years that followed. All the same, Jonah has a musical personality of his own, and he is also one of the few trumpet-players who has battled it out successfully with Sidney Bechet in an ensemble, a task beyond the capacity of quite a few of his contemporaries. He can be heard doing so on 10 Vog LDE127, (A) 12 BN 1207, on which he plays a very moving version of *Black and blue*. In Paris in 1954 he again partnered Bechet, this time on 10 Vog LDE119, performing especially well in *Squeeze me*. While in Paris Jonah also recorded under his own name (1), accompanied by the Alix Combelle Sextet. (Combelle, of course, is the best of the pre-war generation of French tenor-players, a musician capable of holding his own even in the company of Coleman Hawkins.)

[197]

Jonah dominates this LP, playing with particular sensitivity on the slow blues, *Jonah's wail*. The past few years have seen Jonah Jones become popular with a very wide audience, and this success has had the effect of imprisoning him inside a formula. Most of his Capitol recordings are pleasant and tasteful, yet artistically negligible. *Trumpet interlude*, on EmArcy's LP of that name (1944) presents Jonah leading a group including Tyree Glenn (trombone) and Joe Thomas (tenor sax). He is in good but reticent form.

(1) JONAH JONES-ALIX COMBELLE SEXTET – 10 Vog LDE145. *1954*.

DUKE JORDAN (1922)   *piano*

Like Al Haig, Duke Jordan has been continually overlooked in a world of changing fads and fashions. His melodic introductions and solos were a feature of Charlie Parker's 1947 Dial titles (1) and his absence from record for lengthy periods during the nineteen fifties is a sad reflection on the state of jazz. (2) was recorded at the instigation of the French pianist Henri Renaud and contains three charming Jordan originals, including the tune which has since become something of a jazz standard, *Jor-du*, presented here under the title *Minor escamp*. (3) is made up of two sessions with the trio on side one making full use of their opportunities; Jordan exchanges fours with Art Blakey on his own *Forecast* (he imitates Art's drum figures on the keyboard) and turns in a lovely solo performance of *Summertime*. For the quintet tracks Eddie Bert and Cecil Payne are added on trombone and baritone respectively and play Duke's *Flight to Jordan* with great sensitivity and depth of feeling.

(1) CHARLIE PARKER MEMORIAL ALBUM – 12 Vog LAE12002. *1946* and *1947*.

(2) DUKE JORDAN TRIO – 10 Vog LDE099. *1954*.

(3) DUKE JORDAN TRIO-QUINTET – (A) 12 Sig S1202. *1955*.

K

MAX KAMINSKY (1908)   *trumpet*

Max Kaminsky can lead a jazz band with the passion that many other musicians only pour into their solos. A trumpet player with a style based upon the Louis Armstrong of the Hot Five days, Kaminsky is usually associated with the white Chicagoans, although he worked for a time with the bands of Tommy Dorsey and Artie Shaw. (1) and (2) present him leading a small Dixieland group through some rather hackneyed tunes. Only Kaminsky really has anything to say. A much better idea of this musician's talents can be got by hearing him alongside Sandy Williams and Art Hodes in *Jughead boogie* (10 Vog LDE174). The same LP also contains *Blues 'n' booze*, in which Kaminsky plays a series of snarling, plunger-muted blues choruses, and – in complete contrast – a subdued, slightly Bix-like *KMH Drag*. Also outstanding are Kaminsky's solos and lead work with Bud Freeman's band on 'Wolverine Jazz' (10 Br LA8526) and 'Chicago Style' (7 Fon TFE17082), and with Eddie Condon's band in four titles on the 'Chicago Jazz Album' (12 Br LAT8042, (A) 1 Dec 8029). Kaminsky also recorded many titles in the late 1930s and early 1940s for (A) Commodore with groups led by Eddie Condon (1); some are included in (A) 12 Com 30006 and 30010.

(1) DIXIELAND HORN – (A) 12 Com 30013. *circa 1940.*

(2) ALL STAR DIXIELAND – 7 MGM EP600 (*d*). *1953.*

(3) Go, Go, Go – 7 MGM EP656. *1953.*

STAN KENTON (1912) *piano*

In retrospect it seems that the fame of Stan Kenton and his band owed something to the general environment of the war years. Stan has never led an important *jazz* orchestra although the band he had in 1953 came close to the standard of lesser Herman Herds. The pro-Kenton hysteria goes deeper than actual musical values and it may well be that the brassy dissonances, the unusual material, the pseudo-classical approach, all put over with Kenton's unimpeachable sincerity of purpose, appealed strongly to a nation shaken to the core by Pearl Harbour. On record Stan's music has always received ample coverage and his tie with Capitol Records for a lengthy period has enabled that company to put out a set of four twelve-inch LPs, entitled 'The Kenton Era', which surveys the band-leader's ups and downs from 1940 to 1958. The set benefits greatly from the fact that very few previously issued tracks have been included; in the majority of cases concert, broadcast and even rehearsal versions of familiar items have been substituted in favour of the studio-made originals. The first side of (1) is virtually the Kenton Era in microcosm for

Stan speaks of the band's history, interspersing his talk with snippets from about thirty records. The reverse is made up of recordings of the 1940-1 band playing at the Rendezvous Ballroom, Balboa. A Jimmy Lunceford influence is evident not only in the sax section (led by the distinctive alto of Jack Ordean) but also in the punching, rhythmic figures. In many ways this collection of Balboa recordings contains the most interesting music in the entire album; the chief soloists in the band were then Chico Alvarez (one of the most extrovert and pleasing of all Kenton's trumpeters), Jack Ordean and tenor saxist Red Dorris. (2) takes the story from January 1944 up to July 1946, a period which saw the introduction of arranger Pete Rugolo's work, his first score being *Opus a dollar three eighty*. Two mediocre vocalists, Dolly Houston and Gene Howard, are heard but there is also a good rhythmic Anita O'Day track in *I'm going mad for a pad*. The band at this time had yet to find a distinctive style and the more lasting music seems to have been created by soloists Dave Matthews, Boots Mussulli, Kai Winding and Ray Wetzel. The first side of (3) is labelled 'Progressive jazz' and the eight titles, recorded during the April 1947 to July 1948 period, represent the band which seems to have attracted (or repelled) so much attention. Side two was recorded after Kenton's semi-retirement from the business, by the 'Innovations' orchestra. The most remarkable feature of this period was not the music (which was banal and pretentious in the extreme), but that Stan actually toured America with, and presumably found audiences for, the forty-man ensemble. *Salute, Ennui, Coop's solo* and *Samana* were recorded in concert at Cornell Rhythm Club, New York; it is singularly unfortunate that in Manny Albam's *Samana* alto saxist Art Pepper's only solo in the entire Kenton Era is virtually lost through bad microphone positioning. A higher jazz content is evident in (4) which presents more of Kenton's contemporary work. The 'Innovations' band proved economically impracticable so Stan returned to a less esoteric big-band policy. *Swing house*, a Gerry Mulligan original, and *Zoot*, a Bill Holman showcase for the virile tenor playing of Zoot Sims, demonstrate the powerful, healthy sound of the 1954 band. Although these four LPs give a very full picture of Kenton's musical activities over a decade and a half, (5) and (6) are strongly recommended in addition for they represent further the fine band which Stan fronted in 1953. Driven by Stan Levey's extrovert drumming, the ensemble sounds far removed from the monster band which Stan led a few years before. Lee Konitz, Conte Candoli, Richie Kamuca and Frank Rosolino all add their weight to the proceedings to make this the best of Kenton's many line-ups. (7) is a pleasant LP of standards by a slightly later personnel, still with Candoli, Konitz and Rosolino but with Zoot Sims substituting for Richie Kamuca. Somewhat ironically the band swings more, and is more relaxed, on a semi-novelty commercial single featuring singer Chris Connor (*And the bull walked around olay*, Cap 13939, (A) 2388).

(1) KENTON ERA, Vol. 1 – 12 Cap LCT6157. *1940–1*.

(2) KENTON ERA, Vol. 2 – 12 Cap LCT6158. *1944–6*.

(3) KENTON ERA, Vol. 3 – 12 Cap LCT6159. *1947–8*.

(4) KENTON ERA, Vol. 4 – 12 Cap LCT6160. *1952–8*.

NOTE : The American Capitol issue of The Kenton Era consists of four LPs in a box, complete with descriptive booklet, auto-coupled and minus some of the titles included on British Cap LCT6160. The LPs are not available separately and the album number is W569.

(5) STAN KENTON ORCHESTRA – 10 Cap LC6595. (A) 10 Cap H383. *1952*.

(6) STAN KENTON ORCHESTRA – 10 Cap LC6602. (A) 10 Cap H426. *1952*.

(7) STAN KENTON ORCHESTRA – 10 Cap LC6697. (A) 10 Cap H462. *1953*.

FREDDIE KEPPARD (1883–1932)   *cornet*

When a musician is only to be heard through the emaciated recordings made down an acoustic horn it is very difficult to compare his work with that heard on modern recordings and make a fair assessment. Keppard had a great reputation in his day, was obviously a powerful, if not particularly subtle cornettist. The recordings he did make were at a time when he was past his prime and probably give very little idea of his real powers. *Salty dog* and *Stockyard strut* made in 1926 are his best-known recordings. These, together with *Stomp time blues* and *It must be the blues* also made in 1926 under Jasper Taylor's name, are all available on a historically valuable EP (1).

(1) NEW ORLEANS TRUMPET – 7 JC JEL7. *1926*.

BARNEY KESSEL (1923) *guitar*

In his solos Barney Kessel swings more than most other musicians. He has absorbed the teachings of the late Charlie Christian and plays an extrovert, happy kind of jazz in an entirely natural manner. Although he is seldom heard functioning as a rhythm guitarist today it should not be forgotten that he took his place on one of Charlie Parker's 'Dial' sessions in 1947 (along with Dodo Marmarosa, Red Callender and Don Lamond) and fed chords at the most telling points behind the soloists on *Cheers, Carvin' the Bird, Stupendous* and *Relaxin' at Camarillo*. His own groups have been sensitively recorded for the Contemporary label, the clarity of the reproduction being second to none. On (1) he leads a quintet containing Bud Shank and the underrated pianist Arnold Ross through a varied programme. *Salute to Charlie Christian* is a complimentary tribute to Kessel's idol; *Tenderly* and *What is there to say* are equally effective ballad performances with lyrical, tasteful guitar to the fore throughout. Barney's septet captures the mood, if not the sound, of the early-forties Benny Goodman small bands on (2), an effect which is heightened by the presence of Georgie Auld and Harry Edison on some tracks. *Happy feeling*, the title of one track, sums up the atmosphere of a highly recommended LP. (3) and (4) are by a trio comprising Kessel, Ray Brown and Shelly Manne. Both albums consist of vital, swinging jazz born of a closely-knit group feelings; *Satin doll* (3) is played at the perfect tempo while Kessel runs his chords faultlessly on *It could happen to you*. (5) is devoted to songs from the film *Some like it hot* and benefits greatly from the presence of trumpeter Joe Gordon and multi-reed player Art Pepper. (6) is devoted to swinging versions of the melodies from *Carmen* which have been adapted for jazz with reverence and intelligence; Kessel and Vic Feldman are the outstanding soloists on another recommended album.

(1) Easy Like – 12 Vog LAC12082. (A) 12 Con 3511. *1953* and *1956*.
(2) To Swing or Not To Swing – 12 Vog LAC12058. (A) 12 Con 3513. *1955*.
(3) The Poll Winners – 12 Vog LAC12122. (A) 12 Con 3535. *1957*.
(4) The Poll Winners Ride Again – 12 Vog LAC12186. (A) 12 Con 3556. *1958*.
(5) Some Like It Hot – 1t Vog LAC12206. (A) 12 Con 3565. *1959*.
(6) Carmen – 12 Vog LAC12214,(S) SCA5011. (A) 12 Con 3563. *1959*.

ANDY KIRK (1898)   *bass saxophone, bandleader*

Although Andy Kirk's Clouds of Joy worked in and around Kansas City for many years, and although a large number of the sidemen came from that city, the band's style of playing was much smoother and more lightly poised than, say, that of the Bennie Moten or Count Basie orchestras. This relaxed, very individual style was largely the creation of the band's pianist, Mary Lou Williams (q.v.), who wrote most of the arrangements. On *Walkin' and swingin'* (2), she anticipated Johnny Dankworth and scored a trumpet in with the reed section. The other outstanding musician in Kirk's orchestra was Dick Wilson, a tenor saxophonist who died in 1941 at the age of 30. A soloist in the Coleman Hawkins tradition, Wilson possessed a little of Chu Berry's impetuous manner, while his light, dry tone was faintly suggestive of Lester Young's. Wilson was an abnormally fluent and inventive soloist and had he lived he might have developed into a really important tenor player. He can be heard on the records listed below. By 1940 Harold Baker had joined the band, and he, Dick Wilson and Mary Lou Williams all perform on *Twelfth Street rag* and *The Count. 1940.* (A) 12 Dec DL8044 – KANSAS CITY JAZZ, two tracks by a small group from the Clouds of Joy, under the leadership of Mary Lou Williams.

(1) ANDY KIRK AND HIS TWELVE CLOUDS OF JOY – 7 Col SEG7607 (*d*). *1936.* (A) plus extra tracks 12 Cor 56019 (*d*) *1936–41.*

(2) CLOUDS OF JOY, No. 2 – 7 Col SEG7646 (*d*). *1936.* (A) (plus extra tracks) 12 Cor 56019 (*d*). *1936–41.*

LEE KONITZ (1927)   *alto, tenor saxophone*

From a pale and wan sound with the Claude Thornhill band during the late nineteen-forties, Lee Konitz's style has blossomed and matured giving credence to his unusual approach to improvisation. A founder member of the Lennie Tristano school (q.v.) Lee has worked hard at the task of breaking with tradition while maintaining a jazz feeling. Like Tristano he constructs lines which flow across the 'natural' breaks in phrasing and looks on a three-chorus solo as a unified statement rather than a series of eight- or four-bar patterns. He is at his best with such fellow Tristano students as Billy Bauer, Warne Marsh, etc., and despite the drawback of his small, piping tone on alto (1) is a good introduction to his work. Apart from the smooth, swift-moving group tracks the LP also contains a beautiful alto-guitar duet in *Rebecca*. In 1952 Konitz joined the then newly formed Stan Kenton band (the best ever to play under Stan's leadership) and during the next eighteen months of blowing in a sax section he acquired a more forceful approach which has improved his subsequent work. With Kenton he was heard solo on such titles as the driving *Fascinating rhythm* and the moodily smouldering *Loverman*. The listener senses the fight taking place between Konitz and his conscience here; the desire to play nothing but freely improvised jazz on the one hand and the equal desire to subjugate his introversion in favour of a more strident sound on the other. The result of the battle is a surprisingly virile alto style which contrives to avoid banal turns of phrases; *In lighter vein*, from the Kenton period (12 Cap LCT6009, (A) Cap T524) ranks with the best of Lee's work on record while his unique tone adds class to the reed section sound on all the sides made at this time. (2) was made at the Haig Club in Hollywood six months after Konitz joined Kenton and while it is, ostensibly, a collection of titles by the alto player with the Gerry Mulligan Quartet, in fact most of the tracks are solos by Lee with Gerry and his men playing retiring roles. *All the things you are* from this LP contains a magnificent Konitz passage which exhibits the main facets of his new-found style. His knife-edged tone, the savage attack, the long phrases interspersed with gaps of silence, all these qualities give the alto saxist's work its individual character. (3) is a little out of the ordinary in that Konitz is heard playing tenor on five of the tracks. Using the bigger saxophone results in a surface resemblance to Stan Getz and Zoot Sims although the undeniable Konitz method of line construction cuts short the similarities. Billy Bauer is present on four of the tracks, filling out the chords behind the soloist and placing his interjections in the most strategic positions. This LP also introduces a young drummer named Dick Scott whose intelligent appreciation of the situation and well-shaded volume control makes him a valuable addition to the select Konitz coterie. Scott and Bauer are heard again on (4), undoubtedly the best album by Lee on the market. Recorded live at a club in Pittsburgh Konitz edited the tapes and took out any sections on which he considered his playing to be below par. This has resulted in some tracks which fade out or are cut short abruptly but the sections which have been included on the record are superlative; *Sweet and lovely* finds the alto saxist at the peak of inspirational form, constructing a long, floating melodic line which only an unfortunate break in the tape succeeds in disrupting. There are many good solos to be heard on (5), Lee's first LP for Norman Granz; the presence of trumpeter Don Ferrara adds interest (Ferrara is another Lennie Tristano student) although the orthodox drumming of the late Shadow Wilson is less effective than that of Dick Scott. On *Billie's bounce* Ferrara and Konitz pay tribute to Charlie Parker by playing Bird's original solo (from the 1945 Savoy session) in unison. Theoretically (6) should have been an excellent LP for it features a sax section containing Konitz and four similar-thinking musicians (including Hal McKusick, Warne Marsh and Ted Brown). Unfortunately Jimmy Giuffre's well-meaning attempts at arrangements bog Konitz and Marsh – the two principal soloists – in a morass of dullness most of the time, added to which the drummer seems uncertain of the beat on more than one occasion.

(1) LEE KONITZ COLLATES – 12 Esq 32-027. (A) 12 Pre PRLP7004. *1949.*

(2) LEE KONITZ AND THE GERRY MULLIGAN QUARTET – 12 Vog LAE12181. (A) 12 WP PJM406. *1953.*

(3) KONITZ IN HI-FI – 12 Lon LTZ-K15902. (A) 12 Atl 1258. *1956.*

(4) THE REAL LEE KONITZ – 12 Lon LTZ-K15147. (A) 12 Atl 1273. *1957.*

(5) LEE KONITZ QUINTET – 12 Col 33CX10119. (A) 12 Ver 8209. *1957.*

(6) JIMMY GIUFFRE ARRANGEMENTS – (A) 12 Ver 8335. (Four titles on 7 HMV 7EG 8566.) *1959.*

GENE KRUPA (1909)   *drums, bandleader*

Gene Krupa was the first of the showman drummers. Right at the start of the 'swing era' he became aware of the public's appetite for noise and excitement, and with solos like that on *Sing, sing, sing* (7 RCA RCX1026), by Benny Goodman's orchestra, he catered for it. As Goodman's drummer, of course, he was also taking part in such sensitive and gentle performances as the Goodman Trio and Quartet recordings. Some of the drumming he was doing in those days sounds a little dated now (especially when compared with Dave

Tough's work from the same period), but Krupa was always a brilliant technician and he swung at a time when good white drummers were the scarcest of all musicians. Goodman and Krupa had known one another in Chicago, where Krupa played on such famous recording sessions as those by the Chicago Rhythm Kings and the McKenzie-Condon Chicagoans. A whiff of that past (it was past even in 1935) comes through on (1), performed by a contingent from the Goodman orchestra, plus that stalwart bassist, Israel Crosby. The highspot here is Nate Kazebier's trumpet solo in *Blues of Israel*. (2), by another pick-up group, is notable for wild playing by Roy Eldridge and one of Chu Berry's best solos (*I hope Gabriel likes my music*).

In 1938 Krupa left Goodman and formed his own band. Some of the early tracks by this group (together with much later ones) can be heard on (3). Roy Eldridge and Anita O'Day both worked with the Krupa band during the 1940s, and are quite heavily featured in (4) and (5), the latter including Eldridge's frenetic performance of *After you've gone*. (6) contains crisp but slightly staid tracks by the 1945-6 band. With (7) and (8) we arrive at music of real quality, an attempt at re-creating the Goodman Quartet but without a clarinettist. (7), in particular, contains some of the finest solos Hampton and Wilson have put on record. Another attempt at re-creation, and again a success on a slightly lower level, is (9), where Roy Eldridge and Anita O'Day go through some of their old routines from the 1940s. Eldridge is in particularly sparkling form. Two of the noisiest drummers in the world are brought together on (10), but the music – apart from a couple of deafening tracks – is surprisingly pleasant, mainly because Dizzy Gillespie and Roy Eldridge contribute good solos.

The majority of records by Gene Krupa's Trios and Quartets have been disappointing, largely because Krupa has used mediocre soloists. (11), however, bearing the misleading title, 'Krupa Rocks', is uncommonly tasteful, with fine drumming by Krupa and intelligent solos from Gail Curtis (clarinet) and Teddy Napoleon (piano). On (12) Krupa assembled a very competent band to perform some of the arrangements which Gerry Mulligan wrote for him back in the 1940s. But here, alas, with modernists all round him, Krupa seems out-of-place, his on-the-beat style totally out of sympathy with their playing.

(1) CHICAGO STYLE – 7 Par GEP8576 (*d*). *1935.*
(2) GENE KRUPA'S ALL STAR SWING BAND – 7 HMV 7EG8111 (*d*). *1936.* (A) 12 Cam 340 (plus tracks by the 1950 band).
(3) GENE KRUPA – 7 Fon TFE17087. *1938–46.*
(4) GENE KRUPA'S SIDEKICKS – (A) 12 Col CL641. *1940s.*
(5) GENE KRUPA – (A) 12 Col CL753. *1940s.*
(6) LEAVE US LEAP – 7 Ph BBE12173. *1945–6.*
(7) GENE KRUPA, LIONEL HAMPTON, TEDDY WILSON – 12 Col 33CX10027 (*d*). (A) 12 Ver 8066 (*d*). *1955.*
(8) STROLLIN' ALONG – 7 Col SEB10086. *1955.*
(9) DRUMMER MAN – 12 HMV CLP1087. (A) 12 Ver 2008. *1956.*
(10) KRUPA AND RICH – 12 Co 33CX10040. (A) 12 Ver 8069. *1956.*
(11) KRUPA ROCKS – 12 Co 33CX10133. (A) 12 Ver 8276. *1957.*
(12) KRUPA PLAYS GERRY MULLIGAN ARRANGEMENTS – 12 HMV CLP1281. (A) Ver 8292, (S) 6008. *1958.*

L

TOMMY LADNIER (1900–1939)   *trumpet*

Tommy Ladnier played the blunt, economical, attacking kind of trumpet solo that stemmed from the original New Orleans style, as played by Oliver and Bunk Johnson and Keppard, and managed to avoid being strongly influenced by Louis Armstrong as most jazz trumpeters were. Perhaps for this reason a Ladnier recording always sounds fresh and different. His playing is rather mournful and sombre, his tone is slightly rough but loses none of its beauty through this gruff attack, and his ideas are simple, based on the primitive blues; his playing on the trumpet is near in spirit to the piano playing of Jimmy Yancey. Even after years of playing in larger groups like the Fletcher Henderson orchestra this rustic style remained.

His earliest recordings with Ollie Power in 1923 are too indistinct to judge properly. His 1923–4 recordings with Lovie Austin's Blues Serenaders, many of which were as accompaniment to blues singers such as Ma Rainey and Edmonia Henderson, on deleted London and Riverside recordings, afford an interesting contrast between Ladnier's method of supplying an obbligato to a blues singer and Armstrong's very vocalized masterpieces in a similar situation. Ladnier's economy of means, always playing just the right notes and little else, compares interestingly with Armstrong's eloquence.

Dispirited by the growing commercialism of jazz, a trend that he perceived in the requirements of the Henderson orchestra in spite of some great recordings like *Hot mustard, Clarinet marmalade, Snag it, Fidgety feet* and *Sensation* (on deleted Br 78s 02001, 02634 and 02503) made 1926–7, Ladnier left jazz. Hugues Panassié, the French critic, who rates him next only to Oliver and Armstrong, was determined to rediscover Ladnier and with the help of Mezz Mezzrow, managed to find him and bring him back to the jazz scene to record wonderful sides like *Weary blues, Really the blues, When you and I were young Maggie* and *Gettin' together* (most of these were available on a now deleted HMV 10 LP DLP1110, (A) Vic LVA3027 (d)). In 1939 with James P. Johnson he recorded some more fine blues accompaniments, this time to Rosetta Crawford – *Stop it Joe* and *My man jumped salty on me* ((d) Voc V1002. (A) Dec 7567), *I'm tired of fattening frogs for snakes* and *Double crossin' papa* ((d) Br 03461, (A) Dec 7584). He died soon after these recordings, which show in better quality sound his unique and effective economy.

The only good track currently available is *I've found a new baby* a 1932 recording with Sidney Bechet's Feetwarmers, on GREAT JAZZ BRASS – 12 Cam CDN-112, (A) 12 Cam CAL-383.

DAVE LAMBERT (1917) *vocal*

Although his remark was intended as a joke, Dave Lambert's claim to be 'the oldest living bop singer' is near the truth. He and the late Buddy Stewart made some records with Red Rodney in 1947 (*A cent and a half, Charge account, Gussie G* and *Perdido*), with Charlie Barnet (*What's this* and *Bebop spoken here*) and under their own names with Stan Getz and Allen Eager (*Deedle* and *Hot halavah* on Vogue standard play V2050). They blended their voices instrumentally and took off on a number of improvised choruses; Dave's 1949 records with a choir for Capitol (*When the red, red robin, Beban cubop, Always* and *Hawaiian war chant*) were the natural outcome of the earlier experiments and warrant reissue on microgroove. During the late 'fifties Lambert teamed up with the talented Annie Ross and Jon Hendricks to form a unique trio which extended the original idea of King Pleasure (q.v.). Hendricks wrote the unusual, fresh lyrics to established jazz solos and the project reached fruition with (1), an incredible display of unadulterated talent in which the three singers multi-taped their voices to give an accurate imitation of the complete Basie band. Hendricks' solo vehicle, *Little pony* (based on Wardell Gray's original version) is a masterly performance. A second album (2) dispensed with the multi-dubbed idea and added the Lambert singers to the mighty Basie band. Annie Ross's 'lead trumpet' work is fantastic on *Goin' to Chicago*, a track which proves the superiority of Hendricks over Joe Williams as a jazz singer.

(1) SING A SONG OF BASIE – 12 HMV CLP1203. (A) 12 ABC LP1223. *1958.*

(2) SING ALONG WITH BASIE – 12 Col 33SX1151. (A) 12 Rou R52018. *1958.*

YANK LAWSON (1911) *trumpet*

A forceful, attacking trumpet-player, a musician who makes cunning use of mutes, Yank Lawson came to prominence as a member of Bob Crosby's orchestra. With another ex-Crosby musician, the bassist Bob Haggart, he has produced a set of Dixieland performances, using tunes drawn from various eras and areas of jazz. Although the emotional impact is low the playing is highly professional, and the group boasts two fine soloists in Lou McGarity, an exceptionally skilful trombonist who once worked with Benny Goodman, and Lawson himself. (5) is probably the best LP, partly because Billy Butterfield was added to the group, partly because the tunes allow the musicians greater lattitude.

(1) JELLY ROLL'S JAZZ – 10 Br LA8576 (*d*). (A) 12 Dec 8182. *1951.*

(2) KING OLIVER'S JAZZ – 10 Br LA8593 (*d*). (A) 12 Dec 8195. *1951–2.*

(3) BLUES ON THE RIVER – 10 Br LA8580 (*d*). (A) 12 Dec 8196. *1952.*

(4) WINDY CITY JAZZ – 10 Br LA8639 (*d*). (A) 12 Dec 8198. *1953.*

(5) SOUTH OF THE MASON-DIXON LINE – 10 Br LA8703 (*d*). (A) 12 Dec 8197. *1953.*

(6) LOUIS' HOT 5'S AND 7'S – 10 Br LA8698 (*d*). (A) 12 Dec 8200. *1954.*

HUDDIE LEDBETTER (Leadbelly) (1888–1949)
twelve-string guitar, mandolin, piano, accordian, vocal

While Leadbelly was a folk singer – his repertoire was fairly eclectic – rather than a blues singer, his recordings of *Fannin Street*

(3), *Bourgeois blues*, (3), *Becky Deem* (23) and *Roberta* would, alone, justify his inclusion amongst the great blues singers. Blind Lemon Jefferson's most brilliant follower – Leadbelly was Jefferson's guide – he created an enormous number of blues and folk-songs, many of which have been made available in Britain. A comparison with the Jefferson recording of *Stocking feet blues* will immediately show how strong was this influence, although the many personal phrases which appear in Leadbelly's guitar playing give an immediate identity to his songs. The twelve-string guitar is, inevitably, an instrument for producing powerhouse rather than lyrical music and, played by Leadbelly, it was the perfect setting for such songs as *Green Corn* (2) or *Skip to my Lou* (4). It is, nonetheless, amazing that Leadbelly should have achieved such lyricism as he did on *Fannin Street* (3) while, at the same time, propelling this blues with his superb rhythm. Here is demonstrated the fine control which he exercised over his instrumental and vocal techniques, for his voice contained an immensity of sound unmatched by any other singer recorded in this field. *Fannin Street* (3), in fact, is an object lesson in dynamics, one of the truly great blues on record.

Leadbelly's discovery by the Lomaxes, the way in which he sang himself out of prison, his life in the South and in New York, are all, somehow, part of his music. By his proud way of life, he became the style-setter for most of the blues artists around New York and, according to Bill Broonzy, 'When Lead took to wearing a suit on stage, we all started to wear suits on stage.' His only appearance in Europe – Paris, in 1949 – was poorly attended owing to insufficient publicity (this writer was fortunate enough to be present) and, within a few months of his return to New York, he was dead. Not long after his death, this John Henry of the Blues was to be used as the motive power of the skiffle movement and is still the most admired singer/guitarist among enthusiasts of Negro folk-song.

(1) LEADBELLY, Vol. 1 – 10 Mel MLP511. (A) 10 Sti SLP17 *1942–3*.
(2) LEADBELLY, Vol. 2 – 10 Mel MLP512. (A) 10 Sti SLP19. *1943*.
(3) LEADBELLY, Vol. 3 – 10 Mel MLP515. (A) 10 Sti SLP51. *1939*.
(4) PARTY SONGS – 10 Mel MLP517. (A) 10 Sti SLP39. *1941–4*.
(5) SAGA OF LEADBELLY – 12 Mel MLP-12.107. (A) 12 Sti SLP48. *1940–6*. [1]

(6) LEADBELLY'S LAST SESSIONS, Vol. 2 (Part 1)–12 Mel MLP-12.113.
(7) LEADBELLY'S LAST SESSIONS, Vol. 2 (Part 2)–12 Mel MLP-12.114.
(A) 2-12 Fol FA2942. *1948.*
(8) LEADBELLY – 7 Mel EPM7-63. *1943.*
(9) LEADBELLY – 7 Mel EPM7-77. *1942–3.*
(10) LEADBELLY – 7 Mel EPM7-82. *1943.*
(11) LEADBELLY – 7 Mel EPM7-87. *1943.*
(12) CLASSICS IN JAZZ – 10 Cap LC6597. (A) 10 Cap H369. *1944.*
(13) ROCK ISLAND LINE – 7 RCA RCX146. *1940.* [1]
(14) LEADBELLY'S LAST SESSION, Vol. 1 – (A) 2-12 Fol FA2941. *1948.*
(15) LEADBELLY'S LEGACY, Vol. 1 – (A) 10 Fol FA2004.
(16) LEADBELLY'S LEGACY, Vol. 2 – (A) 10 Fol FA2014.
(17) LEADBELLY'S LEGACY, Vol. 3 – (A) 10 Fol FA2024.
(18) LEADBELLY'S LEGACY, Vol. 4 – (A) 10 Fol FA2034.
(19) *Pick a bale of cotton/Alabama bound* – 10 78 HMV MH190. *1940.* [1]
(20) *Packing trunk blues/All out and down* – 10 78 Jcl L2. *1935.*
(21) *Four day worry blues/New black snake moan* – 10 78 Jcl L108. *1935.*
(22) *Becky Deem/Pig meat pappa* – 10 78 Jcl L124. *1935.*
(23) *Diggin' my potatoes/Defence blues* – 10 78 Tem A16 (d). *1946.*

JOHNNY LETMAN (1917)   *trumpet*

Until two British critics, Albert McCarthy and Stanley Dance, visited the U.S. and got him into a recording studio, Johnny Letman was unknown to most jazz collectors, even though he has worked at various times for Count Basie, Cab Calloway and Earl Hines. An aggressive trumpet-player with a vicious edge to his tone, Letman performs in a style very similar to that of Hot Lips Page. Indeed he sounds remarkably like Page in both *Four faces of Johnny* ('the Louis face, the Lips face, the John face and the Cootie face') (1959) and *Blues for baby*, one of four tracks by a group led by Joe Thomas on 'Mainstream', 12 Lon LTZ-K15182, SAH6066, (A) 12 Atl 1303, (S) S1303 (1958). It is on blues, in fact, that Letman's passionate, intense approach is most effective. On other available tracks his playing tends to become a little tousled, a little too untidy.

   1 On (5) Leadbelly is joined by Guthrie and Houston for *Grey goose* and *Ham and Eggs*. On (13) he is accompanied by the Golden Gate Quartet on *Rock Island Line* and *Take this hammer* and on (19) he is accompanied by the Golden Gate Quartet.

GEORGE LEWIS (1900)   *clarinet*

A New Orleans based musician who might never have become the well-known figure he is if he had not been associated with the revival of Bunk Johnson in 1942. Much against Johnson's will, who had no great opinion of either Lewis or Jim Robinson who were crude folk-style musicians with very little of Johnson's technical knowledge but who were thought to be the right people to play with him by his sponsors, Lewis was dragged out of obscurity to play with the rather crusty cornet player. It was said to be an unhappy period and when Bunk Johnson died in 1949 and Lewis took over the band there was no doubt great relief felt all round. It is understandable why Johnson disliked Lewis's playing which is raw and sombre, harsh and often slightly off-pitch with a most disturbing slow vibrato like an air-raid siren. Even when he does play with great feeling and beauty this vibrato can be a destroying factor. However, the many people who admire and like this kind of music will enjoy the band's recordings, which cannot all be mentioned single and all maintain a good standard. Lewis's own *Burgundy Street blues* is usually his best vehicle for improvisation. The best disc is probably (16) and the most unusual (15).

(1) GEORGE LEWIS AND HIS NEW ORLEANS STOMPERS – 12 Vog LAE12005. (A) 12 BN 1205. *1943*.

(2) GEORGE LEWIS AND HIS NEW ORLEANS STOMPERS, Vol. 2 (A) 12 BN 1206. *1943*.

(3) GEORGE LEWIS AND HIS NEW ORLEANS MUSIC – 7 GTJ EPG1182. *1950*.

(4) GEORGE LEWIS AND HIS NEW ORLEANS ALL STARS – 10 Vog LDE082. *1950*.

(5) GEORGE LEWIS AND HIS NEW ORLEANS ALL STARS AND QUARTET – 10 Lon (*d*) HB-U1045. (A) 12 Riv 12-207. *1951–3*.

(6) GEORGE LEWIS AND HIS NEW ORLEANS ALL STARS – 10 Vog LDE012. *1951*.

(7) GEORGE LEWIS AND HIS NEW ORLEANS ALL STARS AND QUARTET – 10 Lon (*d*) H-APB1041. (A) 12 Riv 12-207. *1951–3*.

(8) NEW ORLEANS JAZZ CONCERT (with Freddie Kohlman) – 10 Br LA8627. *1952*.

(9) GEORGE LEWIS AND HIS NEW ORLEANS RAGTIME BAND – 10 Esq 20-067. *1953*.

(10) GEORGE LEWIS AND HIS NEW ORLEANS RAGTIME BAND –
10 Esq 20-073. *1953*.

(11) GEORGE LEWIS AND HIS NEW ORLEANS RAGTIME BAND –
10 Esq 20-085. *1953*.

(12) GEORGE LEWIS AND HIS NEW ORLEANS RAGTIME BAND –
10 Esq 20-086. *1953*.

(13) GEORGE LEWIS AND HIS RAGTIME BAND – 12 Tem TAP13.
1953.

(14) GEORGE LEWIS AND HIS NEW ORLEANS RHYTHM BOYS –
10 Mel MLP504. *1954*.

(15) JAZZ AT VESPERS – 12 Lon (d) LTZ-U15112. (A) 12 Riv 12-230.
1954.

(16) GEORGE LEWIS IN HI-FI – 12 Vog LAE12059. (A) 12 Cav 6004.
1956.

(17) THE PERENNIAL GEORGE LEWIS – 12 Col 33CX10131. (A)
12 Ver 8277. *1957*.

(18) GEORGE LEWIS (and Turk Murphy) AT NEWPORT – (A) 12
Ver 8232. *1957*.

(19) GEORGE LEWIS BAND – 12 Col 33CX10099. *1957*.

(20) RAGGIN' AND STOMPIN' – 10 Col 33C9042. *1958*.

(21) GEORGE LEWIS AND HIS BAND – 7 Col SEB10112. *1958*.

(22) GEORGE LEWIS CONCERT – (A) 12 BN 1208.

(23) DOCTOR JAZZ – (A) 12 Del 201.

(24) GEORGE LEWIS ON PARADE – (A) 12 Del 202.

(25) THE SINGING CLARINET – (A) 12 Del 203.

JOHN LEWIS (1920)   *piano, arranger*

(Although John Lewis is not the leader of the Modern Jazz Quartet
– the Quartet is a co-operative unit in which Lewis acts as musical
director – the MJQ's recordings will be covered under this artist.)
The fragility of the MJQ's music is a far cry from the rough, out-
spoken fervour of the middle-forties Dizzy Gillespie orchestra in
which Lewis gained his first 'name' band experience and it is unfortunate that some of the fervour has not been retained in the music
of the MJQ. Formed originally as the Milt Jackson Quartet (q.v.),
the personnel comprised four men who had, at various times, served
under Gillespie: John Lewis, Milt Jackson, Percy Heath (who
replaced Ray Brown at an early stage in the quartet's history) and

[213]

Kenny Clarke. This personnel was responsible for what must still be considered amongst the best of the MJQ records. (1) and (2) date from the 1952–54 period when the four men seldom worked together as a unit (Lewis was acting as accompanist to Ella Fitzgerald at the time; the other three members were engaged in club work). The healthy vitality of Kenny Clarke's drumming and the uninhibited swing of Jackson's vibes gives the quartet its basic jazz sound and even a relatively coy miniature like *The queen's fancy* (2) is leavened with a foot-tapping beat. *Django* (2) ranks as one of Lewis's best jazz creations for not only does it hit on a suitable mood at the outset but it conjures up an atmosphere strongly reminiscent of the gypsy guitarist's style. Lewis's earlier *La ronde*, written originally for the Gillespie band and recorded by that orchestra under the title *Two bass hit*, is presented on (2) in four separate versions, each instrument being featured in turn to good effect. In 1955 Kenny Clarke left the quartet and was replaced by Connie Kay. Clarke was reportedly dissatisfied with the musical policy line suggested by Lewis and Connie Kay, while an excellent technician, lacked the swaggering jazz spirit of his predecessor. (3), the first LP by the new line-up, has several valuable tracks including *Ralph's new blues*, the fugal *Concorde* and the hard-hitting *I'll remember April*. It also contains a beautifully played but very superficial *Gershwin medley* and some entirely pointless and self-conscious borrowings from Bach during the introduction and coda to *Softly as in a morning sunrise*. About this time Lewis organized and directed a session for Norman Granz under the grand title *The modern jazz society presents a concert of contemporary music* (4). Here Lewis's pretensions as a composer of serious music peeped through the bland surface but the presence of three strong-willed jazz soloists in Jay Jay Johnson, Stan Getz and Lucky Thompson fortunately saved the day. The next MJQ LP (5) was one of the last wholly acceptable *jazz* albums and included Lewis's *Fontessa* – a work of real quality – and some relatively extrovert pieces which recaptured much of the earlier quartet's jazz feeling. Since then, with John Lewis directing the musical policy if not actually leading the unit, the MJQ's ties with jazz have become frequently tenuous. Swing and drive have gone out on the ebb-tide to be replaced by pretention and 'respectability' on the flow. (8) consists of the music which Lewis wrote for the French film *One never knows* (also released under at least two other titles) and, in its way, is masterly although the tintinnabulations of Kay and Jackson are dragged out seemingly endlessly in places. (9) has the addition of Jimmy Giuffre's clarinet on three tracks, a fact almost guaranteed to detract from the jazz value of the surroundings; (10) adds Sonny Rollins' tenor for a pair of titles, surely some of the worst playing this musician has ever committed to record. Away from the MJQ Lewis has made two records using the instrumentation of tenor, piano, guitar, bass and drums. (6) was recorded in Hollywood with Bill Perkins' languorous, Lester Young-like tenor, Jim Hall's guitar, Chico Hamilton on drums and Percy Heath on bass. The result is truly a *Grand encounter* for it represents the best elements in jazz, the long flowing lines, smooth swing and good taste; this is the kind of music which Lewis plays better than almost anyone else and it is unfortunate that he strives at other times for a consciously over-intellectualized form of expression which either fails to swing or sounds insincere. Of equal value is (7), recorded in Paris at the end of 1956 with the young Barney Wilen on tenor (a most interesting soloist), Sacha Distel on guitar, Percy Heath alternating with Pierre Michelot and Kenny Clarke alternating with Connie Kay. The material on both LPs is eminently suitable; (6) includes a tasteful *I can't get started* and *Easy living* (features for Lewis and Perkins respectively) while (7) has captivating readings of Lewis's lovely *Afternoon in Paris* and the Scandinavian folk-song *Ack varmeland du skona (Dear old Stockholm)*. Both (6) and (7) are recommended without reservation.

(1) MODERN JAZZ QUARTET – 7 Esq EP74. (A) 12 Pre PRLP7059 (with four additional titles by Milt Jackson). *1952*.

(2) MODERN JAZZ QUARTET – (A) 12 Pre PRLP7057. Four titles on 7 Esq EP14, remainder on 10 Esq 20-038. *1953* and *1954*.

(3) CONCORDE – 12 Esq 32-024. (A) 12 Pre PRLP7005. *1955*.

(4) MODERN JAZZ SOCIETY – 12 Col 33CX10038. (A) 12 Ver 8131. *1955*.

(5) FONTESSA – 12 Lon LTZ-K15022. (A) 12 Atl LP1242. *1956*.

(6) GRAND ENCOUNTER – 12 Vog LAE12065. (A) 12 WP1217. *1956*.

(7) AFTERNOON IN PARIS – 12 Or MG20036. (A) 12 Atl LP1267. *1956*.

(8) ONE NEVER KNOWS – 12 Lon LTZ-K15140. (A) 12 Atl LP1284. *1957*.

(9) MJQ AT MUSIC INN, Vol. 1 – 12 Lon LTZ-K15085. (A) 12
Atl LP1247. *1956.*

(10) MJQ AT MUSIC INN, Vol. 2 – 12 Lon LTZ-K15173. (A) 12
Atl LP1299. *1958.*

(11) IMPROVISATIONS AND MEDITATIONS – 12 Lon LTZ-K15186. (A)
12 Atl 1313, (S) S-1313. *1959.*

MEADE LUX LEWIS (1905)   *piano*

A boogie woogie pianist of great skill and power, best known for
his recordings of his *Honky-tonk train blues*, a complicated and
exciting piece which no one has played as well as its originator.
The original 1929 recording was available on a now deleted London
AL3506. His *Mr. Freddie blues* and an interesting *Celeste blues* may still
be found in record shops on Brunswick 78s. The second recording of
Honky-tonk train blues, made in 1936 for American Decca, is still to be
found on a Parlophone 78 (R2187). The third recording also made in
1936 for Victor is included on GREAT JAZZ PIANISTS (Camden). (1) is a
good collection of his work, though not too well recorded, for Blue
Note in 1939 and 1944. (2–5) are all worth having, his recent playing
has shown no decline. (6) is a patchy collection of good and awful.

(1) MEADE LUX LEWIS – 7 Vog EPV1065. *1939–44.*

(2) BOOGIE WOOGIE PIANO AND DRUMS, No. 1 – 7 Col SEB10030
(d). *1954.*

(3) BOOGIE WOOGIE PIANO AND DRUMS, No. 2 – 7 Col SEB10052
(d). *1954.*

(4) YANCEY'S LAST RIDE – 12 Col 33CX10094. (A) 12 Ver 1007.
1954–6.

(5) CAT HOUSE PIANO – (A) 12 Ver 1006. *1955.*

(6) OUT OF THE ROARING TWENTIES – 10 HMV DLP1176. (A)
12 ABC PAR 164. *1956.*

TED LEWIS (1892)   *clarinet, bandleader*

Although Ted Lewis was nominally a clarinettist as well as a bandleader, he never in fact played anything resembling jazz upon his
instrument. His stock-in-trade was a specialized brand of sentimental
hocum that earned him the sobriquet, 'the top-hatted tragedian of
jazz'. The only reason for listing Lewis in this book is because his
band contained, over the years, such distinguished musicians as

Mugg y Spanier and George Brunis, while on recording dates Lewis sometimes made use of Benny Goodman, Fats Waller, Tommy and Jimmy Dorsey, Jack Teagarden and that audacious Chicago clarinettist, Frank Teschemacher. Lewis himself cannot be heard at all on (2), apart from once inquiring, 'Is everybody happy?' *Dallas blues* and *Royal garden blues* are outstanding, with Waller playing and singing and Goodman and Spanier featured in solos. Almost as good are *Aunt Hagar's blues* and *Sobbin' blues*; Jimmy Dorsey, incidentally, sounds surprisingly like Jimmie Noone in his clarinet solo on the former track. Both these last-named tracks are included in (1), together with *Farewell blues* (with Teschemacher) and other equally notable performances. *Royal garden blues* and *Dallas blues* (plus other titles) were once available on (A) Col 6127, but this has now been deleted.

(1) EVERYBODY'S HAPPY! – (A) 12 Ep LN3170. *1927–31.*
(2) THE BLUES – 7 Ph BBE12106. *1930–1.*

CRIPPLE CLARENCE LOFTON (1900-1957)   *piano, vocal*

A fine, vigorous and very individual boogie and blues pianist. He has a distinctive staccato style veering towards the ragtime idiom and has provided some fine accompaniments, two good examples being to Red Nelson on *Streamline train/Cryin' mother blues*, probably to Jesse James on *Lonesome day blues/Southern Casey Jones* (Voc V1037 78 (*d*)) and the session with Louise Johnson (2). A Riverside and London LP of 1939 (RLP1037, AL3531) is now deleted, but the Vogue LP gives a good sample of his playing.

Though famous, chiefly, for his piano playing, Lofton was an intriguing singer as he proved on such titles as *Strut that thing* and *Brown skin girls* (recorded in 1935).

(1) *Streamline train/Cryin' mother blues* – 10 78 Br 03508)*d*).
(2) BOOGIE WOOGIE WITH THE BLUES – 10 Lon AL3544 (*d*). *1930.*
(3) PIANO SOLOS – 10 Vog LDE122. *1943.*

JIMMY LUNCEFORD (1902-47)   *saxophone, bandleader*

Just as a comedian can only be as funny as his script-writer, so – a similar aphorism goes – a band is only as good as its arrangers. In the case of Jimmy Lunceford's orchestra, that saying came very near the truth, except that the work of the sections and individual soloists was too masterly to be dismissed quite so glibly. It is true, though, that the shape and sound of the band's music was largely the creation of Sy Oliver, a trumpet-player with Lunceford from 1933 until 1939, when he moved across to Tommy Dorsey. There may have been bands which swung more than Lunceford's (Count Basie's is one), but no band has ever swung with quite the same precision, the same light but thrusting emphasis upon the off-beat. The credit for this belongs partly to Sy Oliver, whose arrangements were designed around this rhythmic pattern, partly to James Crawford, one of the greatest of big-band drummers. The scores on the LPs listed below were mostly written by Sy Oliver, and all exploit formal relation-ships, the to-and-fro between reeds and brass, rather than aspects of texture. Mezz Mezzrow once declared that the Lunceford band had caught 'that old New Orleans up and down'. He probably meant that the trumpet, trombone and reed sections of the band played a similar kind of role to that performed by the front-line instru-ments of a New Orleans band. The opening chorus of *Baby won't you please come home* (3) provides a very concise illustration of this point.

The Lunceford reed section was led by Willie Smith, a musician who impresses his personality upon a section in the same way that Benny Carter does. In addition, of course, Willie Smith is one of the greatest of alto soloists; some of his finest work with Lunceford can be found in *Lonesome road* (the first alto solo), *Uptown blues* and *Chopin's Prelude No. 7* (3). The alto solo in *Margie* (2), incidentally, was played by Ted Buckner. Joe Thomas, the band's tenor player, usually mixed a rich tone with shrewd phrasing in such solos as the one he plays in *Baby won't you please come home* (3). A feature of the Lunceford trumpet section was the presence of at least one high-note specialist, for this kind of showy playing was very much a part of the band's tradition. The best trumpet solos were those played by Sy Oliver, at that time one of the most expert performers with a mute, a master of growl and wa-wa playing. A particularly fine example of his muted work can be heard in *Organ grinder's swing* (1). The other really outstanding musician in this band was Trummy Young, the trombonist, now a mainstay of the Louis Armstrong All Stars. Armstrong, as it happens, has been the dominating influence upon Young's playing for most of his career; many of the trombonist's solos are conceived in a similar fashion, using the same details of phrasing, to an Armstrong solo. Young's style has always been direct, often very forceful. He takes notable – one could almost say famous – solos in *Margie* and *Annie Laurie* (2) and *Lunceford special* (3).

All three LPs contain important tracks by this great orchestra, although (1) is marred by the inclusion of two indifferent performances – *Charmaine* (featuring some of Dan Grissom's plummiest singing) and *Sweet Sue*.

(1) FOR DANCERS ONLY – 10 Br LA8738. (A) 10 Dec DL5393 (*d*). *1934–8*.

(2) JIMMY LUNCEFORD AND HIS ORCHESTRA – 12 Br LAT8027. (A) 12 Dec DL8050. *1934–41*.

(3) JIMMY LUNCEFORD AND HIS ORCHESTRA – 12 Ph BBL7037 (*d*). (A) 12 Col CL634. *1939–40*.

HUMPHREY LYTTELTON (1921)   *trumpet, clarinet, vocal*

Humphrey Lyttelton is one of the very few first-class traditional trumpet players to be born in England. A sincere and skilful player who has modelled himself on the greatest and most difficult model of all, Louis Armstrong, he was particularly fortunate in joining forces at an early stage in his jazz career with the clarinettist Wally Fawkes.

These two men complemented each other's playing so perfectly that between them they created an entirely original body of jazz, firmly based on the Negro tradition, but also completely their own. Lyttelton has always been an adventurer in jazz. Starting with the most elementary forms and ideas he slowly developed and, in order to play what he thought he should be playing, ran the risk of displeasing his earlier followers by becoming more progressive and experimental over the years. It is not with any wish to join the die-hards that we are inclined to believe that his later experiments have been less successful than his earlier ones, not through any decline in skill or sincerity but because he began to follow less universal models. The later attempts to follow the Ellington small band tradition is done so much better by an Ellington small band, such as those led by Johnny Hodges, that the Lyttelton performances suffer by contrast. The very early bands he played with suffered in the same way. It was about 1950 that the band began to sail into its peak period because at this time it was most individual. It only sounded like itself and created what for want of a better term might be called a British-styled jazz. Those intense, highly strung and exciting performances like *Cake walkin' babies* (3), *Tom cat blues* (3) and *1919 march* (3), in spite of the shrill and badly balanced recordings and a sometimes laggardly rhythm section, are classic performances even though Lyttelton himself may have grown somewhat ashamed of them. We shan't forget either, the atmospheric Festival Hall performance of *It makes my love come down* (R3424), the interesting Spanish rhythm experiments like *Original Jelly Roll blues* (3), the original recording of *Trog's blues* (4) and the ever exciting and stimulating *Open house* (R3475) made with some of the Graeme Bell band. This peak was wonderfully captured in the relaxed atmosphere of one of the famous Conway Hall concerts in 1954, a record which we must put first as an acquisition for all Lyttelton collectors. This record is notable not only for Lyttelton and Fawkes but the magnificent playing of Bruce Turner (6). Latterly, in the Hodges and Ellington inspired period, the outstanding saxophone voice with the band has been that of Tony Coe who lacks Turner's relaxed fluency but adds an intensity and power of his own.

(1) HUMPHREY LYTTELTON AND HIS BAND – 7 Tem EXA1. *1948.*

(2) DELVING BACK WITH HUMPH – 12 Esq 32-007. *1948–9.*

(3) HUMPHREY LYTTELTON JAZZ CONCERT – 10 Par PMD1006. *1951–2.*

(4) HUMPHREY LYTTELTON – 7 Par GEP8503 (*d*). *1949–52.*

(5) HUMPH'S JAZZ – 7 Par GEP8734. *1953.*

(6) HUMPH AT THE CONWAY – 12 Par PMC1012. *1954.*

(7) HUMPHREY LYTTELTON – 7 Par GEP8514 (d). *1950–4.*

(8) HUMPHREY LYTTELTON – 7 Par GEP8599. *1951–2.*

(9) HUMPHREY LYTTELTON – 7 Par GEP8534. *1954–5.*

(10) COLOURFUL HUMPH – 7 GEP8700.

(11) JAZZ AT THE ROYAL FESTIVAL HALL – 10 Par PMD1032. *1954.*

(12) HUMPHREY LYTTELTON – 7 Par GEP8546. *1954–5.*

(13) JAZZ SESSION WITH HUMPH – 10 Par PMD1035. *1955.*

(14) HUMPHREY LYTTELTON – 7 Par GEP8572. *1956.*

(15) HUMPHREY LYTTELTON – 7 Par GEP8580 (*d*). *1955.*

(16) HUMPHREY LYTTELTON – 7 Par GEP8584. *1950–1.*

(17) HUMPH SWINGS OUT – 10 Par PMD1044. *1956.*

(18) Here's Humph – 10 Par PMD1049. *1957.*
(19) Humphrey Lyttelton – 7 Par GEP8609. *1956.*
(20) Humph's Blues – 7 Par GEP8645. *1951–6*
(21) Kath Meets Humph – 10 Par PMD1052. *1957.*
(22) It's Mardi Gras – 7 Par GEP8668. *1952.*
(23) I Play As I Please – 12 Dec LK4276. (A) 12 Lon LL-3101. *1957.*
(24) Blue Humph – 7 Par GEP8724.
(25) Humph in Perspective – 12 Par PMC1070. *1958.*
(26) Triple Exposure – 12 Par PMC1110. *1959.*

M

BROWNIE McGHEE (1915)   *vocal, guitar*

Despite the weighty influence which Blind Boy Fuller exerted on McGhee's playing in the early years, McGhee has succeeded in evolving a completely personal style. Warm and endearing as his singing has been for many years, he is able to sing with considerable power and has the advantage of 'coming through' on record. His guitar playing is unmistakable and his strong rhythm has provided the basis for many good blues records since the 1940s. Since the death of Blind Boy Fuller, McGhee has worked mostly with Sonny Terry and, in the twenty-one years of this association, these two have become one of the finest vocal/instrumental duets heard in the blues. After a recent bad patch, McGhee has again attained his proper form and his recent records with Sonny Terry, and by himself, may be recommended. It must be remembered, however, that an artist who records as often as does McGhee, cannot be brilliant at every session. Among his best records are *Knockabout blues, Easy ridin' buggy* and *Woman lover blues* (on Savoy (*d*)), *Secret mojo blues/Me and my dog* (1) and a recent LP on Columbia (2).

(1) Me and Sonny – 7 Mel EPM7-83. *1946.*
(2) Blues Is My Companion – 12 Col 33SX1223. *1959.*
(3) The Bluest – 7 Nix NJE1060. *1958.*
(4) Brownie McGhee, Blues – 10 Fol FA2030.
(5) Brownie McGhee Sings The Blues – 12 Fol FA3557.

(There are many LPs of McGhee with Sonny Terry, available. Those listed above are especially recommended.)

RED McKENZIE (1902–48)   *blue-blowing, vocal*

Here is the old phenomenon of a jazz musician who played none of the recognized jazz instruments and yet achieved fame as a jazz soloist. Red McKenzie performed on the 'paper and comb' with wonderful effect often achieving a really driving, poignant and sometimes beautiful brand of jazz. On *Happy children blues* (1) he achieves a result, with the help of Dick Slevin on kazoo, Jack Bland on banjo and the great Eddie Lang on guitar, that stands comparison with many well-known performances by blues singers. *Morning after blues* (1), *Best black* and *Stretch it boy* (1) recorded in 1924 are naïve but very happy and sincere jazz. *What do I care what somebody said* on a better 1927 recording is worth finding on a deleted Br 78 02507. The Mound City Blue Blowers, as McKenzie called his group, had considerable success in their day and McKenzie began to take greater jazz talent into his recording groups. *Tailspin blues*, *Hello Lola* and *One hour* feature musicians like Jack Teagarden, Glenn Miller, Pee Wee Russell and, on the last two tracks, some very fine Coleman Hawkins solos. These are great recordings which may be found on the collection GREAT JAZZ REEDS. McKenzie also fancied himself as a vocalist; his rather corny and dated efforts in this direction may be found on a number of records.

(1) MOUND CITY BLUE BLOWERS – 7 JC JEL-1. *1924. 1925–35.*

JIMMY McPARTLAND (1907)   *trumpet*

A good player of the white Chicagoan school who followed in the steps of Bix in the Wolverines. He plays a simple, straightforward style with little embellishment and no special distinction, but has taken part in some important sessions. The best under his own name are included on (1) while one of his most notable appearances was with the McKenzie and Condon Chicagoans in 1927.

(1) JIMMY McPARTLAND AND HIS ORCHESTRA (also Condon and Wettling) – 12 Br LAT8042. (A) 12 Dec DL8029. *1939.*

(2) JIMMY McPARTLAND'S JAZZ BAND – 10 Cor LRA10006. (A) 10 Br BL58049 (*d*). *1953.*

(3) AFTER HOURS (with Cozy Cole) – (A) 12 GA 334.

(4) JIMMY McPARTLAND'S DIXIELAND – (A) 12 Ep LN-3371.

(5) 'THE MUSIC MAN' GOES DIXIELAND – (A) 12 Ep LN-3463.

(6) HOT VS. COOL (with Dizzy Gillespie) – (A) 12 MGM 3286.

[222]

JAY McSHANN (1909)   *piano*

Because it was the first group in which Charlie Parker played, the
Jay McShann orchestra has won itself a special niche in jazz history.
Yet the band deserves more than reflected glory. Like Count Basie's,
it was nourished in Kansas City and played lusty, swinging jazz,
mostly blues, using plenty of riffs and sounding like a slightly looser
version of the Basie orchestra. Parker joined the band in 1937 and
worked with it off and on until 1941. He plays solos on several tracks
of (1), his style poised on the brink of maturity. Other soloists include
Paul Quinichette and McShann himself, a pianist in the Basie manner,
while the rhythm team contained that stalwart bassist Gene Ramey
and drummer Gus Johnson. Walter Brown shouts the blues (a little
like Jimmy Rushing) on three tracks.

(1) KANSAS CITY MEMORIES – 10 Br LA8735. *1941–3.*

SHELLY MANNE (1920)   *drums*

After some years of experience with bands of all styles and sizes
Manne seemed to find his true niche when he settled in Hollywood
during the early nineteen-fifties. Previously his work, with big bands
in particular, tended to be tense and is best exemplified by reference
to such records as *More moon* by Woody Herman and *Jolly Rogers*
by Stan Kenton (both on Capitol). Since leaving Kenton he has
developed rapidly into one of the leading drummers of the day, a
man whose work is always interesting and never banal. He makes
extensive use of his kit during his solos and has hit on a method of
playing more melodically than almost any other drummer in jazz.
He has not accomplished this at the expense of drive or swing for
he continues to push big or small bands through their tasks in an
alert but tasteful manner. Manne has appeared on hundreds of
record sessions in Hollywood, both jazz and non-jazz, and he has been
singled out as a founder member of the West Coast movement; he is,
therefore, a familiar name to record enthusiasts all over the world
and it is intended only to single out a handful of the LPs on which
he may be heard. One of his most typical breaks will be found on (1)
during the track entitled *Whose blues*, a passage in which tonal
effects and rubato go hand in hand. He rises to the occasion manfully
on (2) where he is called upon to execute more than the normal
task facing a jazz drummer. Here a number of writers have provided

[223]

a brass-and-rhythm group with a series of scores, some complex and some orthodox. The best track is Jack Montrose's *Étude de concert* in which Manne has to switch quickly from written figures to a swinging 4/4 in the improvised sections. (3) is the quintet which Shelly led for a time featuring Russ Freeman, Stu Williamson and Charlie Mariano in a series of post-Parker settings; Freeman and Manne indulge in some of their telepathic dual solos in which drums and piano are inseparably interlinked. (4) is the record which sparked off a chain-reaction so far as jazz and show tunes are concerned. Andre Previn is, quite naturally, the most prominent soloist in this trio and his adaptation of the tunes from *My Fair Lady* is original but seldom profound.

(1) LENNIE NIEHAUS QUINTET – 12 Vog LAC2167. (A) 12 Con C3518. *1954.*

(2) SHELLY MANNE, Vol. 2 – 10 Vog LDC143. (A) 10 Con C2511. *1954.*

(3) SHELLY MANNE AND HIS MEN – 12 Vog LAC12062. (A) 12 Con C3516. *1956.*

(4) SHELLY MANNE AND HIS FRIENDS – 12 Vog LAC12100. (A) 12 Con C3527. *1956.*

WINGY MANONE (1904)   *trumpet, vocal*

A player of most uneven quality – he has varied between the extremely good sides made under the name of the New Orleans Rhythm Kings (q.v.) in 1934 and the buffoonery of many of his Victor recordings of the 1930s, no longer available. The later recordings for American Decca (1) are fair Dixieland but not the best of Manone. A good track is on SINGIN' THE BLUES (Camden).

(1) TRUMPET ON THE WING – 12 Br LAT8236. (A) 12 Dec 8473. *1957.*

MEZZ MEZZROW (1899)   *clarinet, saxophone*

Mezzrow has earned the title aptly given by Hugues Panassié of 'catalyst'; he has been responsible for stimulating so many jazz musicians into giving their best and been the moving spirit behind so many great jazz recordings that he has acquired a peculiar reputation of playing the best second part in jazz. His own lack of technical ability has stopped him from being a great jazz soloist although he can play a simple unsophisticated blues as well as most Negro clarinettists and far better than any other white musician. The ability to play a second part, as Armstrong once did to Oliver, depends on a sensitiveness and understanding such as one gets in a great accompanist like Gerald Moore. His avowed and known sympathy with the Negro and with jazz has made this a natural part for him, a white musician playing the minor role to a Negro musician; although it seems natural enough to anyone who understands jazz it is still pretty rare.

In 1933 he recorded four sides with a mixed band with great success. We would like to see *Dissonance* and *Swingin' with Mezz* (once available on Par R2881) reissued, also similar and equally successful sides he made in 1934 with Kaminsky, O'Brien, Carter, Freeman, Kirby and Webb amongst others featuring fine arrangements by Alex Hill. He recorded some more great sides for Victor in 1937 and then came the unusual sessions supervised by Hugues Panassié which brought a great trumpet player, Tommy Ladnier, back to public notice just before his death, and brought together players like Sidney Bechet, James P. Johnson, Teddy Bunn to record some memorable tracks like *Gettin' together*, *Really the blues* and *Weary blues*. The HMV LP containing all these (DLP 1110) is now deleted; it is to be hoped that RCA will soon put them back on the market. This was followed by a series of recordings for his own American label King Jazz with Sidney Bechet and a fine rhythm section made up of various experienced musicians. These tracks (1) are more fully discussed under Bechet. After this Mezzrow settled in France and appeared on various recordings. In 1955 an interesting record with one extended improvisation to each side was issued with Peanuts Holland and Guy Longnon on trumpet, Milton Sealey (piano) and Kansas Fields (drums). This appeared on a now deleted Ducretet-Thomson recording (TKL 93092) which may still be found. It is well worth the search.

(1) REALLY THE BLUES – 12 Vog LAE12017. *1945–7*.

(2) MEZZ MEZZROW AND HIS ORCHESTRA – 12 Vog LAE12007. *1954*.

Books: *Really the Blues*, by Mezz Mezzrow and Bernard Wolfe. (Random House, 1946; Musicians Press, 1947; Jazz Book Club, 1959.)

CHARLIE MINGUS (1922)   *bass*

Apart from playing the bass better than almost anyone else in jazz, Charlie Mingus is also one of the most controversial leaders and composers. His works often call for freak effects, for gongs and whistles and other sounds, but the sum total is invariably valid. In his compositional noncomformity Charlie has reached down into the roots of jazz and come up with an original style which owes little or nothing to contemporary writers. (1) was his first important LP, an album which both shocked and amused many listeners; his tone picture of *A foggy day* is extremely effective and, like so many of Charlie's works, it needs to be played repeatedly (most of his scores will stand repetition) before being fully appreciated. (2) and (3) are by basically the same group and, if nothing else, then (3) is notable for the fine trombone playing of Jimmy Knepper. Shafi Hadi is a very accomplished saxophonist capable of interpreting Mingus' scores with great understanding while trumpeter Clarence Shaw shows potential greatness in the unexpected construction of his lines. (3) contains one track, *The clown*, which consists of a poem read against an engaging 3/4 background.

(1) PITHECANTHROPUS ERECTUS – 12 Lon LTZ-K15052. (A) 12 Atl 1237. *1956.*

(2) EAST COASTING – 12 Par PMC1092. (A) 12 Beth 6019. *1958.*

(3) THE CLOWN – 12 Lon LTZ-K15164. (A) 12 Atl 1260. *1958.*

MIFF MOLE (1898)   *trombone*

A pioneer white jazz trombonis , he played in a crisp, agile manner with a keen rhythmic sense that in no way derived from Negro jazz. His tone was classical and in this respect he fitted in well with the Red Nichols school. His music belonged to a ragtime era, but is none the less exciting and worthwhile for that, for he was always a novel and imaginative musician. His early recordings with Nichols on Riverside and London are now deleted. One of his classical sides, *Shim-me-sha-wabble* of 1928 is on VISIT TO JAZZLAND, No. 4. There are some wonderful moments on (1) with an exceptional *Runnin' wild* included.

(1) DOORWAY TO DIXIE (with Cy Touff) – (A) 12 Arg 606. *1949.*

THELONIOUS MONK (1920)   *piano*

For some unknown reason Monk's work remained shrouded in

mystery for several years although he has always been credited with being an influence on Bud Powell during the early, hectic days of the Minton's Playhouse jam sessions. (1) and (2) contain most of the material which he recorded for the Blue Note label in 1947 – at a time when he was looked upon as something of a musical eccentric – and in the early fifties, by which time he was gaining some respect from jazz enthusiasts. Actually, once the listener has become accustomed to Thelonious' tart harmonies and desire to surprise it becomes evident that his playing is much less esoteric than might be expected. The validity of his work as a composer is proved by the timelessness of his tunes *Ruby my dear, Well you needn't, Off minor, In walked Budd, 'Round about midnight, Epistrophy, Misterioso* and *I mean you*, all of which may be heard in prototype form on (1), played by groups containing such men as Ed Gregory, Art Blakey and Milt Jackson. *Midnight* is easily his best-known work and has been recorded by groups of all sizes and styles (including even the Henderson Reunion band on Urania). It is a tune which all but defies improvisation for its character is so strong and so closely bound to the chords that any major departure ends almost inevitably in anti-climax. Monk and Gerry Mulligan give the work a thorough investigation on (12) at a session which, although not entirely successful, contains some rugged, probing lines of rough charm. (2) includes the four titles from a 1952 date with Kinny Dorham, Lou Donaldson and Lucky Thompson, the highlight being the dramatic 6/8 version of *Carolina moon*. (3) and (5) feature the Monk trio recorded two years apart but with Art Blakey present on both occasions. (Blakey is really the only drummer for Monk; both Art and Thelonious are at their best when pitting their wits against strong individualists, and each has developed a form of telepathic communication which enables him to take liberties with phrasing.) There is a splendid, bitter-sweet treatment of *Sweet and lovely* to be heard on (3) and a basic, fundamental blues – *Blue Monk* – on (5) which recalls the direct, uncluttered simplicity of Jimmy Yancey's keyboard style. (4) is by a quintet comprising Ray Copeland, Sonny Rollins, Monk, Curly Russell and Blakey; the LP contains the relentlessly moving *Locomotive*, with Blakey laying down a powerful 'train' rhythm, and the fragmentary arrangement of *Smoke gets in your eyes* in which Monk's piano is offset by the trumpet-tenor front line. In 1955 Thelonious was signed to a contract by

[227]

Riverside who immediately set about the task of selling Monk's music to a wider public. It is unfortunate, to say the least, that the Riverside Monk albums which appeared in Britain on the London label have now been deleted from the catalogues. The first, (6), gave the pianist an opportunity of driving home the fact that his keyboard style is strongly reminiscent of Duke Ellington's at times; (compare Monk's playing with the Duke on the Capitol trio album or on *New piano roll blues*, Vogue V2046. The second, (7), consists of a programme of standard songs with firm underlying support from Oscar Pettiford and Art Blakey as Thelonious strides out in syncopated fashion, particularly on *Tea for two*. (8) has some excellent tracks by Monk and a group which includes Sonny Rollins (who is particularly effective on *Ba-lue bolivar ba-lues-are*) while (9) gives the impression of eavesdropping on the pianist as he plays introspectively through a series of ballads. *Reflection* from this LP is another 'basic' blues and it is reported that Thelonious remarked 'I sound just like James P. Johnson' when listening to the play-back. (10) is a brilliant album in every way, with Monk very much on form, some skilful writing and fine, rolling solos from Coleman Hawkins. Hawk's *Ruby my dear*, played with just the rhythm section (Gigi Gryce, John Coltrane and Ray Copeland are added on the other tracks) is a masterly performance. Replacing the regular pianist Monk quickly takes control of (11) by Art Blakey's Messengers. Bill Hardman and Johnny Griffin respond well to the challenge while Blakey keeps adding fuel to the fire at every turn to make this a first-class LP. Finally (13) and (14), recorded 'live' at a club, benefit greatly from the presence of Johnny Griffin whose supersonic tenor playing tends to overshadow Monk.

(1) THELONIOUS MONK, Vol. 1 – (A) 12 BN BLP1510. *1947*.

(2) THELONIOUS MONK, Vol. 2 – (A) 12 BN BLP1511. *1947, 1951–2*.

(3) THELONIOUS MONK QUARTET – 7 Esq EP75. (A) 12 Pre PRLP7027. *1952*.

(4) THELONIOUS MONK QUINTET – 10 Esq 20-039. (A) 12 Pre PRLP7053 *1954*.

(5) THELONIOUS MONK TRIO – 10 Esq 20-075. (A) 12 Pre PRLP7027 and 7169. *1954*.

(6) MONK PLAYS ELLINGTON – 12 Lon LTZ-U15019 (*d*). (A) 12 Riv RLP12-201. *1955*.

(7) THE UNIQUE THELONIOUS – 12 Lon LTZ-U15071 (*d*). (A) 12 Riv RLP21-209. *1956*.

(8) BRILLIANT CORNERS – 12 Lon LTZ-U15097 (*d*). (A) 12 Riv RLP12-226. *1956*.

(9) THELONIOUS HIMSELF – 12 Lon LTZ-U15120 (*d*). (A) 12 Riv RLP12-235. *1957*.

(10) MONK'S MUSIC – (A) 12 Riv RLP12-242. *1957*.

(11) ART BLAKEY'S JAZZ MESSENGERS WITH THELONIOUS MONK – 12 Lon LTZ-K15157. (A) 12 Atl 1278. *1957*.

(12) MULLIGAN MEETS MONK – 12 Lon LTZ-U15127 (*d*). (A) 12 Riv RLP12-247. *1957*.

(13) THELONIOUS IN ACTION – (A) 12 Riv RLP12-262. *1958*.

(14) MISTERIOSO – (A) 12 Riv RLP12-279. *1958*.

LITTLE BROTHER MONTGOMERY (1907)   *vocal, piano*

One of the most popular pianists of the 1930s, Montgomery is also a fine singer. He has a high voice and often sings in a virtual recitative across the beat. The contrast between voice and piano is most effective as may be heard in his fine *Vicksburg blues* (1). His best-known song, *Vicksburg blues* was re-recorded on several occasions by Montgomery and, under different titles, by other important pianist/singers, among them Roosevelt Sykes and Big Maceo Merriweather.

(1) *Vicksburg blues/No special rider* – 10 78 JCL44. *1930*.

JAMES MOODY (1925)   *alto, tenor saxophones*

Few musicians can play the blues better than James Moody, one of the truly underrated figures in contemporary jazz. His earliest 'name' band experience came with Dizzy Gillespie and it was while working with this orchestra that Moody came to Europe in 1948. He came again the following year as part of a Tadd Dameron-led quintet (Miles Davis was his front-line partner) and stayed on in Paris after the other Americans had returned home. He remained in Europe, dividing his time between Paris and Stockholm, until 1951 when he left to form a new band in New York. Despite his subsequent recording for Prestige, EmArcy and Argo in America the titles he made in Sweden are perhaps the most effective he has ever made. (1) and (2) date from the 1949–51 period and feature Moody on both alto and tenor with bands containing such well-known Scandinavians as Arne Domnerus and Lars Gullin. (2) includes both *Dexterious* and *Good bait*, tenor solos with rhythm (including the talented Gosta Theselius on piano) which convey a distinctive and highly effective mood from the first bars. (3) and (4) are by an interesting small group containing the ex-Gillespie trumpeter Dave Burns and using arrangements written by Quincy Jones. (3) is noteworthy for a touching *Nobody knows the trouble I've seen* and an intense reading of *It might as well be spring*; Eddie Jefferson, a King Pleasure admirer, sings on *I've got the blues* which turns out to be a vocalized translation of Moody's *Lester leaps in* record made in Sweden. (4) benefits from the presence of another greatly underrated but phenomenally talented musician, drummer Joe Harris. Moody turns in a fine alto version of *One hundred years from today* and the band plays Quincy's arrangement of *Keepin' up with Jonesy* (first recorded in Paris by a group of musicians from Lionel Hampton's 1953-vintage orchestra) with accuracy and understanding.

(1) James Moody Blows, Vol. 1 – 10 Esq 20-035. *1949* and *1951*.
(2) James Moody Blows, Vol. 2 – 10 Esq 20-036. *1949–51*.
(3) James Moody and His Band – 10 Esq 20-071. *1954*.
(4) James Moody and His Band – 10 Esq 20-077. *1954*.

JELLY ROLL MORTON (1885–1941)   *piano, vocal*

One of the weaknesses of jazz is the lack of originality to be found amongst its practitioners. It compares to the bulk of European classical music as the circus does to the theatre. The circus has a certain nostalgic atmosphere about it but it is not an entertainment that anyone would want to see every week. Its basis is a series of acts and tricks and the only real interest is to see who does them best. So it is with the majority of jazz – a number of accomplished performers going through a series of set tricks. The number of musicians in jazz who play in an entirely original style and use new material is very few, and the number of composers in jazz who create really new material is even fewer. One of the few was Ferdinand 'Jelly Roll' Morton.

Morton is the Chopin of jazz. A really original composer who mixes the elements of ragtime, blues and Spanish and Creole music to produce a completely unmistakable style of his own. His music is always firmly based on the most basic ingredients of primitive jazz yet even his earliest recordings are unmistakable, the music as clearly and yet as bafflingly Morton as Mozart's is Mozartian. And when he reminisces and plays as he does on the wonderful series of Library of Congress recordings a strong atmosphere and feeling of the early days of jazz is brought to life. The fact that many of Morton's boasts have been proven untrue really doesn't alter the fundamental greatness of his musical imagination and his interpretation of it. Several LPs of early Morton disappeared with the London 'Origins of Jazz' series but can probably still be found, as can his two great piano solos *King Porter stomp* and *The pearls* on Brunswick 78 03564. Two other solos made at the same time, *Fat meat and greens* and *Sweetheart o' mine* might still be found on second-hand copies of Vocalion 78 V1019. All these sides, made in 1926, are worth looking for as they present Morton at his peak as a pianist. (*Mr. Jelly Lord* and *Midnight mama* (1928) are available on 10 Cor LRA 10023.)

Not only could he interpret the music pianistically but knew with certainty how to get the effect he wanted out of a group of jazz musicians, and he also knew how to choose the best. The celebrated series of recordings with his Red Hot Peppers really need no further eulogy. They are classics of jazz that will never be forgotten; practically every side recorded is a gem, individual, original and effective. A good pick of these items recorded between 1926 and 1928 used to be obtainable on 3 HMV 10 LPs which are still worth having for the 1929 recordings including the fine trio sides with Barney Bigard and Zutty Singleton (these were DLP1016, DLP1044 and DLP1071). DLP1044 is the interesting record to search out as the greater part of the first and last mentioned is included on a recent RCA issue (2), a record which is an absolute essential to any balanced and worthwhile collection of jazz. Some of the sides like *Black Bottom stomp*, *Steamboat stomp*, *Grandpa's spells*, *Doctor Jazz* and *Kansas City stomp* are performances of such persuasion and energy that they can never be replaced. On them Morton moulds some of the great men of early jazz – George Mitchell, Kid Ory, Ward Pinkett, Johnny Dodds, Omer Simeon – to his own ideas. We should particularly like to mention here two Morton masterpieces – a wonderful blues performance *Blue blood blues* (on DLP1044) and the beautifully delicate *Mournful serenade*, a trio side until recently only ever available here on a long deleted HMV 78, B9221.

The impressive saga of recordings made by the Library of Congress (3) may not show Morton at his peak as a musician but they are a jazz experience that everyone should try to taste. Unfortunately they have never been issued in Britain. Soon after they were made Morton recorded some of the numbers again for a commercial company and these are available on a depressingly sad and moving record, full of greatness and sincerity (4). Anyone who hasn't got this record should get it before it too disappears.

(1) CLASSIC PIANO SOLOS – (A) 12 Riv 12-111. 10 Lon AL3534 (d). 10 Lon AL3559 (d). *1923–4.*

(2) THE KING OF NEW ORLEANS JAZZ – 12 RCA RD-27113. (A) 12 RCA LPM-1649. *1926–8.*

(3) JELLY ROLL MORTON, Vol. 1 (Boyhood memories) – (A) 12 Riv RLP9001.

JELLY ROLL MORTON, Vol. 2 (The animule ball) – (A) 12 Riv RLP9002.

JELLY ROLL MORTON, Vol. 3 (Discourse on jazz) – (A) 12 Riv RLP9003.

JELLY ROLL MORTON, Vol. 4 (Creepy feeling) – (A) 12 Riv RLP9004.

JELLY ROLL MORTON, Vol. 5 (Georgia skin game) – (A) 12 Riv RLP9005.

JELLY ROLL MORTON, Vol. 6 (The pearls) – (A) 12 Riv RLP9006.

JELLY ROLL MORTON, Vol. 7 (Mamie's blues) – (A) 12 Riv RLP9007.

JELLY ROLL MORTON, Vol. 8 (The murder ballad) – (A) 12 Riv RLP9008.

JELLY ROLL MORTON, Vol. 9 (Jack the Bear) – (A) 12 Riv RLP9009.

JELLY ROLL MORTON, Vol. 10 (Original Jelly Roll blues) – (A) 12 Riv RLP9010.

JELLY ROLL MORTON, Vol. 11 (Buddy Bolden's blues) – (A) 12 Riv RLP9011.

JELLY ROLL MORTON, Vol. 12 (The Storyville story) – (A) 12 RLP9012 (all Library of Congress recordings, *1938*).

(4) JELLY ROLL MORTON – 10 Vog LDE080, 7 Vog EPV1126. (A) Com 30000. *1939.*

Other deleted records include:

JELLY ROLL MORTON'S KINGS OF JAZZ – 10 Lon AL3520. (A) 10 Riv RLP1027. *1923–6.*

JELLY ROLL MORTON SOLOS – 10 Lon AL3519, 3534, 3559. (A) 10 Riv RLP1018, 1038, 1041. *1924–6.*

NEW ORLEANS (JELLY ROLL MORTON AND HIS RED HOT PEPPERS), Vols. 1–3 – HMV DLP1016, 1044, 1071. *1926–30.*

Books: *Mister Jelly Lord*, by Alan Lomax (Cassell); Jazz Book Club, 1956.

BENNIE MOTEN (1894–1935) *piano*

The music of Bennie Moten's orchestra might be said to symbolize Kansas City jazz, beginning that robust tradition of ensemble playing which has been carried forward by Count Basie, Jay McShann, Andy Kirk and Harlan Leonard. The tracks on (1) all date from the 1920s. This is virile, happy music, the work of a ten-piece band, with good solos from Ed Lewis (cornet) and Thamon Hayes (trombone). A large orchestra snorts through *Toby* and *Lafayette* (1932), two noisy but exciting tracks, Count Basie attacking the piano as if he were Fats Waller and Hot Lips Page and Ben Webster contributing passionate solos.

(1) BENNIE MOTEN PLAYS KANSAS CITY JAZZ – 10 HMV DLP1057 (d). *1926–8.*

(2) *Moten Swing* – on (A) 12 Fol 2808. *1932.*

(3) *Lafayette* – on 7 RCA RCX-1027. *1932.*

MUDDY WATERS (McKinley Morganfield) (1915)

vocal, guitar

In any discussion upon the quality of blues lyrics, it is necessary to include Muddy Waters. For, at a time when harshness and clangour have been the mainstay of popular blues, Muddy Waters has succeeded in giving a renewed power to his lyrics. In this, he may be considered the present-day Leroy Carr. His singing has coarsened a great deal since his first recordings, the unfortunate result of excess violence with electricity. However, he can still sing with great majesty, can still envelope an audience with his blues.

(1) THE BEST OF MUDDY WATERS – 12 Lon LTZ-M15152. (A) 12 Chess 1427. *1949–55.*

[233]

(2) MUDDY WATERS – 7 Vog EPV1046. *1949–52.*

(3) MISSISSIPPI BLUES – 7 Lon RE-U1060. *1955.*

(4) *Walking blues/Rolling Stone blues* – 10 78 Vog V2101 (*d*).

(5) *Long distance call/ Hello, little girl* – 10 78 Vog 2273.

(6) *Too young to know/Honey bee* – 10 78 Vog V2372.

(7) *I be's troubled/Country blues* – incl 12 L.o.C. AAFS L4. *1941.*

(The above singles are just examples of the many 45s available in the United States.)

GERRY MULLIGAN (1927)   *baritone, arranger*

The formation of his piano-less quartet in 1952 put Gerry Mulligan on the jazz map although he had already played an important part in several development stages during the late 'forties, notably with the nine-man Miles Davis band (q.v.), and as arranger to the Gene Krupa and Elliot Lawrence orchestras. (1) contains the entire results of the first session under his own name, with a ten-piece unit used on four titles (two trumpets, trombone, tenor, two baritones, piano, bass, drums and maraccas), three saxes and rhythm on two, and a lengthy duet between Allen Eager's tenor and Mulligan's baritone on *Mulligan's too*, an extemporized blues which occupies one complete side of the twelve-inch LP. There are moments of importance in the scoring for the larger group but the chief interest centres around the solo playing of the underrated Eager who, as a more accomplished musician, tends to cut the leader whenever the two are heard in close proximity. (2) presents some of the earliest and best-known quartet titles with Chet Baker's fleet trumpet and the polished brushwork of Chico Hamilton. The effect of this compact, well-integrated music on the jazz world was considerable and since 1952 there has been a vogue for using rhythm sections consisting solely of bass and drums. (Mulligan maintained that the piano tended to dominate the sound of the section and tried to liberate the front line by using arrangements based on harmony arising out of the contrapuntal weaving of two melodic lines.) The success of the formula is demonstrated by comparison of *Walkin' shoes* in the original quartet form (2) and the same tune played by the Tentette (3); the expansion of the implied harmonic progression on (2) is not an improvement and in fact it detracts from the inherent charm of the original. After Baker left the group Gerry recast his instrumentation by bringing in the gruff-sounding valve trombone of Bob Brookmeyer. Although the tonal range of the baritone and trombone are similar a contrast was provided by the differing methods of improvisation; (4), recorded at concerts in Paris during the third *Salon du Jazz*, and (7), taped on location at Storyville Club in Boston, are both good examples of the Mulligan-Brookmeyer unit at its best with Gerry marshalling his forces to give maximum effect and Bob swinging through his choruses with seemingly off-hand unconcern. A feature of (7) is *Storyville story* on which Mulligan plays piano in a chunky, angular fashion. His engaging keyboard style is heard again on one track of (5) entitled simply *Piano blues*. One side of this LP is by a revitalized quartet in which Jon Eardley adds his crackling, exciting trumpet to Mulligan's stately baritone; *Blues going up* is a fine, completely spontaneous twelve-bar played, according to Gerry's announcement, to enable the audience to find its seats and settle down. The reverse side of the record is by a sextet with Brookmeyer and tenor saxist Zoot Sims added to the front line. Although Brookmeyer and Sims were guests at the time they both joined Gerry's later regular sextet which is heard on (6). The happy blend of the four front-liners in which Sims' foot-tapping passages have a catalytic effect, makes for swinging, extrovert jazz which cannot be pigeon-holed stylistically. Since the break-up of the sextet in 1956 Mulligan has concentrated on the quartet format, finding the ideal partner during 1958 in the person of trumpeter Art Farmer. Never before has the Mulligan Quartet sounded so fresh and vital and even the re-recording of earlier material such as *My funny valentine* (12) cannot weaken the considerable impact of the group on record. Farmer, one of the best and most intelligent of all the younger trumpeters, provides the ideal contrast in the solo passages for he has a tendency to construct his phrases across the beat whereas Mulligan comes down heavily and somewhat predictably on top of the beat. Away from his own quartet Mulligan has taken part in a number of record sessions with other artistes, one being with the enigmatic Thelonious Monk (q.v.). The best of these experiments is (8) in which alto saxist Paul Desmond, from the Dave Brubeck Quartet, replaces Bob Brookmeyer; the effect is sometimes startling and never less than interesting for both Desmond and Mulligan are musicians well-versed in the system of two-part invention. Alto and baritone impart a floating quality to the music

[235]

which reaches its greatest heights on *Body and soul*. (9) pairs Gerry
with Stan Getz, a meeting which strikes fire on *This can't be love*.
Unfortunately one side of the LP is largely wasted due to the mistaken
belief that both participants are masters of each other's instrument;
Let's fall in love, *Anything goes* and *Too close for comfort* merely
demonstrate that Getz is as unfamiliar with the baritone as Gerry
is with the tenor. (10) suffers from another serious A and R mistake;
having selected one of the most compatible sax sections of recent
years (Lee Konitz, Allen Eager, Zoot Sims, Al Cohn and Mulligan)
the overall effect is lessened by the inclusion of Freddie Greene on
rhythm guitar whose relentless four-to-a-bar chording is at variance
with the quite different concept of the beat existing in the front line.
(11) is a reunion of Baker and Mulligan after nearly five years apart.
The music is not as good as the early quartet's output (2) but Baker
does not disgrace himself while Mulligan's acute sense of form gives
character and meaning to the music.

(1) GERRY MULLIGAN ALL STARS – 12 Esq 32-014. (A) 12 Pre
    PRLP7006. *1951.*

(2) GERRY MULLIGAN QUARTET – 12 Vog LAE12050. Most of these
    tracks are on (A) 12 WP 1207. *1952* and *1953.*

(3) GERRY MULLIGAN TENTETTE – 10 Cap LC6621. (A) 12 Cap T691
    (remaining titles by Shorty Rogers' Giants). *1953.*

(4) GERRY MULLIGAN QUARTET – 12 Vog LAE12015. (A) 12
    WP1210. *1954*

(5) CALIFORNIAN CONCERTS – 12 Vog LAE12006. (A) 12 WP 1201.
    1954.

(6) GERRY MULLIGAN SEXTET – 12 EmA EJL101. (A) 12 EmA 36101.
    1955.

(7) GERRY MULLIGAN QUARTET – 12 Vog LAE12080. (A) 12
    WP 1228. *1956.*

(8) GERRY MULLIGAN-PAUL DESMOND – 12 Col 33CX10113. (A)
    12 Ver 8246. *1957.*

(9) GETZ MEETS MULLIGAN – 12 Col 33CX10120. (A) 12 Ver 8249.
    1957.

(10) GERRY MULLIGAN SONG BOOK – 12 Vog LAE12128. (A) 12
    WP1237. *1957.*

(11) REUNION WITH CHET BAKER – 12 Vog LAE12185. (A) 12
    WP1241. *1957.*

[236]

(12) Gerry Mulligan Quartet – 12 Ph BBL7320. (A) 12 Col
CL1307. *1958*.

N

FATS NAVARRO (1923–50)   *trumpet*
   Good trumpeters die young, or so it seems; Navarro, Clifford
Brown, Bix Beiderbecke, Bunny Berigan and Sonny Berman
certainly give the statement a ring of truth. Navarro flourished
before the large-scale recording wave hit jazz which means that he is
represented on very few LPs and EPs. (He plays on pitifully few
records released on British labels.) He worked for some time with
bands led by Tadd Dameron and Tadd will be found on several of
Fats' records. The trumpeter was without doubt one of the best of
the new movement with a technique which, on record at least,
exceeded even Gillespie's. His incredibly clean articulation, stamina,
accuracy, full tone and wealth of ideas set him apart from most of his
fellows and it is small wonder that a man of Navarro's capabilities
should have been admired so much by younger musicians. Like
Beiderbecke, Fats was frequently teamed with inferior jazzmen on
record dates, which is what happened on (1); fortunately he was able
to rise above his surroundings and turn in some fine solos, notably on
Ice freezes red. (2) and (3) contain just about all the material he recorded
for Blue Note and the overall standard is much higher than (1).
He duets with Howard McGhee on *Double talk* (readers are warned
that Leonard Feather's sleeve identification of the two soloists is
incorrect), adds fire to the conflagration already created by Bud
Powell on those four brilliant pieces *Wail, Bouncing with Bud, 52nd St.
theme* and *Dance of the infidels* and caps some excellent Allen Eager
and Wardell Gray solos with even greater displays. (Feather is again
incorrect in annotating the Gray and Eager passages.) (4) contains the
titles from his last date, the final track being called, significantly,
Stop. Don Lanphere plays good Warne Marsh-like tenor (he also
composed *Stop* and *Wailing wall* although they are frequently
attributed to Navarro) and the Al Haig-led rhythm section is
completely in context.

(1) FATS NAVARRO MEMORIAL – 10 Lon LZ-C14015. (A) 12 Sav 12011
(with additional titles). *1946* and *1947*.

(2) FATS NAVARRO MEMORIAL ALBUM, Vol. 1 – (A) 12 BN BLP1531.
1947 and *1948*.

(3) FATS NAVARRO MEMORIAL ALBUM, Vol. 2 – (A) 12 BN BLP1532.
1947 and *1948*. (Four titles from (2) and (3) on 7 Vog EPV1033;
three more on 7 Vog EPV1105.)

(4) FATS NAVARRO QUINTET – 7 Esq EP13. *1949*.

RED NELSON (unknown) *vocal*

Nelson's fame as a singer rests, mainly, on his outstanding record
with Cripple Clarence Lofton: *Streamline train/Cryin' mother
blues* (1). Especially on the second side, his high-pitched, mournful
voice gives great poignancy to a particularly fine set of lyrics.
Other recordings, such as *Detroit blues,* do not come up to this
standard. He has recently been rediscovered in the vicinity of
Chicago.

(1) *Streamline train/Cryin' mother blues* – 10 78 Br 03508 (*d*).

NEW ORLEANS RHYTHM KINGS

An early white group that provides the developing link between
the early Negro jazz of New Orleans, which they adapted from the
Oliver Creole Jazz Band stage and considerably diluted, and the thin
and monotonous pipings of most of the Chicago school. The New
Orleans Rhythm Kings were well on the Oliver side of the balance
and played some crisp compact jazz which at the same time had
great character stemming from the robust, rollicking trombone of
George Brunis and the weird piping clarinet of Leon Rappolo. This
was, of course, the original NORK which had no connexion with
the good but more run of the mill Dixieland groups of the same name
led by Wingy Manone in 1934 and Muggsy Spanier in 1935 – except
that Brunis was in them all.

NORK. Original 1922–5.

(1) NEW ORLEANS RHYTHM KINGS – (A) 12 Riv 12-102. (*d*) 10 Lon
AL3536 and AL3552.

Collections: 7 Col 45 SCM5113.

NORK. Manone – 1934.

(*d*) Br 78 01910, 01988, 02040m, 02337. See also LAT8124, 8166.

NORK. Spanier – 1935.
(d) Br 78 02008, 01510, 03447.

FRANKIE NEWTON (1905–1954)   *trumpet*

Frankie Newton's first recording session was, as it happened, the last that Bessie Smith ever made. That was in 1933, and the 18-year-old trumpeter played two of his most restless, violent solos in *Do your duty* and *Gimme a pigfoot* ('The Bessie Smith Story', Vol. 1 – 12 Ph BBL7020, (A) 12 Co CL-856). Newton was to go on, mixing violence with delicacy, making music that was uneasy yet beautiful, until he left the jazz scene in the late 1940s and died in poverty a few years later. A fragile, probing solo can be heard in *Gone at dawn* (1944) on 'Trumpet Interlude' (12 EmA EJL1276, (A) 12 EmA 36017) for Newton's use of mutes was always very sensitive, an outstanding instance being his obbligato on Billie Holiday's *Strange fruit* ((A) 12 Com 30008). Other records currently available in the U.S. that contain Newton solos include *The world is waiting for the sunrise* ((A) 12 Fol 2811), made at a session in 1939 when Newton was in poor health and fluffing a lot of the time, and *Blues for Tommy*, by the Port of Harlem Jazz Men ((A) 12 BN 1202). *Tab's blues* (with one of Newton's finest solos and good alto playing by Tab Smith) and *Frankie's jump*, two recordings made by the little band Newton led at the Café Society in 1939, were once released on a Par 78 but have long been deleted; both titles, together with a third, are included in 'Trumpeter's Holiday' ((A) 12 Ep LN-3252). Two 78s once available in Britain which contain good Newton solos are Mezz Mezzrow's *Mutiny in the parlour* (Regal-Zono) and Willie 'The Lion' Smith's *Blues, why don't you let me alone?* (Br).

ALBERT NICHOLAS (1900)   *clarinet, saxophone*

Albert Nicholas is one of a group of clarinettists who form the hard core of classic jazz clarinet tradition. A modest man and a quietly competent player, he has not become quite so well known as players like Dodds, Bechet and Noone. His own style is very pure, inclining more to the smoothness of Noone except when he plays in the lower register, when, like all traditional clarinettists playing in the lower register, he sounds more like Dodds. But the basic influence on his playing is his Creole origin and his training with Creole

[239]

musicians like Lorenzo Tio. This is most clearly seen in the magnificent recordings of *No pas lemme ca*, *Les ognons* and *Salée dame* with James P. Johnson, Danny Barker and Pops Foster (1), three beautiful sides which illustrate all that is best in the quaint, melodious and smooth Creole style. Having heard these it becomes plainer how this influence remains even in his recordings of traditional jazz tunes such as *Buddy Bolden's blues*, *Wolverine blues*, *Albert's blues* with Don Ewell and Baby Dodds on the same record (1).

His solos should be listened to on many recordings with King Oliver and Luis Russell as he unfortunately made few recordings leading his own group until the 1950s, by which time he had settled in Paris. A recent series of EPs illustrate this period on which he appears with varying French groups and inspires them to varying degrees. The most successful is (4) which includes a good recording of *High society*, *Bugle call rag* and *Black and blue*. *Blues for kicks* (3) features some good clarinet. (5) contains some neat and pleasing clarinet and piano jazz, with Joe Turner. Apart from these few sides under his own name he will be heard to best advantage on Oliver's *Sugar foot stomp* (Vog Cor LRA10020), Morton's *Mississippi Mildred* and *Blue blood blues* (HMV DLP1044), and *High society* (HMV B9216), and Luis Russell's *New call of the freaks* (Par R1645).

(1) CREOLE REEDS – 12 Lon HA-U2035 (d). (A) 12 Riv 12-216. 1946-7.
(2) NICHOLAS WITH REWELIOTTY – 7 Vog EPV1109. 1954.
(3) NEW ORLEANS PARADE, Vol. 1 – 7 Vog EPV1142. 1955.
(4) NEW ORLEANS PARADE, Vol. 2 – 7 Vog EPV1143. 1955.
(5) JOE AND NICK +TWO – 7 Col SEG 7865. 1956.
(6) ALBERT NICHOLAS SEXTET – 7 Col SEG7703 (d). 1956.
(7) ALBERT NICHOLAS AND HIS ORCHEST2A – 7 Col SEG7690 (d). 1956.

RED NICHOLS (1905)   *trumpet*

Nichols is one of those many talented musicians who have plucked from jazz, as it were, some of its essential warmth and excitement, and given it an easy ear-appeal. The result is often like a piano arrangement of a Beethoven symphony. It bears the same relation to jazz as a good poster does to fine art – and there is no reason why a very good poster shouldn't be a bit of fine art. So, the Red Nichols' Five Pennies became immensely popular by virtue of their uncomplicated, tuneful music, and yet still retained many fine jazz elements because of the good jazz players used in the band. Like any art that panders to the taste of a period, much of their work sounds very dated, but nonetheless enjoyable to those whose palates like the vintage. Nichols himself is a good trumpeter with a clear singing tone and he surrounded himself with men of the calibre of Jack Teagarden, Benny Goodman, Gene Krupa, Joe Sullivan, Miff Mole and many more. (1) is a good cross-section of the band's work from 1926 to 1930 and some more good samples are included in various collections. The later revivals of the band have none of the period charm of the originals.

(1) RED NICHOLS AND HIS FIVE PENNIES – 12 Br LAT8307. (A) 12 Br 54008. *1926–30*.

(2) SYNCOPATED CHAMBER MUSIC – (A) 12 Aud 326. *1959*.

(3) HOT PENNIES – 12 Cap T-775 (d). (A) 12 Cap T-775. *1956*.

(4) IN LOVE WITH RED – (A) 12 Cap T-999. *1957*.

(5) PARADE OF THE PENNIES – (A) 12 Cap T-1051, (S) ST-1051. *1958*.

(6) AT MARINELAND – (A) 12 Cap T-1163, (S) ST-1163. *1959*.

JIMMIE NOONE (1895–1944) *clarinet*

Although Jimmie Noone has a reputation quite out of proportion to the number of records he made (the usual criterion as far as collectors are concerned) it was mainly founded on the praises of his fellow musicians (a more reliable foundation for fame). Also he has had a lasting influence on a whole school of clarinet playing. At a time when the rougher, harsher style of playing brought to perfection by Johnny Dodds, held sway, the smooth French-influenced style of Noone which the Creole players had introduced to New Orleans, gradually began to impress itself on several young Negro players. Noone himself was not entirely a hot musician: his genius was for an intricate and exciting counterpoint and a subtle turn of phrase that was to have its most lasting influence on white jazz musicians like Irving Fazola, Jimmy Dorsey and Benny Goodman. He also pioneered a move towards a break-away from the traditional New Orleans line-up, favouring a front-line of alto saxophone and clarinet.

A disappointingly large proportion of the small number of records he did make prove to be rather weak with a strangely sugary, Victor Sylvester type of playing. Noone's liking for a sweet, smooth tone

[241]

and phrase was often indulged in to excess and he hardly ever recorded with a band of musicians of his own calibre. The sides on (1) are notable for the inclusion of Earl Hines on piano and some of Noone's finest solos; a pure-toned and clean kind of playing that has rarely been equalled by any jazz clarinettist. *I know that you know, Four or five times* and others from a first session in May 1928 are probably the best as they are unhampered by a rather plodding tuba on the sides made in August, though Hines and Noone have fine solos on all of them. As the two sessions are conveniently mixed on one LP (1) the weak can happily be taken with the strong. A recording of *It's tight like that* (on a deleted Vocalion V1007 backed with *My daddy rocks me*) is a quaint record with an odd jumpy rhythm very rarely used – Ellington liked it occasionally as in his earliest recordings of *East St. Louis toodle-oo* – and it gives the tune an atmosphere of mild hilarity and infectious enjoyment. This is one of Noone's best recordings, and he plays a fine obbligato to the singer May Alix on the reverse side.

The next easily available session is an unusual one. It has a strangely modern flavour, far more than its 1936 date would suggest. Gedeon Honore on the piano, though no Hines, is a good substitute and Israel Crosby's bass is notable throughout. An intense slow blues, *The blues jumped a rabbit*, is undoubtedly a Noone masterpiece. It is good to have all these available on one EP (2).

The next session in 1936 produced a strange mixture. This was certainly the strongest group Noone ever recorded with, the players all being of a high standard, Charlie Shavers playing, for him, some very warm sounding and restrained trumpet, Pete Brown an excellent partner for Noone on alto in place of his old partner Poston, and Teddy Bunn on guitar at his most brilliant. *Japansy* and *Sweet Lorraine* are peculiarly syrupy but, on the other hand, *Four or five times* is his finest performance of all and Teddy Bunn's solo here is magnificent and memorable. *Bump it* (a speeded up version of the old *Apex blues*) and *I know that you know* are of almost equal merit (3).

Two sides made in 1940 on the American Decca New Orleans album (available on Br LAT8146) are disappointing. Noone revived with a rather unco-ordinated group that should have proved better, although there is a certain rough charm about them – but Noone was never quite this traditional by inclination.

(1) JIMMIE NOONE AND HIS APEX CLUB ORCHESTRA – 10 Cor
LRA10026. (A) 10 Br BL58006 (*d*). *1927*.
(2) JIMMIE NOONE'S NEW ORLEANS BAND – 7 Par GEP8605 (*d*). *1936*.
(3) JIMMIE NOONE AND JOHNNY DODDS – 10 Cor LRA10018. (A)
10 Br BL58046 (*d*). *1937*.

FLOYD O'BRIEN (1905) *trombone*

A remarkably distinctive American white musician who achieves
a unique effect with an absolute economy of notes and an acute
rhythmic sense. All his solos are interesting; worth particular mention
are his sides with Eddie Condon – *Home cooking, The Eel, Tennessee
twilight* and *Madam Dynamite* of 1933, not currently available; with
Mezz Mezzrow on *Dissonance, Swingin' with Mezz*, etc., 1933 – also
not at present available; and sides made with The Chocolate Dandies
in the same year; he recorded with Fats Waller in 1934 and made four
fine sides with George Wettling in 1940 (on 12 Br LAT8042, (A) 12
Dec 8029). Some sides made with Bob Crosby in the 1940s occasionally reveal a fine solo (some on 12 Cor LVA9045, (A) 12 Cor 57089);
thereafter he recorded some small group sides with Matlock and other
Crosby sidemen for the Jump label under the name of La Vere's
Chicago Loopers and Floyd O'Brien's State Street Seven – *Carolina
in the morning* is a good sample (these are available on Tempo 78s –
A1, A3, A44, A91), and some on (1).
(1) MATTY MATLOCK'S DIXIELANDERS – 7 Tem EAP10. *1945–50*.

JOE 'KING' OLIVER (1885–1938) *cornet*

It has always been difficult to assess Oliver's true stature as a
musician because the recordings while he was still at his best are so
badly made by the old acoustical method, and by the time recording
had improved, Oliver was on the decline and very often let other
trumpeters lead his band for him. We have the word of people who
actually heard him that he was a great cornettist. He played a powerful,
driving style that was meant to create excitement and swing and he
was obviously a clever and ambitious musician who led his various
groups through a continual state of progress. Had he been living
today there would have been no question of the music he inspired
having stayed in a narrow and unambitious groove of traditionalism
in the manner of leaders like George Lewis and Kid Ory. He would

have been leading a very advanced group. He was a cornettist who made great use of the mutes and probably sounded like a cross between Tommy Ladnier and Muggsy Spanier both of whom copied his punching, economical style, while Spanier developed his mute technique from Oliver.

No history of jazz and no collection would be complete without the sides made with his Creole Jazz Band on 31 March and 6 April 1923. Not only do they capture Oliver at his peak but also Louis Armstrong at the beginning of his career and some unique two-cornet work which has never been surpassed although often copied. Sides like *Canal Street blues* and *Dippermouth blues*, *Just gone* and *Mandy Lee blues* (all (1)) are compact, driving and inspired – an early model by which to judge traditional jazz in this particular idiom for all times. *Froggie Moore* and *Chimes blues* are also available on (2). These and other sides made in 1923 such as *Krooked blues* (2) and *Alligator hop* (2), *Mabel's dream* (3), *High Society* (3) and *London blues* (3), are the relics of a momentous period of jazz and, without exception, are sides to form the basis of any jazz collection.

The remarkable change of atmosphere and style that marked the Oliver recordings of 1926 that followed show that Oliver was no stick-in-the-mud. His use of musicians like Albert Nicholas, Barney Bigard and Omer Simeon brought a smoother and more rounded feeling to the music, ushering in a period that was to be formalized in the Luis Russell band – Russell was the pianist on most of these groups. The 1926–7 recordings made in Chicago with the exception of *Snag it* (on Cor LRA10023 and Br LAT8124) are to be had on deleted Vocalions (V1004, V1009) and on (4) – this fine LP includes *Sugar foot stomp*, *Willie the weeper*, *Snag it* (*No. 2*), *Someday sweetheart*, *Black snake blues* and *Too bad* from this period.

An even more noticeable sophistication comes in with the New York recordings made in 1927–8. *Speakeasy blues* (4) and *Aunt Hagar's blues* (4) showed the immediate effect of the replacement of Ory by Higginbotham, taking away the last traces of old-timeism from the band. Other studio pick-up groups of 1927–8 can be found on deleted Vocalions V1024 and V1033. Oliver's 1929–31 recordings for Victor are not currently available. They follow this trend and contain some very fine jazz but often with Oliver taking no discernible part in the proceedings. A recording made in 1929 under the name of

Blind Willie Dunn's Gin Bottle Four (deleted Col DE3440, (A) OK8689) is worth finding as a very clearly recorded and highly diverting sample of Oliver's playing, as are his accompaniments to blues singers like Ida Cox and Sara Martin.

(1) LOUIS ARMSTRONG 1923 – (A) 12 Riv 12-122. (d) 10 Lon AL3504. *1923.*

(2) KING OLIVER – 7 JC JEL6. *1923.*

(3) KING OLIVER - 12 Ph BBL7181. (A) 12 Ep LN-3208. *1923.*

(4) KING OLIVER'S DIXIE SYNCOPATORS – 10 Cor LRA10020. (A) 10 Br BL58020 (d). *1926–8. (1929–1931 recordings on deleted HMV DLP1096, 7EG8039, 8091.) Blues accompaniment on deleted AL3510 and recordings with Clarence Williams on deleted AL3526, AL3561.)*

Books: *King Joe Oliver*, by Brian Rust and Walter C. Allen (Jazz Book Club, 1957).

ORIGINAL DIXIELAND JAZZ BAND

One of the pioneering jazz groups, first recorded as far back as 1917, and oddly enough a white band. They played robust, funny-hat sort of jazz with immense spirit and a rather neurotic jumpy near-ragtime rhythm, and revelled in vulgar trombone slurs and comic effects with the clarinet. *Tiger rag* was a natural for them and their earliest recording is to be found on a deleted Br 78 02500. (1) recorded in England in 1919 is the only LP currently available. It is worth having although perhaps not quite as good as the American Victor recordings to be found in a few odd collections.

(1) THE ORIGINAL DIXIELAND JAZZ BAND IN ENGLAND – 10 Col 33S1087. *1919–20.*

KID ORY (1889)   *trombone*

Although this great veteran of jazz is still blowing as lustily as ever and leading his own band, he has the aura of an historic figure. When one considers how many great jazz sessions he was on and what remarkable things he played, the nostalgia must inevitably creep in. Remember his work in the great days of 1926–7 and thereabouts with King Oliver, Jelly Roll Morton (the subtle and exciting work on *Steamboat stomp* and *Black Bottom stomp*) and of course the great recordings with the Armstrong Hot Five and Seven and the New

Orleans Wanderers (1). It is in no way running down Ory to say that these seem to be in another world, played by another man. The present-day Ory is still a great player, perhaps one of the greatest exponents of the tailgate style still playing, always driving, filling in, inspiring with miracles of timing and swing. But the subtlety has gone. As with many veteran players it seems as if the interval when they were forgotten killed off the inspiration and the spark went out. When they began to play once more they went through all the tricks but seemed very little better than a number of players we know to be lesser men. Four rough but exciting sides made in 1944 should be found if possible (on now deleted Voc 78s V1001 and V1012), *Blanche Touquatoux* is brimful of the essence of Creole jazz. The first two Good Time Jazz LPs that came out over here were hailed with excitement for they were fresh and forceful after much we had heard. Since then the standard has not dropped although a certain sameness might be detected. (9) is a better LP than most and has some delightful moments. (10) and (11) are both fine records and can be fully recommended to lovers of good straightforward New Orleans jazz.

(1) JOHNNY DODDS WITH KID ORY – 12 Ph BBL7136. (A) 12 Ep LN-3207. *1926.*

(2) TAILGATE – 12 GTJ LAG12104. (A) GTJ L12022. *1944–5.*

(3) KID ORY – 10 Ph BBR8088. (A) 12 Col CL835. (TIGER RAG.) *1946–50.*

(4) KID ORY'S CREOLE JAZZ BAND – 10 GTJ LDG093. (A) 10 GTJ L21 (*d*). *1953.*

(5) CREOLE JAZZ BAND 1954 – 12 GTJ LAG12004. (A) 12 GTJ L12004. *1954.*

(6) CREOLE JAZZ BAND 1955 – 12 GTJ LAG12064. (A) 12 GTJ L12008. *1955.*

(7) CREOLE JAZZ BAND 1956 – 12 LAG12084. (A) 12 GTJ L12016. *1956.*

(8) KID ORY IN EUROPE – 12 Col 33CX10116. (A) 12 Ver 8254. *1956.*

(9) SONG OF THE WANDERER – 12 Col 33CX10134. (A) 12 Ver 1014. *1957.*

(10) THE KID FROM NEW ORLEANS – 12 HMV CLP1303. *1957.*

(11) KID ORY AND HIS CREOLE JAZZ BAND featuring RED ALLEN – 12 HMV CLP1329. (A) 12 Ver 1018, (S) 6076. *1959.*

HOT LIPS PAGE (1908–54)   *trumpet*

Vehemence is the quality usually associated with Hot Lips Page's music. Few trumpet-players can have played the blues, for instance, with such heated intensity, such eloquent fervour. Yet Page's playing was rarely incoherent or smothered by emotion; even solos performed in the boisterous setting of Bennie Moten's orchestra – as with *Lafayette* (7 RCA RCX1027) and *Moten swing* ((A) 12 Fol 2808) – show that he could keep his head even when he was being most intense. Some of his best work can be found in Chu Berry's *Limehouse blues* (12 Ph BBL7054 (*d*), (A) 12 Ep LG3124) and in *Piney Brown blues* and *627 stomp* (the former with Joe Turner, the latter with Pete Johnson's band) on (A) 12 Dec DL8044. The 'Spirituals to Swing' Concert LP ((A) 12 Van 8523), incidentally, includes a track on which Page is heard playing with the Count Basie orchestra (*Blues with Lips*).

In 1941 the trumpet-player joined Artie Shaw's band and later that year recorded his lengthy version of *St. James' Infirmary blues* (12 RCA RD27065, (A) 12 RCA LPM1570), singing as well as playing. That Page was an uncommonly fine blues-singer is also proved by his work on *My fighting gal*, one of several Trio recordings made in 1940 and released on an HMV 78 (*d*). *South* and *Lafayette*, 1940, on (A) 12 Dec DL8044 – KANSAS CITY JAZZ, are two performances that contain some of Page's most biting and fiery playing. More aggressive trumpet work can be found on the tracks Page recorded with the Mezzrow-Bechet Septet (*House party* and *Blood on the moon* are included in 12 Vog LAE12017). Finally there is (1), recorded at an army camp concert just over a year before Page died. He is accompanied here by the Marian McPartland Trio.

(1) JAZZTIME U.S.A., Vol. 3 – 12 Cor LVA9017. *1953*. (rev. Terry Gibbs.)

TONY PARENTI (1900)   *clarinet*

A classically trained musician who developed a natural affection for ragtime, a spirit which inhabits all his music in the Dixieland vein. Not a great musician but one whose playing is full of an old Creole tradition and worth remembering for the one very fine LP which is available under his own name. It illustrates how ragtime, usually a piano music, can successfully be transcribed into instrumental terms. With Ralph Sutton, Jimmy Archey, George Wettling, Danny Barker and other sympathetic musicians (1) makes up a memorable record that all collectors should have.

(1) RAGTIME – 12 Lon LTZ-U15072 (d). (A) 12 Riv 12-205. *1947–8.*

CHARLIE PARKER (1920–55)   *alto, tenor saxophones*

There have been few, if any, more influential figures in jazz than the late Charlie Parker. His revolutionary style of improvisation is reflected today in the work of thousands of new jazzmen, not only saxophonists but bass players, pianists, drummers, etc. He opened wide the doors of perception yet retained always a strong link with tradition; he was not only the most progressive individualist jazz has ever known, he was also a superb blues player with a feeling for the music which went deep down into his soul. Since Parker there have been many copyists and a lesser number of alto and tenor soloists who have tried hard to find a means of expression not based directly on his sound. Despite his premature death his music lives on in the work of countless jazzmen while even contemporary dance-band arrangements reflect his teachings. His earliest recorded solos will be found on (1) with the Kansas City blues band led by pianist Jay McShann. Although not typical of the period, his solos with McShann are not esoteric and reflect almost equally the influences of Lester Young and Johnny Hodges. *Tiny's tempo* and *Red cross* (7) have solos by a more mature Bird, sweeping through his choruses with confidence and exhibiting his identifying trademarks which were to become so well known in later years. The phrases are long with accents falling on the weak beats; the melodic line is very adventurous harmonically and there is a feeling of bursting, struggling enthusiasm, a desire to say as much as possible in the limited time available. Recorded originally under guitarist Tiny Grimes' name *Red cross* and *Tiny's tempo* are played by a fairly orthodox swing-style group which tends to restrict the free flow of Bird's ideas. The Parker titles on (2), however, are played by a more compatible unit in which Parker is more at home. His front-line partner is the similar-thinking Dizzy Gillespie ('the other half of my heart-beat' according to Bird) while the two rhythm sections include such forward-thinking pianists as Al Haig and Clyde Hart ably supported by two transitional drummers in sympathy with the front-line, Cozy Cole and Sid Catlett. Here on record for the first time are the new interpretations of the *Whispering* and *What is this thing called love?* chords allied to fresh melody lines titled *Groovin' high* and *Hot house* respectively. The inclusion of *All the things you are* more than indicates the desire of the Parker-led school to get away from the established jazz material and to branch out into the more challenging area of the top-quality show tunes. (3) is a most valuable LP for it presents an important jazz session in its entirety, complete with false starts, incomplete takes, scraps of conversation, laughter, etc. Two of Bird's best-known blues, *Billie's bounce* and *Now's the time* are worked over until satisfactory versions are produced. An early attempt at slow-tempo improvisation on a well-known sequence (*Embraceable you*) is included (although the performance breaks down during the piano solo) and the date culminates with the incredible *Ko ko*. Based on the harmonies of Ray Noble's *Cherokee*, *Ko ko* remains one of Bird's best solos on record; although played at very fast tempo the alto player is able to analyse his thoughts, put them into correct sequence and turn in one of the most breathtaking passages ever heard in a jazz context. *Ko ko* is a performance which might be used as a yardstick in measuring the quality of solo work produced by Bird and his contemporaries. (4) and (5) were made in Hollywood by seven-man pick-up groups before and after Parker's breakdown. (These dates were produced and supervised by Ross Russell for his 'Dial' label, as were the fourteen tracks on (10). In recent years the re-issue of the 'Dial' masters has become such a complicated matter that its clarification would require several pages of this book. Suffice it to say here that the 'Dial' titles listed below may well be available on other LPs as well as the Jazztone, Vogue and Roost labels.) (4) contains *Night in Tunisia* with its famous cadenza leading into Bird's brilliant solo; a young Miles Davis and confident Lucky Thompson complete the front-line while the rhythm section contains pianist Dodo Marmarosa – deputizing for Joe Albany – and the surprisingly advanced drumming of Roy Porter. (5) benefits from Bird's improved sound and generally more relaxed approach, Howard McGhee's hot trumpet work, Wardell Gray's beautiful sense of swing and a rhythm section which cannot be faulted on any score – Dodo Marmarosa, Barney Kessel, Red Callender and Don Lamond. In many ways this is one of Parker's most wholly successful dates for every man pulls his weight and the atmosphere is not tense. (6), (7), (8) and (9), together with (3) noted above, contain just about every scrap of music which Parker recorded for the Savoy label. Unfortunately any attempt at programming is non-existent which means that the enthusiast must dig through two or more of the volumes to find all the titles from one session. The search is always worthwhile of course but it would have improved listening conditions if the products of each date had been kept together. All five 'Immortal Charlie Parker' LPs are indispensable to any collection of contemporary jazz on records; here, for example, are the four titles from the semi-novelty session held in Hollywood late in 1945 under the leadership of Slim Gaillard, four titles which contain some excellent Parker and Gillespie passages inset into the *vout* nonsense. Here also are the first examples of Bird playing tenor on a record date (under Miles Davis's name) in place of his usual alto. Two particularly productive sessions held in Detroit during 1948 are included; John Lewis's calm, sympathetic piano provides the backdrop to three takes of *Parker's mood* (take one on (6), takes two and three on (8)), a straight-from-the-heart blues played with simplicity and directness. In contrast *Constellation*, (6) and (8), is a swirling vehicle for Bird at up-tempo while *Ah-leu-cha*, (6), is of interest in that the theme statement is presented contrapuntally by Miles Davis and Parker. (10) continues the pattern but with a greater number of ballads; Duke Jordan is on piano most of the time and it is he who sets the mood for the famous *Embraceable you* in which the alto line floats across the chords to form an extended melody statement greater than anything George Gershwin ever conceived. (11) dates from a concert at Carnegie Hall when Parker was the featured guest with Gillespie's big band. Bird, Dizzy and the rhythm section (John Lewis, Al McKibbon and Joe Harris) are inspired, with Parker adding fresh glory to his cadenza take-off into *Night in Tunisia*. Although the recording fades before the finish, *Confirmation* from this concert must be rated as one of Bird's most effective solos. In 1948 Charlie signed a contract with Norman Granz and was heard – officially – only on Granz-supervised records until the time of his death. One of

Granz's earliest projects was the mating of Parker and a legitimate string section; (12) collates the majority of the alto-plus-strings titles and shows that while Bird occasionally played with marked brilliance, the attempt to please two different audiences with a compromise was not a great success. A better Granz idea is presented on (14) in which three originators of the new jazz style, Parker, Gillespie and Thelonious Monk, play through a set which recalls stormier and hungrier days. Unfortunately Buddy Rich's drumming is not entirely in sympathy with the music and while he is a fine technician it would have been better to have included a younger and more modern drummer with a natural bent for breaking up the beat and using the shifting cross-rhythms so beloved by the three chief participants. (15), or at least one side of the LP, is devoted to more alto-plus-strings but these titles are superior to the ones presented on (12); the session was recorded live at Carnegie Hall and Parker is less inhibited in these surroundings. There are few other records of Parker-in-person available and both (13) and (16) are recommended as examples of the freedom which Bird seemed to feel away from the studio red light and microphone. (13) suffers from some dreadful recording balance (it was taped privately by an amateur) but more than enough of Parker's genius filters through the loud-speaker, particularly on *Now's the time* where the alto saxist inverts the theme and plays generally with more dash and recklessness than before. (16) helps to date Bird's visit to Sweden late in 1950; one side of the LP is devoted to a casual Parker Quintet comprising Bird and an all-Swedish backing. *Loverman* from this Swedish concert helps to dispel the illusion of sickness which pervaded Bird's previous version (10); trumpeter Rolf Ericsson makes a good if not outstanding partner and the rhythm section (with the talented Gosta Theselius on piano) is suitably energetic. On both (13) and (16) Parker has a tendency to close his numbers with a tongue-in-cheek tag based on Percy Grainger's *Country gardens*, a passing whim which several of Bird's imitators copied for a time. There are some very good 1951-vintage quintet recordings to be heard on (17), four titles with Miles Davis on trumpet and four with Red Rodney. *Star eyes* features Parker in confident, swaggering mood and there are some effective twelve-bar compositions included as well, such as *KC blues* and *Back home blues*. (18) finds the alto saxist tied somewhat unnecessarily

[251]

to a Latin American rhythm section and, on four tracks, the inaccurate trumpet playing of Bennie Harris. There are occasional flashes of brilliance here and there but the overall effect lacks impact. Although (19) is by a big band (with two tracks by the alto-and-strings unit) the record is disappointing because the studio-assembled orchestra lacks any rugged individuality while the arrangements are hardly memorable. (20) is unique in that three alto giants – Parker, Johnny Hodges and Benny Carter – are heard playing consecutive solos; all three are extremely effective on the slow *Funky blues* and it is Carter who tends to steal the limelight during the alto exchanges. Undoubtedly (21) contains some of Parker's greatest latter-day work; working with two different quartets (Hank Jones, Teddy Kotick and Max Roach for one date, Al Haig, Percy Heath and Roach for the other) Bird is amongst friends all the way. This is the kind of context in which his genius is at once apparent for it is clear that his commanding personality is responsible for the consistently high level which is maintained throughout. *Now's the time* is a fierce, aggressive blues played with a strident tone and forceful attack; after the theme statement of *I remember you* Parker takes off on a brilliant cadenza passage, telescoping the main phrase of the melody into the final two bars. He sweeps majestically through Kern's lovely *The song is you* and turns in a memorable version of one of his own tunes, *Confirmation*. Although these quartet sessions were not his last, it would be as well to remember Parker from the way he plays here rather than on (25), a drab, lack-lustre collection of Cole Porter songs reputed to be Bird's final work on record. He switches to tenor for (22), an evil-sounding date with Sonny Rollins and Miles Davis. Perhaps the brooding atmosphere helped them to create the intensely moving version of *'Round about midnight* even though Parker was less than a master of the bigger saxophone on this occasion. (24) collates a number of odds and ends from the Granz catalogue, few of which mean much without Parker's own contributions. Three of the tracks, arranged by Gil Evans, set Bird's alto against a background of voices and woodwinds and while the general effect is near-chaotic in places, enigmatically Parker sounds very happy and soars through his choruses as if blissfully unaware of his colleagues' presence. (23), like (22), was made illegally in the sense that Parker appears under a pseudonym ('Charlie Chan') for contractual reasons. Recorded at a concert in Toronto, Bird is heard in typical mid-forties setting with Gillespie, Bud Powell, Charlie Mingus and Max Roach playing through such old favourites as *Hot house*, *Salt peanuts*, etc. This was the first time these five men had played together for some years and their enthusiasm is evident on every track. Parker is in brilliant form, flashing through his solos with an effervescence which matches the outright humour of Gillespie and, as usual, carrying the rhythm section along with him by sheer weight of personality.

(1) JAY McSHANN ORCHESTRA – 10 Br LA8735. (A) 10 Dec DL5503. *1941*, *1942*.

(2) DIZZY GILLESPIE – 12 WRC R29. (A) 12 Sav 12020. *1945*.

(3) IMMORTAL CHARLIE PARKER, Vol. 5 – 12 Lon LTZ-C15108. (A) 12 Sav 12079. *1945*.

(4) CHARLIE PARKER SEPTET – (A) 12 Jazztone J1204. *1946*.

(5) CHARLIE PARKER ALL STARS – (A) 10 Jazztone J1004. *1947*.

(6) IMMORTAL CHARLIE PARKER, Vol. 1 – 12 Lon LTZ-C15104. (A) 12 Sav 12000. *1947*, *1948*.

(7) IMMORTAL CHARLIE PARKER, Vol. 2 – 12 Lon LTZ-C15105. (A) 12 Sav 12001. *1944*, *1947*, *1948*.

(8) IMMORTAL CHARLIE PARKER, Vol. 3 – 12 Lon LTZ-C15106. (A) 12 Sav 12009. *1947*, *1948*.

(9) IMMORTAL CHARLIE PARKER, Vol. 4 – 12 Lon LTZ-C15107. (A) 12 Sav 12014. *1945*, *1947*, *1948*.

(10) CHARLIE PARKER MEMORIAL ALBUM – 12 Vog LAE12002. Seven of these 14 titles are contained in (A) 12 Roo LP2210. *1947*.

(11) NITE AT CARNEGIE HALL – (A) 12 Roo LP2234. *1947*.

(12) CHARLIE PARKER WITH STRINGS – 12 Col 33CX10081. (A) 12 Ver 5004. *1949*, *1950*.

(13) BIRD AT ST. NICKS – 12 Mel 12-105. (A) 12 Jazz Workshop JWS500. *1950*.

(14) BIRD AND DIZ – (A) 12 Ver 8006. Original six takes on 10 Col 33C9026. Alternative takes of four titles on 7 Col SEB10087. *1950*.

(15) CHARLIE PARKER WITH STRINGS – 12 Col 33CX10060. (A) 12 Ver 8189. *1950*.

(16) CHARLIE PARKER IN SWEDEN – 12 Col JGN1002. *1950*.

(17) CHARLIE PARKER QUINTET – (A) 12 Ver 8010. *Au privave/She rote/KC blues* and *Star eyes* on 7 Col SEB10038; *Si si/Swedish*

[253]

schnapps/*Back home blues* and *Loverman* on 7 Col SEB10002.
Alternative takes of *She rote* and *Swedish schnapps* on 12
Col 33CX10117. *1951*.

(18) CHARLIE PARKER QUINTET – (A) 12 Ver 8008. *Un poquito de tu
amor*/*Tico tico*/*Mama Inez* and *La paloma* on 12 Col 33CX10117.
My little suede shoes/*La cucaracha*/*Estrellita*/*Begin the beguine* on
7 Col SEB10032. *Fiesta* on 12 Col 33CX10072. *Why do I love
you?* on 7 Col SEB10053. *1951* and *1952*.

(19) CHARLIE PARKER ORCHESTRA – 12 Col 33CX10004. (A) 12 Ver
5003. *1952*.

(20) JAM SESSION – 12 Col 33CX10008. (A) 12 Ver 8050. *1952*.

(21) CHARLIE PARKER QUARTET – (A) 12 Ver 8005. *The song is you*/
Laird baird/*Kim* and *Cosmic rays* on 12 Col 33CX10117.
Chi chi/*I remember you*/*Now's the time* and *Confirmation* on
7 Col SEB10026. *1952* and *1953*.

(22) MILES DAVIS SEXTET – 12 Esq 32-030. (A) 12 Pre PRLP7044.
1953.

(23) QUINTET OF THE YEAR – 12 Vog LAE12031. (A) 12 Debut
DEB124. *1953*.

(24) JAZZ PERENNIAL – (A) 12 Ver 8009. *Old folks* and *In the still of the
night* on 7 Col SEB10053. Majority of remaining tracks on
12 Col 33CX10117. *1949–53*.

(25) CHARLIE PARKER QUINTET – 12 Col 33CX10090. (A) 12 Ver 8007.
1954.

SANTO PECORA (1902)   *trombone*

Pecora's 1937 recording of *Magnolia blues*/*I never knew what a gal
could do*, (*d*) Par 78 R3050, probably still resides in many jazz collections. On the strength of this and his earlier work with the New
Orleans Rhythm Kings and Sharkey Bonano, Pecora has long had a
reputation as one of the best and most original New Orleans tailgate-
style trombonists, with regrettably little recorded evidence to support
this opinion. He plays in a crisp manner, very agile and adventurous
within the New Orleans pattern. On (5) he is accompanied by a very
well-recorded, very busy and hectic group which plays some exciting
jazz forced along by Pecora's rugged and confident playing. The other
recordings are much in the same vein and only slightly less successful
than (5).

(1) New Orleans Rhythm Kings – (A) 12 Sou 213.

(2) Dixieland Jamboree (with Watters) – 10 Col 33C9036 (d).
(A) 12 Ver 1008. *1950*.

(3) Santo Pecora and His Dixieland Band – 7 Col SEB10079.
1950.

(4) Santo Pecora and His Dixieland Band – 7 Col SEB10104
1950.

(5) Recorded in New Orleans, Vol. 2 – (with Wiggs, Pierson and
Hug) – 12 GTJ LAG12141. (A) 12 GTJ 12020. *1956*.

ART PEPPER (1925)   *clarinet, alto, tenor saxophones*

Pepper is one of the handful of post-war alto players to have
developed a characteristic means of expression. Although his tone
was once thin and Konitz-like, since his return to jazz in 1956 his
sound is full and passionate with much of Benny Carter's elegance.
In short he has become one of the best, if not *the* best, alto soloist
since Parker. *Diane*, a lovely, lyrical original on (1), demonstrates
Pepper's flair for constructing genuinely tuneful lines and com-
municating with the listener in a warm, sincere manner. On (2) and
(3) he is easily the best soloist in Russ Garcia's extrovert big band and
exchanges solo passages with Bud Shank on four tracks. Pepper plays
on one side of (4), with tenor saxist Bill Perkins and a rhythm
section; *What is this thing called love* has one of Pepper's best solos on
record, a floating, airy improvisation underlined with sympathy by
pianist Jimmy Rowles. Similarly *I can't give you anything but love* (5),
on which Art is backed by bass and drums only, is a recommended
example of this musician's considerable ability to play thoughtful
and swinging jazz. (6) is slanted at a wider market and consists of
Hoagy Carmichael singing ten of his own tunes but Pepper bursts
through on most tracks, *Skylark* and *Winter moon* in particular, to
play some telling solo passages. In addition Art shows that he is
capable of contributing really effective obbligatos and generally
assists enormously in the complete success of the LP. The rhythm
section from Miles Davis' quintet supports Pepper on (7) and there
are some indications of a rift between alto and drums in places;
Philly Joe Jones' tempo doubling does not seem to suit Art's tempera-
ment but the slow tunes, *Star eyes* for example, are faultless while
the choice of *Jazz me blues* makes for surprisingly good solos. (8)

is not wholly successful due to the ineptitude of Chet Baker and it is Pepper and Phil Urso who carry the weight of the group on their shoulders. Art plays clarinet, alto and tenor on (9) and indicates that it is within his powers to lead the contemporary field on the first instrument, a supposition which becomes fact on (10) where his clarinet version of *Anthropology* with a medium-sized band directed by Marty Paich is something of a minor classic.

(1) ART PEPPER QUARTET – 10 Lon LZ–U14038. (A) 12 Tampa RS1001. *1956.*

(2) MODERN JAZZ GALLERY – 12 Lon LTZ–R15083. (A) 12 Kap KXL5001. *1956.*

(3) MODERN JAZZ GALLERY – 12 Lon LTZ–R15084. (A) 12 Kap KXL5001. *1956.*

(4) JUST FRIENDS – 12 Vog LAE12088. (A) 12 WP 401. *1956.*

(5) SOLO FLIGHT – 12 Vog LAE12106. (A) 12 WP JWC505. *1956.*

(6) HOAGY CARMICHAEL – 12 Vog VA160112. (A) 12 WP1223. *1956.*

(7) ART PEPPER QUARTET – 12 Vog LAC12066. (A) 12 Con C3532. *1957.*

(8) PLAYBOYS – 12 Vog LAE12183. (A) 12 WP 1234. *1957.*

(9) BARNEY KESSEL – 12 Vog LAC12206. (A) 12 Con C3565. *1959.*

(10) ART PEPPER – 12 Vog LAC12225. (A) 12 Con C3568. *1959.*

RUFUS PERRYMAN (Speckled Red) (1892) *piano, vocal*

Amongst the many and sometimes indistinguishable boogie woogie pianists there are a few great names like Yancey, Johnson, Ammons, Lewis and a few lesser lights who shine out on account of their originality and vigour. Such a one is Rufus Perryman, not of the highest rank but a fresh and exciting performer. Amongst a few sides he recorded in 1929 and 1930 were the exhilarating *Wilkins Street stomp* (1) and two classic versions of *The dirty dozens* (1) which should not be missed. Together with some vivid, spirited but obscure primitive pianists like Billie Pierce, James Robinson and Doug Suggs, Speckled Red was brought to recording light again in 1957 to prove his continued vigour and skill playing *Dad's piece* (2), *Early in the morning* (2) and *Oh, Red* (2). His only other recording revival in 1938 has never been reissued. Singing in a slightly nasal voice, he is, at time, reminiscent of Little Brother Montgomery.

(1) PIANO JAZZ, Vol. 1 (BARRELHOUSE AND BOOGIE WOOGIE) –
(also PineTop Smith, Montana Taylor, Romeo Nelson and
Cow Cow Davenport) – 12 Cor LVA9069. (A) 12 Br 54014.
1929–30.

(2) PRIMITIVE PIANO – (also Billie Pierce, James Robinson, Doug
Suggs) – 12 JC JGN1001. (A) 12 TONE 1. *1957.*

OSCAR PETERSON (1925)   *piano*

Few jazz pianists have been featured on as many records as Oscar
Peterson and this quantity output has led to his summary dismissal
by some critics. A great number of his own LPs have not been
designed primarily for the jazz market (the 'composer' series and the
'Peterson plays pretty' albums, etc.) and it would be incorrect to
castigate Oscar for his glibness and superficiality here. Of his *jazz*
performances (1), recorded during a Jazz At The Philharmonic
concert, is noteworthy if only for *Tenderly*, the electric solo which
remains one of his best on record. Peterson is at his most effective
when not indulging in Tatum-like displays of technique; on the
credit side is the closely knit texture of his trio (completed by guitarist
Herb Ellis and bassist Ray Brown on most LPs) plus the sometimes
overpowering ability to swing with the precision of an aircraft
engine. (2) and (3), recorded live at the Stratford Festival (Ontario)
and the Town Tavern (Toronto) respectively, are two of Oscar's
better LPs in which the bravura excesses are kept to the minimum. He
has an engaging way of playing slow numbers with piano and guitar
laying down separate melodic lines and the harmonies arising
naturally from the juxtaposing of those lines. Ellis left the trio during
the summer of 1958 and his place was taken, not by another guitarist,
but by drummer Ed Thigpen. Before Thigpen took over permanently
Oscar recorded an album of tunes from *My Fair Lady* (a late-entry
in a crowded jazz field) with Gene Gammage playing unobtrusive
drums (4). The revised instrumentation brings about a change for the
better in Peterson's style. He plays in a more direct manner than
before and his uncluttered delivery under the new conditions gives
promise of a better performance level in the future. As an accompanist Oscar's work is usually exemplary and his support to all
manner of soloists – from Louis Armstrong to Sonny Stitt – is
invariably intelligent, helpful and tasteful. It should be stressed that the

four records discussed here represent only a fraction of Peterson's output but they have been chosen because they show the pianist at his best.
(1) CARNEGIE HALL CONCERT – 1952 – 12 Col 33CX10010. (A) 12 Ver 2046. *1952.*
(2) OSCAR PETERSON TRIO – 12 Col 33CX10096. (A) 12 Ver 8024. *1956.*
(3) ON THE TOWN – 12 Col 33CX10135. (A) 12 Ver 8287. *1958.*
(4) MY FAIR LADY – 12 HMV CLP1278. (A) 12 Ver 2119. *1958.*

KING PLEASURE (1922) *vocalist*

Pleasure – whose real name is Clarence Beeks – is one of the few new jazz singers of merit. He was the originator of the idea in which words were added to established jazz solos and he enjoyed a brief spell of fame with his version of James Moody's *I'm in the mood for love* (never released in Britain). Subsequently he has been overshadowed by Annie Ross, Dave Lambert and Jon Hendricks who have worked along the same lines with even greater success but his place as an innovator must not be forgotten. (1) comprises eight intriguing tracks including the moving *Parker's mood* and the lyrical *Just you, just me* (which uses the improvised line from Lester Young's classic record). The lyrics which Pleasure has added are more earth-bound than those composed by Jon Hendricks but the feeling for the music is deep and intense. Although the new versions of the songs are capable of standing alone they still manage to convey the character of the original creators and *This is always* projects as much of James Moody's personality as it does Pleasure's.
(1) KING PLEASURE SINGS – 10 Esq 20-066. (A) 12 Pre PRLP7128 (with four additional tracks by Annie Ross). *1952–3.*

BUD POWELL (1924) *piano*

Tragedy seems to have dogged Bud Powell's career for he has been forced to withdraw from the jazz scene on a number of occasions due to ill-health. When he has been in a position to work he has produced the best piano jazz of two decades. His style developed concurrently with that of Charlie Parker and his vital sense of swing, tremendous technique and long flow of ideas mirrored Bird's manner of playing. (1) is perhaps the best Bud Powell record in any catalogue; it is certainly the most consistent. All the elements of his playing are present here, the ability to play at a seemingly impossible up-tempo (*Indiana*), the unique refashioning of established material to give maximum effect as a jazz vehicle (*Somebody loves me*) and the persuasive treatment of a ballad with full, rich chords (*I should care*). (2) is almost as good and, like so many of Powell's appearances on record, is marked by a feeling of tension which adds vitality and urgency to the music. Bud's dramatic treatment of his own tune *I'll keep loving you* features some exemplary pedal work which adds emphasis to the stately melody line. *Hallelujah* and *Tea for two* (4) find Powell backed by Ray Brown and Buddy Rich and it is Rich who does much to add further fire to the breathtaking *Tea for two*, which uses the Art Tatum idea of ascending figurations; Bud seems to find no difficulty in thinking far ahead even at speed and *Tea for two* ranks as one of his greatest performances. (3) is discussed under the entry under Sonny Stitt's name; suffice it to say here that the excellence of Powell and Stitt makes this a record to play and replay, time and again, for it is the very essence of post-war jazz. (4) and (5) collate nearly all the material which Bud taped for the Blue Note label, a varied selection which includes some alternative takes of the four tracks with Fats Navarro and Sonny Rollins (q.v.), three takes of the trio *Un poco loco* (which improves steadily as Powell attempts each new version), some beautifully played ballads and an outstanding composition by Bud entitled *Glass enclosure*. In addition there is an incomplete version of his lovely tune *Parisian thoroughfare* which, up to the point of the breakdown, contains some of the most swinging modern jazz piano of recent years. During the middle fifties Powell showed signs of an artistic decline which robbed him of his clearcut approach and unbeatable technique. (6) and (7) are worth adding to any collection which already contains (1), (2) and (3) but the reader is warned that there are moments of uncertainty, some misfingered notes and a number of ideas which trail off, unresolved, into space. On the credit side there is the unique atmosphere of '*Round about midnight* (6), the very personal treatment of *Heart and soul* and the nostalgia of *Confirmation* (both on (7)). Fortunately for jazz Bud hit form again a few years later and one side of (8) is only a little below the level of his best performances. *Bud on Bach* is a tremendous *tour de force* based on a Bach exercise and played with the dash and fleet fingering of an earlier period. Unfortunately the second side of this LP has the addition of the Jay Jay Johnson imitator, Curtis Fuller who, although an adequate trombonist, is not in the same street as Powell so far as invention is concerned.

(1) BUD POWELL TRIO – 12 Vog LDE010. (A) 12 Roo 2224 (with four additional titles from a later session). *1947.*

(2) BUD POWELL TRIO – 10 Col 33C9016. (A) 12 Ver 8153 (with additional titles). *1949.*

(3) SPJ JAZZ – 12 Esq 32-049. (A) 12 Pre PRLP7024. *1950.*

(4) THE AMAZING BUD POWELL, Vol. 1 – (A) 12 BN BLP1503. *1949, 1951, 1953.*

(5) THE AMAZING BUD POWELL, Vol. 2 – (A) 12 BN BLP1504. *1949, 1951, 1953.*

(6) JAZZ ORIGINAL – 12 Col 33CX10069. (A) 12 Ver 8185. *1954.*

(7) THE LONELY ONE – 12 HMV CLP1294. Some titles on (A) 12 Ver 8167, remainder on 12 Ver 8301. *1955.*

(8) BUD! – (A) 12 BN BLP1571. *1958.*

SELDON POWELL (1928)   *tenor saxophone*

Juilliard-trained Seldon Powell made his first impact on jazz durring the middle 'fifties. At a time when tenor saxists were divided, stylistically, between the coarse-toned gruffness of Sonny Rollins and the light, smooth approach of the post-Lester Young adherents, it was refreshing to welcome Powell's middle-of-the-road ideas. An instrumental perfectionist, he has succeeded in obtaining the same rounded tone throughout the range of his instrument while his playing reflects those twin giants of the saxophone, Charlie Parker and Lester Young. Briefly his playing falls into the slot previously occupied by Wardell Gray and, like Gray, he swings at any tempo on any thematic material. (1), the first album under his own name, finds him leading a nine-piece band which includes such men as Don Lamond, Tony Aless, Jimmy Nottingham and Billy Bauer; Powell and Aless shared the arranging work which is superbly tailored to meet the requirements of the leader's voice. Apart from the infectious jump tunes such as *Go first class*, there are some splendid ballads rendered with sentiment and a welcome lack of glutinous saccharine. Powell's *Autumn nocturne* and *Summertime* are the very acme of elegance. On his second album (2) the formula is less disciplined in the sense that this is an outing for a free-wheeling sextet (trombonist Jimmy Cleveland, who seems to have left his 'Look-ma-no-hands' tricks at home for once, makes an excellent front-line partner). The choice of material is unusual yet apt; here, for example, is perhaps the first jazz version of *Sleepy time down south* which owes nothing to Armstrong, and here too is a glorious revival of that fine tune *I'll close my eyes*. The rhythm section underlines every phrase with sympathy and accuracy; Freddie Greene is in context here and Roland Hanna's careful piano work is reminiscent of Hank Jones. Powell is not a great innovator in the sense that he does not strive for new methods of self-expression; rather he is content to play as well as he possibly can within the established boundaries of orthodoxy. As examples of first-rate tenor solos both LPs are strongly recommended.

(1) SELDON POWELL PLAYS – 11 Vog LAE12184. (A) Roo 2205. *1955.*
(2) SELDON POWELL SERTET – 12 Vog LAE12201. (A) Roo 2220. *1956.*

SAM PRICE (1908)   *piano*

Sammy Price can play jazz piano, particularly in the confident, two-handed manner of men like James P. Johnson and Fats Waller, but his real strength lies in blues, which he performs in a rolling, barrel-house style. For many years he was virtually the house-pianist for the American Decca 'race' label, and accompanied many blues-singers during the late 1930s and early 1940s. (1) consists of solos which were originally released on King Jazz with Price using the pseudonym, 'Jimmy Blythe, Jr.' Outstanding is *Cow cow blues*, a good performance of the Davenport number. Price also played some impressive solos with Mezzrow-Bechet groups at this time, notably in *Funky Butt, I want some* and *Tommy's blues* (12 Vog LAE 12017). In 1955 he came to Europe with a band which included Emmett Berry (trumpet), Herbie Hall (clarinet) and Pops Foster (bass). (2) contains eight blues (at various paces) by this group, robustly performed and with good solos from Berry, Price and Hall. Five months later the same band worked with Sidney Bechet on (3), helping to make it one of Bechet's finest latter-day recordings. (4), another set of piano solos, includes an exuberant boogie track (*D'accord*) and a subdued, reflective *Sad blues*.

(1) SAMMY PRICE – 7 Vog EPV1146. *1945.*
(2) SWINGIN' PARIS STYLE – 12 Vog LAE12027. *1955.*

(3) SIDNEY BECHET WITH SAMMY PRICE'S BLUESICIANS – 12 Vog
LAE12037. (A) 12 Br 54037. *1956.*
(4) ORIGINAL SAMMY BLUES – 7 R Col SEG7679 (*d*). *1956.*

R

RAGTIME

The real ragtime was something of an unknown quantity to most
jazz collectors for many years. Various band units calling themselves
ragtime groups and many songs with the word ragtime in the title
generally did very little to convey the true meaning of the music.
Ragtime is a root source of jazz but uses very few of the devices of
jazz. Strictly speaking it is a piano music with a regular left-hand
and a strictly and mathematically syncopated melody. It derives from
the French type dances on the one hand, the quadrilles, the cakewalk,
and the American style march as written by Sousa on the other. It is
very melodic and usually follows a march pattern of three or four
distinct sections and a coda. Riverside records opened a whole new
world of delightful music when they began to issue their series of
ragtime recordings taken from old piano rolls made at the beginning
of the century before the gramophone had been fully developed.
They are some of the most important and exciting records ever to
have been released and of tremendous historical value. Although
deleted in England they should be sought out by anyone wanting to
really understand the history of jazz. Artists and composers included
in the series are Scott Joplin, James Scott, Tom Turpin, Joseph Lamb,
to name a handful of the better-known ragtime personalities.
(1) GOLDEN AGE OF RAGTIME – (A) 12 Riv 12-110. *1902–13.*
(2) JOPLIN, SCOTT, TURPIN, etc. – (A) 12 Riv 12-126.
  The original 10 American issues and the 10 London issues (all now
deleted) were as follows:
(3) RAGTIME PIANO ROLL – 10 Lon AL3515 (*d*). (A) 10 Riv RLP1006
  (*d*). *1903–13.*
(4) RAGTIME PIANO ROLL, Vol. 2 – 10 Lon AL3523 (*d*). (A) 10
  Riv RLP1025 (*d*). *1902–10.*
(5) RAGTIME PIANO ROLL, Vol. 3 – 10 Lon AL3542 (*d*). (A) 10
  Riv RLP1049 (*d*).

(6) RAGTIME PIANO ROLL, Vol. 4 – 10 Lon AL3563 (*d*). (A) 10 Riv RLP1060 (*d*).

Books: *They All Played Ragtime*, by Rudi Blesh. (Cassell, 1959.)

GERTRUDE MA RAINEY (1886–1939)   *vocal*

If Bessie Smith developed the 'classic' blues form to its utmost extent then it was Ma Rainey who paved the way. Her relation to the 'classic' blues is approximately the same as Jefferson's is to the country blues for she, it was, who gave her blues formal definition. Her singing, in any event, bears more resemblance to the terse and sombre country blues than does that of her followers. Having started her professional career in the early years of this century she toured the South for many years before she made her first records. She was by then (1922) a popular figure, which accounted for her considerable record sales. She worked steadily until 1933, when the deaths of her mother and sister caused her to return to Georgia. She lived there, in retirement, with her brother, until December 1939.

When she sang it was with primitive and sombre majesty, with 'lowdown feeling' that even Bessie Smith could not equal. Her blues, deep and commanding, had an incantatory quality, as though of some ancient litany. Once again, Joe Smith and Louis Armstrong were two of her featured accompanists and she worked regularly with Tampa Red and Thomas A. Dorsey. And it was for Ma Rainey that Tommy Ladnier played some of his finest blues accompaniments. *New boweavil blues* and *Moonshine blues* (3) are among her best records, but all her work is worthy of interest for, if Bessie Smith was the Empress, then Ma Rainey was the High Priestess of the blues.

(1) MA RAINEY, Vol. 1 – 10 Lon AL3502 (*d*). *1928.*
(2) MA RAINEY, Vol. 2 – 10 Lon AL3538 (*d*). *1924–8.*
(3) MA RAINEY, Vol. 3 – 10 Lon AL3558 (*d*). *1926–7.*
(4) THE GREAT BLUES SINGERS – 10 Lon AL3530 (*d*). *1927–8.*
(5) LOUIS ARMSTRONG PLAYS THE BLUES – 10 Lon AL3501 (*d*). *1924.*
(6) TOMMY LADNIER PLAYS THE BLUES – 10 Lon AL3548 (*d*). *1923–4.*
(7) BLUES – (A) 12 Riv 12-108. *1924–8.*

TAMPA RED (Hudson Whittaker) (1900)   *vocal, guitar*

One of the major figures in the history of 'race' blues, Tampa Red has taken part in a great many sessions. He first recorded in the mid-

1920s and worked as an accompanist for Ma Rainey. His singing is mournful, rather than violent, and his use of a steel in playing the guitar gave a distinctive sound to his recordings. A good technician, he has always produced his best when working with a pianist and, with Big Maceo Merriweather, he formed part of the Victor blues house group which made so many fine sessions in the late '30s and early '40s. It is fair to say that, after Leroy Carr and Scrapper Blackwell, the Merriweather/Whittaker team was the best piano/guitar duo in the blues. In his earlier sessions, with Georgia Tom, Tampa Red also created some fine blues.

(1) MA RAINEY, Vol. 1 – 10 Lon AL3502 (*d*). *1928*.
(2) THE MALE BLUES, Vol. 2 – 7 JC JEL3. *1929*.

DON REDMAN (1900)   *alto saxophone, arranger, composer*
    Don Redman is one of those tantalizing artists, a musician who has failed to live up to his early achievements. After working in the Fletcher Henderson orchestra and with McKinney's Cotton Pickers, both as a musician and arranger, Redman formed his own orchestra and between 1931 and 1933 produced a handful of adventurous and exciting essays in orchestral jazz. His name could then be mentioned in the same breath as Duke Ellington's. Yet since that time Redman has mainly contented himself with working as a free-lance arranger, producing competent but rather unenterprising scores. No doubt the economic depression in the early 1930s (when Negro bands found it particularly hard to get jobs) was partly responsible for this diverting of his talents. Another factor may have been the popularity of his nonsense-songs (pieces like *I heard*, *Two time man* and *Watching the knife and fork spoon*), which he sang in a whimsical, soft-voiced manner.
    Most of the early scores performed by Fletcher Henderson's orchestra were the work of Redman, who played with that band from 1923 to 1929. They include such classic arrangements as *Hot mustard*, *I'm coming Virginia* and *Whiteman stomp* (all recorded by Henderson but deleted years ago). Don Redman, in fact, can be credited with the creation of a style for big-band jazz. In 1929 he became musical director of McKinney's Cotton Pickers, and made it into the finest mid-western orchestra of its day. The band included such talented musicians as John Nesbitt (trumpet), Claude Jones (trombone)

and Prince Robinson (tenor sax), while among those who recorded with the group were Rex Stewart, Sidney de Paris, Joe Smith, Benny Carter, Fats Waller, Coleman Hawkins and James P. Johnson. Four performances from 1930 – *Laughing at life, Baby won't you please come home, Zonky* and *If I could be with you*, the last-named an especially felicitous track – were issued on 7 HMV 7EG8041 but are no longer available.

Like Benny Carter, a musician with whom he has much in common, Redman is an alto saxophonist as well as an arranger and composer. But there is about his solo playing a certain softness, a hint of whimsicality, that results in his solos often sounding uneven. Redman's importance, in fact, rests entirely upon his arranging and composing. The most famous of his works is *Chant of the weed*, one of the finest of all jazz compositions, a genuinely orchestral conception, remarkable for the way in which Redman makes use of texture. *Shakin' the African*, by contrast, is much more boisterous, although scored very distinctively.[1] During the next two years Redman's orchestra was to produce records which gradually became more and more commercial in character, although nearly all of them possess some points of interest. Redman's scoring for the reed section (which he led himself), for instance, was almost always individual and exciting. Between 1931 and 1933 the Don Redman orchestra could be counted among the great bands of jazz.

DJANGO REINHARDT (1910–53)   *guitar*
Django Reinhardt was an exotic, a hybrid, a gypsy guitarist who brought to jazz the technique of the Pyrenees. The result was usually stimulating, imaginative music, but rarely jazz in the normal sense of that ambiguous word. The music Reinhardt played, in fact, was very much a creation of his own, his baroque, flowing solos a blend of two separate traditions. His playing was invariably lyrical; sometimes too much so, for when he played a blues it became too sensuous, too romantic. (*St. Louis blues* (3), for instance, is closer in spirit to Neapolitan music than to jazz.) Not that this mattered very much. Django Reinhardt was a really creative soloist, a guitarist with a magnificent technique and a remarkably sophisticated sense of harmony.

[1] Both once available on HARLEM JAZZ (10 Br LA8565 (d)).

[265]

Most of the records listed below were made with the Quintet of the Hot Club of France, and suffer from rather monotonous rhythm playing (even Django cannot escape criticism here). Stephane Grappelly's violin solos were often timid and rather repetitive, but that he could play in a more spirited fashion is shown by his work on *Minor swing* and *Viper's dream* (3). Most of the pre-war recordings have felicitous moments, but (3) probably contains the finest solo-playing, although Reinhardt's solo guitar tracks – *Parfum* and *Improvisation* – on (5) are outstanding performances. (4), incidentally, contains a number of tracks included in (3) and (6). (7), (8) and (9) were made after the war, by which time Reinhardt had begun playing an electric guitar, an instrument for which his heavy, rococo style seemed singularly unfitted. His best performances using the electric guitar can be heard on (8).

When American jazz musicians recorded in Paris before the war, Django Reinhardt was usually on the sessions as well. Some of his finest solos were recorded in this way. That on *Eddie's blues* (HMV 7EG8361) by Eddie South, for instance, as well as those on *Solid old man* and *Montmartre* by Rex Stewart (7 HMV 7EG8447), and on several tracks (notably *Japanese sandman* and *Hangin' around Boudon*) of 'Dicky Wells in Paris', 12 HMV CLP1054 (*d*). His playing on these sessions was often more gentle, far less flamboyant than his work with the Quintet, perhaps because he no longer needed to carry the entire performance on his own shoulders.

(1) DJANGO – 10 Or MG10019. *1934–5.*
(2) STEPHANE GRAPPELLY AND HIS HOT FOUR – 7 Dec DFE6366. *1935.*
(3) DJANGO – 12 HMV CLP1249. *1936–7.*
(4) DJANGO REINHARDT – (A) 12 RCA LPM1100. *1936–7.*
(5) DJANGO REINHARDT – 7 HMV 7EG8132. *1937.*
(6) THE ART OF DJANGO – 12 HMV CLP1340. *1937.*
(7) SWING FROM PARIS – 10 Dec LF1139 (*d*). (A) Lon LL-1344. *1937–9.*
(8) REINHARDT AND HIS RHYTHM – 10 Fel EDL87005 (*d*). *1953.*

DON RENDELL (1926) — *tenor saxophone*

Rendell came to prominence with the original Johnny Dankworth Seven but left the Dankworth organization when John decided to

[266]

form a big band. Since that time Don has worked with small groups – most of them under his own leadership – apart from a period with Ted Heath and a partial tour of Europe with Stan Kenton during 1956 as a replacement for the American saxist Spencer Sinatra. Lester Young is Rendell's idol, which has resulted in a style of playing close to the 'Brothers' school exemplified by Al Cohn and Allen Eager. Don is a more constructive soloist than such American jazz-men as Phil Urso, Bill Perkins, etc., and his short spell with Kenton (when he worked in a reed section containing both Bill Perkins and Lennie Niehaus as well as Lucky Thompson on baritone) has left an indelible mark of improvement on his playing. *Juno* and *Don't get around much anymore* (1) made within weeks of his Kenton tour show off the new-found confidence. He formed what was to be one of his most effective bands at the beginning of 1957 and led this sextet (with some personnel changes) for fifteen months. During this time the Jazz Six achieved a group style principally through the well-conceived arrangements (and towards the end nearly every member of the band was contributing to the library). (2) is undoubtedly the best record by the most integrated personnel and contains Bert Courtley's masterly *Packet of blues* which features Courtley's strutting, Clark Terry-like trumpet solo. A considerable asset both in person and on record was the presence of the talented Ronnie Ross whose superlative baritone work finally resulted in recognition by the electorate voting in the Down Beat annual poll. (3) is by the Bert Courtley-Don Rendell Jazz Committee, which succeeded the Jazz Six, and shows that the standard of writing and playing equals all but the very best of the contemporary American groups.

(1) DON RENDELL QUARTET – 7 MGM EP615. (A) 12 MGM 3157. *1956.* (In both cases the other titles are by other artists.)

(2) DON RENDELL JAZZ SIX – 12 Dec LK4265. *1958.*

(3) JAZZ COMMITTEE – 7 Dec DFE6587. *1959.*

MAX ROACH (1925)   *drums*

Max was the first modern jazz drummer to add anything to the basic concept of Kenny Clarke, the father of the movement. What he added was a tremendous dexterity and the ability to build shifting rhythm patterns on top of the main pulse without disrupting the beat. His smooth rhythmic continuity is heard at its best behind such artists as Miles Davis (Capitol) and Fats Navarro (Esquire/Prestige); while working in Los Angeles during 1954 he played on one session with Howard Rumsey's Lighthouse All Stars (featuring Bud Shank and Bob Cooper on flute and oboe) and the clarity of the recording enables the listener to appreciate every nuance of his logical but intricate drumming (2). An unaccompanied drum solo made at a concert in Toronto is included on (1) and, allowing for the low fidelity of the reproduction, this will repay investigation for it is one of the few examples on record of a percussion display which commences with a recognizable theme pattern and develops through a series of improvisations. During 1954 Roach formed a quintet with trumpeter Clifford Brown and the reader is referred to the entry under Brown's name for details of these recordings. Following Clifford's death in 1956 the Roach group went into a decline which reached rock-bottom two years later; (3), made at the Newport Jazz Festival, consists of whirlwind tempos which only Roach seems capable of maintaining while the weak front-line soloists pour forth empty, multi-noted passages.

(1) MODERN JAZZ HALL OF FAME – 12 Gal GLP328. (A) Design 29.
    1953. (Other tracks by various artists.)
(2) HOWARD RUMSEY'S ALL STARS – 12 Vog LAC12146. (A) Con
    C3520. *1954*.
(3) MAX ROACH AT NEWPORT – 12 Mer MMB12005. Some tracks on
    (A) 12 Mer MG36140, remainder on (A) 12 Mer MG36141.
    1958.

JAMES 'Bat The Humming Bird' ROBINSON   (1903–57)
vocal, piano

Little is known about James Robinson but he is mentioned here for his fine recordings of *Bat's blues* and *Four o'clock blues* (1). He is a convincing singer, though hardly a good technician, and his piano playing is simple, with the 'all night long' feeling of a Montana Taylor.

(1) PRIMITIVE PIANO – 12 JC JGN1001. (A) 12 Tone 1. *1957*.

SHORTY ROGERS (1924)   *trumpet, flügelhorn*

Although the name Shorty Rogers is synonymous with jazz from Hollywood it should not be forgotten that the trumpeter's career has

[268]

taken in the big bands of Benny Carter and Woody Herman as well as Stan Kenton and Pete Rugolo. He played with Herman during the exciting First Herd days and stayed on to work with later editions of the band. As an arranger he was responsible for such extrovert items as *Keen and peachy*, *That's right*, etc., and succeeded in giving the Kenton band a real jazz sound with *Round Robin*, *Art Pepper* and the commercially-slanted *Orange coloured sky*. As a soloist he has favoured the more introvert style of Miles Davis but his playing is relatively unadventurous both melodically and harmonically. One of the best dates under his own name is (1) which might be considered the fore-runner of many, many similar sessions held in Hollywood during the middle and late 'fifties. Art Pepper's lyrical alto and Hamp Hawes' driving piano give the six titles a vitality which was all too often absent from later dates. As the leader of a studio-assembled big band Rogers was reponsible for some fine, swinging music, the best of which will be found on (2) – unfortunately deleted from the British catalogues – in which the six trumpets (led by Conrad Gozzo with Maynard Ferguson doubling an octave above on some passages) have a bite which few other bands have bettered. Rogers' composi-tional talents seem to be limited to writing melodies based on the bare minimum of notes and while this simplicity gives Shorty's scores great individuality, it throws the responsibility for achieving success on the soloists and sidemen. When the original impetus behind the West Coast movement grew less, the effectiveness of Rogers' work suffered accordingly simply because the soloists no longer played with a sense of urgency. (3) is a good, but hardly outstanding, big-band LP devoted to songs by Richard Rodgers and the air of flaccidity may be sensed in places. The best moments on this particular album occur whenever Bill Holman plays his tenor into the solo mike. In retrospect much of Rogers' middle 'fifties recordings have failed to withstand the test of time although the ones noted below are generally exempt from this criticism.

(1) SHORTY ROGERS GIANTS – 10 Cap LC6549. (A) 12 Cap T691
   (other tracks by Gerry Mulligan). *1951*.

(2) COOL AND CRAZY – (A) 12 Vic LPM1350. 10 HMV DLP1030,
   three more titles on 7 HMV 7EG8250. *1953* and *1956*.

(3) SHORTY ROGERS AND HIS GIANTS – 12 RCA RD27018. (A)
   Vic LPM1428. *1957*.

WALTER ROLAND (unknown)   *vocal, piano*

Walter Roland was a popular accompanist of the late '20s and early to mid '30s. The best-known record made in his own name, *Big Mama*, is an outstanding example of city blues and he recorded under several pseudonyms. Among the recorded examples of his work are some accompaniments to Bessie Tucker (7 HMV 7EG8085) recently deleted.

(1) *Big Mama/Every morning blues* – 10 78 Per 0504 (*d*).
(2) THE MALE BLUES, Vol. 1 – 7 JC JEL2.

SONNY ROLLINS (1929)   *tenor saxophone*

Rollins is one of the most important of the post-Charlie Parker saxophonists; unfortunately, at the time of writing (1960) there are indications that he has passed his zenith and some of his most recent records seem to lack conviction and sincerity of purpose. Starting out as a Parker adherent (and alto was Rollins' first instrument, incidentally) Sonny was virtually alone in adding a strong, Coleman Hawkins-like sound to his playing at a time when most other new soloists on the instrument had pinned their faith on Lester Young. Many of Rollins' earlier records showed off his lack of instrumental control; reed squeaks abounded and the coarseness of tone did not make for pleasant listening. (1) contains the first eight titles made under his name with a quartet comprising Kenny Drew, Percy Heath and Art Blakey on eight of the tracks. (Miles Davis, on piano, Heath and Roy Haynes support Rollins on the exhilarating *I know*, based on the chords of Bird's *Confirmation*.) Although there are defects in the tenor work here, the assets outweigh the liabilities. Sonny's version of *Shadrack* contains an example of the unusual phrasing in the theme statement which has since become an identifying characteristic of the tenor saxist's work; *Slow boat to China* and *With a song in my heart* are also worthy of note. On the same LP are four tracks, made two years later, with the MJQ; *The stopper* is unusually effective while Sonny's bleak tone suits the atmosphere of *In a sentimental mood*. (2) is an excellent collection of titles by Rollins and a supple, swinging rhythm team (Ray Bryant, George Morrow and Max Roach). Humour is present in large quantities throughout *There's no business like show business* on which Sonny positively bristles, spitting out notes with machine-gun accuracy, slurring phrases across three or four bars and then following quickly with the same phrase telescoped into one. Like Art Farmer, Rollins seems to go out of his way to look for unusual tunes which accounts for the presence here of *There are such things* and Ellington's *Raincheck*. (3) is somewhat disappointing as a sequel, the disappointment being occasioned by an overlong track entitled *Tenor madness* (a tune better known as *Royal Roost* some years ago) on which an immature John Coltrane swaps solos with the leader. Fortunately (4), made a month later, restores the standard; in fact this is perhaps the best LP Rollins has ever made. With Tommy Flanagan, Doug Watkins and Max Roach behind him Rollins hits a peak of creativity from the first bar of the first tune and keeps up this incredible standard to the end of the LP. *St. Thomas* is a catchy, calypso-style original by Sonny while the rolling *Moritat* is a tune sometimes known as *Mack the knife*. But *Blue seven* is the outstanding performance of this highly recommended LP; it is almost as much a virtuoso display for Roach's drumming as for Rollins' tenor. (5), dating from the same period, is a well-intentioned waste of time with one entire side devoted to a medley of tunes associated with Charlie Parker. There are few moments here which warrant replaying. The same remark applies to (6) which contains some hideous, cacaphonous solos played at perfectly ridiculous tempos and two very poor vocals by an otherwise acceptable singer, Earl Coleman. This LP marked the termination of Rollins' contract with the Prestige company in New York and it seems that he could not shake the Prestige dust from his shoes quickly enough. (7) was made three months later in Hollywood with just tenor, bass (Ray Brown) and drums (Shelly Manne). Despite Sonny's insistence on including such incredible tunes as *Wagon wheels* and *I'm an old cowhand* the overall standard is very high (it is almost as good an LP as (4)) with Brown providing a firm foundation and Manne inventing new and intriguing patterns. *There is no greater love* and *Solitude* from this set are exemplary. On (8) Sonny faces the challenge of equally strong sidemen in a very much on-form Jay Jay Johnson, Thelonious Monk and Horace Silver alternating on pianos (they both sit at the keyboard for one number) and the aggressively alert drumming of Art Blakey. *Wail march* from this LP brings everyone to boiling point but it is Jay Jay who raised the temperature highest. A plunging nose-dive is experi-

[271]

enced on (9) where Rollins' two performances with the effete music produced by the MJQ are an affront to human intelligence; on this, and some of his other appearances dating from the late 'fifties, it seems that Rollins no longer cares for his listeners and treats them with contempt. By contrast (10) is an LP to place alongside (4); one side is devoted to four tracks by Sonny and a big brass-laden band (no saxes) playing arrangements by Ernie Wilkins. Although this is the first time on record that Rollins has been heard in this context he quickly converts the situation to meet his own requirements and charges headlong through the scores, scattering the brass and generally demonstrating his superiority. The reverse of the LP is made up of three tracks by a trio (Rollins, Henry Grimes and Specs Wright) and one unaccompanied solo, *Body and soul*. The latter is much more successful than Coleman Hawkins' *Picasso* for it is easy to follow the shape and direction of Sonny's line in relation to a known harmonic and melodic base. The trio tracks are amongst the best solos Sonny has ever recorded and serve as a text-book of his individualism. *If you were the only girl* is complete with tempo rubato in the theme statement, the deliberately off-pitch notes and the unexpected phrasing all adding up to a fresh and invigorating style. Unfortunately this is not maintained, or even approached, on (11) where Sonny joins Hamp Hawes, Leroy Vinnegar, Barney Kessel and Shelly Manne for his second Contemporary LP. The fire seems to have gone out of his playing and the most memorable work comes from Vic Feldman who plays vibes on one track only.

(1) SONNY ROLLINS QUARTET – 12 Esq 32-035. (A) Pre PRLP7129. *1951* and *1953*.
(2) SONNY ROLLINS QUARTET – 12 Esq 32-038. (A) Pre PRLP7020. *1955*.
(3) TENOR MADNESS – 12 Esq 32-058. (A) Pre PRLP7047. *1956*.
(4) SAXOPHONE COLOSSUS – 12 Esq 32-045. (A) Pre PRLP7079. *1956*.
(5) SONNY ROLLINS QUINTET – 12 Esq 32-075. (A) Pre PRLP7095. *1956*.
(6) TOUR DE FORCE – 12 Esq 32-085. (A) Pre PRLP7126. *1956*.
(7) WAY OUT WEST – 12 Vog LAC12118. (A) Con C3530. *1957*.
(8) SONNY ROLLINS, Vol. 2 – 12 (A) BN BLP1558. *1957*.
(9) MJQ AT MUSIC INN, Vol. 2 – 12 Lon LTZ-K15173. (A) Atl 1299. *1958*.

(10) SONNY ROLLINS AND THE BIG BRASS – 12 MGM C776. (A)
MJ1002. *1958.*

(11) SONNY ROLLINS AND THE CONTEMPORARY LEADERS – 12 Vog
LAC12213. (A) Con C3564. *1958.*

JIMMY RUSHING (1903)   *vocal*
'The Blues are really spreading around the world now,' said
Jimmy Rushing on one of his recent tours, 'people everywhere are
getting to know what it's all about.' And it is true to say that a large
measure of thanks for this is due to Jimmy Rushing himself. His
arrival in New York, with the Count Basie Orchestra (1936) created,
one might say, a sensation within a sensation. When he left, in 1950,
he had become part of the Basie sound, and Basie's ultimate replacement for Rushing, Joe Williams, made Little Jimmy's absence more
noticeable than ever.

Though he is generally described as a 'blues shouter' this term is not
really accurate. Rushing's voice is not big, it carries by virtue of its
cutting edge rather than its weight. Melancholy is an obvious
adjective with which to describe his singing and, in this, he is closely
related to Leroy Carr. But it is not only a matter of atmosphere,
it is also a matter of technique and phrasing, for Rushing's similarity
to Carr has, on occasion, been fairly pronounced.

Whatever Jimmy Rushing sings it comes out as the blues and while he
rarely sounds unhappy, he almost always sounds sad. Two of Rushing's
devices, both of which have become increasingly noticeable, are
essential to his delivery. Quite unexpectedly, he breaks his voice on a
descending slur, creating a momentary break in rhythm. Again,
towards the end of a song, he may suspend his phrasing in such a way
as to carry over the metre for two or three bars at a time. This device
of singing out of tempo was a trademark of Billie Holiday but,
though Rushing does the same thing, he achieves a quite different
result. Although he has recently lost some of his power and mobility
Rushing is still the finest male jazz blues singer of our day; his voice
does not sound as if it is likely to give out in the near future. And,
when it comes to swinging a band, Rushing still remains far ahead,
of his rivals. He made many fine records with Count Basie (q.v.) but
none better than *Good morning blues, Blues I like to hear* and *Don't
you miss your Baby.* However, they are all worth hearing. But then,

that statement applies to practically every record that Jimmy Rushing has ever made.

(1) THE JAZZ ODYSSEY OF JAMES RUSHING, ESQ – 12 Ph BBL7166. (A) Col CL1152, (S) CS8060.

(2) IF THIS AIN'T THE BLUES – 12 Van PPL11008. (A) 12 Van 8513. *1957.*

(3) LITTLE JIMMY RUSHING AND THE BIG BRASS – 12 Ph BBL7252. (A) Col CL1152, (S) CS8060.

(4) RUSHING LULLABIES – 12 Ph BBL7360. (A) Col CL1401.

(5) JIMMY RUSHING – 10 Van PPT12002 (*d*).

(6) JIMMY RUSHING – 10 Van PPT12016 (*d*). *1955.*

(7) THE WAY I FEEL – 7 Par GEP8695. *1951–2.*

(8) CAT MEETS CHICK – 12 Ph BBL7105.

(10) GOIN' TO CHICAGO–(A) 12 Van 8518.(Some tracks dupl on (5).)

(11) LISTEN TO THE BLUES – (A) 12 Van 8505. (As above for (6).)

LUIS RUSSELL (1902)   *piano, bandleader*

The Luis Russell orchestra had an identity of its own for about seven years, from 1927 up to 1934, the year that Louis Armstrong took the band over. The most creative period, however, lay between 1929 and 1931, when J. C. Higginbotham, Henry 'Red' Allen (then at his most flamboyant and exciting), Charlie Holmes, Albert Nicholas, Pops Foster and Paul Barbarin were all playing in the band. Most of these musicians were New Orleans men, many of them (including Russell himself) had worked with King Oliver in Chicago. It was hardly surprising, therefore, that the Russell orchestra displayed a greater affinity with the old New Orleans bands than any other group of its size, making use of fairly simple arrangements that allowed plenty of scope for the soloists. At its best, Luis Russell's band could play with quite extraordinary verve and passion. Recordings were also made by contingents from the band, led either by Henry Allen or by J. C. Higginbotham (an outstanding example is Allen's *It should be you*, 12 Fol 2807). Most of Russell's soloists are dealt with elsewhere, but space should be found here for the alto player, Charlie Holmes, a musician with a style rather like Hodges', yet lyrical in a very individual way. Some good latter-day playing by Holmes can be found on two Al Sears EPs (7 Par GEP8681, 8688, *1951*).

PEE WEE RUSSELL (1906)   *clarinet*

Kingsley Amis once described Pee Wee Russell as 'the greatest lyric poet since Yeats'; an exaggeration, but not an absurdity. Pee Wee, in fact, can be called many things – satirist, poet, magician, clown – without any of them actually pinning down the uniqueness of his music. A clarinettist who heard the great Negro bands in Chicago during the 1920s, who drew inspiration about equally from the spiky, sweet and sour playing of Johnny Dodds and Frank Teschemacher, Pee Wee developed into a very personal kind of virtuoso, adroit in the use of the briefest cadences, able to twist many tones out of a single note, a musician of quite extraordinary subtlety and wryness. Pee Wee exploits, as nobody else has ever done, all the illegitimate sounds his instrument can utter, all the flutters, growls and turkey-gobblings. Occasionally, particularly during the mid-1940s, he has grown stale or has lost heart and fallen back upon his mannerisms, but that happens to every artist who relies upon the inspiration of the moment rather than (as, say, many New Orleans clarinettists do) upon a set of lyrical conventions.

It is a pity that (1) is such an uneven LP. Pee Wee plays pleasantly enough (though he's far from at his best), but Wild Bill Davison's solos are brash and Vic Dickenson's irrelevant. (2) presents Pee Wee in a larkish mood, gurgling and rasping away, and creating a near-masterpiece in *Sugar*. (3) is gentler, more persuasive, with the clarinettist accompanied by Nat Pierce, Steve Jordan, Walter Page (he died not long afterwards) and George Wettling. *Blues* (on Fontana's THE SOUND OF JAZZ) is an absorbing duet with Jimmy Giuffre (whom Pee Wee 'cuts' without much trouble), recorded during rehearsals for the T4 show, 'The Sound of Jazz'. During most of his life, though, Pee Wee has worked in other mens' bands, so many of his finest solos must be sought elsewhere. 'Great Jazz Reeds' (12 Cam CDN-139 (A) 12 Cam CAL-339), for instance, contains *Hello Lola* and *One hour*, recorded in 1929 by the Mound City Blue Blowers, with Pee Wee contributing splendidly capricious solos. Just before and during the war, he recorded many sides for (A) Commodore (some can be found on (A) 12 Com 30010 and 30006), usually in groups led by Eddie Condon. It was in a Condon group, too, that he helped to make four impassioned tracks for the 'Chicago Jazz Album' (12 Br LAT8042, (A) 12 Dec 8029) in 1939. The following year saw him

[275]

record two good sessions with groups led by Bud Freeman –
'Wolverine Jazz' (10 Br LA8526) and 'Chicago Style' (7 Fon
TFE17082). Excellent post-war examples of his playing can be heard
in 'Jazz At Storyville' (12 Lon LTZ-15061, (A) 12 Sav 12034) and
(on half of 12 Col 33CX10104, (A) 12 Ver 8241) 'The Ruby Braff
Octet at Newport'.

(1) WILD BILL, VIC AND PEE WEE – 10 Vog LDE134. *1954*.

(2) WE'RE IN THE MONEY – (A) 12 Sto 909. *1950s*.

(3) PEE WEE RUSSELL PLAYS PEE WEE – (A) 12 Stereocraft RTN105.
1958.

S

BUD SHANK (1926)   *flute, alto, tenor, baritone saxophone*
Versatility and consistency are Shank's major qualities. He has
appeared on hundreds of record sessions held in Los Angeles, both
jazz and non-jazz, usually in the company of such established Cali-
fornians as Shelly Manne, Shorty Rogers and Russ Freeman. It is
obvious from Shank's alto work (and it is on this instrument that he
has made most of his records) that Art Pepper has been a great
influence; they played together in the Stan Kenton band for some
time then in 1959 teamed up to form a quintet for Hollywood club
dates. Like Pepper, Shank's style owes about as much to Charlie
Parker as it does to Lee Konitz although the pale, transparent tone
lacks much individuality. Nevertheless Bud's innate professionalism
makes him a useful soloist for his playing rarely falls below the expected
standard. Some of his earlier (and best) work will be found on (1)
where he joins forces with Shorty Rogers on one side of the LP,
putting aside his alto in favour of the flute for a memorable *Lotus
bud*. (Despite the presence of Bill Perkins and Hamp Hawes the reverse
of this LP is disappointing.) (2) presents a quintet of unusual instrumentation (Shank on flute, Bob Cooper on oboe plus rhythm)
playing a tuneful, somewhat superficial kind of 'chamber jazz'. As
a flautist Shank must be reckoned as one of the best in jazz for his
technique on the instrument is far superior to that of other saxophonists who have elected to double. Bud rises to great heights on
both (3) and (5), two excellent LPs made with the talented Brazilian

[276]

guitarist Laurindo Almeida. These records are perhaps the best examples ever of the fusion of jazz and Latin American music. Unlike the heavy-handed attempts to infuse jazz into the music of such big bands as those led by Machito and Perez Prado, Shank and Almeida – aided by bass and drums – divide the North and South honours equally for each has a great understanding of the other's native style. (4) presents the quartet (Bud, Claude Williamson, Don Prell and Chuck Flores) which Shank fronted for some time in the late 'fifties. There is more bite to the alto here, particularly so on such an uncompromising number as *Walkin'*, a quality which gives Bud's playing greater individuality and presence.

(1) BUD SHANK-SHORTY ROGERS – 12 Vog LAE12020. (A) WP 1205. *1954.*

(2) HOWARD RUMSEY'S ALL STARS – 12 Vog LAC12146. (A) Con C3520. *1954.*

(3) ALMEIDA-SHANK – 12 Vog LAE12019. (A) WP 1204. *1954.*

(4) BUD SHANK QUARTET – 12 Vog LAE12041. (A) WP 1215. *1956.*

(5) ALMEIDA-SHANK – 12 Vog LAE12215. (A) WP 1259. *1959.*

CHARLIE SHAVERS (1917)   *trumpet*

Prominent before the war with the fine John Kirby Sextet, Charlie Shavers has now found his true niche as one of jazz's great trumpeters. Many listeners have been put off by Charlie's sense of humour and technical eccentricities which have sometimes overridden his fundamental good taste. Leading a workmanlike sextet, containing trombonist Benny Morton and pianist Kenny Kersey, Shavers wastes a lot of time on (1) in so-called imitations of Armstrong, Eldridge, Cootie Williams, Ziggy Elman, Harry James and Dizzy Gillespie; in each case he sounds like Charlie Shavers and the best tracks are those on which his sextet is allowed to play without added gimmicks. Sy Oliver arranged and conducted (2) on which the Shavers trumpet is placed in a somewhat saccharine setting complete with strings. (3) is much better for here Charlie is heard in an orthodox jazz context, trading choruses with Urbie Green and Hank D'Amico and generally producing music of high quality. His hard-hitting excitement does much to keep things moving on (4) where he partners that underrated tenor saxist Hal Singer.

[277]

(1) The Story of The Jazz Trumpet – 10 Lon LZ-N14009. (A) 12 Beth 67 (with additional tracks). *1954.*

(2) Gershwin, Shavers and Strings – 10 Lon HB-U1053. (A) 12 Beth 27. *1955,*

(3) Jazz For Tonight – 12 Cor LVA9025. (A) 12 Cor 57018. *1955.*

(4) Hal Singer-Charlie Shavers Quintet – (A) 12 Pre PRLP7153. *1959.*

ARTIE SHAW (1910) *clarinet, bandleader*

At least part of Artie Shaw's success as a bandleader has sprung from his flair for picking good drummers. George Wettling, Cliff Leeman, Buddy Rich and Dave Tough all worked for him at one time or another. This helped to offset the essential blandness of Shaw's music, a blandness encountered both in the orchestral work and in Shaw's clarinet playing. Although he is a brilliant technician, Artie Shaw rarely produces solos that are much more than exercises in ingenuity. His first band, however, built around a string quartet (1), was quite a stimulating group, but the success of Benny Goodman's orchestra, and the growing vogue for big swing bands, resulted in this idea being dropped. The band heard on (2) is a fairly conventional group, brassy rather than subtle. This LP contains the two-part *Blues*, but an inexplicable omission is *Shoot the likker to me John boy*, the recording Leo Watson made with Shaw's band. (Watson, who died in 1950, was a member of the Spirits of Rhythm and the most inspired scat singer in jazz.) (3) includes an extended version of *St. James' Infirmary blues* (featuring Hot Lips Page) and the theatrical but exciting *Concerto for clarinet*; the highspot of this LP, though, is Billie Holiday's singing in *Any old time*. All these later records, apart from (7), contain tracks by both the 1938–9 band and the larger orchestras of the 1940s, the latter usually complete with a string section. As well as Hot Lips Page singing and playing *Blues in the night*, (4) contains several smooth arrangements of show tunes and two Gramercy Five tracks also found on (7). Page turns up once more on (5), also Roy Eldridge (one track is the 1945 *Little Jazz*). *Special delivery stomp* (included in (6) along with *September song, Carioca* and *Frenesi*) is duplicated on (7), an LP which presents every recording made by the Gramercy Five of 1940 (Billy Butterfield plays the trumpet, Johnny Guarnieri the harpsichord), plus four by its successor of five years later, this time with Roy Eldridge and Dodo Marmarosa.

(1) ARTIE SHAW WITH STRINGS – (A) 12 EP LN3112. *1936.*

(2) ARTIE SHAW AND HIS ORCHESTRA – (A) 12 Ep LN3150. *1937.*

(3) ANY OLD TIME – 12 RCA RD27065. (A) 12 RCA LPM1570. *1938–45.*

(4) THE GREAT ARTIE SHAW – 12 Cam CDN127. (A) 12 Cam CAL-465. *1938–45.*

(5) BOTH FEET IN THE GROOVE – (A) 12 RCA LPM1201. *1938–45.*

(6) ARTIE SHAW – 7 RCA RCX1011. *1939–45.*

(7) ARTIE SHAW AND HIS GRAMERCY FIVE – (A) 12 RCA LPM1241. *1940–5.*

DON SHIRLEY (1927) *piano*

One of the most original talents to appear on the scene for some time and one of the most impressive pianists now recording. Although it has not been much noted, he has experimented more successfully in the direction of combining classical piano with jazz than Brubeck or John Lewis. The phenomenal technique applied to *How high the moon* (2) makes it a unique and breathtaking performance.

(1) TONAL EXPRESSIONS – 12 Lon HA-A2004. (A) 12 Cad 1001. *1954.*

(2) PIANO PERSPECTIVES – 12 Lon HA-A2003. (A) 12 Cad 1004. *1955.*

(3) ORPHEUS IN THE UNDERWORLD – (A) 12 Cad 1009. *1955.*

(4) IMPROVISATIONS – 12 Lon HA-A2046. (A) 12 Cad 1015. *1956.*

(5) SOLOS – (A) 12 Cad 3007. *1956.*

(6) WITH TWO BASSES – (A) 12 Cad 3008. *1957.*

OMER SIMEON (1902–59) *clarinet*

One of the greatest clarinettists within the New Orleans tradition. He had a clear smooth tone like Albert Nicholas, being infused with the same Creole tradition, and the same technical dexterity and smooth flow of ideas as Jimmie Noone. Jelly Roll Morton always regarded him as the best clarinettist and used him often, notably for most of his best Red Hot Pepper recordings like *Doctor Jazz, Black Bottom stomp, Steamboat stomp* and *Original Jelly Roll blues* and fine trio and quartet sides like *Shreveport stomp* and *Mournful serenade.*

[279]

He also played with King Oliver's bands, with Fletcher Henderson, Lionel Hampton and Jimmie Lunceford. He led very few recording groups of his own; these included some fine sides made with James P. Johnson and Pops Foster in 1945 not currently available. His last few years were spent with the great Wilbur de Paris band and he can be heard to good advantage on these, keeping alive and enlarging a strongly kicking New Orleans tradition of clarinet playing.

ZOOT SIMS (1925)   *clarinet, alto, tenor, baritone saxophones*
There are very, very few artists in jazz whose recorded output is of such a consistently high quality that the collector can buy 'blind' (or perhaps 'deaf') and be sure of satisfaction. Zoot Sims is one of that select coterie. Like Stan Getz, Allen Eager, Al Cohn, etc., Zoot has taken Lester Young as his model so far as tone and melodic approach are concerned. Unlike Lester he swings in a more forthright and direct manner, emphasizing the beat strongly and generally inducing all but the paralytic to tap their feet as he plays. He was one of the original 'Four Brothers' and took the first sixteen-bar solo on the Woody Herman recording of that name. Since leaving Herman in 1949 he has worked occasionally with big bands (he added fire to the Stan Kenton sax section during the latter half of 1953) but has been heard most frequently with small groups. Almost any Sims record can be recommended in its entirety and the final decision and selection must rest with the individual collector. The records listed below are all representative of Zoot's tremendous ability to play commanding, swinging solos irrespective of material or tempo; his inherent sense of time means that he is never brought down by a weak rhythm section and he has been known to carry a group containing inept performers by the sheer strength of his playing. The four titles on (1) were recorded in Paris during Zoot's visit to Europe with Benny Goodman's sextet; the tenor saxist demonstrates his trick of driving himself forward with short, jabbing phrases on *Night and day* while on the slower *Don't worry about me* he picks up the tail end of Jerry Wiggins' piano chorus, repeats it and uses it as the foundation for his own solo. Zoot is closer to the breathy Hawkins school than Lester during *Memories of you* (2) and its three session mates from the 1950 New York date; the accompaniment here is superb with John Lewis, Curley Russell and Don Lamond fusing to

give Sims unified support. (3) dates from the Kenton period and comes from a broadcast which the band did in Paris; Sims is featured at great length on Bill Holman's specially designed *Zoot* and the full band responds to his infectious beat with alacrity. (4) is a fourteen-track survey of Hollywood and Zoot's concert version of *I'll remember April* is a highlight. Bob Brookmeyer is on piano and Larry Bunker on drums for this exemplary performance which, even by Sims' own high standards, is masterly. While with the Gerry Mulligan Sextet Sims made three LPs with his Mulligan colleague Bob Brookmeyer; (5) and (6) feature this two-man front line playing through two programmes of material which owes more to the Kansas City type of small band than the Charlie Parker quintet. Zoot is not an adventurous player from the harmonic standpoint and his beautifully simple style has gained acceptance from a wide range of jazz admirers. On (7) Sims has built up a complete sax section by multi-taping his own alto, tenor and baritone work while (8) takes the process a step further with the tenor saxist presenting himself as a four-alto team. Despite the obvious mechanical trickery both LPs are enormously successful for Zoot achieves the perfect 'sax section' blend throughout. (9) is a return to orthodoxy (and the tenor, apart from one track); backed by one of those hand-picked rhythm sections – Johnny Williams, Knobby Totah and Gus Johnson – Zoot is heard at his most fluent, pouring out a glorious version of *The man I love* at slow tempo, a foot-tapping *Blue room* and a romping version of *Tea for two* under the title *55th and State*.

(1) ZOOT SIMS QUARTET – 7 Vog EPV1086. *1950*.

(2) ZOOT SIMS QUARTET – 10 Esq 20-002. (A) 10 Pre PRLP118. *1950*.

(3) THE KENTON ERA – 12 Cap LCT6160. (A) 12 Cap W569. *1953*.

(4) JAZZ WEST COAST, Vol. 1 – 12 Vog LAE12038. (A) 12 WP JWC500. *1954*.

(5) ZOOT SIMS-BOB BROOKMEYER – (A) 12 Dawn DLP1102. *1956*.

(6) ZOOT SIMS-BOB BROOKMEYER – 12 Vog LAE12047. (A) 12 Sto 907. *1956*.

(7) ZOOT SIMS QUARTET – 12 HMV CLP1165. (A) 12 ABC 155. *1956*.

(8) ZOOT SIMS PLAYS FOUR ALTOS – 12 HMV CLP1188. (A) 12 ABC 198. *1956*.

(9) ZOOT SIMS QUARTET – (A) 12 Arg LP608. *1956*.

[281]

ZUTTY SINGLETON (1898) *drums*

One of the greatest of all New Orleans drummers, equalled perhaps by only Baby Dodds, with a highly developed and modernized sense of swing, which has carried him beyond the strictly traditional field of jazz. He combines power and precision with imaginative variety and uses the full battery of percussion with a constant occurrence of drumming surprises. One of the few drummers, who while indulging in very little exhibitionism, compels one often to listen to him rather than to the rest of the band. While he is to be heard on many great jazz sessions, including some fine trio sides with Morton and Bigard in 1929 and further sides with Bigard in 1944 and some of the greatest of all Louis Armstrong Hot Five sides made in 1928, there is little available under his own name with the exception of two good tracks on NEW ORLEANS JAZZ (12 Br LAT8146, (A) 12 Dec 8283, *1940*) a record which features two even better tracks by an identical group under the name of Red Allen.

BESSIE SMITH (1898–1937) *vocal*

Bessie Smith's life could be briefly described as 'rags to riches . . . to rags'. Now that twenty-three years have passed since her death, we are able to look back, to see more clearly the confines of her life and music. And there is an irony, a sad logic in the titles of her first and last issued records, for they were *Downhearted blues* (1) – February 1923 – and *Down in the dumps* (2); here was the rise and fall of a great artist in less than eleven years.

Bessie's great achievement was the crystalization of the 'classic' blues form, as intent upon conscious dramatic effect and theatrical device as the country blues of Jefferson were lean and dour. The unbridled, emotional swoops of Bessie Smith's style were balanced only by her magnificent voice and impeccable technique. It was all 'balanced on a knife edge' as is so often the case with genius; a slight push may, so easily, overbalance it into monstrous distortion. As Bessie sang, so she lived her life: flat out. There was nothing held back.

Working on the basis laid by the great Ma Rainey, Bessie took the blues from the tent show into the large theatre. But, they were still the blues and, to back her she needed real blues musicians. In Joe Smith she found her most perfect accompanist. His cornet playing provided the lyricism which answered her majestic declamations, searching out the edges of Bessie's phrasing, answering with complete understanding. Charlie Green, Louis Armstrong at his most brilliant, Frankie Newton, Ed Allen, James P. Johnson, Clarence Williams and Fletcher Henderson all worked with Bessie Smith on recording sessions; none achieved the same perfection of musical intimacy as did Joe Smith.

It is often said that Bessie Smith did not make a bad record. This implies that her voice, alone, irrespective of her material, made every record worthwhile. If one agrees with such a suggestion, then the statement may be regarded as true. If, however, lyrics and melody have some importance – which seems likely – then it must be admitted that all Bessie Smith's records were not masterpieces. One could hardly place *Kitchen man* in the same class as *Young woman's blues* (3).

St. Louis blues and *Reckless blues* (with Armstrong) are both *tours de force*. *Lost your head blues*, *Baby doll* and *Weeping willow blues* prove Joe Smith's right of place as her most perfect accompanist. *Black Mountain blues* and *Blue spirit blues* have notably fine lyrics and her famous *Backwater blues* is enhanced by James P. Johnson's rich accompaniment. Since Bessie Smith's death, only one recorded artist has produced the same warmth, the same timeless magnificence, the same controlled brilliance: Mahalia Jackson. She, however, is dedicated to the Gospel and has steadfastly refused to sing 'sinful' songs. So it seems that, for many years to come, Bessie Smith, even in death, will remain the Empress of the Blues.

(1) THE BESSIE SMITH STORY, Vol. 1 – 12 Ph BBL7019. (A) Col CL855. *1923–5.*

(2) THE BESSIE SMITH STORY, Vol. 2 – 12 Ph BBL7020. (A) Col CL856. *1924–33.*

(3) THE BESSIE SMITH STORY, Vol. 3 – 12 Ph BBL7042. (A) Col CL857. *1925–7.*

(4) THE BESSIE SMITH STORY, Vol. 4 – 12 Ph BBL7049. (A) Col CL858. *1927–31.*

(5) THE GREAT BLUES SINGERS – 10 Lon AL3530 (*d*). *1927–46.*

JOE SMITH (1902–37)   *trumpet*
'Nobody plays that sweet horn like Joe,' said Bessie Smith of her

favourite accompanist – and she was right. There is a tenderness in Joe Smith's trumpet-playing that cannot be found anywhere else in jazz; he could evoke pathos without being sentimental, and he could also play a firm, strong lead (as in *There'll be a hot time in old town tonight* – 12 Ph BBL7042, (A) 12 Col CL857). Joe Smith took many solos on recordings by Fletcher Henderson's band during the time he sat alongside Tommy Ladnier in its trumpet section, most of the best ones on such long-deleted 78s as *Fidgety feet* (Br), *What-cha-call-'em blues* (Par), *Sensation* (Br) and *Livery stable blues* (Par). But it is his work with Bessie Smith, the intimacy between trumpet and voice on those records in the 1920s, that most perfectly preserve the lyrical quality of Joe Smith's playing. Among the finest of the tracks he made with the blues singer are *Weeping willow blues* (12 Ph BBL7020, (A) 12 Col CL856), *Trombone Cholly* (12 Ph BBL7049, (A) 12 Col CL858), *Baby doll, One and two blues, Young woman blues, Alexander's Ragtime Band, There'll be a hot time in old town tonight* and *Money blues* (12 Ph BBL7042, (A) 12 Col CL857).

PINETOP SMITH (1904–29)   *piano, vocal*

Pinetop Smith was one of the handful of extremely gifted pianists who transformed the rough and ready blues piano into a classical form of boogie woogie. He is also credited with inventing the name in *Pine Top's boogie woogie* (1) recorded in 1928. He was a pounding, carefree type of pianist with great technical skill and natural blues singing voice; it was unfortunate that his career was cut short in a shooting incident or he would obviously have developed along with Pete Johnson and Albert Ammons to become one of the greatest boogie pianists. On the brief evidence of the above title and *Pine Top's blues* (1), *I'm sober now* (1) and *Jump steady blues* (1) he more or less qualifies anyway.

(1) PIANO JAZZ (BARRELHOUSE AND BOOGIE WOOGIE) (also Montana Taylor, Romeo Nelson, Cow Cow Davenport and Speckled Red) – 12 Cor LVA9069. (A) 12 Br 54014. *1928–30.*

STUFF SMITH (1909)   *violin*

Hezekiah Leroy Gordon Smith – better known as 'Stuff' Smith – led an exuberant little band at the Onyx Club in New York during the years just before World War II. Jonah Jones was on trumpet, Cozy Cole behind the drums. Wearing a battered top-hat, Stuff would mix comedy routines with some of the most dazzling violin-playing ever heard in jazz. But his talents as a comedian did him harm at the time, for many critics refused to take his playing seriously. Some still do. But even the most serious-minded critic must admit that of all the hopeful men who have attempted to play jazz on the violin, only Eddie South and Stuff Smith have really succeeded. Joe Venuti played too many clichés, Ray Nance tries to sound like a gypsy fiddler. Eddie South is undoubtedly the more profound musician of the two, but at the same time he cannot equal the sheer audacity of many of Stuff Smith's solos. Stuff plays his instrument (nowadays he uses an amplified violin) as forcefully as if it were a trumpet or tenor saxophone, bowing fiercely at the same time that he soars in extravagant melodic flights.

Unhappily none of those pre-war records (*You'se a viper*, *Old Joe's hittin' the jug* and *After you've gone* were three of the best, all issued on British Vocalion and long ago deleted) is now obtainable. Stuff Smith's newer recordings, however, show that his skill and spirit are undiminished. On (1), apart from a diffuse trifle of his own composition (*Time and again*) he attacks nearly all the time, excelling himself on *Things ain't what they used to be* and *It don't mean a thing*. (2) brings together Stuff Smith and Dizzy Gillespie, both brilliant but capricious virtuosi. Luckily the two musicians resist the temptation to take their art too lightly and this unlikely partnership produces splendidly pugnacious jazz. One track, *Rio Pakistan*, has Asiatic undertones, the cunning interplay between violin and trumpet suggesting the relationship between the *sitár* and *tambourá* in Indian classical music. Devotees of this unusual musician should also hear him playing around and behind Nat Cole on three tracks of 'After Midnight', 12 Cap LCT6133, (A) 12 Cap W782 (*1956*), while two volumes of 'Ella Fitzgerald Sings the Duke Ellington songbook' (12 HMV CLP1214, 1227, (A) 12 Ver 4008/2, 4009/2) (*1956*), contain more irrepressible solos.

(1) STUFF SMITH – 12 Col 33CX10093. (A) 12 Ver 8206. *1957*.
(2) DIZZY GILLESPIE AND STUFF SMITH – 12 HMV CLP1291. (A) 12 Ver 8214. *1957*.
(3) IT'S SWINGIN' STUFF – 7 Col SEB10113. *1957*.

[285]

WILLIE SMITH (1908)   *alto saxophone, clarinet*

The most remarkable thing about Willie Smith's alto playing is its thrusting enthusiasm, the way he will push his ideas across at the listener. Hodges may be more lyrical, Carter more elegant, Parker incomparably more intense, but none of them can surpass Willie Smith for sheer vigour and swing. His finest playing can be found on records by the Jimmy Lunceford orchestra, with which he worked from 1926 until 1942. For a time he led the Duke Ellington reed section (he takes a number of powerful solos on 10 Vog LDE035, by Duke Ellington's Coronets), but for most of the last decade he has been the star performer in Harry James' orchestra. His solos are still as audacious as ever, and played with the same massive tone. Apart from *Experiment perilous* (2), an informal recording on which there are also solos by Lucky Thompson, Howard McGhee and Arnold Ross, the items cited below are not very exciting.

(1) WILLIE SMITH SEXTET – 7 Vog EPV1090. *1946.*
(2) WILLIE SMITH SEXTET – 7 Vog EPV1110. *1945.*

WILLIE 'THE LION' SMITH (1893)   *piano, vocal*

One of the best-known comedians in the jazz world, Willie 'The Lion' is one of the most erratic and unpredictable pianists. He fits into the same school as James P. Johnson, and Fats Waller but has none of their professional polish. Practically everything he plays is exciting and has a powerful swing but can be marred by a bull-headed roughness. His own compositions, making an odd contrast, are unusually delicate and intricate and his performances of these are amongst his best. Some of his 1935 recordings on American Decca will always be remembered but none of these are now available. Some of the performances on (1) are excellent, including a fine performance of *Carolina shout*. (2) and (3) are two extraordinary performances where Smith reminisces in a most unreliable and incoherent way about some of the great jazz pianists that he remembers through the mists of time. His pianistic imitations are sometimes a bit wide of the mark while his vocal ones are complete misses, some of them rather embarrassing. His claims as to his own contribution to jazz history probably even surpass some of Morton's, but, in spite of all these quibbles, these two records are full of good music and are certainly amongst the most amusing jazz recordings ever made.

[286]

Smith is at his best as a rhythm pianist within a group and there has been a recent good sample of this on some sides made with Rex Stewart (12 Fel FAJ7001, (A) 12 Fel FAJ7001).

(1) THE LION STEPS OUT – 10 Lon H-APB1017. *1953.*
(2) REMINISCING THE PIANO GREATS – 10 Vog LDE177. *1950.*
(3) THE LEGEND OF WILLIE 'THE LION' SMITH – 12 TR RX3015. (A) 12 GA 368. *1958.*
(4) ACCENT ON PIANO – (A) 12 Ur 1207. *1955.*
(5) THE LION ROARS – (A) 12 Dot 3094. *1957.*

EDDIE SOUTH (1904) *violin*

The fact that Eddie South has never become particularly famous indicates how possible it still is for a major jazz soloist to remain in obscurity. If South had not spent most of the 1930s in Europe and made the records listed below, in fact, it seems quite likely that his talents might have escaped attention altogether. The truth is that Eddie South is the most brilliant of all jazz violinists, a performer with more depth, an even greater range of expressiveness, than Stuff Smith, his only rival. Eddie South claims that he was inspired by Darnell Howard, the New Orleans clarinettist, who played violin in many of the bands he worked with. As far as tone and technique are concerned, Smith is in a class by himself; no other jazz violinists can approach his virtuosity. And to this technical brilliance he adds the sensitivity and imagination which are the possessions of the really creative soloist. On (1) he is partnered by the French violinist, Stephane Grappelly, a very competent performer, in two straight-forward tracks (*Dinah* and *Fiddle blues*) and two interpretations of a section from the first movement of Bach's Concerto in D minor. At first the violinists perform the music more or less as written, then they improvise upon the same passage. (2) contains the superb *Eddie's blues*, a ravishing performance, the greatest example of violin-playing in jazz. On this track South's only accompanist is the guitarist Django Reinhardt. Another solo by South can be found on 12 HMV CLP1249 ('DJANGO'), where he is one of three violinists (the others are Grappelly and Michel Warlop) playing *Lady be good*.

(1) EDDIE SOUTH AND STEPHANE GRAPPELLY –7 HMV7 EG8324. *1937.*
(2) EDDIE SOUTH – 7 HMV 7EG8361. *1937.*

[287]

CHARLIE SPAND (unknown) *vocal, piano*

Noted as a leading blues/boogie pianist of the '20s and '30s, Charlie Spand was also a good singer. His recordings, with Blind Blake in particular, are excellent examples of city blues piano/guitar duets.

(1) PIONEERS OF BOOGIE WOOGIE, Vol. 1 – 10 Lon AL3506 (*d*). 1929.

(2) PIONEERS OF BOOGIE WOOGIE, Vol. 2 – 10 Lon AL3537 (*d*). 1929.

MUGGSY SPANIER (1906) *cornet*

One of the hottest white jazz musicians, he has achieved a Negro approach, tone and swing to his work that makes it quite exceptional and unique. Plus the obvious Armstrong influence that possesses almost any hot trumpeter he has made the use of the mute a trademark, probably modelling himself in this respect on players like King Oliver and Bubber Miley. The bubbling, effervescent quality of his playing has added spark and drive to many small groups such as the Charles Pierce Orchestra (10 Lon AL3503 (*d*), (A) 12 Riv 12-107) and a group known as the Jungle Kings on the same record, and the Bucktown Five sides made in 1924–5 (10 Lon AL3528 (*d*)), (A) 12 Riv 12-107). For many years he played in the largely non-jazz Ted Lewis Orchestra but even here Spanier's vigorous playing, particularly at times when the band contained other hot men like George Brunis, Benny Goodman and Fats Waller, produced some memorable recordings like *Royal Garden blues* and *Dallas blues*, both on 7 Ph BBE12106. He also played with Miff Mole, Ben Pollack, Eddie Condon and Bob Crosby on record. Spanier's moment of glory came, however, with the recordings he made in 1939 with his Ragtime Band. These recordings, sixteen sides of compact vibrant, tearaway Dixieland music were responsible to some extent for the great revival of interest in traditional jazz which started in the 1940s. Brunis' trombone had much to do with their success. Outstanding are *Relaxin' at the Touro* (1), *Someday sweetheart* (1), *At the jazz band ball* and *Riverboat shuffle* (1), but as all sixteen are happily contained on one valuable LP we needn't be choosy. It is safe to say without in any way denigrating Spanier's later work, most of which is excellent, that he never reached such a peak again, for none of the later recordings ever utilized a group which knit together so well.

(1) The Great 16 – 12 RCA RD-27132. (A) RCA Vic LPM-1295. *1939*.

(2) Muggsy Spanier – 7 Tem EXA3. *1945*.

(3) This Is Jazz – 10 Vog LDE015. *1947*.

(4) Dixieland Band – 12 Mer MPL6516. (A) 12 Mer 20171. *1950–1*.

(5) Hot Horn – 10 Br LA8722. (A) 10 Dec DL5552 (*d*). *1954*.

THE SPIRIT OF MEMPHIS   *vocal group*

Some time in the early 1930s, we do not know exactly when, the Spirit of Memphis gospel group was formed. Four young men started singing in the Mount Olive Baptist Church, Memphis. It was a rather casual beginning for one of the greatest gospel groups in America. Soon the group had increased to six men and, within a short time, they were broadcasting regularly over local stations. Since then the size of the group has varied between four and seven members, but the music has remained the same. The antiphonal patterns which have formed the basis of Afro-American music, are most clearly heard in gospel song, though jazz has used antiphonal devices in all its periods. In The Spirit of Memphis, the excitement and swing of gospel music is perfectly exposed to the listener. The varying weights and textures of the lead singers' voices add to the element of surprise which such passionate music usually inspires. For those who have never heard a gospel group in action, recordings by The Spirit of Memphis will be a revelation.

(1) Negro Spirituals – 12 Vog LAE12033.

(2) Highway To Heaven – 12 Par PMC1085.

(3) Negro Spirituals – 10 Par PMD1070.

(4) Spirit Of Memphis – (A) 12 King 573.

(5) Spirit Of Memphis – (A) 12 King 577.

JESS STACY (1904)   *piano*

Stacy is one of the most exciting pianists in jazz. He plays in a brilliant, bouncy, propulsive style which might be described as Earl Hines without the surprises. His touch is crisp but has the un-ruffled calm of Teddy Wilson's playing. Yet. although these two other great pianists come to mind when thinking of Stacy, there is no questioning his complete originality, and the remarkable tone he seems to conjure out of a piano which makes his playing immediately recognizable. One of his great recordings is still available on a 78 – *Barrelhouse* recorded in 1936 (Par R2187) and an excellent side with orchestra, *Daybreak serenade*, recorded 1945, is on GREAT JAZZ PIANISTS. Some of his finest work was done with the Benny Goodman orchestra during the latter half of the 1930s. Many a flashing solo is to be found in the band's recordings of this period and connoisseurs will always refer to his inspired improvisation on *Sing, sing, sing* at the famous Carnegie Hall concert – a completely unpremeditated flash of genius. Some fine solos of a high standard are included on (1) while (2) is a nostalgic flashback to the Goodman days with many of the old sidemen, an exciting record which includes a wonderful solo, amongst several, called *Blues for Otis Ferguson*.

(1) JESS STACY PIANO SOLOS – 10 Br LA8737. (A) Br BL54017. (d) *1951*.

(2) TRIBUTE TO BENNY GOODMAN – 12 Lon LTZ-K15012. (A) 12 Atl 1225. *1955*.

HERBIE STEWARD (1926)   *alto, tenor saxophones*

'Underrated' is an over-used term in jazz but it happens to describe Herbie Steward's work with accuracy. A contemporary of Stan Getz and Zoot Sims, Herbie spent some time with Artie Shaw during the middle 'forties, soloing on such Shaw records as *Summertime* and *The maid with the flaccid air* (long since deleted from the catalogues) and on the small group *Man I love*, released some years ago on Parlophone under Barney Kessel's name. He joined Woody Herman's new band in 1947 and was an original member of the *Four brothers* sax section, being featured on the record of that name. (Herbie is the third of the four soloists and takes his sixteen bars between those of Serge Chaloff and Stan Getz.) (1) is the only recording currently available under his own name, which is some reflection on a record industry which over-uses lesser artistes while ignoring genuine talent. All four titles are by small groups; *Medicine man* (by Al Cohn) and *Passport to Pimlico* (by Johnny Mandel) are played by Steward and a near-perfect rhythm section (Al Haig, Jimmy Raney, Curley Russell and Roy Haynes) and point up the truth in the comment that Steward's enviable tone is a contemporary translation of Eddie Miller's. In recent years Herbie has been heard on few jazz records

(Buddy Childers' Liberty LP, made in 1955, is an exception) and has
been playing alto in studio bands and pit orchestras. However, in
1957 he came to New York to take part in a reunion session by the
Four brothers (with Al Cohn in place of the contractually debarrde
Stan Getz) and, on his feature number *So blue* (2), he proved that his
powers of jazz invention had not diminished in the slightest.

(1) HERBIE STEWARD – 7 Vog EPV1085. (Recorded originally for
Roost.) *1950–1.*

(2) FOUR BROTHERS TOGETHER AGAIN – 12 (A) Vic LX1096. *1957.*

REX STEWART (1907)   *cornet, trumpet*

Rex Stewart must surely be the most versatile trumpet-player in
jazz, even if he does use a cornet. Stanley Dance has given what is
probably the most concise listing of his diverse styles. 'There is his
unique half-valved tone and style,' he has written, 'a Bix-like open
tone, and sometimes a pure brass tone like the best of Shavers; a
growl tone and style *à la* Cootie; and – best of all – a tight-muted
fierce and angry tone which no one else ever quite attains.' These are
the talents Stewart took with him when he joined Fletcher Henderson's
orchestra in 1926. A couple of his solos with Henderson – in *Sugar
foot stomp* and *Singin' the blues* – can be found on 10 HMV DLP1066
(*d*). From 1934 to 1945 Stewart played with Duke Ellington's band.
His ability to play Bix-like choruses can be heard in *Kissin' my baby
goodnight* (10 Col 33S1044 (*d*)), while a currently available example of
his work is his solo in *Across the track blues* (12 RCA RD27133 (A)
12 RCA LPM1715).

(1) and (3) are played by contingents from the Ellington orchestra,
including Ben Webster and Harry Carney (who plays the alto sax
solo in *My Sunday gal* (3)). Rex himself performs with typical pun-
gency, and both these and (2) can be recommended. One of Stewart's
most aggressive growl solos, incidentally, a solo worthy of Bubber
Miley, is that on *Subtle slough* (3). (2) was recorded in Paris in 1939
(the group includes Django Reinhardt) and has some brilliant open
playing by Stewart in *Finesse*, and a splendid half-choked, bullying
solo in *I know that you know*. (4) was made during a visit to London,
but finds the trumpet-player handicapped by a poor rhythm section.
(6) is not quite the success it should have been, Rex himself sounding
rather dull and the rest of the musicians – apart from Willie 'The

'Lion' Smith – following his example. Finally there is (5), containing a set of old Fletcher Henderson scores performed by a band of ex-Henderson musicians under Stewart's leadership. These performances never quite capture the excitement of the originals, but there are good solos and some enthusiastic (if fallible) ensemble work.

(1) REX STEWART'S 52ND STREET STOMPERS – 7 HMV 7EG8266 (*d*). *1937.*
(2) REX STEWART'S FOOTWARMERS – 7 HMV 7EG8447. *1939.*
(3) REX STEWART ORCHESTRA – 7 HMV 7EG8137. *1940.*
(4) REX STEWART'S LONDON FIVE – 7 Tem EXA8. *1949.*
(5) COOL FEVER – (A) 12 Ur 1212, (S) S2012. *1957.*
(6) RENDEZVOUS WITH REX – 12 Fel FAJ7001, (S) SJA2001. (A) Fel FAJ7001, (S) SJA2001. *1958.*

SONNY STITT (1924) *alto, tenor saxophones*

Sonny Stitt is the most convincing and natural-sounding of all the Parker-derived saxophonists. In addition he has a longer history and was playing like Bird long before most other musicians had grasped the fundamentals of the new jazz style. In an attempt to get away from the omnipresent Parker shadow Sonny switched to tenor in 1949 and it is on this instrument that he is heard throughout (1). Not only is Stitt at or very near his best on the nine quartet tracks but his playing is matched in standard by the plunging, driving piano work of Bud Powell. Rarely has there been a more productive pairing in recent years. Piano and tenor swap ideas throughout the course of the entirely apt programme which includes such firm favourites with jazzmen as *Fine and dandy* (two different takes), *All God's children* and a sinewy *Bud's blues*. There is rather more than a nod in the Parker direction with *Sonnyside* which is, in fact, Bird's tune *Dexterity*. The remaining five tracks are from a different session, with Jay Jay Johnson and John Lewis, and includes Lewis's wholly delightful *Afternoon in Paris* and two takes of the twelve-bar *Blue mode*. Still on tenor Sonny is the chief soloist on (2) which was made at four sessions during 1950. Here Stitt seems unable to decide whether to pin his hopes on Lester Young (whose ghost smiles through on the very slow numbers such as *Mean to me*) or Parker (who might almost have been the author of *Blazin'*). Three of the tracks are by the band which

Stitt and tenor saxist Gene Ammons co-led for a time, an extrovert and exciting unit having strong ties with the small jump bands of an earlier era. (3) is an LP of a different kind, apart from the fact that Sonny plays alto on all eight tracks; Stitt is the featured soloist in a series of arrangements designed to show off his talents against a ten-piece band accompaniment scored by Quincy Jones. The scores are tailor-made with Sonny sounding suitably nostalgic on tunes such as *My funny valentine* and swinging in a direct, uncluttered manner on the blues (*Quince*). His second and third albums for the Roost label, (4) and (5), are much less disciplined affairs in which his alto is deployed against the subtle pulsations of the Hank Jones-Wendell Marshall-Shadow Wilson rhythm section. With just this trio behind him Stitt's imagination knows no bounds. He soars aloft, skimming gracefully across the contours of a set of tunes which include a whirlwind *Cherokee*, a bitter-sweet *It might as well be spring* and a number labelled *Bird's eye* which turns out to be Parker's *Steeplechase*. One side of (4) has its value reduced by the inclusion of Freddie Green who strums his rhythm guitar in steady, Basie style; unfortunately Stitt's conception of the beat is such that the guitar chords, occuring four times in every bar, tie him down unnecessarily so producing a static, earth-bound effect. (Freddie may be one of the greatest rhythm guitarists in the world but that does not mean his presence will improve the sound of *every* section; he is frankly out of context here.) (6) is a raw-edged, unsentimental sequel to Norman Granz's 'Nothin' but the blues' set (see Stan Getz). Stitt (on alto again) and Roy Eldridge make up an unusually good front line as they complement each other with tough, searing phrases. The Oscar Peterson Trio (plus Stan Levey on drums) provides the necessary base and Stitt seems to be closer to Parker than usual, including in his solos outright quotations from *Bird's nest*, *Cool blues*, etc. The presence of Eldridge indicates that Sonny is not just an esoteric and minor artist but a thoroughly accomplished jazzman capable of fitting in with a variety of stylists whose common denominator is a deep understanding of the blues.

(1) SPJ JAZZ – 12 Esq 32-049. (A) 12 Pre PRLP7024. *1949.*
(2) STITT's BITS – 12 Esq 32-078. (A) 12 Pre PRLP7133. *1950.*
(3) PLAYS QUINCY JONES ARRANGEMENTS – 12 Vog LAE12171. (A) 12 Roo 2204. *1955.*

(4) SONNY STITT QUARTET – 12 Vog LAE12196. (A) 12 Roo 2208. *1956.*

(5) STITT AND THE NEW YORKERS – 12 Vog LAE12191. (A) 12 Roo 2226. *1957.*

(6) ONLY THE BLUES – 12 HMV CLP1280. (A) 12 Ver 8250. *1958.*

JOE SULLIVAN (1906)   *piano*

A thoughtful but not very adventurous pianist who recorded some delightful sides in 1933 including his own *Gin mill blues* and *Little Rock getaway* (1). Four further sides made in 1935, including another *Little Rock getaway*, are perhaps even better than these 1933 sides, and still amongst the best Sullivan available (2). These are certainly worth finding. His jazz is tempered with a certain amount of classical restraint and more recent LPs like (4), (5) and (6) show no change or advance, and although they meander along in a pleasing enough way, they add up to little and are not particularly exciting. Some of the best sides he made were with Sidney Bechet, Pops Foster and George Wettling in 1945 (3).

(1) GIN PARLOUR PIANO – 7 Col SEG7652 (*d*). *1933.*

(2) JOE SULLIVAN – 7 Br OE9276. *1935.*

(3) BECHET-SULLIVAN QUINTET – 7 Tem EXA7. *1945.*

(4) MR. PIANO MAN – 12 Col 33CX10047. (A) 12 Ver 1002. *1955.*

(5) NEW SOLOS BY AN OLD MASTER – 12 Lon HA-U2011 (d).
(A) 12 Riv 12-202. *1953.*

(6) JOE SULLIVAN PLAYS FATS WALLER – 10 Ph BBR8091. *1955.*

RALPH SUTTON (1922)   *piano*

A young white musician who has steeped himself in and thoroughly mastered several kinds of Negro-style music and at the same time drawn these elements into his own style, which has become increasingly individual over the years. He spreads a great feeling of enjoyment in his playing and, apart from the fact that he has never been adventurous enough, is one of the best pianists playing in a traditional idiom today, and a very fine technician. Some of his early recordings should be dug out on 78s as they are amongst his best; two very enjoyable ragtime performances *The Cascades/Frog legs rag* authentically played on Vog V2108, *Dill pickles/Whitewash man* both driving and enjoyable performances on Vog V2112, *St. Louis blues*

[294]

and *Carolina in the morning* in the Harlem idiom on Vog V2113 and, with his quartet, *Up jumped you with love/Sweet and lovely* on a recently deleted Br 05564.

A number of LPs are available and all can be recommended for those who admire this pianist, particularly PIANO MOODS (2) with a flashing *Keep your temper* and other pieces in the Harlem vein and BACKROOM PIANO (1) which shows off his ragtime technique to best advantage.

(1) BACKROOM PIANO – 12 Col 33CX10061. (A) 12 Ver 1004. *1949.*
(2) PIANO MOODS – 10 Col 33S1018 (*d*). *1950.*
(3) MUSIC OF FATS WALLER – 10 Col 33S1025 (*d*). *1951.*
(4) RALPH SUTTON AT THE PIANO – 10 Vog LDE014. *1952.*
(5) I GOT RHYTHM – 10 Br LA8719 (*d*). (A) Dec DL5498 (d). *1953.*
(6) A SALUTE TO FATS – 10 Fon TRF6002. (A) 12 Har 7019.
(7) CLASSICAL JAZZ TRADITON – (A) 12 Riv 12-212.
(8) BIX BEIDERBECKE SUITE – (A) 12 Com 30001.

T

BUDDY TATE (1915) *tenor saxophone*

Buddy Tate holds the record for the longest stay that any tenor player has made in Count Basie's orchestra. He joined in 1939 (replacing Herschel Evans) and remained there until 1948. His style, aptly enough, was rather similar to Herschel Evans', although Tate has always been a more straightforward soloist, at once less decorative and less lyrical. He still remains a remarkably fluent, often a very exhilarating musician, however, capable of rhapsodizing gently or of whipping up excitement at faster tempos. During the 1950s Tate led a band of his own, playing at New York clubs and dance-halls, and it is this group – eight pieces in all – which performs on one side of (1). The ensemble work may be a bit ragged but there is much warmth, plenty of swing and good solo playing from Skip Hall (piano), Pat Jenkins (trumpet), Ben Richardson (clarinet) and Tate himself. The other side features a pick-up group, including Buck Clayton, Dickie Wells and Earl Warren; most of the tracks are pleasant, but nobody strikes fire. Supported by rather a lumpy rhythm section, Tate performs a very static *Vonce*, and the genuinely lavish *Teeny Weeny* (on which Tate might be mistaken for Coleman Hawkins) and *Blues for Vi*. All in CASCADE OF QUARTETS Vols. 1 and 2 on Columbia. Some excellent playing by Tate can also be heard on 'Songs for Singers', 12 Ph BBL7317, (A) 12 Col CL1320, by the Buck Clayton All Stars (1959).

(1) SWINGING LIKE – TATE – 12 Fel FAJ7004, (S) SJA2004. (A) Fel FAJ7004, (S) SJA2004. *1958*.

ART TATUM (1910–56)   *piano*

Not only was Art Tatum one of the most accomplished musicians in jazz, he was one of the world's most talented pianists. His instrumental command has never been surpassed and while he has been criticized for indulging in flights of technique for their own sake, it must be made clear that a simpler, less involved method of approach would have been foreign to Art's natural style. By the time he made his first records (1) in his early twenties he was already the possessor of a formidable degree of keyboard dexterity. Over the years he added little to his method of approach; he was not a great innovator but rather a craftsman who had matured early in life. Any one of his records might be taken as a copybook example of the Tatum style complete with the unexpected changes of tempo, the breathtaking runs of semi-quavers and demi-semi-quavers, the modulations and all the other ornate decorations which made him such a difficult musician to accompany. (2) is made up of solos (including the famous *Tea for two*) and trio performances with Tiny Grimes (guitar) and Slam Stewart (bass) playing the part of musical telepathy experts. (3) is no longer available but is worth obtaining second-hand if only for the wholly delightful version of *Aunt Hagar's blues*. In 1954 Norman Granz signed Tatum to a recording contract and it is reported that the pianist made the equivalent of fourteen twelve-inch LPs of solos at three sessions. Eleven of these have been released in America; they consist largely of new versions of previously recorded Tatum classics and it is not surprising that few of the re-recordings are the equal of the originals. Later Granz sessions teamed Tatum with Benny Carter and Louie Bellson (4) for a series of occasionally brilliant trio works, a better set with Roy Eldridge plus bass and drums (5), a superb programme with Lionel Hampton and Buddy Rich (6) and a slightly inferior but nevertheless interesting collection with

[296]

Hampton, Rich, Barney Kessel and Harry Edison (7). Throughout the course of this gargantuan effort there are many moments when Tatum and one or other of the soloists hits on a high level of communication and *rapport* but too much of the time is taken up by Art easily outstripping the limited technical resources of his colleagues. Strangely enough one of the better Tatum-plus-added-soloists sessions involved Buddy De Franco whose flying fingers matched those of the pianist whenever Buddy succeeded in throwing caution to the winds (8). But one of the best records from this period is (9), a trio date with Art romping merrily through such tunes as *If*, *Isn't it romantic* and *Just one of those things* unobtrusively backed by Red Callender and Jo Jones. Fittingly Tatum's last session before his death on 5 November 1956 was his best in years. (10) pairs the pianist with that giant of the tenor saxophone, Ben Webster. Here is true greatness in jazz, a combination of muscular strength and graceful decoration akin to the fan-vaulted roof of a Gothic church. By any known standards the Webster-Tatum version of *All the things you are* is a jazz classic, the remaining tracks only a little less so.

(1) ART TATUM SOLOS – 12 (A) Ep 3295. (Other tracks not by Tatum.) Tatum titles only on 7 Fon TFE17235. *1933*.

(2) ART TATUM – 12 Cor LVA9047. (A) Br 54004. *1937* and *1940*.

(3) ART TATUM SOLOS – 10 Cap LC6524. (A) Cap H216. *1949*.

(4) TATUM-CARTER-BELLSON – 12 (A) Ver 8013. (Two titles on 7 Col SEB10062, three titles on Col SEB10027 and one title on 12 Col 33CX10115.) *1954*.

(5) ART TATUM-ROY ELDRIDGE – 12 Col 33CX10042. (A) Ver 8064. *1955*.

(6) HAMPTON-TATUM-RICH – 12 Col 33CX10045. (A) Ver 8093. *1955*.

(7) LIONEL HAMPTON'S GIANTS – 12 Col 33CX10063. (A) Ver 8170. *1955*.

(8) ART TATUM-BUDDY DE FRANCO – 12 (A) Ver 8229. (Two titles on 7 Col SEB10101, one title on Col 12 33CX10115.) *1956*.

(9) ART TATUM TRIO – 12 (A) Ver 8118. (Seven titles on Col 10 33C9039, two titles on Col 12 33CX10115.) *1956*.

(10) ART TATUM-BEN WEBSTER – 12 (A) Ver 8220. (Six titles on 12 Col 33CX10137, remaining track on 12 Col 33CX10115.) *1956*.

JACK TEAGARDEN (1905) *trombone, vocal*

A master musician by any standards, Teagarden's easy mastery of the trombone has made him almost the counterpart of Armstrong on the trumpet, in spite of the number of great Negro trombonists in jazz. He has created an exact and classical style which many other jazz musicians have copied, with clean phrasing, an elegant tone and relaxed timing. The company he has played with has unfortunately not always been up to his own level; he positively towers above most of the Chicago gang. His tired singing is as famous as his tromboning; and shows many of the same characteristics. He has combined on many occasions vocally with Louis Armstrong, their voices blending admirably. The 154 recordings on Bethlehem (2) were not really very exciting because of a rather weak group and it is all a bit stereotyped while on (3) he never gets a chance to shine. (1) includes some good Teagarden vocals and solos and the same can be said of (4–7); the best is probably (6). The verdict is that it would be nice to hear Teagarden record with some really distinguished company; perhaps he was heard to the best advantage for some years in the touring band he fronted with the genius of Earl Hines to spark his imagination.

(1) Big T's Jazz – 12 Br LAT8229. (A) 12 Dec 8304. *1944–55.*
(2) Jazz Great – 12 Lon LTZ-N15078. (A) 12 Beth 32. *1954.*
(3) Accent on Trombone – (A) 12 Ur 1205. *1954.*
(4) This Is Teagarden – 12 Cap T-721. (A) 12 Cap T-721. *1956.*
(5) Swing Low Sweet Spiritual – 3 - 7 Cap EAP-1-820, 2-820 and 3-820. (A) 12 Cap T-820. *1956–7.*
(6) Jazz Ultimate (with Bobby Hackett) – 12 Cap T-933. (A) 12 Cap T-933 (S) ST-933. *1957.*
(7) Big T's Dixieland Jazz – 12 Cap T-1095. (A) 12 Cap T-1095. *1958.*
(8) Shades of Night – 12 Cap T-1143. (A) 12 Cap T-1143, (S) ST-1143. *1958.*

CLARK TERRY (1920) *trumpet*

Originality in jazz is something of a myth. It is the quality which many soloists try all their lives to possess yet Clark Terry can claim to be an original stylist. His perky phrasing and semi-closed manner of playing are immediately identifiable while his presence in Duke Ellington's trumpet team for some years gave the band an important solo voice. Like Lucky Thompson and Bennie Green, Terry is frequently found in the company of contemporary-style jazzmen although he is not, basically, a modernist. It seems certain that he was an early influence on Miles Davis although Terry himself claims that there is a St. Louis trumpet style to which he and Miles (as St. Louis residents) merely adhered. Terry's tone recalls the cornet work of Rex Stewart with Ellington while his flügelhorn playing on (2) sometimes takes on the quality of an Army bugler. Many of the effects which sound as if they have been made with a mute are achieved merely by holding the bell of the instrument; in this way Terry succeeded in making his trumpet 'talk' during Duke's *Such sweet thunder* suite. Apart from his occasional solo with Ellington Clark was given his own full-length showcase on (1) in the company of Horace Silver, Cecil Payne, Jimmy Cleveland, etc. Despite the quality of some tracks this is a disappointing LP so far as Terry is concerned and he is better represented on (2) with the enigmatic Thelonious Monk. Although the sleeve contains no mention of any personnel it is Terry who solos so well on Bobby Timmons' tune *Moanin'* (3) where he finds no difficulty in making himself heard above Quincy Jones' enthusiastic band.

(1) CLARK TERRY – 12 EmA EJL1256. (A) 36007. *1955.*

(2) IN ORBIT – 12 (A) Riv 12-271. *1958.*

(3) QUINCY JONES ORCHESTRA – 12 Mer MMC14038. (A) 12 Mer 60129. *1959.*

SONNY TERRY (Saunders Terrell) (1911)   *vocal, harmonica*
The amazing technical virtuosity of Sonny Terry's harmonica music has, on occasion, tended to obliterate all thought of his singing. It is hard to believe, until it is witnessed personally, the dynamic power which Terry can generate with his voice alone. It is strong, rough but not excessively loud; the pitching is often a fraction sharp. It is a voice which bears down upon the beat and can accept no compromise. Terry started singing with gospel groups around North Carolina and occasional performances of gospel songs like *This little light of mine* show his thorough grounding in the idiom. He began to gain a reputation as a harmonica player after recording with Blind Boy Fuller and went on to become famous as the greatest blues harmonica player of all. There is one possible exception, the only

man who Terry acknowledges as his equal: Sonny Boy Williamson. In recent years, Terry's playing has become slightly less intricate, his melody lines bent rather than twisted. But this is by his own choice for, when he wishes to use it, his technique, if anything, is even finer than before. One feels, simply, that Terry's blues playing has become more reflective, more finely shaded than it used to be.

(1) FOLK BLUES – 10 Vog LDE137. *1953*.

(2) CITY BLUES – 10 Vog LDE165. *1953*.

(3) ME AND SONNY – 7 Mel EPM7-83. *1946*.

(4) WHOOPIN' THE BLUES – 10 Mel MLP516. *1949*.

(5) THE BLUEST – 7 Nix NJE1060. *1958*.

(6) SONNY AND BROWNIE IN LONDON – 12 Nix NJL18. *1958*.

(7) BLUES IS MY COMPANION – 12 Col 33SX1223. *1959*.

(8) SONNY TERRY – 10 Top 10T30. *1954*.

(9) SONNY TERRY AND HIS MOUTH HARP – (A) 12 Riv 12-644.

(10) SONNY TERRY AND BROWNIE McGHEE – (A) 12 Fan 3254.

There are also a great many recordings of Sonny Terry in the Folkways catalogue. These are too numerous to list and it is advisable to hear as many as possible before making a choice.

SISTER ROSETTA THARPE (c. 1910) *vocal, guitar*

Unhappily, some years ago, Sister Rosetta Tharpe went all electric, at least her guitar did. Since then we have had no opportunity to hear her exciting acoustic solo work any more. Fortunately, she can still sing, though the addition of somewhat flabby backing has not tended to increase the interest of her more recent recordings. However, for about ten years – approximately 1940 to 1950 – Rosetta Tharpe sang and played with a drive which has characterized only the best gospel singers. Her playing was particularly fine; it had a fierce, masculine sound. Technically able, Tharpe played whines and runs with perfect timing and, the second she came in, there was a great lift in the rhythm. Her work with pianist Sammy Price and her duets with Marie Knight are among the most exciting gospel records. One is still hoping for the opportunity to hear Sister Rosetta Tharpe without her electric guitar for, technically, she has in no way deteriorated. 'Gospel Train' (1) contains reissues of many.fine tracks

(1) GOSPEL TRAIN – 12 Br LAT8290. (A) 12 Dec 8782.

(2) SISTER ROSETTA THARPE – 7 Br OE9284. *1956.*

GOSTA THESELIUS (1922)   *arranger, piano, tenor saxophone*
There are few, if any, more talented European jazz arrangers than
Gosta Theselius. In addition he is a remarkably good tenor soloist
and a capable pianist, which makes his retirement from jazz as an
instrumentalist since 1955 all the more regrettable. He cites
Stravinsky, Ravel and Duke Ellington amongst his favourites and has
a grasp of jazz orchestration which would be the envy of many
American arrangers and composers. In September 1951 he was
elected as top Swedish arranger by *Estrad* magazine and scored three
numbers for a band of Scandinavian poll winners (including Rolf
Erikson, Arne Domnerus, Ake Persson, Lars Gullin and Bengt
Hallberg). These records have never reappeared on microgroove
and were not given their share of praise when first issued. All three
numbers (*Pick yourself up*/*Summertime* on Esq 10-238 and *Cream of the
crop* Pts. 1 and 2 on Esq 10-233) will repay investigation not only for
the solos but also for the intelligent writing which adds so much to
the quality level. A year later Theselius again won the *Estrad* poll and
wrote two arrangements for the same line-up of poll winning
instrumentalists (*L'Estrado*/*Sophisticated lady* on Esq 10-313); Duke's
Lady is handled superbly by Theselius and his men as they add further
charm and beauty to this sensuous tune. As a tenor saxist Gosta is
heard at his best on (1), recorded during the 'Jazz Club U.S.A.' tour of
Europe. Theselius, Jimmy Raney and a rhythm section play through
Raney's ingenious *Invention* and Leonard Feather's *Jumpin' for Jane*
as if they had been working as a group for several months. (2) forms
part of a series devoted to European jazz and is, by Theselius's own
standards, relatively unadventurous. Nevertheless the scoring is neat
and efficient and there are some good solo passages from Rolf
Blomquist (flute), Bengt Hallberg and an uncredited trumpeter
(presumably Bengt-Arne Wallin) on *Kreta*, the Norwegian tenor
player Bjarne Nerem on *Brewin'* and Domnerus and Gullin respectively on *Chips* and *The swingin' thirds.*
(1) SWINGIN' IN SWEDEN – 12 (A) EmA 36121. (*Invention* on 7 Esq
    EP17; *Jumpin' for Jane* on 7 Esq EP45.) *1954.*

(2) GOSTA THESELIUS ALL STARS – 7 Or EP7014. (A) 12 Bally 12002 (plus eight additional tracks). *1956*.

JOE THOMAS (1912) *trumpet*

Although he has been playing professionally ever since 1929, and during that time has worked with such bands as Fletcher Henderson's and Benny Carter's, Joe Thomas is still not a familiar soloist to many jazz *aficionados*. He has never, of course, been a showy trumpeter, and this probably contributed to the neglect he has suffered over the past decade. His style owes much to Louis Armstrong, and while he is capable of performing with a burning, ravishing tone, many of his solos are sober in character. On *Pocatello*, 1946, for instance – a good track – his playing has a distinctly wistful air about it. In 1941 Thomas distinguished himself with a set of moving blues choruses on Art Tatum's *Lucille* and *Lonesome graveyard blues* (both issued on British Br and now deleted), his obbligato work behind Joe Turner's singing being particularly impressive. A more recent appearance on record found Thomas playing, as part of Tony Scott's All Stars, along with J. C. Higginbotham, Wilbur de Paris and others, a lengthy *Blues* on '52nd Street Scene' (12 Cor LVA9109, (A) Cor CRL57239). But Joe Thomas's finest work of all can be heard in 'Mainstream', 12 Lon LTZ-K15182, (S) SAH6066, (A) 12 Atl 1303, (S) S1303, on four tracks of which he leads a group that includes Johnny Letman, Dicky Wells and Buddy Tate, with Jimmy Crawford on drums. Thomas's solo in the fourteen-minute *Blues for baby* is a beautifully sustained creation, powerful as well as lyrical.

SIR CHARLES THOMPSON (1918) *piano*

Sir Charles has nailed his colours to the Basie style and can sound even more like Basie than the Count himself at times. His light, feathery touch and supple swing have been heard on many records in recent years, nearly always with a Basie-style rhythm section. (1) presents a somewhat heterogeneous personnel which includes Danny Barker, Buck Clayton and Dexter Gordon, but the moments of greatest interest occur whenever Charlie Parker takes his turn before the microphone. Thompson is in the ideal context on both (2) and (3) where he underlines the various solos (and takes some of his own) during the superior jam sessions organized by Buck Clayton; (2)

includes one of his own tunes, *Robbins nest*, which has become
something of a jazz standard. When the Vanguard record label
launched its jazz series the following year Sir Charles was virtually
house pianist and may be heard on several Vic Dickenson dates
(q.v.). He was given his own chance to show his paces as featured
soloist with three members of the original Count Basie rhythm
section (4) and turns in a quartet of lightly-swinging performances of
great charm. (5) presents a well-integrated band under his own
leadership and is noteworthy chiefly for the work of Emmett Berry
and Coleman Hawkins, the latter turning in a memorable version of
Talk of the town.

(1) SIR CHARLES AND HIS ALL STARS – 10 Vog LDE032. (A) 10
    Apo LP103. *1945*.
(2) BUCK CLAYTON JAM SESSION – 12 Ph BBL 7032. (A) 12 Col
    CL548. *1953*.
(3) BUCK CLAYTON JAM SESSION – 12 Ph BBL7040. (A) 12 Col
    CL567. *1953*.
(4) SIR CHARLES THOMPSON QUARTET – 10 Van PPT12007. (A) 10
    Van VRS8006. *1954*.
(5) SIR CHARLES THOMPSON BAND – 10 Van PPT12011. (A) 10 Van
    VRS8009. *1954*.

LUCKY THOMPSON (1924)　　　　　　　　*tenor saxophone*

Lucky Thompson made it clear very early on in his career that he
was destined to become a major jazz artiste. His rich, soulful sound
owes much to Chu Berry and Don Byas for he is, stylistically, a
Hawkins adherent rather than a follower of Parker or Lester Young.
Nevertheless he has played on several sessions with *avant-garde*
jazzmen such as Miles Davis and Charlie Parker. Ideally he is at home
with 'fringe' modernists such as Dodo Marmarosa (the Marmarosa-
Thompson version of *How high the moon*, recorded in 1946, is a minor
jazz classic and its deletion from the Parlophone catalogue during the
early nineteen-fifties will be regretted by all those collectors whose
libraries do not contain copies). In more recent years he has been
provided with better settings since the 'discovery' of the so-called
mainstream jazzmen; (1) finds him in the company of Basie musicians
(with the Count himself on two of the tracks) plus trombonist
Bennie Green, another talented jazzman whose playing falls between

two pigeon-holes. Lucky is almost at home in this context, sweeping through his solos in the grand manner with his gorgeous tone and forceful personality. Yet there are aspects of his playing which run counter to the 'four-heavy-beats-in-the-bar-and-no-messing' approach of the Basie rhythm team and it would be interesting to hear Lucky in a group composed entirely of men with a similar not-quite-modern outlook (Thompson, Bennie Green, Dodo Marmarosa or Ray Bryant, Clark Terry and Gus Johnson, for example). One side of (2) comes close to the ideal for here Thompson is supported by just Skeeter Best on guitar and Oscar Pettiford on bass. These are perhaps the finest examples of Thompson's work in the current catalogues for the tenor saxist is allowed maximum freedom of expression. The reverse is only a little less effective and despite the presence of a frustrated trumpeter playing trombone (Jimmy Cleveland) Thompson instills into the group a consistency of style which allows him to present his relaxed *Body and soul* in the right atmosphere. It is Lucky who adds most of the gilt to the gingerbread on (3) and (4) where he blows away the air of enervation which so frequently surrounds Milt Jackson-led groups. In February 1956 Thompson came to Europe where he embarked on a hectic programme of recording in Paris; (5), (6) and (7) date from this period and are listed in downward order of merit. (5) is no longer in the catalogue, which is singularly unfortunate since it contains some of Lucky's best solos from this period. *Thin ice* is a remarkable piece played by tenor, bass (Benoit Quersin) and drums (Dave Pochonet) only. On the remaining tracks the gifted Emmett Berry and Henri Renaud are added on trumpet and piano. (6) is made up of pleasant, sometimes outstanding, performances on such established material as *Tenderly*, *My funny valentine*, *Indian summer*, etc. Here Lucky receives the adequate but generally uninspired support of five French musicians on piano, vibes, guitar, bass and drums. (7) has several good tracks but is less consistent than the previously mentioned LPs; some of Thompson's 'originals' bear striking resemblance to better-known tunes! Back in America (after playing baritone with Stan Kenton) Lucky graced some big band sessions for the ABC-Paramount label; he may be heard on *Deep passion*, *Perdido* and *The gentle art of love* (8) and on most of the tracks comprising Quincy Jones' *That's how I feel about jazz* album (9). In most cases he tends to steal the limelight with his personable solos. The records mentioned here will give an adequate picture of Thompson although he has appeared on many more dates. (The assertion by certain writers, and Thompson himself, that the tenor player has been overlooked by the various record companies is completely without foundation. Anyone attempting a Thompson discography will know that Lucky has played on a tremendous number of dates.)

(1) Jo Jones Special – 12 Van PPL11002. (A) Van 8053. *1955.*
(2) Lucky Thompson Orchestra – 12 HMV CLP1237. (A) ABC Para LP111. *1956.*
(3) Milt Jackson – 12 Lon LTZ-C15074. (A) Sav 12070. *1956.*
(4) Milt Jackson – 12 Lon LTZ-C15091. (A) Sav 12080. *1956.*
(5) Lucky Thompson – 10 D-T D93098. (A) Lon D-T D93098. *1956.*
(6) Lucky Thompson – 12 (A) Dawn 1113. (Four titles each on 7 Vog EPV1150 and EPV1152.) *1956.*
(7) Lucky Thompson – 12 Vog LAE12022. *1956.*
(8) Oscar Pettiford, Vol. 1 – 12 HMV CLP1171. (A) ABC LP135. *1956.*
(9) Quincy Jones Orchestra – 12 HMV CLP1162. (A) ABC LP149. *1956.*

JOE TIMER (Theimer) (*1923–55*)   *drums*

Timer was the original leader of an exciting rehearsal band based in Washington, a band formed by local musicians principally for their own pleasure and enjoyment. (1) is the only example of the group on record but the LP gives a clear indication that THE Orchestra possessed a spirit and drive not often encountered in post-war big bands. Trumpeters Irving Markowitz and Charlie Walp, trombonists Earl and Robbie Swope and bass player Mert Oliver all played with Woody Herman before joining THE Orchestra and there is a blazing enthusiasm about the band's music which recalls the best of the Herds. Bill Potts, who played piano with the band, wrote some of the arrangements as did Timer himself (who was responsible for the exciting four-trumpet feature *One for Kenny*); Johnny Mandel contributed the beautifully shaded *The song is you*. Timer's own drumming was completely in keeping with the context and his powerful style combined elements of both Tiny Kahn and Art Blakey. (1) is a record which seems to have been overlooked by many

[305]

discerning jazz enthusiasts and any lover of swinging orchestral jazz
as played by Woody Herman, etc., is advised to investigate THE
Orchestra's sole LP without delay.
(1) WILLIS CONOVER PRESENTS THE ORCHESTRA – 12 Cor LVA9008.
   (A) Br 54003. *1954.*

LENNIE TRISTANO (1919) *piano*

The Tristano school is something of a jazz phenomenon. Paralleling
the exciting developments of Charlie Parker, Lennie's select coterie of
musicians developed a low-temperature approach to improvisation
based largely on linear invention. Unusual harmonic twists are rare
in the pure Tristano style but the construction of flowing melodic
lines which sweep across the normally accepted breaks in phrasing –
even across the bar-line subdivisions – have an important place in
Lennie's teachings. Prominent amongst his associates have been Lee
Konitz, Warne Marsh, Billy Bauer, Jeff Morton, Arnold Fishkin,
Ronnie Ball and Sal Mosca – and that is almost the complete list, for
Tristano followers in America are few in number. In fact Europe has
reflected a greater acceptance of the school; Lars Gullin, Arne
Domnerus, Duggie Robinson, Derek Humble, Hans Koller and
Max Bruel have come under the spell of Lennie (via Lee Konitz) for
varying periods in their careers. As a pianist Tristano's work is
marked by a graceful touch, long lines and great keyboard dexterity;
(1) finds him in the company of Konitz and Bauer on four tracks
with Lee and Lennie achieving a high degree of *rapport.* (2) and (3)
comprise the seven tracks Lennie made for Capitol in the spring of
1949, seven titles which have weathered the test of time remarkably
well and sound fresh by present-day standards. *Yesterdays* (2) is an
abstruse piano solo which will repay repeated playings. *Intuition* and
Digression are unusual experiments in completely free improvisation;
all six musicians commence playing with no pre-set time signature,
chord sequence or key yet during the course of the performances
they succeed in evolving a sense of group form. (4), or at least one
side of the LP, aroused a certain amount of controversy at the time of
its issue. A certain amount of tape splicing, editing and speeding up
has been done deliberately to achieve the desired effects; however
much doctoring has gone into the making of the finished record
there can be no denying the success of the end-products or the deep

sincerity inherent in *Requiem*, a two-piano track dedicated to Charlie Parker.

(1) LEE KONITZ COLLATES –12 Esq 32-027. (A) Pre PRLP7004. *1949.*

(2) LENNIE TRISTANO SEXTET – 10 Cap LC6598. (A) Cap H371. (Remaining tracks not by Tristano.) *1949.*

(3) LENNIE TRISTANO SEXTET – 7 Cap EAP491. (A) Cap EAP491. *1949.*

(4) LENNIE TRISTANO – 12 Lon LTZ-K15033. (A) Atl LP1224. *1955.*

BRUCE TURNER (1923) *alto saxophone*

A musician of imperturbable mien, Bruce Turner was for five years a cornerstone of the Humphrey Lyttelton band, being its most lyrical and most consistent soloist during the whole of that period. Many of his best solos, in fact, will be found on Lyttelton recordings. Bruce Turner's style blends the phrasing of Johnny Hodges with the poise and tenacity of Willie Smith, an admirable conjunction, although a close observer may also detect traces of Lee Konitz and Charlie Parker. Nevertheless, Turner's approach is very individual, his tone easily identified. (1) and (2) are actually by the Wally Fawkes-Bruce Turner Quintet and use a similar instrumentation to that of the old Jimmy Noone Apex Club band. This is pleasant but rather timid music, the best solos coming from Bruce Turner. (3) features Turner's own little 'jump band' (a raw but virile group); the best tracks on this rather uneven EP are *Donegal cradle song*, and *Jumpin' at the Woodside*, mainly because of the leader's alto playing.

(1) TAKIN' IT EASY, Vol. 1 – 7 Dec DFE6192. *1954.*

(2) TAKIN' IT EASY, Vol. 2 – 7 Dec DFE6193. *1954.*

(3) THE CONTROVERSIAL BRUCE TURNER – 7 Nix NJE1051. *1957–8.*

JOE TURNER (1907) *piano*

A pleasant and easy-swinging player in the James P. Johnson tradition. Nothing particularly profound, *Hallelujah, I've got the world on a string, Frankie and Johnny* and *Sweet and lovely* make an enjoyable set of recordings on (1).

(1) JOE TURNER PIANO MOOD – 7 Vog EPV1038. *1952.*

JOE TURNER (1911) *vocal*

Joe Turner, of course, started singing very early. He was so young that he had to be smuggled in and out of the Kansas City cabarets to avoid trouble with the police. He arrived in New York in 1938 and, in the next two years, sang at Café Society, recorded and appeared at Carnegie Hall. After moving to Chicago he dropped out of sight for a time but, fortunately, the early Rock period brought him back to records. There is no one singing today who has Turner's panache or his majesty. His voice, enormous and stupefyingly rich, is an extraordinary vehicle for the transformation of dross into pure gold.

Turner has recorded at a consistently high standard but has never surpassed the magnificent records which he made with Pete Johnson in 1938. And here, the lyrics, especially on *Roll 'em Pete* (1), were outstanding.

(1) *Gone away blues/Roll 'em Pete* – 10 78 Par R2672 (*d*). *1938*.
(2) Boss Of The Blues – 12 Lon LTZ-K15053, (S) SAH-K6019. (A) 12 Atl 1234, (S) S1234. *1956*.
(3) Rockin' The Blues – 12 Lon HA-E2173. (A) 12 Atl 8023.
(4) Joe Turner – 7 Lon RE-E1047.
(5) Joe Turner – 7 Lon RE-E1111.
(6) Careless Love – (A) 12 Sav 14016.
(7) Joe Turner – (A) 12 Atl 8005.
(8) Kansas City Jazz (one track: *Piney Brown Blues*) – (A) 12 Dec 8044.

DICK TWARDZIK (1931–55)   *piano*

Had he lived it seems likely that Dick Twardzik would have become an important pianist in jazz. He made very few records during his short life but those few records show tremendous individuality. In fact it is true to say that there has never been another pianist quite like him. His formal musical education gave him a distinctive keyboard approach in which a Tatum-like instrumental dexterity was allied to an acute perception of light and shade. (1) is by a section of Herb Pomeroy's Boston band under the leadership of the late Serge Chaloff; *Fable of Mabel*, a Twardzik composition, is the highlight of the programme, while Dick's own solos stand out from their context with sharpness and clarity. He contributed six tracks to (2) – the reverse of the LP is by the Russ Freeman Trio – and was due to record a further set of titles to complete the album after his return from Paris in 1955. Although his death prevented the completion of the album, those six titles are of great value in themselves. *Bess you is my woman* is an outstanding piano solo played mostly out of tempo and with intelligent use of the pedals. The final eight bars, which crash brashly into a swinging 4/4, give the performance an unexpected climax and indicate that Twardzik's sardonic humour equalled that of Monk.

(1) THE FABLE OF MABEL – 12 Vog LAE12052. (A), two 10 Sto LPs, LP310 and LP317. *1954.*

(2) DICK TWARDZIK TRIO – 12 Vog LAE12117. (A) WP1212. *1954.*

V

SARAH VAUGHAN (1924)   *vocal*

Even when Sarah Vaughan was performing in the company of such fiery modernists as Charlie Parker and Dizzy Gillespie, back in the 1940s, she maintained a certain detachment in her singing. It made the listener much more conscious of the melodic line she was creating, of the daring intervals and implied harmonies, than of the song as an entity in itself. This impassive approach, in fact, was the exact opposite of what Billie Holiday accomplished with similar material. Later on, some of Sarah Vaughan's innovations hardened into mannerisms, used sometimes largely to emphasize the superb range of her voice. During the last five or six years, however, Miss Vaughan's iciness has begun melting, her singing has become more human, using words as allies rather than enemies. The result is that she is now singing better than at any time in her career.

(1), (2), (3) and (4) were originally issued on the Musicraft label, the products of some of Sarah Vaughan's earliest sessions. They include some of her best work from that period. On several tracks the orchestra was directed by Tadd Dameron, and there are brilliant performances of two Dameron songs – *I could make you love me* (with well-controlled octave jumps in the last eight bars) (1) and *If you could see me now* (3). (4) was made eight years later, Sarah being accompanied by a trio which included that fine drummer, Roy Haynes; he also drums on (7) and (8). This LP contains distinguished versions of *Lover man* and *Body and soul*. A dazzling performance of *Why can't I?* is the highspot of (6), an excellent LP, but near-perfection is reached with (7), a recording of Sarah at work in a night-club and full of a warmth and relaxation missing from most of her studio recordings. (8), made in an adjoining club only a week or so later, is less satisfactory. The second half is much superior to the first, including a dynamic performance of *All of you* that makes brilliant use of the occasional asperity, the cunningly flattened note. (9) presents Sarah Vaughan accompanied by the Count Basie orchestra (but without Basie himself) – a stirring partnership.

(1) I'm Thru With Love – 7 MGM EP637. *1946.*
(2) Sarah Vaughan Sings After Dark – 7 MGM EP538 (*d*). (A) 12
    MGM 3274. *1946–7.*
(3) Sarah Vaughan Sings After Dark, No. 2 – 7 MGM EP572 (*d*).
    (A) 12 MGM 3274. *1946–7.*
(4) My Kinda Love – 7 MGM EP605. (A) 12 MGM 3274. *1946–7.*
(5) Swingin' Easy – 12 EmA EJL1273. (A) 12 EmA 36109. *1954.*
(6) In The Land of Hi-Fi – 12 EmA EJL100. (A) 12 EmA 36058. *1955.*
(7) At Mister Kelly's – 12 Mer MPL6542. (A) 12 Mer 20326. *1958.*
(8) After Hours At The London House – 12 Mer MMC14001.
    (A) 12 Mer 20383, SR60020. *1958.*
(9) No 'Count Sarah – 12 Mer MMC 14021. (A) 12 Mer 20441,
    (S) 60116. *1959.*

JOE VENUTI (1904)   *violin*

Although not in the really hot tradition of Stuff Smith and Eddie South, as far as violins can ever be said to get hot, Venuti doesn't fall so far the other way as to come into the insipid gypsy-styled category of Stephane Grappelly and Ray Nance. His partnership with Eddie Lang in the 1930s produced some of the best white jazz ever to be put on record, including the classic *Farewell blues* which, with three other sides made in 1931, contain some fine work by Jack Teagarden, Benny Goodman and the rest of the group. The later rather more sophisticated and less jazzy recordings are not available, though there is some merit in a showcase album he recorded in the 1950s (2).

(1) The Venuti-Lang All Star Orchestra – 7 Br OE9468. *1931.*
(2) Fiddle On Fire – (A) 12 GA 33-351. *1950s.*

W

FATS WALLER (1904–43)   *piano, organ, vocal*
Thomas 'Fats' Waller was one of the most successfully commercialized jazz musicians to still retain a great prestige as a jazzman.
He was a powerfully swinging, highly skilled pianist with a humour,
exuberance and style that made him almost too individual. He had a
very popular touch and, from the jazz point of view, he probably
over-used it. A pupil of James P. Johnson, he inherited much of the
master's approach to Harlem piano with few of its finer points. For
Johnson's inventiveness, delicacy and variety, he substituted power,
broad humour and some stock tricks. The result is that a little Fats
Waller is a tonic, too much of it can become monotonous. Nevertheless, there can be few people who like jazz who haven't got their
favourite Fats Waller recording and who don't feel an affection for a
wonderful entertainer and showman. The removal of Victor
recordings to the Decca group meant the wholesale deletion in Great
Britain of what was becoming a vast and confused collection of
Waller recordings. Their deletion is a cause of sorrow to the Waller
collector, but it does simplify the choice of recordings for the time
being for the general collector. His work was of such a general high
standard and followed the same successful formula so often that,
although your own favourite track might at present be unavailable,
the records now reissued by RCA give as good a cross-section as any
of his work. Three London 'Origins of Jazz' series have also been
deleted which showed Waller as a soloist on organ, piano and piano-
roll transcriptions, but these can still probably be found, and are still
available in America on Riverside (1), (2). Two sides made in 1929
start our modern Waller saga, with Charlie Gains, Charlie Irvis,
Arville Harris and Eddie Condon, *The minor drag* (3) a sprightly little
number which was intended to be called *Harlem fuss* and *Harlem fuss*
(4), a slow number which was intended to be called *The minor drag*.
These are two of the jazziest sides Waller made. After that the selection
is random because all Fats Waller sides seem as good. We might
single out *Until the real thing comes along* (3), *B flat blues* (4), *Ain't
misbehavin'* (4) – the extended and immortal performance that graced
the film 'Stormy Weather', *Rosetta* (4), featuring Waller on celeste,

Rhythm and romance (5), *I'm on a seesaw* (5), *Black raspberry jam* (5),
There's honey on the moon tonight (6), *Come and get it* (6), *Up jumped
you with love* (6). Also available in Britain, two boring EPs featuring
Waller in London in 1938 playing organ solos (8) and with British
jazz players (9).

(1) YOUNG FATS WALLER – (A) 12 Riv 12-103. *1923–6.* Some of this
    material available on (d) 10 Lon AL3507. *1923–6.*

(2) THE AMAZING MR. WALLER – (A) 12 Riv 12-109. *1939.* (d) 10
    Lon AL3522 and AL3521.

(3) FATS WALLER – 7 RCA RCX-1010. (A) 7 RCA Vic EPA-5005.
    1929–38.

(4) THE REAL FATS WALLER – 12 Cam CDN-131. (A) 12 Cam
    CAL-473. *1929–43.*

(5) FATS 1935–37 – 12 RCA RD-27047. (A) 12 RCA Vic LPM-1246.
    1935–7.

(6) FATS 1938–42 – 10 RCA RC-24004. (A) 12 RCA Vic LPM-1502.
    1938–42.

  The two American LPs above titled AIN'T MISBEHAVIN' *and*
  HANDFUL OF KEYS *do not coincide exactly with the British issues as
  for technical reasons the two British LPs had to be rearranged.*

(7) HANDFUL OF KEYS – 12 RCA RD-27185. *1934–9.*

(8) FATS WALLER IN LONDON, No. 1 – 7 HMV 7EG8304. *1938.*

(9) FATS WALLER IN LONDON, No. 2 – 7 HMV 7EG8341. *1938.*

GEORGE WALLINGTON (1924) *piano*

Although he was one of the earliest of all the new, post-Bud
Powell pianists, it was not until 1951 that George Wallington
emerged as a soloist of note. The occasion is marked by (1), his first
trio LP on which he received the expert support of Curley Russell
and Max Roach. His percussive manner of playing owes much to
Powell but harmonically his approach is different; similarly his own
compositions have great individuality (and there are five of his tunes
on (1)) and seem to have had a minor influence on the work of Mose
Allison. *Lemon drop* and the excellent *Godchild*, both from George's
pen, have gone into the libraries of several well-known orchestras
while in recent years he and his wife Billie have turned out a number
of better-class popular songs. (*Way out there*, a Wallington product,
has been recorded by Chris Connor.) (2), by the same personnel as (1),

contains amongst other tracks an extended version of the earlier *Polka dot* (1) under the title *Variation*. George plays the theme slowly and thoughtfully at first before changing both mood and tempo. Joining the Lionel Hampton band during the summer of 1953 Wallington came to Europe with Hamp where he made a few records before leaving the band in mid-tour. Both (3) and (4) date from this period; (3) was made in Sweden with a group of Scandinavians and contains George's folk-song treatment of Monk's *'Round about midnight*, a moody and appealing version of a familiar tune. (4) was made in Paris with Pierre Michelot and Jean-Louis Viale on bass and drums respectively. Despite the recording balance, which tends to give Viale's cymbals undue prominence in places, this LP is strongly recommended as an example of Wallington the soloist. His choice of material is excellent, ranging from a swinging *Star eyes* to a reflective *These foolish things* by way of an unexpectedly Tatum-like solo on *Just one of those things*. In addition there are some excellent Wallington originals – *Ny*, *A day in Paris* and *Fairyland* – which would warrant investigation by other artistes. Records dating from 1955 onwards indicate that Wallington's solo style has undergone a change; (5), recorded 'live' at the Café Bohemia, and (6), by virtually the same group but with Phil Woods in place of Jackie McLean, feature a nervous, fragmentary kind of solo style closely allied to the 'pecking' system of playing adopted by the front-liners. ('Pecking' consists of two instrumentalists soloing together, each playing short, jagged phrases which should interlock to form a cohesive line. They seldom do and the result is usually cacophonous.) However, on *What's new* (6) George returns to his previous ballad style for a solo which creates a suitable atmosphere; Phil Woods' contribution maintains the mood but Donald Byrd's complete lack of understanding on ballads destroys the effect later on.

(1) GEORGE WALLINGTON TRIO – 10 Esq 20-025. 12 (A) Sav 12081 (with four additional titles). *1951*.

(2) GEORGE WALLINGTON TRIO – 10 Esq 20-076. 10 (A) Pre PRLP158. *1951*.

(3) GEORGE WALLINGTON – 7 Esq EP2. 12 (A) EmA 36131 (remaining titles by Jimmy Raney). *1953*.

(4) GEORGE WALLINGTON TRIO – 10 Vog LDE059. *1953*.

(5) GEORGE WALLINGTON QUINTET – 12 (A) Pro PLP1001. *1955*.

[313]

(6) JAZZ FOR THE CARRIAGE TRADE – 12 Esq 32-032. 12 (A) Pre PRLP7032. *1956*.

CHICK WEBB (1907–39)   *drums*

Harlem's Savoy Ballroom was not only the 'home of dancing feet' in the 1930s, it was also home for Chick Webb's orchestra. Although hunch-backed and fragile in build, Webb was one of the greatest of all jazz drummers, and his band included such fine soloists as Sandy Williams, Taft Jordan and Elmer Williams; the orchestrations, mostly light and swinging, were usually written by Edgar Sampson. Ella Fitzgerald began singing with the band in 1934, and it was she who helped Webb to achieve commercial success outside of Harlem. Unfortunately the records listed below only give a partial idea of how stimulating this orchestra could sound. *I want to be happy* is probably the best, including passages by Chick Webb's Little Chicks (a 'band within a band'), featuring Wayman Carver's flute; *Hallelujah* contains some particularly splendid drumming by Webb himself (note his delicate use of the high-hat cymbal), good singing by Ella and a sultry trumpet solo from Taft Jordan. Both are available on the collection FIVE FEET OF SWING, on Brunswick, (A) Decca. Chick Webb's hit-record, *A-Tisket A-Tasket* (1937), is included in an Ella Fitzgerald LP, 'Ella and her Fellas,' 12 Br LAT8223, (A) 12 Dec 8477.

GEORGE WEBB (1917)   *piano*

George Webb will always be remembered as the jazzman who appeared at the Royal Festival Hall in his shirt-sleeves and braces and as the leader of a remarkable band which burst upon the British jazz scene in the 1940s. Until this Yerba Buena modelled group came along nobody had thought that British jazz musicians could make such a loud and unrefined noise. The full-blooded clarinet playing of Wally Fawkes stood out of this group while Webb's own enthusiastic Zurke-styled piano playing made sure that there were no gaps left in the commanding welter of sound. The tracks on (2), some of which appear on 12 Dec LK4139 and LK4205, still sound full of spirit if perhaps a little more ragged than they seemed at the time. The best side, *South*, is not now available in England.

(1) GEORGE WEBB AND HIS DIXIELANDERS – 7 Mel EPM-7-70. *1945*.

[314]

(2) George Webb and His Dixielanders – 7 Dec DFE6351. *1945–6.*
(A) Dixie-London Style (with Mark White) – 12 Lon
LL-1337. *1946.*

BEN WEBSTER (1909)   *tenor saxophone*
'The Clark Gable of the tenor saxophone, at once a brute and a
hero.' Leonard Feather's description of Ben Webster is a good one,
for in Webster's music can be found both the extremes of tenderness
and aggression. Webster belongs, of course, to the school of Coleman
Hawkins; in fact he was rather overshadowed by Hawkins in the
1930s, just as he was during the next decade by Lester Young and his
imitators. It has only been comparatively recently, in fact, that
Webster's true stature has become apparent, that his real individuality
has begun to shine through. For Webster is that rarest of things, a
jazz musician who is actually playing better as he grows older. If,
nowadays, he resembles another saxophone player, then it is –
unlikely as it seems – Johnny Hodges, particularly when Webster
performs one of his light, feathery solos, exploiting the alto range
rather than the deeper register of his instrument.

Webster first achieved prominence as a member of Bennie Moten's
Kansas City orchestra (he can be heard playing an aggressive solo in
Lafayette, 7 RCA RCX1027). Subsequently he worked with Fletcher
Henderson's orchestra. But it was during the three years he spent
with Duke Ellington's orchestra (from 1940 to 1943) that his real
quality as a musician seems to have emerged. Up to that time his
playing had been very much dominated by Hawkins; now he started to
assert a style of his own – or rather two styles. There was the leathery,
attacking playing found in *Cotton tail*, the lyrical, graceful improvising on *Just a-sittin' and a-rockin'*. Both these recordings, together with
What am I here for?, *Perdido* and *All too soon*, on which Webster also
plays outstanding solos, are contained in 12 RCA RD27134, (A) 12
Vic LPM1364. Another good solo – in *Chloe* – can be found on
12 RCA RD27133, (A) 12 Vic LPM1715.

During the 1940s Webster passed through a period when he
frequently took the two extremes of his playing – the aggression and
the tenderness – beyond the point of artistry, sounding either too
rowdy or too sentimental. By the time he made the records cited
below, however, all of them fairly recent, he had entered a period of

[315]

fresh maturity, performing with superb control and remarkable eloquence. His use of light and shade is particularly masterly, the way he will vary his tone to suit the cadences of the melodic line. With the exception of *Night and day*, all the tracks on (1) move at very slow tempos, but Webster has an uncanny capacity for being able to swing at even the most leisurely pace. And the *rapport* between his playing and that of Art Tatum (not always the easiest pianist to work with) is ideal. (One track included in the U.S. release – *All the things you are*, a dazzling performance – is omitted from the British LP but included in ART TATUM, 12 Col 33CX10115.) On (2) Webster was accompanied by an Oscar Peterson group, and is at his most authoritative on the two blues – *Soulville* and *Late date*, sending a genuine frisson up the spine at some points. Once again the tempo scarcely edges above a trot, but there is no slackening of tension or interest. (3) brings Webster together with his old mentor, Coleman Hawkins, in a set of absorbing performances. Webster is the smoother player on this LP, Hawkins getting a stronger, more virile sound, but as far as inventiveness goes there is little to choose between them. Once again, most of the tracks are slow – either ballads or blues. Webster and Hawkins come together once more (this time with Budd Johnson and Roy Eldridge) on (4). An extended performance of *In a mellow tone* takes up the whole of one side. *Almost like being in love* in TENOR SAXES (12 Col 33CX10056) is light and airy, but *Tenderly* is fuzzy and rather maudlin. REEDS THAT MATTER (Mer) finds Webster working with a medium-sized band in *Iron hat* and *Pouting*, the first pugnacious, the latter lyrical, while on *You're my thrill* (with a small group) he performs with an Olympian magnificence.

There are many recordings which contain good solos by this remarkable tenor player. Among the most accessible, however, are BENNY CARTER, JAZZ GIANTS (12 Vog LAC12188, (A) 12 Con 3555), SWEETS (with Harry Edison) (12 Col 33CX10087, (A) 12 Ver 8097), BILL HARRIS AND FRIENDS ((A) 12 Fan 3263). He also appears on four tracks of LEGRAND JAZZ (12 Ph BBL7238, SBBL510, (A) 12 Col CL1250 CS8079), and – this time in unusually fine fettle – on one LP in each set of ELLA FITZGERALD SINGS THE DUKE ELLINGTON SONG-BOOK (12 HMV CLP1213/4, CLP1227/8, (A) 12 Ver 4008/2, 4009/2).

[316]

(1) ART TATUM-BEN WEBSTER QUARTET – 12 Col 33CX10137. (A)
12 Ver 8220. *1956.*

(2) SOULVILLE – 12 Col 33CX10122. (A) 12 Ver 8274. *1958.*

(3) BLUE SAROPHONES – 12 Col 33CX10143. (A) 12 Ver 8327, (S) 6066.

(4) BEN WEBSTER AND ASSOCIATES – 12 HMV CLP1336. (A) 12
Ver 8318, (S) 6056.

DICKY WELLS (1907)   *trombone*

When a man plays the blues he usually tells the truth about himself,
for simplicity reveals the poverty as well as the richness of an artist's
imagination. The seven trombone choruses which Dicky Wells
plays in *Dicky Wells blues* (1), therefore, are more than enough to
illuminate the rare quality of this musician. Violent, stabbing phrases,
or notes blown in a low, husky whisper – Wells seems able to play
anything he likes, manipulating his tone to make the melodic line
more expressive, always implying much more than he actually
states. Dicky Wells, in fact, is one of the two greatest trombonists in
jazz (the other is Jimmy Harrison), an opinion apparently shared by
André Hodeir, the French critic, who devotes a whole chapter of
'Jazz, Its Essence and Evolution' (Secker & Warburg, 1956) to an
analysis of the trombonist's work.

(1) was made when Dicky Wells was touring Europe with Teddy
Hill's orchestra. The trombonist plays superbly on every track, but
reaches the peak of his brilliance in the two solo items – *Dicky Wells
blues* and *Lady be good*. The whole LP is remarkable, though, for in
addition it includes outstanding solos from Bill Coleman and Django
Reinhardt. Four years earlier Wells took part in the sessions organized
by Spike Hughes, and some of his most expressive playing can be
found on *Sweet sorrow blues*, *Arabesque*, *Fanfare*, *Sweet Sue* and
How come you do me (12 Dec LK4173). In 1938 the trombonist joined
Count Basie's orchestra, staying with it until 1946, and among the
many good solos he recorded with the band were those in *Texas
shuffle*, *Panassié stomp*, and *Jive at five* (all on 12 Br LAT8028, (A) 12
Dec 8049), in *Dickie's dream* (12 Fon TFL5064, (A) 2-12 Ep SN6031),
and in *Jimmy's blues* (12 Fon TFL5077, (A) 12 Col CL754). He also
played well on four tracks by the Kansas City Seven (especially
After theatre jump), recorded in 1944. These were released on both
Mercury and EmArcy LPs but are no longer available.

From the time he left Count Basie until comparatively recently, Dicky Wells remained in obscurity. Whenever he did appear on the odd record, his playing usually sounded indifferent, lacking the audacity and vigour of the older solos. His re-emergence as a creative soloist has largely been due to the revival of interest in 'mainstream' jazz, and the various recordings made in the last few years. It would be silly to claim that Wells' playing on (2) and (3) is equal to his best work of the 1930s, but it is still uncommonly fine. On (3) and several tracks of (2), Wells leads a trombone section consisting of himself and three other old stalwarts of the Basie band – Vic Dickenson, Benny Morton and George Matthews. Unhappily an organ was used instead of a piano on several of these tracks. (3) is probably the better LP, for (2) also includes few disappointing performances by a different group. Dicky Wells visited Britain in 1959 with the Buck Clayton band and he can be heard playing in audacious fashion on 'Songs for swingers' (12 Ph BBL7317, (S) SBBL533. (A) 12 Col CL1320, (S) CS8123). He also performs well with a Joe Thomas group on 'Mainstream' (12 Lon LTZ-K15182, (S) SAH6066, (A) 12Atl 1303).

(1) DICKY WELLS IN PARIS – 12 HMV CLP1054 (d). *1937.*
(2) BONES FOR THE KING – 12 Fel FAJ7006, (S) SJA2006, (A) 12 Fel FAJ7006, (S) SJA2006. *1958.*
(3) TROMBONE FOUR IN HAND – 12 Fel FAJ7009, (S) SJA2009. (A) 12 Fel FAJ7009, (S) SJA2009. *1959.*

GEORGE WETTLING (1906)   *drums*

A crisp, bouncing style drummer similar to Ray Bauduc who can always be relied upon to keep a session going with plenty of variety and a rock-steady beat. One of the few drummers who can lend his own character to a session without the use of long drum solos. The classic sides with his Chicago Rhythm Kings (1) made in 1940 have some fine playing by Floyd O'Brien and Jess Stacy. (3) is a very pleasing and sprightly session.

(1) CHICAGO JAZZ ALBUM (with Condon and McPartland) – 12 Br LAT8042. (A) 12 Dec 8029. *1940.*
(2) JAZZ TRIOS – (A) 12 Kap 1028.
(3) RAGTIME DUO (with Signorelli) – (A) 12 Kap 1005.
(4) DIXIELAND IN HI-FI – (A) 12 Har 7080.
(5) SOUNDS OF JAZZ – 7 Fon TFE17083. *1951.*

BUKKA WHITE (?–1943) *vocal, guitar*

Here is the singing of a man condemned. Bukka White's songs, powerful and desperately twisted, have rarely been surpassed in their feeling of hatred. One other singer, Jesse James, on his terrifying *Lonesome day blues* has succeeded in imparting to us the same violence in such an unequivocal manner.

Little is known of White's life but it is believed that he died in Parchman, Mississippi, at the State Penal Farm. According to Big Bill Broonzy, he was the finest of the younger singers from Northern Mississippi, but an extremely hard and bitter man. He usually plays guitar with a steel, sliding around notes and twisting them to suit his voice. *Strange place blues* (1) is an average performance and, to hear Bukka White at his best – both for words and music – one must listen to *Parchman Farm blues* (2) or *Fixin' to die blues* (3).

(1) *Strange place blues* – including 12 Ph BBL7369. *1942.*

(2) *Parchman Farm blues/District Attorney blues* – 10 78 OKo5683 (d). *1942.*

(3) *Fixin' to die blues/Black train blues* – 10 78 OKo5588 (d). *1942.*

JOSH WHITE (1908) *vocal, guitar*

When, in the early 1940s, Josh White became a major night-club attraction around New York, he had reached the point where sophistication was swamping all folk feeling in his work. It was quite a jump from leading Blind Lemon Jefferson to starring at the Blue Angel and the Café Society. His repertoire had become more and more eclectic and, though he was still singing the blues, he was making them intelligible to everyone. This may have increased the significance of his social message; it certainly decreased the quality of his music. But it was largely thanks to Josh White that Big Bill Broonzy and others were given a hearing in places which had hither-to been barred to them. Whatever opinions there may be of his singing, he has long been accepted as a fine guitarist with a strong sense of rhythm. The reason for his inclusion, then, is twofold: his quality as a guitarist and, more importantly still, as a reformer.

(1) JOSH WHITE – 12 Nix NJL2. *1956.*

(2) JOSH WHITE STORIES, Vol. I – 12 HMV CLP1159. (A) 12 ABC 124 *1957.*

(3) Josh White Stories, Vol. 2 – 12 HMV CLP1175. (A) 12 ABC 166. 1957.

(4) Southern Blues – 7 Mer YEP9504.

(5). John Henry, Ballads, Blues and Other Songs – 12 Elek 123

JOHNNY WIGGS (1899) *cornet*

An amateur player in the New Orleans tradition with a clear and easy cornet style, he leads a pleasantly bouncy and nicely balanced group on (1), very well recorded, with other New Orleans stalwarts like Emile Christian, Raymond Burke and Armand Hug giving of their best. Edmond Souchon gives a lusty vocal on *Everybody loves my baby*. (2) is slightly less successful being rather more ponderous in its approach.

(1) Recorded in New Orleans, Vol. 2 (with Pierson, Pecora and Hug) – 12 GTJ LAG12141. (A) 12 GTJ 12020. 1956.

(2) Dixieland Of Old New Orleans – (A) 12 GC3021. 1957.

(3) Papa Laine's Children – 12 Or MG20002. 1951.

CLARENCE WILLIAMS (1893) *piano*

The composer of famous jazz standards like *Royal Garden blues* and *Baby won't you please come home*, his own talents as a musician have never been particularly outstanding, but are by no means negligible. A competent pianist in the blues–cum–barrelhouse tradition he has welded together a number of historical groups of widely differing characters. Most of these will be found listed under famous artists. A delightful 78 (Voc V1034 (d)) of *Cushion foot stomp/PDQ blues*, 1927, is worth searching out. A wide selection of his various groups (1) is a must for those who like the slightly eccentric and fanciful in traditional jazz.

(1) Back Room Special – 10 Col 33S1067 (d). 1923–30.

(2) Clarence Williams' Washboard Band – 7 Par GEP8733. 1927–9.

(3) Clarence Williams' Jazz Kings – 7 Fon TFE17053. 1928.

COOTIE WILLIAMS (1904) *trumpet*

Although it is the cunning with which he manipulates the wa-wa mute, the briskness and sting of his more bizarre playing, for which Cootie Williams is most renowned, this particular side of his technique was acquired almost accidentally. He joined the Duke Ellington orchestra in 1929 as a replacement for Bubber Miley, the greatest of the 'growl' trumpet-players, and it fell to his lot to play the Miley solos in Ellington's earlier compositions and to construct fresh ones, using a similar technique, for the new ones. Miley had been a natural 'growler', achieving a wonderful integration between accent and melodic line; Williams played the style in a more self-conscious fashion, and although he created many fine solos in this way they never possessed the inspired abandon of Miley's best work. Cootie's most satisfying solos, in fact, have generally been those played with an open horn, those allowing his rich, majestic tone to be heard in its natural state. The best proof of this can be found in his solos in *Saratoga swing* (12 Cam CDN119 (A) Cam 459), in the old HMV 78s (*d*) of *Blue feeling* and *Troubled waters*, all by Duke Ellington's orchestra, and in *On the Alamo* and *Waitin' for Benny* (more or less by the Benny Goodman Sextet) on 12 Ph BBL7178 (*d*), (A) 12 Col CL500 and 12 Ph BBL7172 (A) Col CL652 respectively.

Most of Cootie Williams' finest recorded work was done during the eleven years he spent with Duke Ellington. During that period Ellington wrote two 'concertos' for him: *Echoes of Harlem* (also known as *Cootie's concerto*) (Br and Vog 78s (*d*)) and *Concerto for Cootie* (12 RCA RD27133, (A) 12 RCA LPM1715). Other outstanding solo playing can be heard in *Shout 'em Aunt Tillie* (12 Cam CDN119, (A) 12 Cam 459), *Hyde Park* (7 Dec DFE6376), and *Prologue to the Black and Tan Fantasy* and *Gypsy without a song* (10 HMV DLP1172), all by Duke Ellington's orchestra; in *Pyramid* (12 Ph BBL7163, (A) 12 Ep LG-3108) by Johnny Hodges' orchestra; and in *Buzzin' around with the bee* (12 Cam CDN129, (A) 12 Cam 402) by Lionel Hampton's orchestra. Four tracks by Williams' Rugcutters – including *Mobile blues* – are contained in ELLINGTON SIDEMEN (12 Ph BBL7136 (*d*), (A) 12 Ep LN3108, 3237) while (1) includes the fine *Delta mood*.

During the year he spent with Benny Goodman, Cootie Williams took many excellent solos on recordings by the Goodman Sextet A fine selection of these, including *Breakfast feud*, can be found on 12 Ph BBL7172 (A) Col CL652. During the middle 1940s Cootie led his own band for several years, making plenty of records, none of which is now available. Evidence that Cootie Williams can still play as boldly and enthusiastically as ever, though, can be found on (2), an LP made for an American mail-order record company, on which the trumpet-player is joined by Rex Stewart and Lawrence Brown (two old confreres from his Ellington days), J. C. Higginbotham, Bud Freeman and Coleman Hawkins.

(1) COOTIE WILLIAMS' RUG-CUTTERS – 7 HMV 7EG8266 (*d*). *1938*. (rev. Rex Stewart.)

(2) THE BIG CHALLENGE – (A) 12 Jazztone 1268.

JOE WILLIAMS (1903)   *vocal, guitar*

One of the most exciting country singers to record in the early '30s was King Solomon Hill, whose *Tell me Baby* (1) and *Dead gone train* (1) are magnificent examples of Texas-style blues. The high falsetto voice working over free guitar patterns is so perfectly matched with the instrumental sound that, occasionally, the guitar tone could almost be mistaken for the singing. Who was King Solomon Hill? Years of research have suddenly produced the startling information – now corroborated – that his real name was Joe Williams, from Crawford, Mississippi. Under his real name, Williams had made several fine recordings for Bluebird, singing in a much deeper voice and playing in a totally different guitar style. His falsetto swoops were always noticeably clear and, in a series of recordings made in 1957, this vocal control is effectively demonstrated. A most forceful guitarist, he is quite at ease as a soloist or with piano, harmonica, mandolin.

(1) BACKWOODS BLUES – 10 Lon AL3535 (*d*). *1931*.

(2) JOE WILLIAMS, Vol 1 – 7 JC JEN3. *1957*.

(3) JOE WILLIAMS, Vol. 2 – 7 JC JEN4. *1957*.

MARY LOU WILLIAMS (1930)   *piano*

There have been very few women instrumentalists (as distinct from singers) in jazz. Easily the most distinguished is Mary Lou Williams, who started playing professionally back in 1929 and ever since has constantly kept herself busy developing and revising her style. In her early days, when she was both playing the piano and arranging for the Andy Kirk band, she adopted a very direct, down-to-earth approach, e.g. *Drag 'em* and *Night life*, on Coral LRA10022 (A) Br 54015. Her playing was incisive, staccato, influenced about equally by Earl Hines and the boogie-woogie pianists who worked around Kansas City. After moving East with the Kirk band she seems to have absorbed some of Fats Waller's style, a fact reflected in some passages on (1), an EP containing such fine solos as *Corny rhythm* and *Mary's special*. Meanwhile she was playing equally virile solos on most recordings which the Andy Kirk band made during this period.

Since the early 1940s Mary Lou Williams has worked as a solo performer and her playing has become increasingly modern in style, particularly after she came under the influence of Bud Powell and Thelonious Monk around 1946. (2) demonstrates this change quite clearly, although not so completely as some later records. The best track on (3), for instance, is Mary Lou Williams' version of *Monk's tune*. (4) is an extremely good LP, recorded in London, with the pianist accompanied by Alan Ganley and Kenny Napper; as well as some of her own 'originals', the tracks include Tadd Dameron's *Ladybird* and Thelonious Monk's *'Round midnight*. In Paris Mary Lou recorded a set of very warm, relaxed performances in partnership with Don Byas (5). Perhaps (6) lacks dynamics, but it does present some pleasant and inventive playing, particularly of a blues, *Nicole*.

As well as playing the piano, of course, Mary Lou Williams had constantly been at work arranging and composing. She wrote scores for Benny Goodman and Duke Ellington (*Trumpet no end*) as well as for the Andy Kirk band. Her most ambitious work, however, and one rather removed from the jazz field, is the 'Zodiac Suite'. She made a solo piano recording of it in 1945 and a year later she performed the complete work with the New York Philharmonic. Finally, at the 1957 Newport Jazz Festival, Mary Lou Williams played three sections from the suite (plus *The Carioca*) accompanied by the Dizzy Gillespie Orchestra, available on Col 33CX10111 (A) Ver 8244.

(1) MARY LOU WILLIAMS – 7 Col SEG7608 (*d*). *1936*.

(2) PIANO PANORAMA – 10 Esq 20-026. *1951*.

(3) MARY LOU WILLIAMS QUARTET – 7 Esq EP66. *1953*.

(4) MARY LOU WILLIAMS PLAYS IN LONDON – 10 Vog LDE022. (A) 10 Con 2507 (*d*). *1953*.

(5) DON CARLOS MEETS MARY LOU – 7 Vog EPV1042. (A) Included in 12 Sto 916. *1953*.

(6) MARY LOU WILLIAMS IN PARIS – 10 Fel EDL87012 (*d*). *1954*.

SONNY BOY WILLIAMSON (1912-48)   *vocal, harmonica*

Williamson's harmonica playing, though completely different in theme and phrasing, is equal to Sonny Terry's in quality. It is upon Williamson, rather than Terry, that present-day players such as Little Walter Jacobs and James Cotton base their styles. On his earlier records Williamson often played with a high-pitched 'vocal' tone, rather like a fierce Noah Lewis but, with the start of the '40s he began to 'modernize' his approach. By 1942 his playing bore a pronounced resemblance to that of the early jump saxophonists and this 'country-jump' style, according with the beginnings of R & B, helped to make him immensely popular with Negro urban audiences.

His singing, also, was unmistakably personal. Due to an impediment of speech, Williamson often had to stammer a word – this was particularly noticeable with 'm's – giving a sense of physical strain to his songs. It is worth noting that Muddy Waters, among others, has used this 'm' sound on record, a considerable tribute to Williamson's impressive singing.

(1) BLUES IN THE MISSISSIPPI NIGHT – 12 Nix NJL8. (A) UA UA4027. *1942*.

TEDDY WILSON (1912)   *piano*

Time has not really touched Teddy Wilson. An elegant, rather reserved pianist (he has even been dubbed 'gentlemanly'), Wilson goes on creating subtle, essentially melodic solos in very much the same way that he was doing twenty-five years ago. His solo in *Once upon a time* by the Chocolate Dandies ((A) 12 Fol 2811), made in 1933, for instance, one of his earliest and best, is not so very different from the playing on his latest LPs. In the early days the influence of Earl Hines was perhaps a little stronger, but Wilson had already begun softening the outlines of Hines' staccato manner, mixing in a little of Waller, achieving in the process a remarkably personal and sensitive style, one that uses under-statement more often than rhetoric.

Between 1935 and 1939 Teddy Wilson was the pianist in the Benny Goodman Trio and Quartet, and most of his solos on records by these groups are worth hearing, particularly those in *Smiles* ((A) 12 RCA LPM1226) and *Someday sweetheart* (HMV 78, (*d*)). He also played a memorable solo in Mildred Bailey's recording of the latter tune

(Br 78, (*d*)). Meanwhile Wilson was making records under his own name, using such musicians as Lester Young, Buck Clayton, Johnny Hodges and Jonah Jones and with Billie Holiday as his singer. A selection of these performances (mostly of very high quality) can be found on (1), and there are two more in a Billie Holiday EP, 'Lady Day' (7 Fon TFE17010). Although (3) was made by a group which included Ben Webster and Buck Clayton, the music is rather too casual, with Wilson taking the best solos. (10) and (11) were recorded at the same time as 'The Jazz Giants '56' (12 Col 33CX10054, (*d*) (A) 12 Ver 8146) – indeed (10) contains one track, *Gigantic blues*, taken from that LP. All three records contain some of Wilson's most fluent and sprightly playing.

When a musician keeps up such a consistent standard of performance as Teddy Wilson does, it is hard to single out records for special praise. The pianist is certainly at his very finest, however, in *Blues for the oldest profession*, included in ANATOMY OF IMPROVISATION (Col, (A) Ver), and on (6), an LP that has been deleted but is worth searching for. His playing on all the tracks is outstanding, but the three crisp, springing choruses in *Avalon* must rank among his greatest work. (7) comes from the same session but has not quite the same sparkle.

(1) TEDDY WILSON AND BILLIE HOLIDAY – 10 Ph BBR8061 (*d*).
    (A) (plus extra tracks) 12 Col CL637. *1935–8.*
(2) MR. WILSON – 7 Ph BBE12284. (A) (plus extra tracks) 12 Col
    CL748. *1941.*
(3) TEDDY WILSON ALL STARS – 7 MGM EP648. *1945.*
(4) TEDDY WILSON TRIO – 10 Esq 20-009. *1952.*
(5) FOR QUIET LOVERS – 10 HMV DLP1162. (A) (plus extra tracks)
    12 Ver 2029. *1954.*
(6) GENE KRUPA, LIONEL HAMPTON, TEDDY WILSON – 12 Col
    33CX10027 (*d*). (A) 12 Ver 8066 (*d*). *1955.*
(7) STROLLIN' ALONG – 7 Col SEB10086. *1955.*
(8) AFTER YOU'VE GONE – 7 Ph BBE12196. *1956.*
(9) I GOT RHYTHM – 12 HMV CLP1230. (A) 12 Ver 2073. *1956.*
(10) PRES AND TEDDY – 12 HMV CLP1302. (A) 12 Ver 8205. *1956.*
(11) PRES AND TEDDY – 7 Col SEB10099. *1956.*
(12) TEDDY WILSON AT NEWPORT – 12 Col 33CX10107. (A) 12 Ver
    8235. *1957.* (rev. Gerry Mulligan.)

(13) THE IMPECCABLE MR. WILSON – 7 HMV 7EG8567. (A) (plus extra tracks). 12 Ver 8272. *1958.*

(14) MR. WILSON AND MR. GERSHWIN – 12 Ph BBL7344. (A) 12 Col CL1318, CS8120. *1959.*

JIMMY WITHERSPOON (1924)   *vocal*

The next finest blues shouter of today, after Joe Turner, Jimmy Witherspoon is finally receiving proper recognition. He started singing professionally with the Jay McShann band, in 1944. In 1952 he left, in order to freelance, and came up with a big hit, *Big fine gal* (2). Although he uses many of Joe Turner's mannerisms (it would be hard for any shouter not to do so) he still has a personal style which makes him easily recognizable. His voice, in any event, is almost halfway between Joe Turner's and Jimmy Rushing's so enabling him to move a little farther away from the shadow of Joe Turner. Witherspoon's fine sense of timing, together with his clarity of line, has helped him to success. As with Joe Turner, his singing has an instrumental approach which generates an immediate swing; he sings sounds as much as words. He is continually improving.

(1) JIMMY WITHERSPOON SINGIN' THE BLUES – 12 Vog LAE12218. (A) WRC 1267. *1959.*

(2) JIMMY WITHERSPOON AND HELEN HUMES – 7 Vog EPV1198. *1949.*

(3) *Failing by degrees/New Orleans woman* - 10 78 Vog V2261.

(4) *Who's been jiving with you/Rain, rain, rain* – 10 Vog V2295.

(5) *Jump Children/Take me back* – 10 Vog V2356.

(6) NEW ORLEANS BLUES – 12 Lon LTZ-K15150(A) 12 Atl 1266. *1957.*

(7) GOIN' TO KANSAS CITY – (A) 12 Vic LPM1639.

(8) JIMMY WITHERSPOON AT MONTEREY – (A) 12 HiF J421.

(9) FEELIN' THE SPIRIT – (A) 12 HiF R422.

PHIL WOODS (1931)   *alto saxophone*

Since the very earliest records Phil Woods seemed destined to emerge eventually as a soloist of note. He possessed that indefinable presence, or personality, in his playing although his ideas were based almost exclusively on those of Charlie Parker. Gradually he has worked his way towards greater individuality of expression and while the Parker influence is still present (few young alto saxists can hope to exist without reference to Bird occasionally) he now plays with such fierce determination that the listener is never in doubt about the soloist's identity. (1) is the Parker Quartet type of approach (alto, piano, bass and drums) and it says much for Woods that he succeeds in maintaining interest throughout the course of this twelve-inch LP; the throbbing, leaping keyboard work of Johnny Williams seems ideally suited to Phil's style. The chief interest in (2) is not Woods (although he plays well as does Donald Byrd) but the presence of pianist Al Haig who makes one of his rare appearances on record. At the time of this session Haig and Woods were both members of the big Dizzy Gillespie band. (3) is typical of the Phil Woods-Gene Quill group (two altos and rhythm) in which Quill's stutterings and multi-noted solos merely go to show that Woods is a better and more direct improviser. The power of Woods' playing is such that he finds no difficulty in stealing the thunder even when partnered by longer experienced soloists such as Zoot Sims and Gerry Mulligan. This is just what happens on (4) and although Phil was suffering from a heavy cold at the time of the sessions he managed to create solos of such intensity that he emerged the real star of the record. Woods' strident shout-it-from-the-rooftops style of playing seems at times to be a modernized version of the jump alto associated with Pete Brown.

(1) PHIL WOODS QUARTET – 12 Esq 32-020. Pre PRLP7018. *1955.*
(2) THE YOUNG BLOODS – 12 Esq 32-060. (A) Pre PRLP7080. *1956.*
(3) PHIL AND QUILL – 12 Esq 32-050. (A) Pre PRLP7115. *1957.*
(4) MANNY ADAM'S JAZZ GREATS – 12 Cor LVA9064. (A) Cor 57173 *1957.*

Y

JIMMY YANCEY (1898–1951)   *piano, vocal*

There were and are more brilliant boogie-woogie pianists than Jimmy Yancey, but never one who brought more poetry and beauty to what is, mainly, a rather brash and indelicate form of jazz. The bass figure gives a boogie performance its basic character; Yancey's were almost invariably light and delicate in structure often no more than the sparse, four-note to a bar habanera or tango rhythm. Even if he employed more notes he was not a pounding pianist and always left the treble part a 50 per cent share. His melodic line was constantly changing and developing using very tuneful phrases as opposed to the riff-like percussive phrases of the commercialized boogie. By these means he preserved the feeling of the blues with its long melodic lines far more than most pianists. His singing was rather harsher than his playing, a hard, soulful, uncompromising statement of fact rather than an artistic performance. There are two good samples on (3), *Cryin' my sleep* and *Death letter blues* made in 1940. The vintage Yancey year was 1939. In the spring of that year he recorded a number of titles for a small label that specialized in early piano music – Solo Art run by an enthusiastic amateur called Dan Qualey. Eight of these are included on (1) and although they are fine performances by any standards, the recordings he made for Victor later the same year, basically the same performances with different titles are better recorded and more rounded performances and it is these, which are essential to any collection of jazz piano. The four tracks on (2) the habanera based *Five o'clock blues* and *State Street special*, both graceful, and supple pieces and *Yancey stomp* and *Tell 'em about me* which are Yancey at his most exhilarating. *Yancey's bugle call* (3) is another delightfully easy yet exciting performance. Later recordings made for the Session label in 1943 do not quite recapture this peak period but there are some delightful tracks, notably *At the window* (4).

(1) JIMMY YANCEY – a lost recording date: 10 Lon. AL3525. YANCEY'S GETAWAY – (A) 12 Riv 12-124. *1939.*

(2) JIMMY YANCEY (piano) – 7 HMV 7EG8062 (*d*). (A) 10 Vic LX3000. *1939-40.*

(3) JIMMY YANCEY (piano) – 7 HMV 7EG8083 (*d*). (A) 10 Vic LX3000. *1939-40.*

(4) JIMMY YANCEY (piano) – 10 Vog LDE166. *1943.*

(5) PURE BLUES (with Mama Yancey) – (A) 12 Atl 1283. *1951.*

MAMA YANCEY (1896)   *vocal*

On the few occasions when Jimmy Yancey sang, working also under the pseudonym of Faber Smith, he proved that he was no singer. No one could ever doubt that he felt the blues, for he played them with simple genius and, accompanying his wife, Estelle 'Mama' Yancey, he recorded some of his best latter-day blues for the defunct Session label. Mama Yancey is one of the most expressive singers of the St. Louis school and her intense delivery, with twisting notes and fast vibrato, makes her records with Jimmy extraordinarily moving.

[328]

Their *How long blues* is a great record. After Jimmy's death, Mama Yancey only recorded very occasionally and some sides recorded with Don Ewell, on piano (1), show that she was no longer singing as she had with her husband.

(1) MAMA YANCEY WITH DON EWELL – 10 Tem LAP7. *1952.*
(2) PURE BLUES – (A) 12 Atl 1283. *1951.*

YERBA BUENA JAZZ BAND

This vigorous and brash jazz group was formed in 1940 by trumpeter Lu Watters (1911) and had much to do with the fervour and enthusiasm of the jazz revival of the forties. They played as they imagined the King Oliver Creole Jazz Band would have played had it still been going strong. On the whole they overemphasized the corny element, the plonking banjo and the thumping tuba and stereotyped instrumental phrases. Our guess is that the Creole Jazz Band on modern recordings would have sounded much more supple and subtle than this and in all probability Muggsy Spanier got nearer to the sound with his famous Ragtime Band. The Yerba Buena Jazz Band could never be criticized for lack of spirit and they have done much valuable work in preserving some of the old blues and rags and bringing them back to light. They have done much bad work, though they can hardly be blamed for it, in giving inspiration to a lot of inferior imitators. Their music is emphatic and exciting but tends to get monotonous in too large doses, but it is infinitely more alive and kicking than the emaciated offerings of the Condon and Chicago-inspired type of Dixieland which co-existed with it. No special collection need be sorted out, they all sound much the same, and a Yerba Buena devotee will like them all.

(1) YERBA BUENA JAZZ BAND – 10 GTJ LDG038. (A) 12 GTJ12024. *1941.*
(2) BUNK JOHNSON AND THE YERBA BUENA JAZZ BAND – 12 GTJ LAG12121. (A) 12 GTJ12024. *1941–44.*
(3) 1942 YERBA BUENA JAZZ BAND – 12 GTJ LAG12123. (A) 12 GTJ 12007. *1942.*
(4) SAN FRANCISCO STYLE, Vol. 1 – 12 GTJ LAG12025. (A) 12 GTJ 12001. *1946–7.*
(5) SAN FRANCISCO STYLE, Vol. 2 – 12 GTJ LAG12030. (A) 12 GTJ 12002. *1946.*

(6) SAN FRANCISCO STYLE, Vol. 3 – 12 GTJ LAG12035. (A) 12
   GTJ 12003. *1946.*
(7) YERBA BUENA JAZZ BAND – 1947 – (A) 12 Riv 12-213. (also
   Helm). 10 Lon (*d*) HB-U1061. *1947.*
(8) YERBA BUENA JAZZ BAND – 10 Vog LDE009. *1949.*
(9) DIXIELAND JAMBOREE – (A) 12 Ver 1005 (also Pecora). 10 Col
   33C9036. *1950.*
(10) LU WATTERS AND HIS YERBA BUENA JAZZ BAND – (A) 12 Ver
    1005. 10 Col 33C9004 (*d*). *1950.*

LESTER YOUNG (1909–59) *tenor saxophone, clarinet*

Lester Young came into prominence at a time when jazz was
predominantly 'hot', when – to use André Hodeir's handy phrase –
tension dominated over relaxation. The style of Coleman Hawkins,
a musician who created, almost single-handed, a jazz technique for
the tenor saxophone in the 1920s, epitomized this warm, emotional
approach. By contrast, Lester Young's music appeared detached,
oblique, almost dispassionate. His tone was pale where Hawkins' had
been rich, he phrased leanly where Hawkins seemed florid, he would,
as Benny Green has observed, concentrate upon extreme subtleties of
sound, employing false fingerings to obtain an effect of two or three
different densities on the same note. He was fond, too, of using
intervals hitherto neglected in jazz. Yet although Lester Young's
musical stance, the angularity and paleness of his playing, were radical
enough, even foreshadowing the 'cool' jazz of the 1950s, harmonically
he belonged to the 1930s. His vision was primarily melodic. The
ease and relaxation of his improvising arose from his ability to
anticipate, to phrase ahead, preparing for and leading into the next
chord change several beats before he reached it.

In common with Louis Armstrong and Jelly Roll Morton, two
other great innovators, Lester Young grew up in New Orleans (he
was actually born just outside that city, in Woodville, Mississippi).
There is even an ingenious theory, propounded by Ross Russell,
which claims that the pattern of New Orleans clarinet playing can
be discerned in the work of Young and a number of other musicians
who became associated with Kansas City jazz. After spending a year
touring with King Oliver's band, Young began working around
Kansas City with groups led by Bennie Moten and Walter Page.

In 1934 he replaced Coleman Hawkins in Fletcher Henderson's band when that tenor-player left for Europe, but he lasted only a short time. 'He didn't sound like Hawk,' said Mrs. Henderson afterwards. Then, in 1936, he went to New York as one of the tenor-players in Count Basie's orchestra (the other was Herschel Evans, a musician whose style derived from Hawkins'). That year he also made his first recordings – four sides by Jones-Smith, Inc. (a quintet drawn from inside the Basie band), two of which, *Shoe shine swing* and *Lady be good* are included in (1) and (2) respectively. Young's playing was already completely mature, and the first thing a listener notices about his style is its austerity. During the first four bars of *Lady be good*, for instance, he uses no more than ten notes in all, but deploys these with great precision. This reticence, this severely functional manner of playing, lay at the core of Young's music, as well as his fondness for lagging behind the beat, then suddenly catching up with it.

Lester Young worked with Count Basie's orchestra from 1936 until the end of 1940, then played with it again for a short time during the winter of 1943. Within that first period of four years he created some of his greatest solos. Outstanding examples can be found in *Roseland shuffle*, *Every tub* and *Shorty George* (10 Br LA8589; the last two titles are also on (A) 12 Br 54012) and in *Honeysuckle rose*, *One o'clock jump*, *John's idea* and *Panassié stomp* (12 Br LAT8028, (A) 12 De 8049). (1) and (2), of course, are collections of Young's solos with Basie, although three tracks on these LPs – *Rock-a-bye Basie*, *Jump for me* and *Moten swing* – actually contain tenor solos by Buddy Tate and not by Lester Young. (1) includes the splendid *Clap hands here comes Charlie* (one of Young's favourites among his own solos), *Taxi war dance* and *Lester leaps in* (this track by a small group, the Kansas City Seven), while (2) contains *Tickle toe* (another favourite), *Twelfth Street rag*, *Louisiana* and *I never knew* as well as others nearly as good. While Billie Holiday was singing with Basie's band in 1937 she started using Lester Young on her own recordings, and he also played on many that she made with Teddy Wilson's orchestra. These two artists thought alike in many ways. The musical *rapport* they established, in fact, was comparable to that between Bessie Smith and Joe Smith. Lester Young, too, always believed that a jazz soloist should know the lyrics of the songs he played, while Billie

Holiday was a singer for whom the words were as vital as the melody, who would actually recast a melody, in fact, in order to heighten the impact of the lyric, wrenching it into poetry. Together they created some classic performances. Three of the best, *I must have that man*, *Easy living* and *Foolin' myself*, are contained in 10 Phi BBR8061 (*d*). (The same titles can be found on (A) 12 Col CL637, together with two more featuring these artists – *Me, myself and I* and *Sailboat in the moonlight*.) But the majority of recordings which Billie Holiday and Lester Young made together, including *Mean to me*, *Sun showers*, *Yours and mine*, *This year's kisses*, *I'll never be the same*, *Without your love*, *I can't get started*, *Getting some fun out of life*, *All of me* and *Trav'lin' alone* still wait to be reissued by Philips or (A) Columbia. (Two new Holiday EPs include several. See Appendix A.)

At one time there was available on (A) 12 Commodore 20021 a set of the recordings which Lester Young made with the Kansas City Six and Seven, consisting (in 1938) of musicians drawn from the Basie band and (in 1944) of another group which included Bill Coleman and Dicky Wells. The earlier of these sessions is the more important, for it produced such notable playing as Lester Young's tenor solo in *Way down yonder in New Orleans*, as well as some rare examples of his clarinet work in *Pagin' the devil*, *Countless blues* and *I want a little girl*. Young achieved a remarkably personal tone upon his all-metal clarinet; the only clarinettists who have got anywhere near it, in fact, have been Jimmy Giuffre and (to a lesser extent) Pee Wee Russell. Another Kansas City Seven session was recorded in 1944, this time for EmArcy, producing two of Young's most sinuous and oblique solos in *After theatre jump* and *Lester leaps in*, solos that also swing superbly. All four tracks from this session were once available on 10 EmA EJ751 but the LP has since been deleted. Some outstanding tracks dating from Young's period with the Basie band can be found in 'Spirituals to Swing', 12 Van 85234, recordings of a concert at Carnegie Hall in 1938, a concert at which both the Basie band and the Kansas City Six performed. As well as playing superb solos with both groups (especially in *One o'clock jump*) Young is heard playing a clarinet obbligato to a Helen Humes blues.

About a year after leaving Count Basie, Lester Young recorded four tracks – including wiry but eloquent versions of *Indiana* and *Tea for two* – in the company of Nat Cole and Red Callender. These tracks, together with three titles (*Jumpin' at Messner's, S.M. blues* and *Jammin' with Lester*) included in (6) and (7), have now been reissued on (A) 12 Score SLP4029. Two more of Lester Young's happiest performances from this period can be found in *Afternoon of a Basie-ite* and *Sometimes I'm happy* on REEDS THAT MATTER, his solos here teeming with ideas and stimulated by Sid Catlett's fine drumming. (3) is the product of three separate sessions. The first, made in 1944, has some of Young's softest, most seductive improvising (the kind of playing which so much influenced Stan Getz) as well as brisk piano solos by Johnny Guarnieri and (in *Exercise in swing*) good trumpet playing by Billy Butterfield. A session recorded a fortnight later resulted in even finer music, this time with Young assisted by a rhythm section comprising Count Basie, Freddie Green, Rodney Richardson and Shadow Wilson. The tracks from the third session, however, featuring a sextet which the tenor saxist led at the Royal Roost in 1949, are very lumpy and uninspired. (4), incidentally, contains alternative 'takes' of many of the recordings on (3).

Lester Young spent fifteen months in the U.S. Army during 1944 and 1945. When he was released he took up his recording career again, starting with a sequence of very worthwhile sessions. Tracks from one of these can be heard on (5) where Young is accompanied by Nat Cole and Buddy Rich. Another (with Vic Dickenson and Dodo Marmarosa in the band), the first of a series he made for Aladdin, produced an outstanding performance in *These foolish things* and three good tracks in *Jumpin' at Messner's, D.B. blues* and *Lester blows again*. The first two items can be found on (7), the second pair on (6). Many of the Aladdin sessions which took place during the next four years, however, recorded not only Lester's music but also a bewildering inconsistency in his standards of performance. Some of the tracks on (6) and (7) present a soloist whose playing goes beyond the edge of coherence. Nevertheless, although the brilliance often flickered it still shone occasionally, as when Young recorded *You're driving me crazy* (it includes one of his very best solos) and three other titles (all with that fine but reclusive pianist Joe Albany in the group) (6) and in the set of five choruses which Lester plays in *No eyes blues* (7), a track that also includes a nicely astringent piano solo by Argonne Thornton.

At the beginning of the 1950s Lester Young began working for

[333]

Norman Granz, both as a recording artist and as a member of 'Jazz at the Philharmonic'. His track on ANATOMY OF IMPROVISATION, in fact, presents him in action at a JATP concert; the track has historical significance too, for he is heard playing alongside Charlie Parker. Most of the recordings which Young made during this last decade of his life, however, are sadly uneven in quality. Some of the best sessions were also some of the earliest, where he was accompanied by John Lewis, Gene Ramey and Jo Jones. He can be heard with this group in (8) and on three tracks of (9), both recordings including a beautifully relaxed *Let's fall in love*. Otherwise (9) consists of some remarkably listless performances, apart from *I can't believe that you're in love with me* and *This can't be love*. One complete side of (10) is also sadly uninspired, but the other half contains four tracks – *It all depends on you*, *Count every star*, *September in the rain* (all with fine John Lewis piano playing) and *Slow motion blues* – which have very adroit and muscular tenor solos. The first title can be found on (A) 12 Ver 8162, the last three on (A) 12 Ver 8181, two LPs which otherwise include little of interest.

To discover Lester Young's finest recorded work from this period, one has to go to three records – (11), (12) and 'Jazz Giants '56' (12 Col 33CX10054 (d), (A) 12 Ver 8146) (one track on the last record, *Gigantic blues*, is also included in (11)). The title, 'Jazz Giants', was correctly used on this occasion, for the group comprises Roy Eldridge, Vic Dickenson, Lester Young, Teddy Wilson, Freddie Green, Gene Ramey and Jo Jones, and the session found these men living up to their reputations. It is particularly good to hear Lester Young in such relaxed form, playing pawky, curiously warm-toned solos, especially in *This year's kisses* and *I guess I'll have to change my plans*. (11) and (12) were recorded at the same time as the 'Jazz Giants' LP but are just by Young alone with the rhythm section. Indolence creeps in here and there, yet on the whole Young's playing here towers above most of his recorded work during the preceding ten years.

(1) LESTER YOUNG MEMORIAL ALBUM, Vol. 1 – 12 Fon TFL5064. (A) 12 Ep LN3167/8 or 2-12 SN6031.[1] *1936-40.*

(2) LESTER YOUNG MEMORIAL ALBUM, Vol. 2 – 12 Fon TFL5065. (A) 12 Ep LN3167/8 or 2-12 SN6031.[1] *1936-40.*

(3) BLUE LESTER – 12 Lon LTZ-C15132. (A) 12 Sav 12068. *1944-9.*

(4) THE MASTER'S TOUCH – (A) 12 Sav 12071. *1944–9.*

(5) LESTER YOUNG TRIO – (A) 12 Ver 8164. *1945.*

(6) LESTER YOUNG – 12 Vog LAE12016. (A) 12 Aladdin 801/2[1]
1945–9

(7) THE GREATEST – 12 Vog LAE12194. (A) 12 Aladdin 801/2.[1]
1945–9.

(8) LESTER YOUNG ORCHESTRA – 7 Col SEB10008 (*d*). *1951.*

(9) LESTER'S HERE – (A) 12 Ver 8161. *1951–3.*

(10) THE PRESIDENT – 12 Col 33CX10031 (*d*). *1951–2.*

(11) PRES AND TEDDY – 12 HMV CLP1302. (A) 12 Ver 8205. *1956.*

(12) PRES AND TEDDY – 7 Col SEB10099. *1956.*

(13) THE LESTER YOUNG STORY – (A) 12 Ver 8308. *1945–56.*

---

[1] NOTE: All the tracks on (1) and (2) can be found on (A) 12 Epic LN3167 and 3168, while those on (6) and (7) are included on Aladdin 801 and 802. The distribution of the tracks, however, does not correspond with that on the British LPs.

RECORD LABEL ABBREVIATIONS

(A)—U.S.A.   (B)—Great Britian   (S)—Stereo

ABC—ABC Paramount (A)
AL—Audio-Lab (A)
Am—American Music (A)
Arg—Argo (A)
Atl—Atlantic (A)
Aud—Audio Fidelity (A & B)

Bal—Baltimore Jazz (A)
Beth—Bethlehem (A)
BN—Blue Note (A)
Br—Brunswick (A & B)

Cad—Cadence (A)
Cam—RCA Camden (A & B)
Cap—Capitol (A & B)
Cav—Cavalier (A)
Cir—Circle (A)
Col—Columbia (A & B)
Coll—Collector (B)
Com—Commodore (A)
Con—Contemporary (B)
Cor—Coral (A & B)
Cou—Counterpoint (A)

Dec—Decca (A & B)
Del—Delmar (A)
DJ—Dixieland Jubilee (A)
Dot—Dot (A)

EmA—EmArcy (A & B)
Ep—Epic (A)
Esq—Esquire (B)
Fan—Fantasy (A)

Fel—Felsted (A & B)
Fol—Folkways (A)
Fon—Fontana (B)

GA—Grand Award (A)
Gal—Gala (B)
GC—Golden Crest (A)
GN—Gene Norman (A)
GTJ—Good Time Jazz (A & B)

Har—Harmony (A)
HMV—HMV (B)

JC—Jazz Collector (B)
Jub—Jubilee

Kap—Kapp (A)

Lib—Liberty (A)
Lon—London (A & B)

Mel—Melodisc (B)
Mer—Mercury (A & B)
MGM—MGM (A & B)
MJ—Metro Jazz (A)

Nix—Nixa (B)

Or—Oriole (B)

Par—Parlophone (B)
Ph—Philips (B)
PJ—Pacific Jazz (A)
Pre—Prestige (A)

Pro—Progressive (A)
Pye—Pye (B)

RCA—RCA (B), RCA Victor (A)
Reg—Regent (A)
Riv—Riverside (A)
Roo—Roost (A)
Rou—Roulette (A)

Sag—Saga (B)
Sav—Savoy (A)
Sco—Score (A)
Sig—Signal (A)
Sou—Southland (A)
Sto—Storyville (A)

Tem—Tempo (B)
Top—Topic (B)
TR—Top Rank (B)
Tra—Transition (A)

UA—United Artists (A)
UR—Urania (A)

Van—Vanguard (A & B)
Ver—Verve (A)
Vic—Victor (A)
Voc—Vocalion (A & B)
Vog—Vogue (B)

WP—World Pacific (A)
WRC—World Record Club (B)

APPENDIX A

THE following important records were issued in Britain too late to be included in the body of this book.

BIX BEIDERBECKE – 7 Ph BBE12368. *1927.*

ORNETTE COLEMAN ('Tomorrow is the Question') – 12 Vog LAC12228. (A) Con 3569, (S) 7569. *1959.*

ORNETTE COLEMAN ('Change of the Century') – 12 Lon LTZ-K15199, (S) SAH-K 6099. (A) 12 AH1327, (S) S1327. *1959.*

MILES DAVIS – 12 Esq 32–100. *1954–6*

MILES DAVIES/GIL EVANS ('Sketches of Spain') – 12 Fon TFL5100. *1959–60.*

DUKE ELLINGTON ('Blues in Orbit') – 12 Ph BBL7381, (S) SBBL567. (A) 12 Col CL1445, (S) CS8241. *1959.*

GIL EVANS ('Great Jazz Standards') – 12 Vog LAE12234. (A) 12 WP1270, (S) 1270, *1959.*

FOLKWAYS RECORDS.

The whole of the Folkways catalogue is now available in Britain. Outstanding among the new issues are the four listed below:

SNOOKS EAGLIN (a young guitarist and blues singer of major stature) – 12 Fol FA2476.

JOSEPH LAMB ('Classic Ragtime') – Fol FG3562.

FURRY LEWIS – 12 Fol FS3823.

THE COUNTRY BLUES (Big Bill Broonzy, Leroy Carr, Gus Cannon's Jug Stompers, Sleepy John Estes, Peg Leg Howell, Blind Lemon Jefferson, Lonnie Johnson, Robert Johnson, Blind Willie Johnson, Tommy McClennan, Blind Willie McTell, Memphis Jug Band, Washboard Sam, Bukka White) – 12 Fol RF1.

JOHNNY HODGES – 7 Fon TFE17234. *1938–9.*

BILLIE HOLIDAY ('Fabulous Billie') – 7 Fon TFE17214. *1935–8.*

BILLIE HOLIDAY – 7 Ph BBE12359. *1937.*

BILLIE HOLIDAY ('Blue') – 7 Fon TFE17026. *1939–41.*

J. J. JOHNSON ('Jay Jay in Person') – 12 Fon TFL5041, (S) STFL512. (A) 12 Col CL1161, (S) CS8009.

JAMES P. JOHNSON (*1929*)/JOE SULLIVAN – 7 Fon TFE17246.

QUINCY JONES ('The Great Wide World of Quincy Jones') – 12 Mer MMC14046, (S) CMS18031. (A) Mer 20561, (S) 60221. *1959*.

JUNIOR MANCE ('Junior') – 12 HMV CLP1342. (A) 12 Ver 8319, (S) 6057. *1959*.

REVS. MOSLEY, BURNETT & GATES (Gospel artists) – 7 Fon TFE17265.

CHARLIE MINGUS ('Mingus Ah Um') – 12 Ph BBL7352. (A) Col CL1370, (S) CS8171. *1959*.

CHARLIE MINGUS ('Blues and Roots') – 12 Lon LTZ-K15194, (S) SAH-K6087. (A) At 1305, (S) S1305. *1959*.

GERRY MULLIGAN/BEN WEBSTER – 12 HMV CLP1373. (A) Ver 8343, (S) 6104. *1959*.

CHARLIE PARKER – 7 Vog EPV1264. *1947*.

RED ONION JAZZ BABIES (with Louis Armstrong) – 7 JC JEL9. *1924*.

SONNY STITT ('Sits in with the Oscar Peterson Trio') – 12 HMV CLP1384. (A) Ver 8344, (S) 6108. *1959*.

SPIRITUALS TO SWING, Vol. 1 (Goodman, Basie, Kansas City Six, James P. Johnson, Bechet-Ladnier) – 12 TR 35/064. (A) Van 8523. *1938–9*.

SPIRITUALS TO SWING, Vol. 2 (Goodman, Golden Gate Quarter, Ida Cox, Sonny Terry, Joe Turner, Johnson-Lewis-Ammons, Bill Broonzy, Mitchell's Christian Singers, Kansas City Six) – 12 TR 35/065. (A) Van 8524. *1938–9*.

ART TATUM ('The Art Tatum Discoveries') – 12 TR 35/067. *1956*.

JOE TURNER ('Big Joe Is Here') – 12 Lon HA-E2231. (A) At 8033. *Early 1950s*.

CLARENCE WILLIAMS BLUE FIVE ('Sidney Bechet Memorial') – 12 Fon TFL5087. *1923–5*.

SINGIN' THE BLUES (Leadbelly, Lizzie Miles, Hot Lips Page, Louis Armstrong-Jack Teagarden, Billy Valentine, Billy Eckstine, Lil Green, Fats Waller, Wingy Manone, Jimmy Rushing, Lucy Reed, Hazel Scott) – 12 Cam CDN-147. (A) 12 Cam CAL-588. *1930–50*.

APPENDIX B

COMPLETE LIST OF LONDON 'ORIGINS OF JAZZ' SERIES
(all deleted in *1959*)

AL 3501 LOUIS ARMSTRONG PLAYS THE BLUES.
AL 3502 MA RAINEY, Volume 1.
AL 3503 MUGGSY, TESCH AND THE CHICAGOANS.
AL 3504 LOUIS ARMSTRONG WITH KING OLIVER.
AL 3505 JOHNNY DODDS, Volume 1.
AL 3506 PIONEERS OF BOOGIE WOOGIE, Volume 1.
AL 3507 REDISCOVERED FATS WALLER SOLOS.
AL 3508 FOLK BLUES OF BLIND LEMON JEFFERSON.
AL 3509 NEW ORLEANS HORNS.
AL 3510 KING OLIVER PLAYS THE BLUES.
AL 3511 JAMES P. JOHNSON – EARLY HARLEM PIANO.
AL 3512 THE FABULOUS TROMBONE OF IKE RODGERS.
AL 3513 JOHNNY DODDS, Volume 2.
AL 3514 COLLECTORS' ITEMS, Volume 1.
AL 3515 RAGTIME PIANO ROLL, Volume 1.
AL 3516 THE ROARING 'TWENTIES, Volume 1.
AL 3517 IDA COX SINGS THE BLUES.
AL 3518 ROY PALMER AND THE STATE STREET RAMBLERS.
AL 3519 JELLY ROLL MORTON SOLOS.
AL 3520 JELLY ROLL MORTON'S KING OF JAZZ.
AL 3521 FATS AT THE ORGAN. Fats Waller (*vocal and organ*).
AL 3522 JIVIN' WITH FATS. Fats Waller (*vocal and piano*).
AL 3523 RAGTIME PIANO ROLL, Volume 2.
AL 3524 BLUES AND STOMPS, Volume 1 – TOMMY LADNIER.
AL 3525 JIMMY YANCEY – A LOST RECORDING DATE.
AL 3526 CLARENCE WILLIAMS AND HIS ORCHESTRA, Volume 1.
AL 3527 SOUTH SIDE BLUES PIANO – JIMMY BLYTHE.
AL 3528 MUGGSY SPANIER AND THE BUCKTOWN FIVE.
AL 3529 SOUTH SIDE CHICAGO JAZZ.
AL 3530 THE GREAT BLUES SINGERS.
AL 3531 CRIPPLE CLARENCE LOFTON – A LOST RECORDING DATE.
AL 3532 BIX BEIDERBECKE AND THE WOLVERINES.

AL 3533 COLLECTORS' ITEMS, Volume 2.
AL 3534 CLASSIC JAZZ PIANO, Volume 1.
AL 3535 BACKWOODS BLUES.
AL 3536 GEORGE BRUNIS WITH THE NEW ORLEANS RHYTHM KINGS.
AL 3537 PIONEERS OF BOOGIE WOOGIE, Volume 2.
AL 3538 MA RAINEY, Volume 2.
AL 3539 WILL EZELL – GIN MILL JAZZ. *Piano solos.*
AL 3540 JAMES P. JOHNSON – EARLY HARLEM PIANO, Volume 2.
AL 3541 NEW YORK JAZZ OF THE ROARING 'TWENTIES.
AL 3542 RAGTIME PIANO ROLL, Volume 3.
AL 3543 BIX BEIDERBECKE, Volume 2.
AL 3544 BOOGIE WOOGIE WITH THE BLUES.
AL 3545 TOMMY AND JIMMY DORSEY. *With* The California Ramblers.
AL 3546 PENITENTIARY BLUES.
AL 3547 BIRTH OF BIG BAND JAZZ.
AL 3548 TOMMY LADNIER WITH MA RAINEY AND EDMONIA HENDER-
        SON.
AL 3549 JUMPIN' WITH PETE JOHNSON. *Piano solos.*
AL 3550 COLLECTORS' ITEMS, Volume 3.
AL 3551 THE DUKE – 1926.
AL 3552 GEORGE BRUNIS WITH THE NEW ORLEANS RHYTHM KINGS,
        Volume 2.
AL 3553 HARLEM PIANO ROLL.
AL 3554 MIDWESTERN JAZZ.
AL 3555 JOHNNY DODDS, Volume 3.
AL 3556 LADD'S BLACK ACES.
AL 3557 NEW ORLEANS HORNS, Volume 2.
AL 3558 MA RAINEY, Volume 3.
AL 3559 CLASSIC JAZZ PIANO, Volume 2.
AL 3560 JOHNNY DODDS, Volume 4.
AL 3561 CLARENCE WILLIAMS AND HIS ORCHESTRA, Volume 2.
AL 3562 JAZZ OF THE ROARING 'TWENTIES, Volume 2.
AL 3563 RAGTIME PIANO ROLL, Volume 4.
AL 3564 BLIND LEMON JEFFERSON SINGS THE BLUES.
AL 3565 JAZZ PIANO RARITIES.

INDEX

It was impossible, in a book of this size, to give all the musicians and singers a separate entry. The discerning reader will immediately notice that some artists who would seem to deserve a full entry do not get one, while others, perhaps less deserving, do. There are not many instances – Kenny Clark, Hank Jones, Horace Silver, Harry Carney, Eddie Lang, Ray Nance, Frank Teschemacher – these seem to be the main ones. In all these instances, it seems that the artist in question has made his most important contribution on records under other people's names. This complete index will help to refer to these examples of their work. The bold numbers indicate a main entry; the other numbers help to complete the recording history of each artist included in the book.

Gillespie, Dizzy, 50, 74, 93, 94, 95, 110, **141-4,** 170, 189, 206, 213, 214, 229, 237, 248, 250, 251, 253, 277, 285, 309, 323, 327
Gillum, Jazz, 51
Giuffre, Jimmy, 58, 171, 205, 215, 275, 332
Glenn, Tyree, 117, 198
Golden Gate Quartet, **53**
Goldkette, Jean, 43
Golson, Benny, 60, 62, 70, 131, 144
Gonella, Nat, 131
Gonsalves, Paul, 32, 33, 117, 118, 119
Goodman, Benny, 30, 43, 79, 81, 94, 100, **145-50,** 151, 152, 155, 159, 167, 187, 202, 205, 206, 209, 217, 241, 278, 280, 288, 290, 310, 321, 323, 324
Gordon, Dexter, 141, **150,** 151, 302
Gordon, Joe, 70, 143, 202
Gowans, Brad, 88
Gozzo, Conrad, 170, 269
Grainger, Percy, 251
Grant, Bobby, 52, **150-1**
Grant, Jewel, 85
Granz, Norman, 100, 138, 143, 166, 205, 214, 250, 252, 293, 296, 334
Grappelly, Stephane, 164, 266, 287, 310
Gray, Al, 33
Gray, Wardell, 32, 33, 126, 136, 150, **151-2,** 209, 237, 249, 260
Green, Bennie, 11, 80, 95, 299, 303, 304
Green, Benny, 330
Green, Charlie, 168, 283
Green, Urbie, 80, 148, 171, 277
Greene, Freddie, 30, 108, 236, 261, 293, 333, 334
Greer, Sonny, 18
Gregory, Ed, 227
Greig, Stan, 64
Griffin, Johnny, 49, 228
Grimes, Henry, 272
Grimes, Tiny, 67, 167, 248, 296
Grissom, Dan, 219
Gryce, Gigi, 60, 61, 70, 93, 127, 228
Guarnieri, Johnny, **152-3,** 278, 333
Guerin, Roger, 55
Gullin, Lars, 61, 105, 138, **153-4,** 230, 301, 306
Guy, Fred, 114
Guy, Joe, 79

HACKETT, BOBBY, 18, **154-5**
Hadi, Shafi, 226
Haggart, Bob, 91, 209
Hagood, Kenny, 124, 141
Haig, Al, 9, 64, 138, 141, **155-6,** 166, 198, 237, 249, 252, 290, 327
Halcox, Pat, 27, 28
Hall, Al, 24
Hall, Edmond, 8, 18, 19, 91, **156**
Hall, Henry, 73
Hall, Herbie, 261
Hall, Jim, 58, 157, 158, 162, 215
Hall, Skip, 295
Hallberg, Bengt, 61, 105, 106, 138, **156-7,** 301
Hamilton, Chico, 85, **157-8,** 215, 234
Hamilton, Jimmy, 117, 119
Hampton, Lionel, 45, 55, 60, 61, 68, 73, 79, 91, 126, 127, 129, 145, 147, 148, **158-61,** 178, 184, 187, 206, 230, 280, 296, 297, 313, 321
Hampton, Slide, 131
Handy, W. C., 18
Hanna, Roland, 261
Harden, Wilbur, 86
Harding, Buster, 143, 152
Hardman, Bill, 49, 228
Hardwicke, Otto, 112
Harriot, Joe, 126
Harris, Arville, 311
Harris, Bennie, 252
Harris, Bill, 74, 170, 171
Harris, Joe, 230, 250
Harris, Otis, **52**
Harris, Wynonie, 53, **161**
Harrison, Jimmy, 78, 106, **161,** 168, 317
Hart, Clyde, 248
Hastings, Lennie, 25
Hawdon, Dickie, 94
Hawes, Hampton, **161-2,** 269, 272, 276
Hawkins, Buddy Boy, **52**
Hawkins, Coleman, 12, 34, 44, 55, 57, 67, 69, 73, 78, 80, 159, **162-7,** 169, 172, 183, 197, 203, 222, 228, 265, 270, 272, 280, 296, 303, 315, 316, 322, 330, 331
Hayes, Tubby, 102
Hayes, Thamon, 233
Haynes, Roy, 127, 156, 270, 290, 309
Heath, Percy, 96, 97, 143, 185, 213, 215, 252, 270

[345]

Heath, Ted, 25, 267
Heckstall-Smith, Dick, 64
Hefti, Neil, 33, 152
Henderson, Edmonia, 207
Henderson, Fletcher, 14, 22, 30, 31,
  45, 146, 147, 148, 161, 163, 164,
  167–70, 207, 208, 227, 264, 280,
  283, 284, 291, 292, 302, 315, 331
Henderson, Horace, 68, 169
Hendricks, Jon, 208, 209, 258
Herman, Woody, 11, 25, 35, 75, 80, 81,
  82, 107, 129, 137, 138, 140, **170–2,**
  199, 223, 269, 280, 290, 305, 306
Heywood, Eddie, **172–3,** 177
Hibbler, Al, 117
Hicks, Robert, **51**
Higginbotham, J. C., 91, 169, **173,**
  244, 274, 302, 322
Hill, Alex, 225
Hill, Bertha 'Chippie', 53, **173**
Hill, King Solomon, 52, **322**
Hill, Teddy, 317
Hines, Earl, 16, 17, 18, 37, 54, 55, 74,
  83, 110, 130, 151, 172, **174–5,** 189,
  192, 211, 242, 289, 298, 322, 324
Hinton, Milt, 123
Hobbs, Jack, 167
Hodes, Art, 39, **176,** 199
Hodeir, André, 317, 330
Hodges, Johnny, 18, 22, 23, 36, 46, 72,
  73, 112, 114, 115, 117, 118, 119,
  120, 147, 159, 163, 171, 172, **176–9,**
  219, 248, 252, 274, 286, 307, 315,
  321, 325
Holiday, Billie, 57, 74, 80, 128, 146,
  179–82, 239, 273, 278, 309, 325,
  331, 332
Holland, Peanuts, 223
Holman, Bill, 77, 140, 200, 269, 281
Holmes, Charlie, 46, 274
Honore, Gedeon, 242
Hooker, John Lee, **52**
Hopkins, Claude, 103, 123
Hopkins, Lightnin', 52, **182**
Horn, Paul, 85
Hoskins, Jerry, 10
Houston, Dolly, 200
Howard, Darnell, 287
Howard, Gene, 200
Howell, Peg Leg, **52**
Howlin' Wolf, **52**
Hucko, Peanuts, 18

Hudson, Will, 153
Hug, Armand, **182,** 320
Hughes, Spike, 44, 73, 164, **183,** 317
Humble, Derek, 102, 306
Humes, Helen, 332

IRVIS, CHARLIE, 112, 311
Isaacs, Ike, 67

JACKSON, BO WEAVIL, **52**
Jackson, Chubby, 140
Jackson, Cliff, 44
Jackson, Mahalia, 54, 119, **183,** 283
Jackson, Milt, 76, 90, 97, 129, 141,
  142, 166, **184–6,** 213, 214, 215, 227,
  304
Jackson, Quentin, 24, 117
Jackson, Rudy, 112
Jacobs, Little Walter, **52,** 324
Jacquet, Illinois, 32, 75, 131, 193
James, Harry, 146, 170, **187–8,** 277,
  286
James, Jesse, 217, 319
Jaspar, Bobby, 77
Jefferson, Blind Lemon, 51, 52, 59, 70,
  188–9, 210, 263, 282, 319
Jefferson, Eddie, 230
Jefferson, Hilton, 169
Jenkins, Gordon, 18
Jenkins, Pat, 295
Johnson, Angeline, 196
Johnson, Bil Bill, 52, 60
Johnson, Blind Willie, 51, 54, **196–7**
Johnson, Budd, 142, **189,** 316
Johnson, Bunk, **189–91,** 207, 212
Johnson, Charlie, 161
Johnson, Dick, 90
Johnson, Dink, **191**
Johnson, Gus, 223, 281, 304
Johnson, James P., 91, 125, **191–2,**
  208, 225, 228, 240, 261, 265, 280,
  283, 286, 307, 311
Johnson, Jay Jay, 32, 95, 96, 139, 142,
  166, 186, **192–4,** 214, 260, 271, 292
Johnson, Lonnie, 16, 53, 59, 68, 78,
  194–5
Johnson, Louise, 217
Johnson, Pete, 10, 191, **195–6,** 247,
  256, 284, 308
Johnson, Professor, **54**

[346]

Machito, 277
Mackintosh, Spike, 129
McCarthy, Albert, 211
McCoy, Kansas Joe, **52**
McGarity, Lou, 148, 209
McGhee, Brownie, 28, 52, 135, **221**
McGhee, Howard, 151, 165, 237, 249, 286
McHugh, Jimmy, 25
McKenna, Dave, 57
McKenzie, Red, 163, 206, **222**, 222
McKibbon, Al, 141, 250
McKinney, William, 264
McKusick, Hal, 205
McLean, Jackie, 11, 49, 96, 313
McPartland, Jimmy, 146, **222**
McPartland, Marian, 247
McRae, Carmen, 67
McShann, Jay, **223**, 233, 248, 326
Mance, Junior, 11, 49, 144
Mandel, Johnny, 139, 290, 305
Manne, Shelly, 23, 74, 162, 172, 177, 202, **223-4**, 271, 272, 276
Manone, Wingy, 145, **224**, 238
Margolis, Sam, 56
Mariano, Charlie, 224
Markowitz, Irving, 305
Marmarosa, Dodo, 202, 249, 250, 279, 303, 304, 333
Marsh, Arno, 171
Marsh, Warne, 35, 203, 205, 237, 306
Marshall, Wendell, 90, 117, 293
Martin, Sara, **53**, 245
Martinez, Sabu, 99
Marx, Dick, 64
Matlock, Matty, 91, 243
Matthews, Dave, 146, 200
Matthews, George, 318
May, Peter, 167
Mayerl, Billy, 42
Memphis Slim, **52**
Merrill, Helen, 62
Merriweather, Big Maceo, 51, 229, 264
Mezzrow, Mezz, 12, 38, 63, 68, 82, 159, 208, 218, **224-5**, 239, 243, 247, 261
Michelot, Pierre, 77, 215, 313
Middleton, Velma, 18, 19
Miles, Lizzie, **53**, 55
Miley, Bubber, 112, 113, 288, 291, 321

Miller, Eddie, 44, 91, 290
Miller, Glenn, 44, 94, 155, 222
Mills Brothers, 17, 132
Mingus, Charlie, **226**, 253
Mitchell, Billy, 33
Mitchell, George, 104, 231
Mobley, Hank, 49
Mole, Miff, 106, 161, 183, **226**, 241, 288
Moncur, Grachan, 22
Monk, Laurie, 94
Monk, Thelonious, 48, 49, 50, 58, 79, 96, 120, 153, 165, 167, 185, 194, **226-9**, 235, 251, 271, 299, 309, 313, 323
Monterose, J. R., 108
Montgomery, Little Brother, 53, **229**, 256
Montgomery, Wes, 75
Montrose, Jack, 224
Moody, James, 105, **229-30**, 258
Moore, Brew, 81, 107
Moore, Gerald, 225
Morand, Herb, 105
Morello, Joe, 65
Morgan, Lee, 144
Morrow, George, 62, 270
Morton, Benny, 8, 31, 103, 110, 168, 277, 318
Morton, Jeff, 306
Morton, Jelly Roll, 25, 38, 101, 111, 125, 147, 191, **230-3**, 240, 245, 279, 282, 330
Mosca, Sol, 306
Moss, Danny, 94
Motian, Paul, 90
Moten, Bennie, 30, 203, **233**, 247, 315, 330
Moule, Ken, 77
Muddy Waters, 52, **233-4**, 324
Mulligan, Gerry, 23, 58, 75, 77, 94, 95, 107, 108, 119, 123, 128, 154, 157, 200, 204, 206, 227, 281, **234-7**, 327
Mundy, Jimmy, 131
Mussulli, Boots, 200

Nance, Ray, 23, 116, 117, 118, 119, 172, 178, 189, 285, 310
Nanton, Joe, 112, 115, 116
Napoleon, Teddy, 206

[348]